The Game of Death in Ancient Rome

WISCONSIN STUDIES IN CLASSICS

General Editors
Richard Daniel De Puma and Barbara Hughes Fowler

The Game of Death in Ancient Rome

Arena Sport and Political Suicide

Paul Plass

The University of Wisconsin Press

The University of Wisconsin Press
2537 Daniels Street
Madison, Wisconsin 53718

3 Henrietta Street
London WC2E 8LU, England

5 4 3 2 1

Printed in the United States of America

Library of Congress Cataloging-in-Publication Data
Plass, Paul, 1933–
    The game of death in ancient Rome: arena sport and political suicide / Paul Plass.
    300 p.   cm. — (Wisconsin studies in classics)
    Includes bibliographical references and index.
    ISBN 0-299-14570-0 (cloth: alk. paper)
    ISBN 0-299-14574-3 (paperback: alk. paper)
    1. Games—Rome—History. 2. Rome—Politics and government. 3. Suicide—
Rome. 4. Violence in sports—Rome. I. Title. II. Series.
GV31.P53   1995
796'.0937'6—dc20   94-40884

The gorgeous delirium of gladiatorial shows . . .
　　　　　　　　　　—George Eliot, *Theophrastus Such*

The saying goes, to die is easy but to live is hard.

　　　　　　　　　　—Admiral Ugaki, *Fading Victory*

Contents

viii   Contents

Acknowledgments

A grant from the University of Wisconsin Graduate School made a period of uninterrupted work possible. In addition to the members of the research award committee, I owe thanks to Thomas Habinek, Alessandro Schiesaro, and Denis Feeney for commenting on the project at various stages, and particularly to Richard Saller and Carlin Barton for their interest encompassing everything from details to overall organization and emphasis. Professor Barton's own work on the place of gladiatorial combat in Roman society has been a major stimulus for me. Some readers saw the manuscript only in earlier versions which have undergone substantial revisions. Improvements are often due to their suggestions, and what they have not seen is my own responsibility through omission or commission.

I am also grateful to Barbara Fowler, a general editor of the Wisconsin Studies in Classics series, for the support and encouragement she has once again offered, as well as to Raphael Kadushin, Carol Olsen, and Angela Ray for efficient editorial work.

Finally, the book is dedicated to my son, Mark.

Note on References

References to Latin and Greek authors follow abbreviations in the second edition of the *Oxford Classical Dictionary* (1970). Dio Cassius is cited as Dio. All citations of Dionysius of Halicarnassus refer to the *Antiquitates Romanae*. In the Notes and Selected Bibliography, *Aufsteig und Niedergang der römischen Welt* is abbreviated *ANRW*.

The Game of Death in Ancient Rome

Introduction

I am concerned in this study with two facets of Roman society—bloodshed in the arena and political suicide. Their historical origins were quite different, and while the first was an institution in the usual sense of the word, the second was a socially sanctioned practice in vogue principally during the earlier Empire. Both were relatively uncommon, but the need to process violence that was met particularly by gladiatorial games is a cultural universal, however peculiar the Romans' way of doing so. In fact, processing violence is a common denominator I want to isolate and examine on the relatively general level of social logic, where axioms at work in institutions and practices are to be found and differences give way to deeper connections. Though my interest is principally in Rome, inclusion of some Greek material seems justified, inasmuch as social logic typically spans cultures, especially cognate ones.

Axioms commonly are propositional statements, logic the broader rules under which they operate. But rigid definitions along these lines are not appropriate to social or political life, where axioms covering any number of activities are more like general attitudes and assumptions about what is so or ought to be so. They are seldom reduced to exact propositional form or related to each other in any fixed hierarchical order, but they work together, instead, in broad tendencies making up a loose system. Thus while personal freedom or group consensus are general attitudes each entailing a further set of practical procedures for specific situations, theory and practice cannot be kept clearly apart. Very general procedural tendencies become operative in axioms, and axioms reflect broad procedural rules giving direction to how things are done.

As these are rather abstract notions, a few examples by way of illustration are in order. Tacitus reports that silver and clay vessels had equal value in Germany, that worship was conducted without temples in the open, and that gods were not represented with human faces (*Germ.*

5.2, 9.2). The first he connects with a simple system of utilitarian values, the two religious customs with an innate sense of awe before the divine. What is being accounted for are facts (of which the third is apparently wrong) about particular practices or institutions, while the explanations are broader axioms about German society. The natural piety of undeveloped peoples was a general principle commonly employed in contemporary theory of religion, and a distinction between use value and display value was familiar in Rome. So Tacitus attempted to understand Germanic culture through religious or economic axioms that lay behind customs, giving them meaning and embodying fundamental social tendencies. Initially, differences among the three specific practices are a good deal more evident and numerous than any connections. Two are then subsumed under a broader religious principle, and all three finally come together thematically under a still broader axiom of natural simplicity.[1]

Whatever the soundness of Tacitus' views in these instances, the truth of social axioms is different from the truth of facts, in that the former are valid as well as true. What was valid *for* Germans was factually true *about* them for an observer like Tacitus. At Rome itself, under one rule governing divination, signs were valid only when they had been officially accepted. Under another, even when reported falsely, they remained valid for the official acting on them, with the consequences of the mistake falling on the reporter. This second case is something like holding brokers liable for losses from bad financial advice, and to those who invest heavily in high-risk political ventures, as the Romans did, an operational axiom to the effect that *official* action *constitutes* reality can be most useful. Axioms, moreover, are frequently implicit—the more implicit, in fact, the more effective. For the most part, social reality is taken for granted as something objective and is not thought of as an arbitrary set of rules. Everyone knows that laws are passed and policies are decided on by other people, but while social reality is *made* through political action, it is valid because it is also made *real*.

A special application of this principle is propaganda designed to create false facts: Nero publicly dumped spoiled grain, for example, to create the impression of food in plenty when the supply actually had been reduced by storm and fire (Tac. *Ann.* 15.18.2). Crude as outright falsification usually is, Nero's action does show some imagination in tricking the public into drawing a false conclusion which then becomes politically true. The ambiguities of political reality exploited by Nero's simple tactic are, in fact, implicit in variant textual readings representing two different facets of the situation. The spoiled grain was gotten rid of either "to show the reliability of the food supply" (*quo securitatem annonae osten-*

taret) or "to maintain confidence in it" (. . . *sustentaret*). With the one, the aim is to make the fact of ample supplies plain; with the other, it is to create a public sense of confidence in them.

The second of these alternative readings again has to do particularly with the subjective, conceptual social reality constituted on a large scale by rules that work more subtly and pervasively to make things true.[2] This is, by way of contrast to Nero's ad hoc maneuver for making people think that something was so, what we might call permanent propaganda—the received way of thinking about what is real, the public fiction (or public reality) common enough in all societies, not least in Rome, where it could encompass everything up to the vast ideological project of acting as though the Principate were a restoration of republican values.[3]

Somewhere between these two comes the incident of the Caudine Forks (Livy 9.1–11). Trapped in a hopeless position, a Roman army surrendered to the Samnites under a pledge of peace guaranteed by the consuls on the scene. The Senate then repudiated the arrangement by refusing to ratify it formally. Livy's focus at this point shifts to the issue of political reality. Canceling the agreement entails that Postumius, one of the consuls, be handed back, naked and with hands bound, to the Samnites, whose angry general points out that if Rome wants to repudiate the agreement, its army ought to go back into the position from which it was extricated by the pledge (an awkward point already raised at Rome by supporters of the truce; 8.14). Along with the anomalous status of Postumius—now a nonperson, fallen out of history into limbo between an enemy city which will not take him and his own which does not want him—the Samnite demand that "everything should be as though it had not happened" (*omnia pro infecto sint;* 11.4) dramatizes the oddity of making and unmaking political reality at will. Everything runs at cross-purposes to everything else, and the conceptual puzzle putting both sides at a loss about exactly what to think or do is highlighted with a flourish of Senecan paradox: "The Samnites were tricked by a dream happier than they could imagine, our army was freed by the same luck that trapped it, a vain victory was made invalid by a still vainer peace, and the guarantee bound no one except the guarantor" (Livy 9.9.14–15).

Livy is as interested in the dilemmas faced by both sides as he is in the military situation. The consuls themselves were originally unable to say anything "on behalf of a treaty so shameful or against one so necessary" (4.7; cf. 8.4), and nothing is done for Roman integrity when Postumius, after being handed over to the Samnites, knees the Roman envoy in the crotch to give Rome grounds for action due to violation of their representative's diplomatic immunity by someone who now is a "Samnite" (10.10).[4] The principle of socially constituted reality appears in more familiar guise at Rome in the axiom of *patria potestas,* which while applying in practice with some restrictions, in theory carried nearly absolute authority. It granted the father power of life and death *(ius vitae necisque)* over his children along with extensive control of decisions made by them, even as adults, so long as he was alive.[5] Since children were defined negatively in this way by their radical inferiority to the father, their existence and status as persons under the axiom of *patria potestas* were socially constituted in an unusually strong sense of the term.

Because axioms are broad rules, transferability is a feature of them. Transferability can appear in a variety of cultural contexts, including societies where authority to declare or deny a fetus' right of survival is formally vested in the mother and inferred from a larger principle of personal autonomy. The job of axioms is to define norms and minimize anomaly in social logic—in the case of abortion, the perceived anomaly of a woman denied control over her own body, in *patria potestas* that of a man without paramount power though bearing paramount responsibility for the ultimate social unit (the family). The logic of Roman social organization dictated that in the domestic sphere the father should have the unrestricted authority given to the general by *imperium* in the public sphere.

Axioms naturally come into play where danger to order is most strongly felt, but as they establish normalcy in one respect, new anomaly is apt to spring up in another, as is clear enough from the case of the Caudine Forks. The dilemmas entailed by abortion in respect to the relation between real and potential personhood, between biological realities on the one side and social and personal ones on the other, between women's ambivalent status vis-à-vis society at large and unborn prospective members accorded many other protections but not that of survival, have counterparts in the incongruities to which the axiom of paternal authority in Roman society led: "Suppose the head of a family was ninety, his two sons seventy-five and seventy, their sons between sixty and fifty-five, the sons of these in their forties and thirties, and the great-great-grandsons in their twenties, none of them except the ninety-year-old Head owned a penny. If the seventy-five-year-old senator or the forty-year-old General or the twenty-year-old student wanted to buy a box of chocolate, he had to ask the *senex* for the money. This is really quite extraordinary." So much so that one might, in fact, "well wonder how such a society can possibly have worked."[6]

It worked because a good deal of flexibility was available in actual practice to get around the hard cases that make bad law. But hard cases bring out with special clarity the broader logic that may be no less significant than what is done to make adjustments. In the political sphere, economic anomalies of *patria potestas* were eliminated. There, in his capacity as magistrate, a son was legally free from his father's authority. But since officeholders moved back and forth from civic to domestic status, the one inevitably influenced the other, so that as a magistrate with the highest authority, a man might well be under considerable pressure from his father's still higher authority, while little boys *(impuberes)* could juridically possess *patria potestas. Patria potestas* had no specific legal basis; what was done depended on a traditional social logic of *mos maiorum* and *auctoritas* so powerful as to hold even when the father was insane *(Dig.* 1.6.8). Speaking of the *ius imaginum,* another of these highly effective implicit axioms, Eberhard Bruch remarks on its "illustration of an essential feature of the unwritten constitution of the Roman Republic: the contrast between law and reality."[7]

The keen interest shown by declamatory rhetoric in social logic, particularly its vagaries, is a good measure of the attention it attracted. On occasion, sober legal principles could lead to situations quite indistinguishable from the mad world of declamation. In accordance with correct procedure for execution of women, Sejanus' young daughter was officially raped before being garroted. Seeing an opportunity to make a point about the logic of autocracy, Tacitus adds that when she was first taken to prison, she asked to be spanked for whatever it was she had done wrong *(Ann. 5.9)*. Suetonius' indication that the procedure of rape before execution was used more than once may be exaggeration, but it again has a suggestion of absurdity *(Tib.* 61.5).[8]

The execution of Sejanus' daughter is doubly pertinent for our purpose because it involves intense violence of the kind that recurred on a larger scale under public auspices in the arena and in political suicide. The absurdity or anomaly in question, though, is not so simple a matter after all. Dysfunctional as legal logic appears to be here, there is nothing dysfunctional about getting done what one wants done, and Roman society as a whole was remarkably good at doing just that. As social axioms are not exact rules, so the dilemmas they spawn are generally not so much contradictions as awkward trade-offs out of which social order is composed at every level—ensuring social welfare, for example, through aid that predictably increases dependence and thereby also decreases the welfare of its recipients. Deterrent capital punishment—safeguarding life by taking it—is another notorious instance, of which both gladiatorial combat and political suicide are very special cases. At Rome, systemic contradiction was detected by Seneca and others in antisocial effects of socially sponsored arena violence, while for Tacitus suicide forced by the emperor or used by his opponents as a gesture of defiance exemplified the Principate's political irrationality.[9]

Disparate social institutions, then, can be considered to exhibit a deeper logic or shared "patternment" in the Whorfian linguistic sense of general submerged cryptotypes that shape explicit phenotypes and themselves "easily escape notice, may be hard to define and yet have profound influence on linguistic behavior."[10] Social axioms, too, disclose covert cultural patternments, much as iron pieces of diverse shape disclose the single underlying pattern of an invisible magnetic field in which they lie. For our purposes the field is security reaffirmed, anomaly set right, and irregularity regularized.

Some axioms deal with values specific to a culture (say, conformity or freedom); others, such as those involving security, are global. No society chooses to perish on principle except as the price of attempting to preserve its principles. In this sense self-destruction can itself be entailed by the logic of security, and just that anomaly played a major role in political suicide at Rome. Either imposed by those in power for their own security or chosen by those in opposition as a final way of preserving political integrity, suicide was both a functional political move and a dysfunctional failure of politics.

The two facets of Roman society which concern us are held together by a loose organizing principle broad enough for heuristic analysis moving in a single direction (Roman responses to violence) along several lines (bloody arena sport and political suicide). At the general level of social logic, the same issue is dealt with by many societies and in many related guises by the same society. The similarity of gladiatorial combat and suicide lies in a quest for security through incorporation of disorder into order—an interlude of controlled disorder sponsored by society in order to (re)affirm its own security. As a universal social need or value, security is then given content in particular societies by axioms defining simultaneously what a normal state of affairs is and what anomalies subvert it.[11] If *patria potestas* was a norm at Rome, anomaly was anything that called male authority into question. Public norms, though, are not simply identical with public interest. Society is not an actor; individuals and groups are, and so normalcy and stability are the aim chiefly of those whose interests are best served by whatever system is in place. As a practical matter, then, dominant interests largely determine or constitute public values as a whole. In comparing divination with modern sociological techniques, R. Bastide contends that divination dealt with anxieties about the future felt by individuals, while sociological forecasting is concerned with impersonal laws or tendencies.[12] But since, as he remarks, divination was often performed on behalf of the public, its efficacy was rooted in a more abstract social logic extending beyond individual or specific political interests. It could be exploited by the elite for their own particular ends only because its validity seemed plain to everyone in the first place. It is this social dimension of institutions, rather than the single actors or groups who used them, that will concern us.

If "human societies are problem solving organizations" and if the paramount problem to be solved is disruption of order, then social institutions are instruments for preserving or restoring systemic regularity.[13] Social life depends on rules, and insofar as rules can guarantee order at best only very imperfectly, disorder has to be managed through accommodation. Suicide ought not to be necessary at all; mass violence ought not to be a major activity (though this was less obvious to Romans). But they in fact do occur, and social systems must contend with them as "normal" disruptions requiring acknowledgment and adjustment, complete prevention being out of the question.

As a result, violence or, more generally, disorder falls under an axiom of anomaly, that is, an abnormal or disruptive factor formally institutionalized in one way or another to be internalized, in a process characteristic of any immune system. Divination is a particularly clear case. Normal signs (e.g., bird behavior), solicited through routine impetrative procedures, represented the control made possible by rituals at the disposal of society. Here the factor of order and security was salient. Oblative signs, on the other hand, which were frequently queer and came uninvited, bore on their face an unmistakable indication of breaches in the ordinary state of affairs. As they were then repaired through often bloody expiation (which might well consist of *munera*, or public shows), so in gladiatorial combat external danger was dealt with through a special mode of violence, and internal political conflict peculiar to the Principate was addressed through still another mode in suicide. Anomaly, accordingly, is a logical precondition of normalcy (as disease is of health) and brings with it the risk of serious dysfunction (as powerful drugs have dangerous effects and healing involves the risk of killing). A little chaos is a necessary and useful thing, provided it does not go too far. If it does, disorder is no longer processed but actually produced by the system itself, as was the case with both *munera* and political suicide in the view of some critics. If *patria potestas* can actually confuse lines of authority or divination can foster panic through too many alarming signals, then mayhem in the arena may encourage brutality in the stands and political suicide may create the tension it also reduces. This is clearly a fertile field for unintended consequences, which along with illusion and self-deception play a major role as general political phenomena in Tacitus.

The anomalous state of affairs threatening security is itself also in part socially constituted, with normality or abnormality in large measure defined by expectations of how things will or should happen. The hideous damage done to men or animals gave public bloodshed its social meaning only because it was done by society itself. Games were a normal part of entertainment, eagerly awaited and immensely popular, but that does not preclude a powerful element of incongruity, since entertainment is by no means as simple as it might seem. The serious rioting which plagued Roman sporting events was routine only in an unfortunate sense of the word, and entertainment more generally is a routine part of life in that it permits routines to be routinely broken. More specifically, much of the entertainment value of *munera* came from an intensity and scale of violence felt to be out of the ordinary. The principle is familiar from modern circuses and carnivals, which also inhabit an anomalous marginal domain that is alluring because rules as a rule are broken. And again like dangerous circus acts with wild animals, carnage in the arena afforded the special vicarious fright that comes from watching anything which seems potentially threatening. As for suicide, though there anomaly took on a far more narrowly personal and political guise, the peculiar concept of self-destruction as a civil right lent death the same oddly routine quality that lethal games in the arena had. And in both, social meaning derives from violence that is understood to be perfectly normal yet decidedly unusual.

In *munera* the break in routine is effected through ceremony, and in a few cases of suicide there is evidence for some degree of ritualization, enough at any rate for Petronius to parody (Tac. *Ann.* 16.19). If a special occasion of one kind or another, then, is the formal aspect of anomaly—games have times set aside, suicide is the last of all resorts—its material aspect is violence causing and filling the interludes in routine. Bloodshed in the arena took its effect directly from the impact made by concentrated violence. In the absence of efficient methods such as gunfire or reliable poisons, suicide, too, gained political significance partly from the dramatic ordeal it inflicted, an aspect heavily emphasized in accounts of Cato's death. Each in its own way thus administered a dose of cultured (in the medical-biological sense) violence, working like an immune system to bring the body politic back into balance.

Gladiatorial combat and political suicide, though, are not *reducible* to the notion of disrupted/restored social routine, an important proviso caught in the analogy of iron filings shaped by a magnetic field. While focusing principally on the emergence of an underlying pattern, the comparison leaves unrestricted the pieces' capacity to enter alternative relationships, form new configurations, reveal other patterns, and, above all, retain properties differentiating each from the others as well as from larger patterns all have in common.

In addition to the potential pitfalls of reductive explanation, concentrating on formal aspects of institutions introduces structuralism of a kind and its chronic problem of artificial connections. Anything, after all, sooner or later is (trivially) somehow related to everything else. But that knife cuts the other way as well: anything is finally dissimilar from everything else, too, and so detection of structures is to some extent necessarily a matter of partial paradigms, heuristic rules, and functional definitions. In contemporary American society, laws liberalizing abortion, restricting dissemination of personal information by credit agencies, or forbidding involuntary blood tests are concerned with unrelated areas while nonetheless all being inferences from a single principle of individual rights. In Rome, too, so far as lethal games and suicide used divergent means to serve distinct purposes, they made up a pair with quite different historical sources and original purposes. At the same time, as components of one social system, diverse elements also address similar problems, preeminently so in respect to the problem of security and survival that is crucial to every society and must be met wherever it presents itself.

Part I

Arena Games and Public Uses of Violence

1

Public Spectacles as Broken Routine

"Arrachion won . . . an Olympic victory thanks to the fairness of the judges and to his own courage. For while competing with his last opponent (whoever he was), Arrachion was caught in a hold, scissored by the other man's legs and squeezed by his hands. After dislocating his opponent's toe, Arrachion died from suffocation, but the man who had killed him was forced to give in at that very moment owing to the pain in his toe. The Eleans crowned and proclaimed the corpse of Arrachion victor" (Paus. 8.40). In a second, highly rhetorical account, Philostratus (*Imag.* 2.6) concentrates on the crowd's hysterical admiration for the victor, and in *On Gymnastics* (21) he adds that as Arrachion was himself about to give up, his trainer inspired him "to love of death" by shouting, "How glorious a monument it is not to yield at Olympia!" While the archaic statue described by Pausanias, which was erected to Arrachion in the marketplace of the Phigalians and was once accompanied by an inscription, may attest to a core of fact in the story, this detail and others in the several versions are likely to be anecdotal elaborations. Even when they overshoot fact, though, elaborations normally aim at symbolic reality and make sense by conveying the truth of social paradigms or exempla.

As elementary rules, paradigms are global in extent, appearing thematically everywhere from explicit procedures enshrined in a legal system to unwritten laws that, in turn, cover fundamental moral attitudes as well as the countless rules governing daily life. The author of anecdotes and of the social logic they sum up thus is ultimately society itself, in this instance the creator of a public statue as well. The story is paradigmatic because the peculiar circumstances of Arrachion's death make up a limiting case to mark out how far the logic of competition reaches. Its scope is in fact surprisingly large, with the paradoxical *notion* of posthumous

15

athletic success sharpened by the overwrought rhetoric in Philostratus' suggestion of religious transfiguration: "Greater than his two previous Olympic prizes is this last victory by which he is ushered into the chorus of the blessed covered with dust." Interest in finding a rationale prompts Philostratus to discount any idea that the situation really was just queer or a mere accident: "Don't imagine that this was chance, for he planned his victory with great care" (*Imag.* 2.6.2). (Claims to posthumous glory and noble intention reappear in efforts to rationalize political suicide at Rome.) To the extent that the incident is historical, it stands in relation to the fictional enhancement it has undergone as actual legal dilemmas stand in relation to the melodramatic scenarios devised by the declaimers. Fact or fiction, however, the axiomatic truth the story represents is the supreme value of competitive victory conveyed by the honorary statue itself, the judge's decision (called "fair"), the crowd's frenzied approval, and the trainer's exhortation.[1]

Here, however, that particular axiom is not the story's point but its presupposition. The true point lies in the odd connection of victory with death, an idea that can be accommodated only at the outer edge of the rationale for sports. In warfare the two go together readily, in gladiatorial games less easily (e.g., Suet. *Claud* 34.2, where both contestants die), and athletic combat is assimilated to military combat by the echo of familiar epitaphs to fallen victors in the trainer's encouragement. Though in sports death is anything but normal, it does happen; in the episode of Arrachion it is doubly exceptional in happening to the man who wins. When the live loser is depicted as a corpse in a painting described by Philostratus whereas the dead Arrachion is blooming with vitality, what is disclosed is anomaly implicit in competitive violence even as it is rationalized under civilized rules. Limiting cases are naturally bound to be anomalous, and their anomaly is bound to seem contrived, designed as these cases are to address the full potential of situations.

Pausanias' second example, a boxer also awarded victory though disemboweled by his opponent's jab, is a plain case of cheating and poses no conceptual problem, though it does again demonstrate the extraordinary violence associated with sport. While doing that, Arrachion's death in addition discloses a dilemma within the system, a dilemma which transforms competition either positively, as it does here when it transcends life, or negatively into absurd consequences. In the case of another athlete, there is no doubt about Pausanias' own opinion on the limits of rational competition: Timanthes' leap into a fire after realizing that he can no longer pull his bow is "more madness than manliness" (6.8.4).

Games in general are rule-bound procedures reflecting deeper social patterns and performing several complementary functions. Entertainment, the most obvious and quite possibly the most important function, is still only one aspect of a complex whole, and bloodshed in the arena at Rome assuredly was complex. Taken solely at face value, the entertainment it afforded was simply a social custom not pointing beyond itself and requiring no further explanation. Yet it was also a less straightforward social euphemism, helping mask other more disturbing things, much as publicly sponsored lotteries and the revenue they bring in seem more acceptable when packaged as "gaming" instead of "gambling." Lethal gladiatorial combat between humans was no more mere diversion than elaborate animal hunts were staged solely to satisfy public curiosity about exotic fauna, although they did that, too. Like other kinds of entertainment, both had a second, separate social dimension. For if simple entertainment is in the first instance what *munera* meant to each spectator, all spectators together comprised another, collective reality in which arena games took on a quite different significance determined not by individual attitudes but by social effects. Public events are programs, acts of social communication with a distinctively social significance of their own. The new, separate mass identity which can emerge for individuals comes not solely from the easy avoidance of personal responsibility and the weakening of normal private inhibitions facilitated by crowds. It may also constitute a larger political presence, which at the games in Rome embodied popular opinion either conflicting with authority in occasional mob action or expressing solidarity with it through participation in the spectacle. The possibility of dysfunction in this public domain is what concerned Seneca.

Like divination, games had a religious side connected with threats of one kind or another—war, plague, famine—to communal well-being.[2] Some formed part of funeral ceremonies or were directly linked to divination when they were given to expiate offenses. But here again it is useless to look for exclusive meanings. The purpose of gladiatorial combat in its original form at the tomb of the dead was richly overdetermined: to pacify spirits through entertainment, to flatter them with special attention, to give them a share of the energy expended in competition, and to fortify the living in the face of their own danger from death. The last of these in particular is strongly suggested by the general connection of sports to military training and to warfare, preeminently an occasion of possible death.[3] Particularly in the later development of the games, the threat they entertained comes from death more generally rather than from the dead: as an institution, what gladiatorial violence has in view is death as such, not the individual deaths of marginal people who were in fact of no importance.

The contrast between instrumental uses of ritual on the one side and more general symbolic ones on the other can help clarify the social role of gladiatorial combat. The former focuses on optimal means, whereas the latter incorporates broader aims, including values, and goes beyond immediate, purely practical considerations. Institutions, accordingly, can be simultaneously symbolic on one level and instrumental on another, insofar as their symbolic ends also fulfill specific functions. Voting is a familiar case in point. It is a purely practical means for settling issues as well as a powerful symbolic act (e.g., asserting popular sovereignty or, in the event of low participation, rejecting a regime's legitimacy) which may, in turn, have concrete effects.[4] Originally, stylized combat at tombs aimed in a relatively narrow, concrete way at reinforcing vitality and perhaps at enhancing wider feelings of collective security also. As the direct tie between means and end was weakened, ritualized violence developed in one direction into entertainment, while in another it took on a larger social meaning that continued to lie in display of power, but one now to some extent cut loose from its religious roots. The original simple expenditure of physical energy was transposed into conspicuous consumption of public resources measured by both blood and money and carrying the symbolic meaning which frequently accompanies consumption. Costly armor worn by gladiators or the vivid colors and jewelry in which animals killed in the arena might be decked out were expansive/expensive symbolic shows at odds with more normal, instrumentally rational expenditure.

In light of the extremes to which games were often taken in various directions and the unusual situations that might be played out in them, it is worth considering to what extent their meaning lay in the sense of anomaly that they aroused. The routine diversion they provided could be a very sharp departure from ordinary life: "But finally the excitement of bloody combat and the fairytale charm of the scenery were not enough to arouse the dulled nerves of the higher or lower crowd. What was rare had to be devised, what was most unreasonable and unnatural had to be found in order to give new spice to the cannibalistic show."[5] More exactly, it is worth considering whether the meaning of Roman games lies in restoration of order by working—or rather, playing—anomaly both into and out of the social system, as happens on a small scale in the story of Arrachion, whose death becomes part of the athletic code, but a very unusual one. If *procuratio* in divination was inoculation administered when symptoms occurred, then perhaps bloody games were a symptom deliberately induced to forestall more serious infection. The danger which that entails is overdosage, as the critics of *munera* in fact insisted: "A culture is a tissue of exceptions, whose incoherence goes unnoticed by those involved in it, and in Rome spectacles were such exceptions."[6]

Though sometimes decreed in response to signs, lethal games normally had no connection with divination and dealt more often with the general possibility of danger than with particular threats. While divination as a result responded to breaches in order, the exceptional violence of arena games itself was a breach, sociologically all the more interesting for being artificial, whereas the anomaly with which divination concerned itself occurred of its own accord. *Munera* were artificial also in the narrower sense of being contrived from violence so unusual in circumstance, manner, and concentration that combat and hunting became something quite different in the arena. Carnage in the games thus was rationalized under an axiom of greater violence managed through episodes of stylized, lesser violence. Its logic called for a staged exercise, a "show" of strength, or a war "game" "played" on society's own initiative in symbolic rehearsal of the permanent possibility of violence. *Munera* accordingly canvassed a full range of possible outcomes: winning and killing, sparing or dying; losing and killing, dying or being spared; both parties surviving or both dying.

The resolute performance expected from good gladiators is a direct corollary of their role as institutional transformers and conduits of violence. They felt (or ritually feigned, as modern wrestlers do) a rage for killing (Cic. *Tusc.* 4.48), and Cicero also speaks of the "hatred we [spectators] have for gladiators who die weak, suppliant and begging to live" (*Mil.* 92). Though it is not clear what phase of the show Seneca has in mind, the crowd's howl, "Kill, hit, burn! . . . Why does he die so slowly?" (*Ep.* 7.4–5) betrays the love of pure violence detected by Juvenal, too, behind the sex appeal exercised by ugly gladiators (*ferrum est quod amant;* 6.112).[7] On reflection, Romans might well have granted that there was something—psychologically if not morally—to the contention that "seeing a man killed [in the arena] is much like killing him" (Athenagoras *Embassy* 35; cf. Lactant. *Div. Inst.* 6.20.9–14: the spectator becomes *particeps;* Sen. *Clem.* 1.25.1: throwing a man to the lions is like tearing him apart with your own teeth). Some of this was ordinary bad temper at goods not delivered as advertised, the bloody-mindedness being no more earnest than, say, tough sport-talk in Petronius about "first rate iron, no quarter given, with the butchershop in the center so the whole amphitheater can see it" (*Sat.* 45; cf. "Kill the umpire!" in modern times, and in a noncontact sport at that). Lively engagement, moreover, would be a natural adjunct to the genuine expertise of many Romans in the technical side of gladiatorial combat. All the same, the fantasies of mayhem accompanying modern sports are not actually realized as they were at Rome, where there was little need for make-believe.

An angry crowd "insulted" by gladiators reluctant to die seems like peevish children to Seneca (*De Ira* 1.2.4–5). But spectators are in fact adults, and lack of what Seneca regards as grounds for genuine anger does not mean that their hostility is unreal, as is plain enough from the powerful physical reactions which are distinguished from true anger (2.2–3) and include defensive fear at such things as the sound of a war trumpet, the "depressing" (*tristis*) sight of deserved punishment, or an account of Hannibal at the gates of Rome (2.2.4). These kinds of fear, again directly pertinent to what went on in the arena, register threats to physical security, and several other military dangers that occur to Seneca also resemble arena action in being at one remove from real violence, either through representation (reports, pictures, enactments) or anticipation. It is the bare thought of combat, for example, that turns even a brave man pale when he handles arms, and it is the idea of violence that engages spectators at a *munus* as they think about what they are seeing. What is more, instinctive reactions can ultimately develop into an equally irrational lust for carnage on a vast scale, termed a "spectacle" by Seneca, doubtless with a glance at the arena (2.5.4). Though true single combat is exceptional in real war, combat is experienced individually, and so the spectacle of a fight to the death was bound to trigger powerful empathy.[8]

It takes little imagination to see what even a casual sporting taste for toughness on the part of the crowd under the circumstances could do to those on the sand. Many must have died benumbed by sheer terror; others were driven to suicide at the prospect of what would happen (Sen. *Ep.* 70.20–26 mentions three instances during one of Nero's shows). At the same time, courage frequently is a brutal business, indispensable even in less obviously military sports testing physical performance at its limits. In the arena spectators were close to the action. Claudius liked to watch the faces of gladiators as they died (Suet. *Claud.* 34.1), and if that was exceptional, *munera* still did their job by forming a highly unstable psychological and social compound of courage, skill, and violence.

Since what was advertised was a display of ferocity, it would not be possible to watch toughness being replaced by terror without some measure of disquiet at a deeper, less simply entertaining level as well. Like a fire drill deemed successful only when the building burns down, public rehearsals of violence are always in danger of going too far. In bringing out the internal contradictions of violence, Seneca cites the fear felt by the brutalizer himself of a victim he has dehumanized into a veritable *monstrum* kept in a cage and so dreadful to look at that those who do so are incapable even of pity (*De Ira* 3.17). Seneca is thinking primarily about what unrestrained savagery can do, but fear one feels at one's own atrocity and the loss of compassion by others who witness it are also perceptive psychological insights into the negative dimensions of violence. The former suggests a disfigured sense of guilt that makes up yet another aspect of the connection tying aggression and fear together (cf.

Tac. *Agr.* 42.3: people hate those they have wronged). Though violence in the arena was normally nothing so extreme as what Seneca envisages, the element of fear bears more directly on the disturbing or demoralizing effect of public spectacles and could well suggest that spectators cannot feel pity because it has become intolerable. In situations unthinkable for themselves, people may lose compassion not because they do not feel it but because, self-defensively, they cannot endure to feel it (a principle which leads to the Stoic depreciation of pity).

In any case, public brutality cannot do without a reassuring sense of order by which it is underwritten and made entertaining. Once violence threatens to become seriously disturbing, ferocity can mask a sense of fear felt at the naked fact of carnage unredeemed by any show of skill or courage. Cowardly death is unseemly because it reveals that the victims were just that—cowards, perhaps, but mere victims, too.[9] Fear must again have been a major ingredient in the sudden upwelling of pity that led to powerful swings of emotion. The spectators' abrupt turning against Pompey out of sympathy for the elephants at one of his shows (Dio 39.38.2–4; Pliny *HN* 8.20–21), public disapproval of Drusus' relish for bloody games (Tac. *Ann.* 1.76.3), and the popular favor Caracalla won for crying or averting his gaze when criminals were thrown to wild animals (*Hist. Aug.* 1.5) all suggest that the appeal of *munera* depended heavily on the deeply anomalous effect they had. Though a tired fighter could not perform up to standard, forcing a man to fight for his life twice on one day (Suet. *Calig.* 35.2) must have been thought to be cruel by some because double jeopardy seemed unfair.

Though speculation concerning crowd psychology is a hazardous business, it is less so in connection with the logic of institutions. Games are absorbing, to begin with, because they ultimately reflect absorbing interests of daily life, epitomized in the case of bloodshed at Rome by the competition for survival experienced in one form or another by every spectator, most of all by the political elite who sponsored *munera*. In Tertullian's phrase, gladiators were taught enough "to know how to die" (*De Spect.* 12), and when the arena was used as a place for execution, the game was, plainly enough, simply death itself in its frightening or fascinating aspects and in the pity or cruelty it aroused.[10] Varied as private reactions were bound to be, the social meaning was at bottom public realization of the possibility of death, realization in a literal sense for those fighting, in a richer social sense for those watching. Thus anger, as Cicero says, and fear—the one aggressive, the other defensive, and the two often closely paired by historians (Tac. *Hist.* 4.2.2) or ethical philosophers—were twin key ingredients in the social psychology of the games as well.

High-stake competition at Rome was a powerful stimulus to betting, particularly in the circus, and though it is true that gambling typically involves direct participation by individual players while games are a spectator sport, both can induce so strong an emotional identification with the action that chance is replaced by raw risk. Even the most mathematical gambling games may lose their connection with quantity and become qualitative, irrational passion for nothing but pure danger. The rush of momentary power, the intoxication of hazarding success or failure for its own sake, is an exaggerated form of what is at work in the intense highs and lows well attested in mass sports at Rome and elsewhere. Psychological approaches to gambling focus on its initially liberating effect along with the potential to go beyond entertainment and become a destructive breakdown of routine. Seen sociologically as an occasion for risk taking, controlled vicarious danger affords a break in routine, remains within the system, and socializes what otherwise would be disruptive behavior—all things that lethal sports did, too, in their own way. The power directly exercised by the gambler with a throw of the dice or a pull of the slot machine's handle is analogous to the crowd's thumbs-up or thumbs-down decision at the arena.

> One of the functions of society is to provide mechanisms that enable people to deal with and control potentially dangerous situations. Many social rituals perform this function. . . . [Gambling] provides escape from both the uncertainty and the boring routine of modern life by reinforcing, in familiar and highly ritualized surroundings, conventions and roles that let gamblers feel, at least for the duration of the game, that they are the masters of their fates. Some of the more structured gambling situations, such as horse-race betting, allow gamblers to confront the probabilistic, chancy nature of existence within the comforting bounds of ritual order.[11]

High risk in this form provides relatively benign interruption of routine. The machismo of Spanish bullfighters, whose contempt for danger can approach the suicidal fascination with empty risk characteristic of compulsive gamblers, has more unsettling effects close to the atmosphere of the arena.[12]

In their scale and focus on physical danger, *munera* have few parallels and seem most comparable as an institution to the mass human sacrifice practiced in ancient Mesoamerica. At the tops of pyramids, victims, sometimes by the thousands, had their chests slit open and their hearts torn out in a spray of blood to be offered, still throbbing, to the sun. The bodies were then tumbled down steep, blood-smeared steps running to the ground, where they might be skinned and have parts taken for consumption at banquets. Those even less fortunate were thrown into beds of glowing ashes before being pulled out for sacrifice. Next to the pyramids stood great racks containing thousands of skulls from previous sacrifices, to register, as the scale of games at Rome did, the importance of extraordinary violence publicly consumed.[13]

This is, of course, in many respects quite different from anything that happened at Rome, but comparison is actually all the more instructive because differences in substance go with formal similarities at more abstract levels of social rationale. Political intimidation was one specific feature which Aztec celebrations and Roman games had in common.[14] Moreover, besides dangerous ball games requiring protective equipment like that worn in the arena, the Spaniards describe what they call a "gladiatorial" contest reminiscent of the Etruscan Pherseu game, calling for one contestant to be handicapped in defending himself from lethal attack.[15] Differences, though, are initially more striking. At Rome public violence was less overtly religious and had relatively narrow, practical aims, such as winning political favor, affording public entertainment, and serving as a method of capital punishment. The first two of these are directly represented in the term *munus*, "owed gift." Aztec sacrificial mayhem, in contrast, was a much more ambitious institution, cosmic in scope and essentially religious, resting on the belief that the universe itself would perish if the sun failed to receive its regular ration of human blood. While raw material for public bloodshed was supplied as a by-product of warfare at Rome, the mission of the Aztec military was more urgently and exclusively to furnish victims, and so mock battles could be conducted to produce pretended captives for very real sacrifice.[16]

Considered formally, however, the ultimate rationale of violence in both institutions centers identically on the need for responding to danger. More exactly, it centers on furious, brutal physical activity releasing and making raw energy available to deal with the threat of disorder— political disorder at Rome, in Mexico a vastly greater cosmic entropy.[17] The purpose of the pain and carnage lay in tapping vital power by provoking, appropriating, and finally "taming" death. The problem is ultimately not death and danger, as they are elemental facts about which nothing can be done, but the insecurity they create in the scheme of things. About that, something can be done through ritual mediating between the fact of death and human attitudes to form a socially constituted substitute, a *corpus vile*, available for public uses.[18] This is similar to reinforcement of security in divination by projecting danger onto officially accredited substitutes (the sign and the price of averting the danger it signals), which can then be readily gotten rid of through *procuratio*.

Several other things entailed by the central axiom of danger embraced to be mastered appear in both systems. Orgies of blood are occasions as much for recognizing danger as for celebrating security and victory. Vulnerability, moreover, is kept at bay through brutality which is reassuring precisely through its excess.[19] Aztec celebrations thus were at once negative and positive, undesirable as well as indispensable, and occupied a marginal position in the scheme of social values like that of gladiators and gladiatorial combat. Again like Roman games, Aztec ritual could exorcise violence only by incorporating it directly into the ceremony.[20] At Rome death was originally brought under a measure of control by additional death staged at the dead man's tomb. Much later a mime about the capture and crucifixion of the highwayman Laureolus must have owed its very long run in part to its power to exorcise anxiety about threats to law and order. In the anecdote of Arrachion, the limits of sporting violence are extended to include death; in the arena, violence is concentrated at the center, squarely within the domain of social control in a highly militaristic society. In both cases the crucial factor is a two-way border transaction breaching normalcy to permit processing and elimination of disorder. Arrachion's fate is deeply anomalous, but he still comes under the reassuring category of winner; *munera* are a routine feature of public life, whose social meaning, however, derives from their deeply abnormal character, as the meaning of Laureolus' story did when performance became reality and actual crucifixion was carried out under Domitian.

2

Games and Liminoid Ritual

In arena games, then, sets of fundamental opposites (life/death, security/ danger) are tied to each other in a distinctive reciprocal relationship allowing social contradiction or anomaly to be both acknowledged and resolved. Acknowledgment is no less important than resolution; normalcy must be breached before it can be repaired. *Munera* do both by confirming order through disorder, controlling violence by means of violence, injecting fear into entertainment, and transforming ritual into reality through actual death.

The concept of liminoid social institutions is of special value for exploring the complex logic of how this process worked at Rome. Liminal ritual is commonly treated as a three-stage process of separation, transition (ordeal), and reintegration, through which individuals or society at large recognize, deal with, and dispose of threats. The pattern is pertinent for our purpose mainly in its formal aspect. Though especially important in rituals of initiation, it is in fact a pervasive principle with a much wider application, termed liminoid in the distinction made by Victor Turner between liminal ritual proper and more general forms of social anomaly.[1] In this definition, liminoid institutions, found in industrial societies where liminal ritual has undergone substantial attenuation, tend to be socially marginal rather than central, individual rather than communal, and a matter for leisure time rather than serious activity. The last applies to *munera,* the first two much less so, and Rome in any case was not an industrial society. Still, liminality was not rigidly limited to ritual procedures even in ancient societies but extended into broader regions. In that aspect, liminality can be a useful organizing principle for cultural features that constituted ritual only in a loose sense.

As specific purposes are lost sight of, liminal ritual is attenuated in

25

one way or another into a vaguer liminoid procedure that still preserves the underlying scheme of threat and response. Attenuation is most often caused by gradual changes in the nature of the problems addressed by rituals. A. van Gennep noted the tendency of some phases in *rites de passage* to assume autonomy, and one specific form of attenuation consists of normal liminal elements present but relocated.[2] Certain components of the pattern may become unusually prominent or be repositioned in new combinations. The chief point of contact with arena games is in the stylized danger characteristic of the ordeal in the middle phase. To this extent gladiatorial combat can be thought of as incorporating a ritual component without being ritual in a precise sense of the term. Before experiencing vicarious participation in lethal combat, the spectators were separated from normal outside activities by gathering in the arena (whose barriers mark separation from the combatants inside, too) and afterward were reintegrated into society by returning to daily routine with an enhanced sense of solidarity.

In connection with the central element of danger, another formal ritual component comes into play. This one, from rites of expulsion, primarily concerns the gladiator in his role as a dangerous stranger isolated from normal contact, as strangers are, though not in order to be accepted into society (as usually happens in liminal rituals) but to be eliminated from it.[3] The pattern is again faded, since gladiators had no "role" in a proper ritual sense. But ritual functions permeate social institutions, and participants in the games as a rule were in fact expelled either literally through death or, less directly, through the marginality entailed by their status. They were, that is to say, isolated as outsiders in a place reserved for aliens (the arena), were then subjected to ceremonial violence, and sooner or later were gotten rid of permanently. Powerful feelings of participation engendered in those who watch competition of this kind can come either through symmetrical violence between equals or asymmetrical, unequal violence between an entire group and a minority or individual.[4] The former defines winners and losers, as in combat between two well-matched fighters or in chariot racing. The latter expels victims, as in gladiatorial combat observed by a crowd either identifying itself with the victor or viewing all participants as victims. We can thus speak of expulsion as an inverse corollary of reintegration, in that it achieves solidarity not by directly restoring a normal state but indirectly, by way of getting rid of aliens and losers.

A dual, inverse relationship of this kind between negative expulsion and positive reintegration in the two sides of a single liminoid process is common in funeral ceremonies, where survivors and the dead are formally opposites, yet opposites composing a single social group, as crowd and gladiators do.[5] Both dead and living are separated from normal life; both are in a transitional stage (mourning in the case of the living; in that of the dead, the corpse's incongruous condition represents someone/ something—like Arrachion—between life and death); both share in integration, though quite differently—survivors through resumption of normal life, the dead by expulsion from it into their own proper world.[6] Taken as a separate autonomous phase, gladiatorial combat for those in the arena may be terminal violence, while for those watching, it is entertainment, that is, the immediate object, the "show" they go to see in a special place at a special time. But violence becomes more than diversion as it is transformed on the safe side of the barrier in the crowd's consciousness into an interiorized "representational space," where, in a sense, the spectators see themselves as a social entity confronted with violence and as a social hierarchy defined by their own segregated seating arrangements.[7] Blurring of the line between theater and reality, between spectacle and audience, turns games in the arena into a highly effective medium for the anomalous state of affairs which they simultaneously represent and are, by enacting, in an exceptionally direct way, carnage as part of public order.

Resemblances of one kind or another between gladiatorial games and modern sports readily come to mind: with hockey or football on the score of special equipment, with boxing on that of brutal hand-to-hand combat, with soccer or again football on that of team tactics in the case of mass gladiatorial military games, with auto racing on the score of real and imminent danger. The social meaning of games and of public events in general lies in the sense of reality each creates. In one important respect the peculiar sense of reality attached to gladiatorial shows is most closely reproduced by a form of modern entertainment normally not thought of as sport at all. Among violent spectator sports, professional wrestling as it is conducted in the United States is perhaps the most remote from a legitimate game and for that reason closest to bloodshed in the arena. The elaborately choreographed outcome turns competition into a melodrama of good against evil violence, whose manifest artificiality calls for a special kind of involvement through self-deception on the part of the spectators. It is true that the violence here is not authentic as it was in the arena. But the messages it carries are no less socially real, since while genuine danger is absent, at the level of public performance it persists in the form of ceremonial violence, largely replacing what is done with what is thought.[8]

Security and insecurity, order and disorder, are fundamental possibilities faced by all societies. They are what divination in its countless varieties was concerned with, and arena games belonged to an equally extensive class of public occasions for suspending the routine of daily life and attending to the pressures and threats it posed. Festivals were experienced not only one by one but as parts of the larger yearly social rhythm, reflecting the rhythm of nature with its positive and negative phases. Some were a time of celebration, others of anxiety, with both together representing the ultimate polar possibilities of success and failure. As the function of institutions is, of course, to reinforce, not undermine, morale, periodic breaks for the most part are vacations from trouble. Recall Mary Douglas' rule: "Where there is dirt, there is system."[9] Order, that is to say, is prior to disorder and defines it. But the relationship runs the other way as well. Order implies disorder, and so all festivals are at the same time determined by the opposite of what they ostensibly celebrate: harvest festivals by famine, fertility rituals by sterility, parades of military strength by military danger. The same uneasy conjunction is operative again in liminal rituals, as order reemerges only after an interlude of its opposite. To the extent, then, that disorder was processed in much the same way through ritualization in public shows of violence at Rome, *munera,* too, can be understood in accordance with the antithetic logic of liminal institutions and their peculiar incorporation of potential dysfunction to assure proper functioning.

3

Gladiatorial Combat

In the case of *munera* the dysfunction in question is lethal physical violence, preeminently the violence of warfare, although games could be associated with danger more generally in time of crisis due to plague or famine or other natural disaster. Originally gladiatorial combat was a ritual response to the death of prominent members of the community.[1] Racing games seem to have been similarly connected with renewal of life through vigorous, hazardous physical activity. Stylized combat was an instrument for safeguarding communal vitality, and as the connection between the two weakened, concern with violence and public welfare persisted, but now only in a general way as part of routine celebrations of civic power. What originally had been close to sacrificial dueling lost much of its overtly sacrificial substance, without ceasing to have a powerful symbolic afterlife in the sense of danger that always goes with combat.

Roman religion catered especially to fear, which in the case of gladiatorial games was at first due to the threat posed by the dead man's spirit, probably from its desire for blood and vengeance. Until about the time of Constantine, blood taken from dead gladiators was still ritually poured by a high official onto a statue of Jupiter Latiaris, perhaps into its throat. But any original notion of strengthening corporate vitality was no longer salient, nor were th⌐ ͏͏͏͏͏͏͏͏ ͏͏͏͏ ͏͏͏͏ ͏͏͏͏͏ by Augustus or Marcus Aurelius (Dio 55.8.5; *Hist. Aug.* Marcus 8.2) thought of very strongly as a genuinely efficacious offering of blood.[2] Games were essentially ceremonies for the living, not sacrifice for the dead. When Christians detected behind bloodshed in the arena sinister demonic spirits feeding on gore, their understanding of the rationale of gladiatorial combat remained tied to notions of sacrifice. Non-Christians, more positively, found a larger social purpose in the military utility of staged violence. Though for many years gladiatorial combat was a feature only of private ceremonies, its gradual expansion in scale from the mid–third century B.C. and later adoption as public entertainment were perhaps influenced by the escalation of military violence that accompanied imperial expansion. In any event, *munera* continued to play an important role, because shifts in emphasis on specifically religious anxieties had no effect on the anxiety deeply colored by military violence prominent in Roman experience, to say nothing of the more general background fear in daily life experienced as vague uneasiness about what might happen.

Games in general, not only gladiatorial contests, aimed at renewal of the community's vigor through furious discharge of energy, especially on the part of young people, who for that reason occupied a prominent place in public sport. The general connection of sport with crises of one sort or another is rooted in the elemental threat of failing vitality. Danger from this direction can be dealt with by events scheduled regularly to tap into natural rhythms, while those given only on occasion have more narrowly political aims. The threat posed to civil peace by the latter led to some measures for state control that were later taken over and extended by the emperors, under whom the games became an important factor in maintaining political equilibrium. As direct connections with funeral rites weakened, the editor's freedom to give games at his own convenience greatly enhanced their political value. Long delays became common in the late Republic, since favor could best be won by entertainment sponsored during a term of office.

While explaining the political uses of public bloodshed, this says nothing about why it had an appeal in the first place. In addition to warning about a demonic dimension to games, Christian critics also addressed themselves to more accessible aspects which throw light on the psychological and sociological role of the games. In the arena, they charged, the appeal was sheer brutality *(saevitia)*, in the theater lust *(lascivia)*, in the circus *furor*.[3] *Furor* is the emotional violence tied to victory or defeat and intensified by the acute uncertainty between the two evoked in Seneca's account of a sporting crowd's mindless roar echoing distantly to those who have stayed at home (*Ep.* 83.7, 80.2; cf. Juv. 11.197).[4] While the aims of Christian social criticism were chiefly judgmental and not descriptive, it was made through a genuine grasp of communally shared passions as aspects of an underlying social logic, though a logic seen as morally abnormal rather than as incorporating a principle of liminoid abnormality to help preserve equilibrium in the social system by dealing with what threatens to disrupt it.

Ancient theories of catharsis recognized the social utility of vicarious emotions, especially those aroused in the theater, in venting dangerous impulses under controlled conditions. A cathartic approach to the games and to sport more generally receives a good deal of support from theories that emphasize the effect of periodically relaxing the inhibitions on which social order normally relies.[5] Theaters, of course, are not the same as circuses or arenas; the emotions in question are somewhat different and perhaps not so simply released. Still, a Freudian model of relaxed inhibition applied to the games at Rome does take account of sado-masochistic gratification perhaps touched on by Ovid when he links the ambience of sexual excitement dating back to the rape of the Sabine women (*sollicitos ludos; Ars Am.* 1.101) with the more violent arena (*sollicito tristis harena foro;* 1.164), where stimulation gains additional spice from betting and there is again a sexual component ("the son of Venus has often fought there, and the spectator who has watched men being wounded is wounded himself . . . as he chats, brushes her hand and asks who is winning after he places a bet, he groans from the blow, feels the dart and himself becomes part of the game," 1.165–70; cf. the women who "come to see and to be seen," 1.99).

It is hard to know how far this textbook description of a game flooding the spectacle can be pressed, and so far as sport goes, some research suggests that aggression may actually be increased by participation, whose chief effect is not to relieve tension but to foster a reassuring sense of membership in a group.[6] Aggressiveness, in other words, may not be felt to come from internal pressure needing release, but from an external target against which it can be directed. Sharp distinctions in such matters are artificial, since they are largely different ways of looking at the same thing. Tensions may be built up in order to provide relief, inhibitions may be relaxed, and fantasies of power may be indulged in ways that all work together to increase a feeling of security and solidarity through aggressive activity. Definitions of ritual as a general rule can be "recast in terms of psychological function . . . especially in light of . . . emphasis on the emotional dimension of ritual."[7] Since there is every reason to suppose that carnage in the arena had multiple psychological roots, enhancement of security or reduction of anxiety would naturally be parts of its ritual function.

In celebrating victory, violent sport expressed a sense of power and gratification at survival: for example, games were vowed during the Aetolian war and were later given, together with a lion and panther hunt, on a very large scale (Livy 39.22.1–2). Games given while war was in progress, on the other hand, would bring with them a stronger element of anxious wishful thinking, which served as a psychological protective coloring in the face of current danger. Thus *munera* given for the funeral of a former consul at the height of Hannibal's invasion (Livy 23.30.15) must have reflected the "special *religio*" (anxiety) at impending war mentioned in connection with later games (Livy 36.36.7). That would have been true, too, of the lavish performances and hunts offered by Caesar amid serious civil strife (App. *BCiv.* 2.2.13). Dio's remark that, in turning attention for a time from political brutality to games, Caracalla showed himself no less fond of sporting bloodshed (77.6.2) again treats the latter as a disturbing, aggressive extension of, rather than escape from, the former.

In the language of ritual, public bloodshed provided a liminoid interlude during which a high level of public tension was "entertained," in both senses of the word: "diverted" by the absorbing performance, more seriously "dealt with" as something demanding attention. What in real crises is a matter of life and death becomes absorbing entertainment precisely because at another place and time it *is* an extraordinary matter of life and death. In accordance with the structure of liminoid ritual, this institutionalized anomaly mediates the poles of normal/abnormal, secure/vulnerable states by passing from the former through the latter and back to the former. That is why those who fought in the arena were as much a symbolic threat to Roman society as they were actual victims of it, and why their death or that of someone like the highwayman Laureolus was not murder even when it was not execution either. In its own way, the death of Arrachion, too, escapes being merely accidental or criminal and receives positive social meaning precisely through its exceptional character. So disturbing to the populace was an attempted breakout by gladiators at Praeneste that it led to much talk about Spartacus (Tac. *Ann.* 15.46.1). Fears along this line were normally allayed by brutal discipline in the gladiatorial schools and, in the games themselves, by ritual disposal of those who embodied the perennial possibility of violence.[8] Anxieties about enemy invasion or gladiators and slaves set loose on society could be safely addressed in combat whose outcome was assured, as the death of Laureolus in the mime show again was.

Sham danger was thus the key not only for the games' power to entertain but also for the more serious dimension of the violence they involved. Real threats cannot be gotten rid of in complete safety, and so the efficacy of ritual substitutes depends on how strongly their reality is felt. The very similar dilemma caught in the axiom *si pacem vis, bellum para* has direct pertinence to arena combat, whose peacetime logic hinged on its being waged with wartime consequences but in total safety. Dummy weapons occasionally used in playful arena ritual were at two removes from the real world, while genuine weapons and genuine bloodshed were kept off at one remove by real ritual. The aim was to acknowledge danger without losing control; the violence is real enough where it is, but where it is is not the everyday real world. The transition from make-believe performance to reality was brought about largely through obtrusive brutality, which as an aspect of the logic of gladiatorial combat is not explicable solely through the sadistic gratification it undoubtedly provided but through the very opposite as well—stylized fear of violence.[9] Violence may not be in the real world, but it is real enough where it is. The shock therapy delivered by human sacrifice, called for in times of unusual social stress, is effective in the same way through the deeply anomalous reversal it creates by sanctioning what is normally forbidden. Disease is cure, as it is again in the shock treatment of decimation, when the general turns on his own army.

In this way arena violence, which is in Tertullian's mind when he writes that the Romans "relieve" or "allay death with murder" (*mortem homicidiis consolantur; De Spect.* 12), has a separate, social dimension. In fact, if his own language about "relief" is taken without the strong irony running through the section on *munera,* it points to a genuine social need addressed by the violence Tertullian calls public murder. It is true that what is allayed is primarily the dead man's anger at dying, while his survivors derive pleasure (with a hint of sadism) from funeral games, and magistrates later win political favor for sponsoring them. But since blood is shed in the first place because of the fear felt by society at the dead man's anger, gratification from the show is colored by the perception of danger already present in the original rationale of gladiatorial combat. As bloodshed was then later socialized in full-scale public games, the source of danger shifted from the dead to gladiators themselves. The ambivalent combination of relief and fear which their death occasions is what comes out in the delight felt by people when Constantine destroyed the enemy by throwing German war prisoners to the animals (*Panegyrici Latini* 6.12.3, 12.23.3) or in the arena games put on at Beirut "so that as criminals are punished, the business [*ergon*] of war can be the pleasure of peacetime" (Joseph. *AJ* 19.335–37; cf. the cheer raised at the public execution of Simon ben Giora, Joseph. *BJ* 7.154–55; Symmachus *Relat.* 47.1: *voluptati/formidini*). When 225 ringleaders of a Samnite revolt were scourged and beheaded in the forum *summo gaudio plebis* (Livy 9.24.15), satisfaction again came from the action taken to alleviate insecurity felt by colonies. The anomalous "serious pleasure" entailed by dependence of public security on institutions of violence is marked by the slight oxymoron in Josephus' phrase about business being pleasure, as it is in Tertullian's "murderous allayment" of death.

In 20 B.C. Augustus dedicated a temple of Mars Ultor to celebrate the recovery of military standards lost earlier in the East (Dio 54.8.1–3). Then in 2 B.C. he had 260 lions and 36 crocodiles killed and a naval battle staged in conjunction with gladiatorial combat at the dedication of a second temple to Mars Ultor (Dio 55.10). Many years before at Philippi, he had vowed a temple to Mars in return for success in avenging Caesar's death (Suet. *Aug.* 29.2; cf. Dio 59.22.7). The original personal motive of *ultio paterna* was diluted by recapture of lost standards in 20 B.C., and the length of time which had elapsed before the vow was carried out in 2 B.C. naturally tended to make any connection with vengeance remote. The delay was probably due to the same concern for political timing that created lengthy gaps between *munera* and the deaths they marked. Once Augustus had assumed power, the security of his regime was of primary concern, hence his provision that officials should set out for their provinces from the new temple.[10]

If vengeance had been modified by the passage of time, however, it was not eliminated, nor had Mars become an administrator. As thoughts of narrow revenge faded, the significance of the violence it entailed was transformed into a more general concern with security, much as after gladiatorial combat had been transformed into a social institution, its original retrospective connection with individual vengeance for the dead gave way to the broader, prospective communal function of violence represented on the occasion of Augustus' celebration by hunting games *(venationes)* and war games. If his current position made vengeance unnecessary, he knew that need for it always remained a possibility, and the awareness of danger implicit even in ceremonies of power is apparent in his plan to have standards that were lost in future campaigns returned here. What is more, the nails he wanted driven into the temple by the censors revived an old procedure for dealing with social disorder and plague through magical *defixio* (Dio 55.10.4).

Apart from the association with vengeance, positive/negative polarity was seen very strongly within Mars himself, who had been permitted no temple within the *pomerium* at Rome until Augustus' dedication because he defined two incompatibile phases of social life. As Quirites, Romans were at peace, as *milites* they were at war, and so the military *comitia centuriata* could not meet within the *pomerium* either. Mars thus had *saevus* and *tranquillus* faces, the former when he was marching out to war (as Gradivus), the latter when he presided over internal peace. "Since his divinity was dedicated outside the walls, there will be no armed quarrel among the citizens, yet he will defend the walls from the danger of war" (Vitr. *De Arch.* 1.7.1; as god of fire, Vulcan has the same ambivalent status). Mars's *saevus* face, too, was ambivalent in external warfare so long as he was "still impartial to both sides [*communis*] and fortune had not yet made a decision where she would apply her power"

(Livy 10.28.1). And when showing two faces internally, he embodied civil *furor* whose wild manifestations had to be fenced off, as gladiatorial violence was in the Saepta, Forum, or arena. Like the *pomerium,* rituals of lustration associated with warfare traced a confining, internal safety zone around violence. The procession in strength made before battle around the Roman fleet or army transferred potential danger to an animal which could be gotten rid of deep in the sea or buried on land.[11] Dangerous influences clinging even to victorious troops after their foreign excursion were removed upon their return from campaign, and behind all such cathartic measures looking to the past or apotropaic ones looking to the future lay a fundamental sense of the danger inseparable from any exercise of power.

Although war is divided ritually into two aspects, wild and tame (negative danger and positive victory), what is conveniently separated in ritual substitutes remains linked in reality. Catiline's "incredible" toughness in the field and unyielding courage to the bitter end, his passion for civil strife, his "tricky, unstable mind," the "newness [i.e., anomaly] of dangers and crimes," and the no less anomalous "joy and grief, mourning and celebration" that greeted his downfall (Sall. *Cat.* 4, 5, 60, 61) all made him and other such figures into living embodiments of Mars *anceps* (Livy 21.1.2) in a new, more disturbing political guise, epitomizing the doubly problematic nature of violence during civil war, when social order was most radically breached.[12] The same ambivalence was embodied again in the ambivalent social status of gladiators, central figures in an institution through which the threat of violence could be played out under more favorable circumstances by Roman society.

If "the Romans . . . conceived of *pax* as a condition that could only result from successful war," their military displays would naturally have an implicitly defensive side, insofar as peace was a function of war and the possibility of defeat an inseparable twin of victory.[13] Three hundred seventy Roman deserters were taken to Rome, scourged, and thrown from a rock (Livy 24.20.6); more than three hundred captured at Rhegium were scourged and beheaded in the Forum "to restore Roman credibility among the allies" (Polyb. 1.7.11–12 [the number is put at four thousand in Livy 28.28.3]; cf. Polyb. 11.30; Dion. Hal. 6.30.1; App. *Hisp.* 6.32). It is true that such measures were vigorous assertions of power and that plain entertainment came in as well when Scipio the Younger threw non-Roman deserters to wild animals or Lucius Paulus had them mashed by elephants at public shows (Val. Max. 2.7.13–14). But the dose of official terror to stiffen military discipline achieves its effect precisely through the unusual scale of brutality, which in turn may express not only power but also consciousness of threats that make good discipline imperative at any cost. Posing danger to order by their very existence, captives and deserters are anomalies, "dirt" in the system most efficaciously disposed of by means of the violence they represent. At times of victory, when danger is remote, the violence seems gratuitous, but for a militaristic society where desertion is treason, overkill is an axiomatic response. The example cited immediately before these cases by Valerius Maximus is Scipio's crucifixion of Roman deserters (2.7.12). After first apologizing for the impropriety of servile punishment in the case of Roman citizens, Valerius Maximus goes on to cases of discipline "that can be mentioned without reopening patriotic wounds." His unease, like Livy's at human sacrifice in Rome (*minime Romano sacro;* 22.57), again signals the inordinate intensity which makes crucifixion so inappropriate for Roman victims and, by the same token, so effective in meeting the danger posed by slaves.

The impact of decimation, too, comes from excess both exactly quantified (every tenth man and a full 10 percent) and wholly random (any and every tenth man, guilty or innocent alike, a proportion further reduced by Antony on one occasion to better focus the terror; App. *BCiv.* 3.7.43). Decimation is the clearest example of how shows of violence can spring from an acute sense of fear or failure which may finally transform itself from self-defensive anger into self-destruction when no other target is available, as happens in an incident mentioned by Plutarch. Antony's troops *ask* to be decimated out of shame at a poor performance, and he *asks* the gods to inflict on himself the disaster due for previous successes (Plut. *Ant.* 44.3). It is not too much to speak in some cases of a paroxysm of violence whose social meaning lies in insistence on the extraordinarily high cost to be paid (see Addendum 2). Taste for violence seems normal enough in such sentiments as "bravery is eager for danger" or "soldiers glory in wounds," nor is there anything surprising about the gladiator Triumphus's complaint at the rarity of *munera* under Tiberius ("The good old days are gone!"; Sen. *Prov.* 4.4). On the other hand, Tacitus' ambiguously admiring description of German women eagerly examining their menfolks' wounds (*Germ.* 7.2) is vaguely disturbing, and the gladiator who enjoyed having a doctor probe his wounds (Gell. *NA* 12.5.13) is clearly a pathological case, as are troops eager for decimation.

Quantitatively excess cost, as we will see, became a central factor in the social pathology of arena bloodshed, and other, more routine rituals of public power underwent inflation, too. On the axiom "no pain, no gain," a minimum level of violence ensuring that the victory was not "dustless and bloodless" (Gell. *NA* 5.6.21) had to be met for authorization of a triumph (see Addendum 3). Valerius Maximus (2.8.1) sets the number at five thousand enemy dead, adding that to avoid an inflated body count, generals were required to certify the total. A negative corollary to heavy losses inflicted on the enemy is the cost in lives to oneself, and so minimum and maximum casualties on both sides had to be taken into account. If failure to reach a minimum number of enemy dead could preclude triumph, so could exceeding the maximum of friendly casualties (Dion. Hal. 9.26.8–9). After a battle that produced "more grief than joy" due to heavy losses, the Romans fought again and won; only then did they celebrate a triumph (Livy 4.17–20.1). The consul Marcus Fabrius voluntarily "decimated" his own reputation when he declined a triumph owing to the loss of his fellow consul and his brother (Dion. Hal. 9.13.4), while disgruntled troops inflicted another species of decimation on their commander's prestige by abusing him for the losses they had incurred (Dion. Hal. 9.3.4) instead of saluting him imperator.

Both origin and meaning of the triumph—Rome's quintessential power ceremony—are highly controversial, the latter particularly so owing to political changes which affected religious content.[14] On any account, however, the two antithetic elements we have been examining were always present: proclamation of success and assertion of power on the one hand, defensive gestures acknowledging cost and risk on the other. Whether or not the triumph and other public games *(ludi)* like those in the circus originated specifically from the pattern of New Year's festivals, tension between success and failure, and ultimately between life and death, characteristic of seasonal festivals did appear in later, more heavily politicized celebrations of victory.[15] The success of society triumphant was forever shadowed by the dangers facing society militant. Insofar as it seemed prudent to admit that as much thanksgiving was due to the gods as recognition to the general, what the triumph expressed was human dependence. And even if the victory parade did not actually purify the army from blood guilt, negative elements were still much in evidence: the cathartic power of the laurel worn by the general and his troops, the apotropaic abuse he received from them, and a variety of other apotropaic devices revealing anxiety even as they tried to disarm it. One detail was intended quite specifically to represent a larger understanding of what victory meant: the slave who, standing behind the triumphator, held a golden crown over his head and reminded him to look behind to his own mortality.

Though denial of a full triumph was frequently the result of political intrigue, the *ovatio* which replaced it again expressed a wider symbolic sense of human limits: the victor's (relative) humiliation, entering the city on foot or horseback and not in a chariot, embodied what he had not achieved. The curious report of Caesar crawling up the Capitoline steps on his knees, oblivious to the symbols of glory around him, seems connected to some such idea. Claudius is supposed to have done the same thing, and Dio thematically couples Caesar's gesture with the humiliation he had suffered earlier when an axle on the victory chariot broke as he was passing the temple of Fortuna (Dio 43.21.1–2, 60.23.1). Whatever effect the slave's cautionary message to the triumphator had on the public at large, stories of pity for some captives (Plut. *Aem.* 33.3–4) suggest that old anxieties about divine jealousy being most apt to strike when least expected were at times felt by spectators, too, as pity was in the arena. In a variation on the Arrachion theme, explored in chapter 1, the danger attached to military success for the victor came to pass in another anecdote when, in answer to his own prayer asking for the cost of victory to be paid by himself rather than by Rome, Aemilius Paulus lost two children shortly before and after his triumph (Plut. *Aem.* 35–36).

Institutionally, then, victory and defeat—as general possibilities—are deeply implicated with each other. The folkloristic character of some of the stories probing that idea and the frequency with which they are repeated attest to its powerful grip. Psychologically, too, as disquieting elements inherent in the nature of triumphs made themselves felt also in the arena, the taste for brutal entertainment there again became a function of insecurity. While risk was played out in the combat being waged between those who might actually die, it was being played out on another level of symbolic meaning between them and the spectators.[16] In that respect, violence did not indulge sadistic impulses so much as it imposed measure on the possibility of unmeasured violence; ritually disciplined violence done to outsiders was reconstituted as the security of insiders who could return home safe, sound, and victorious, as those who witnessed a triumphal spectacle did. For if society is to flourish, others must not, and decisive violence is the unmistakable medium or "show" of decisive strength.[17] Like the imperial politics which it reinforced ideologically, gladiatorial combat was for the most part a zero-sum game playable under rules guaranteeing that losers lose everything (most clearly in *munera sine missione*). At this microcosmic level, each duel is all or nothing, while, at a higher systemic level, all gladiators together lose everything before a public which loses nothing. The game accordingly had to be played at cross-purposes as one game within another, "pieces" being the players themselves whose aim was to see how often they could win individually, while society played to see how good it could be at losing "men."

In this process, combat is transformed into a secondary, substitute game available for public use. The uncertain outcome of normal contests must be settled anew at each playing, as gladiatorial combat was by the participants. Rituals, on the other hand, are privileged games, "fixed" to assure the same (correct) outcome, so that to the uncertainty which guarantees the entertainment value of normal games there is added in ritual games the security of a controlled outcome keeping the danger of defeat in check. Reassurance is achieved mainly through elaborate ceremonies which distance intense action occurring at the immediate level of competition, minimize individual intentions, and focus attention on the social conception or logic of the occasion. This is a larger code which members of a society "learn to learn" and which Tertullian has in mind when he remarks that gladiators must know enough to die (De Spect. 12).

> Symbolic protection of society reaches its high point in *munera* when the spectators, arranged in good order—important people dressed in signs of their status, soldiers in their parade uniforms, and the emperor in triumphal garb—assist with eliminating, crushing, and forcing submission of all enemies, real or potential, of order: those condemned to the beasts or the sword, rebels and brigands, prisoners of war, dangerous barbarians, or slaves, always the object of fear. How better to associate the masses with rejection of all rebels and troublemakers of every sort, enemies internal and external? What better way to spread among the masses the lessons of fear overcome, of discipline, submission, courage, and virile violence— all of which these diminished creatures, even women and on occasion dwarfs or children, exemplify?[18]

The mainly military danger which gladiatorial violence rehearsed was immediately established by the equipment, the trumpet blast that started proceedings, and prisoners or regular troops sent into staged but still lethal combat.[19] Military violence had permeated Roman society to a remarkable degree throughout the Republic, and once Rome was free from any serious external enemies, much of its aggression was directed internally at civil threats. Though the Empire depended on a professional military establishment, armed force continued to be a source of disorder, especially in Italy, and the possibility of civil violence remained deeply engrained in the Roman consciousness.[20] The military (*miles*), seen by Tacitus as a separate factor along with Senate and people, was itself dangerous because of its role in civil war. Institutionally, however, personal dangers of warfare, no longer so familiar a part of life, were replaced for many by vicarious gladiatorial combat that could help exorcise the ever-lurking alternative of disorder.[21]

Gladiatorial games were on occasion used to bolster the morale of military units, while actual land or sea battles were reenacted to do the same on the home front. In combat staged by Scipio before some troops in Spain, all participants had freely volunteered for various reasons of honor (Livy 28.21). Claudius staged a simple *munus* without *venationes* in the praetorian camp (Suet. *Claud.* 21.4), and a pageant of Rome receiving the surrender of British kings presided over by Claudius in general's uniform seems to have been political ceremony, morale enhancement, and historical reenactment all at once (21.6). Complexities in the sociology of violence at Rome come out again in complaints that a sport like boxing, the most brutal of nonmilitary games, might entirely replace military experience (Tac. *Ann.* 14.20.4). It is perhaps not surprising that where gladiatorial combat, with its heavily military trappings, was regular entertainment or served as a morale builder, boxing could seem to be a sign of weakness. For ferocious and entertaining as boxing might be (it was added to gladiatorial combat by Caligula; Suet. *Calig.* 18.1), public security, after all, was a matter of large-scale military violence and therefore tied to symbolic rituals which addressed the special anxieties associated with it.

Some aspects of racing, too, had military uses. The physical prowess at Rome's disposal was the obvious point made by Augustus' celebration of Actium with gymnastic contests, prisoners of war in gladiatorial combat, and boys and men from the nobility taking part in horse races (Dio 53.1.4–6). War dances occasionally figured in circus performances (Livy 44.9.4–7), while grotesque effigies of threatening demons (Manducus, the "Cruncher") carried in the *pompa* added menacing ideas of defeat. But racing was less directly paramilitary than gladiatorial combat was, and so the danger it embodied took a different form, though one which could be fully as hazardous as combat. Risk was focused at the turning point in the circus, the most treacherous spot on the track, marked in Greek horse racing by the *taraxippos* (the place where horses panic) and in Rome perhaps by the underworld associations of Consus.[22] What is more, the violence of racing often spread into serious civil disturbances, which (like the violence of modern soccer crowds) could make symbolic political statements and express the elemental tensions and risks of competition that pervaded real life as well.

The fanatic mentioned by Pliny the Elder who immolated himself on a charioteer's funeral pyre (*HN* 7.186) must have done so in part because he saw his own vicarious feelings of success intolerably threatened. Partisans on the other side, feeling no less threatened by his death, minimized its significance by spreading a rumor that he had accidentally fallen into the fire during a fainting spell. Nothing could better illustrate the crucial symbolic role of danger and violence in Roman games than this deeply anomalous response, treated not as truly irrational (as Pausanias treats Timanthes' suicide; Paus. 6.8.4), but as something with a powerful meaning that cannot be dismissed out of hand but must be normalized and made to disappear in the routine flow of trivial events. By at last "realizing" the many earlier potential deaths shared vicariously with his idol, the dead man had brought what the games represented directly into life, in the process again touching on the larger issues raised by Arrachion's death. Spectators' intense engagement is the subject of comment by other observers. For Tertullian it is a sign of panic and moral collapse in Roman society (*De Spect.* 16), while Augustine echoes Ovid's notion of violence spreading from arena to stands (Ov. *Ars Am.* 1.165–70). Even someone who tries to resist is "struck with a worse wound in his mind than the gladiator is in his body" and loses his identity in that of the crowd (August. *Confessions* 6.8). With a somewhat lighter touch, Dio Chrysostom satirizes the vicarious thrill acted out through wholly useless body language by spectators (*Or.* 32.80–86; cf. John Chrysostom *Homily on I Cor. 12.5*).

These are acute evocations of mass psychology, whose narrowly ethical focus, however, does not do full justice to the logic of group solidarity created by public participation in violence. Pliny the Younger is shrewdly aware of the overwhelming desire to be with the winner—*any* winner—at work in devotion to sports when he remarks that if a team of horses changed party color halfway through a race, its partisans would instantly change their loyalty (*Ep.* 9.6). Stuffy or not, his complaint that the color, not the horses' speed or drivers' skill, is what counts recognizes a brute need for victory and a fear of defeat whose intensity suggests that meaning is being attached to games on a relatively abstract plane where victory-as-such produces powerful feelings of rightness, success, and security.[23] The corollary is violence-as-such producing a special symbolic sense of power through which theater and circus (Suet. *Ner.* 16.2, 26.2) are linked to arena despite their many differences. Stories of emperors' overwrought, on occasion lethal, sporting passions (Suet. *Calig.* 30.2, 55.2; Suet. *Ner.* 22.1–2; Suet. *Dom.* 10.1) hint at the substitute political activity which games represented and which helped make them so engrossing for the general public, too. Some common people who had insulted the racing faction that Vitellius favored were executed by him for political subversion (Suet. *Vit.* 14.3). But fanatical partisanship of this kind goes beyond either sport or even politics in any normal sense, to involve self-assertion at a much deeper, elemental social level where the exaltation of association with the winner in popular sports is further transformed into feelings of membership in a triumphant group. The special place of gladiatorial bloodshed in this comes from the ultimate social incarnation of all such groups in the victorious army, whose deeply anomalous appeal, felt also in the Roman triumph and in *munera*, prompted Robert E. Lee's paradox that it is good for war to be so horrible, as otherwise we might grow too fond of it—and Spengler's that few men can stand a long war without moral deterioration, but none can stand a long peace.

Deeper roots to the urgency of sports are touched on again by Cassiodorus. Races cause disturbances, he says, and "what in an earlier age began as religion, a quarrelsome later one has turned into sport. . . . [partisans] become as passionately engaged as if the state were in danger" (*Var.* 3.51; cf. Juvenal's quip that if the Greens lose, the city is shocked "as though Cannae had happened" [11.199–201] and Ammianus Marcellinus' account of sleepless nights endured by those torn with precarious hope about the outcome of races [28.4.31]). Cassiodorus' remark comes close to isolating an abstract desacralized feeling of danger devoid of any reasonable object—the classic definition of anxiety. What is in fact feared is the threat of a wrong outcome, a threat concentrated for the sport addict in games, for the devoted gambler, more abstractly, in pure risk. Cassiodorus has no formal categories for exploring this sort of thing, though he sees that racing is not religion or politics or really even diversion but is concerned rather with a vague danger beyond all three that has to be averted again and again because of its persistent possibility.

The self-understanding represented by Nemesis/Fortuna in her role as patron goddess of gladiators was ultimately imposed by society at large. The arena or circus became a ruthlessly simple microcosm: victory and security on the one hand, danger, defeat, or death on the other. So far as the former is concerned, gladiatorial combat had from early times celebrated military triumphs and brought an added sense of expansive well-being when it was used for entertainment at social events. Some very old aspects of public violence perhaps helped give a semblance of reason to Caligula's practice of having torture and capital punishment carried out while he was lunching or partying (Suet. *Calig.* 32.1).[24] When it began to serve as a place to display the Empire's wealth and scope, the microcosmic arena was at the same time inflated into a macrocosmic symbol, the elephant, for example, being reserved for the emperor as a sign of outsized power. By the same token, the wide range of animals trapped and set in elaborate artificial settings, mimicking natural ones, for slaughter during *venationes* constituted a political zoo symbolizing the reach of imperial authority over nature itself. To show that even animals must feel the power of Rome, Pompey spent several days hunting during a campaign in Africa (Plut. *Pomp.* 12.5). The universal authority represented by a parade of captives from all over the world, also, is ideologically idealized in the fantasy of obeisance to Caesar in Virgil's *Aeneid* (8.700–28).

To make the same point through some extraordinary political color-coding, Nero celebrated a visit of the Parthian king Tiridates with a costly show of performers both male and female, young and old, and all of them black (Dio 63.3.1). As Ovid notes in another connection (*Ars Am.* 1.99), spectators were as important as the show itself, since their attendance in great numbers at a public event *was* the show in a political and social sense. Seating arrangements could occasion riots, and Augustus introduced elaborate regulations for ensuring that the crowd would mirror the larger political order. *Ordo* is both "row of seats" and "social rank," hence the special subversiveness of Caligula's attempts to foment trouble over seating in the theater (Suet. *Calig.* 26.4). The precise geometry of the arena's architecture and blocks of spectators wearing clothing of the same color helped draw sharp lines of status among the 50,000 or so spectators in the Colosseum, who represented the body politic secure from the actual carnage down on the sand, though deeply involved in the symbolic defeat or victory they had assembled to view. The circus held from 200,000 to 250,000 people, and foreign visitors were customarily shown the crowd in Pompey's theater as a microcosm of the Roman public (Tac. *Ann.* 13.54.3).[25]

This was the positive side of the games, the entertainment they furnished, the public prosperity they proclaimed, the fruits of empire they permitted everyone to share.[26] On the far side of the barrier—yet exactly in the center, too—was the violence on which the surrounding show of social harmony, solidarity, and security focused. Feelings of unity and power became stronger still when the decision of life or death was handed over to the crowd by the game's patron. And a wider, more disturbing significance to what was happening could scarcely be ignored even by the most unreflective of spectators as dying contestants were finished off and their corpses dragged out through the Gate of Death (Porta Libitensis) by attendants dressed as Charon and Mercury.[27] Seen schematically, the gladiator's passage from life to death through this gate was exactly what the triumphant general needed reminding of when he passed in the opposite direction through the Porta Triumphalis. Though familiarity must have bred contempt as such symbolism gradually became popular burlesque, the entertaining show of public power was still delivered by means of a close encounter with death for the spectators, too. Most *munera* given in the several hundred amphitheaters or theaters throughout the Empire could not offer the lavish display of games at the centers of power. Still, if the symbolic message conveyed by provincial spectacles was less imposing, like solo high-wire or tiger-taming acts in contrast to a three-ring circus, they could make up through concentration some of what was lost in scale, particularly with regard to violence, which may well be experienced more compellingly when individuals rather than large groups are its victims, close up, caught in a spotlight and with a minimum of pomp. The death of the man who committed suicide on his favorite charioteer's pyre was no less dramatic for being solitary.

The games came to depend even more heavily on an overload of violence when *venationes* were added as a morning attraction to *munera* (sometimes along with *sparsiones,* yet another form of unusual expenditure and consumption). Raw material for these shows flowed into the arena or circus through an organization closely matching its gladiatorial counterpart. Animals were sought throughout the Empire with the help of the military and, once gathered, were set against unarmed victims, amateurs with some skill, or trained professionals. Exhibition of animals at victory celebrations or games dates back to republican times and could be entirely free of killing, but fascination with unusual fauna at Rome never led to the establishment of a true zoo, perhaps because display for its own sake could not meet Roman social needs. Instead, an element of danger, along with strangeness and vast scale, was again a major ingredient in the appeal of animal shows.[28] As the military costume of gladiators carried its own clear message about the potential seriousness of what was going on, so here danger was immediately evident in equipment such as protective barriers with the same dual function, alarming and reassuring, that makes safety nets part of the show in modern circuses.[29]

Venationes were given further spice by connections with military danger, notably in the case of elephants.[30] According to Pliny the Elder, elephants captured and taken to Rome to adorn a triumph in the circus were either killed in the course of staged combat or chased around with harmless weapons to reduce the fear they inspired by making them look ridiculous (*HN* 8.16–18). The second of these versions again betrays the threat implicit even in triumphal displays of power, and Pliny adds another anecdote that makes the same point in reverse. A captured Roman soldier matched with an elephant and besting it in single combat was executed by Hannibal to forestall damage to its fearsome reputation. Beyond special military applications of this kind, hunting in all of its forms naturally involved situations posing physical danger as acute as any met in combat. Killing the elephant is killing the animal we have reason to fear; we fear it because it is dangerous, and killing the dangerous animal is killing the dangerous enemy we have good reason to fear, too. Augustus seems to have made a point of exploiting the salutary effect of hunting shows on discipline and moral fiber. Parallels with gladiatorial games emerge on several other counts as well: hunting had its socially reputable and disreputable aspects, it became a valuable political tool owing to the messages it conveyed, it had roots in religious sacrifice, and with its pseudo-natural settings it appealed to Roman fondness for the real make-believe of symbolic political theater.[31]

So far as bloodshed in the arena was a surrogate for uncontrolled violence in the surrounding world, it lent itself especially well to quantification through unusual scale and intensity of violence. When the throats even of gladiators who had accidentally fallen were slit, Claudius eagerly watched their faces as they died (Suet. *Claud.* 34.1). This seems to be mentioned by Suetonius as the personal quirk of an emperor lavish with games anyway (*Claud.* 21). But the violence, rather than skill, which Claudius found interesting (34.2) was in fact an essential axiom in the social logic of *munera,* an axiom of anomaly through excess from which their special function sprang. The large number of days set aside, the vast sums spent, and the inordinate concentration of violence all helped make the breach in order unmistakable.

4

Extravagant Expenditure, Conspicuous Consumption

The impression of anomaly made by lavish displays is in the first instance quantitative and statistical, though quality and rarity can make a vital contribution, too. While six hundred ostrich brains served by Elagabalus were an astonishing abundance (*Hist. Aug.* 30.2), the eight bald men invited to another banquet (29.3) or two hunchbacks smeared with mustard sauce and then displayed on a silver platter by Commodus (11.2) made imperial dinners amazing—like Samuel Johnson's dog walking on its hind legs—not because they were done well (that is, in excess) but because they were done at all. And even if stories such as these are a hopeless farrago of fact, exaggeration, and fabrication, the notional categories they and many reports like them filled were real enough. Divination operated with the same dual criterion for the same purpose of attracting attention through signs that were bizarre or had the wrong size. A fire, widely believed to have been set during a riot, was also counted as a portent simply because of its large scale (Dio 50.10.6).[1] If oversize fires, storms, footprints, or snakes are ominously special, then productions with a cast of thousands are specially good because they are too much— or, in the case of undersize gladiators, too little—of a good thing. The skeleton of a forty-foot creature would have nicely complemented the live hippopotami and crocodiles shown at a *ludus* (Pliny *HN* 8.96, 9.11). The distinctively formal nature of such exercises in superlatives is again crucial to the liminoid role of arena games, where interruption in routine was effected not only by what was exceptional about the show but also by the fact that it was exceptional.

Suetonius says that Nero admired Caligula for nothing so much as for having squandered in just one year an enormous sum, including all the surplus of 2.7 billion sesterces left by Tiberius (*Calig.* 37.3). Seneca mentions a single dinner costing 10 million sesterces, roughly a quarter of the annual revenues from Egypt under Augustus (*Helv.* 10.4). Since imitation is the sincerest form of admiration, Nero himself proceeded to squander 2.2 billion (Tac. *Hist.* 1.20.1), spending "the scarcely believable" amount of 800,000 a day on entertainment for a royal guest and presenting him with a gift of more than 100 million on his departure (Dio has 200 million; 63.6.5), playing dice for 400,000 per pip, and never traveling with fewer than 1,000 vehicles in his entourage (Suet. *Ner.* 30.3). Cicero had counted 600,000 sesterces per year sufficient for a life of luxury (*Stoic Paradoxes* 49). Vitellius, who was said to have gone through 900 million in a few months (Tac. *Hist.* 2.95.3; or merely on dinners, Dio 65.3.2–3), demanded banquets costing a minimum of 400,000 each (though one for Nero had cost 4 million; Suet. *Ner.* 27.3). Other details, like the 2,000 choice fish and 7,000 birds served on one occasion (Suet. *Vit.* 13.2), come in principle to much the same sort of thing, a principle pertinent also to *munera* in respect to their lavish "consumption" of animal and human life.

Dio, in fact, uses just that notion. When people were thrown to the beasts, "few animals but many humans died this way, some fighting each other, others eaten by animals. . . . that is how he [Claudius] used them up [*analiskein*]" (60.13.1–2). Though *analiskein* is a common metaphor for "kill," in this context its wider semantic field ("use up money, time, food") introduces a special way of looking at death in the arena that catches its peculiar abstractness (the implicit commodification brings to mind the revealing use of "waste" current during the Vietnam war). In lending itself to extravagance, consumption acquires a broader, symbolic social meaning beyond considerations purely of quantity.

For lethal games were part of two economies at Rome. In the first, monetary factors were concrete. *Lanistae* had contracts with gladiators, some of whom entered the arena because they had lost their property (Suet. *Tib.* 35.2) and therefore saw combat as an opportunity for employment in an ordinary sense of the word. Both parties, moreover, made further financial agreements with editors who provided entertainment for consumption by the public. Since money ultimately buys value, it circulates in a second economy of symbolic worth, one of whose primary forms at Rome was status exchanged in reciprocal transactions of social recognition between ruler and ruled. In this larger sphere, the rate or scale of consumption became an index of symbolic values. The death of high-priced gladiators made a show particularly good, because what the editor was willing to spend meant something different socially and politically than what he in fact spent.

As quantity, that is to say, becomes quality, extravagance represents political capital. Expenditure thus was exclusively a qualitative matter of status when people of rank and wealth appeared in the arena (Suet. *Ner.* 12.1). Since they did so for no financial reasons, the transaction would seem unreasonably wasteful, and a concept of anomalous or irrational political consumption lies behind otherwise inexplicable reports such as one in Dio about Caligula's having some lower-class bystanders seized and used as food for the show beasts during a shortage of condemned criminals (59.10.3–4). True or false, the story measures the convertibility of life understood as a simple economic resource (in the food supply) into symbolic social values (entertainment as a vehicle of unrestricted imperial power). Use of violence as political currency entirely independent of normal rational standards is brought out by several parallel accounts which seem to have contaminated each other. In Dio, Caligula has the victims' tongues cut off to prevent protest and extends the social range of violence by forcing a knight to fight in the arena (59.10.3–4), while Suetonius tells of an innocent knight who is thrown to the animals with his tongue cut off when he does protest (*Calig.* 27.4).

Crazy forms of consumption like this aside, ancient economies did show bias against investment and production toward pure expenditure and display, whose dangers at both monetary and symbolic levels were clearly recognized. In *Precepts of Statescraft* Plutarch comments specifically on disjunction between the two. Authentic social ambition *(philotimia)* is "not financial but symbolic" (820E); purchased status—and he includes that gotten by paying for *munera*—is useless (821F) because real status cannot be bought. The present system, he complains, therefore has all the signs of irrationality: it encourages "absurd and pathetic" display, knows no bounds, and requires heavy borrowing in order to afford shows that cannot be afforded. Dispensing illusory wealth, however, gains "not reputation and power but shame and contempt" (822D). As a matter of formal social analysis, this argument detects on a monetary and symbolic level the counterfinality seen by Seneca in gladiatorial carnage on a moral level, when he contends that some aspects of *munera* dehumanize their human public, to say nothing of their participants (*Ep.* 7.3). When Plutarch, too, deprecates games that excite brutal and bloody feelings (*Precepts of Statescraft* 822C), he comes close to seeing massive violence as well as colossal numbers as part of an unbalanced social equation.

Economic statistics, properly speaking, are hard quantities, and that is in the first instance how they are recorded in the historical tradition. Even hard economic data, however, are still a function of many other factors—purchasing power, inflation rates, spending preferences, and so on. Direct comparison between systems is hazardous for any number of reasons, not least because benchmarks are difficult to come by in ancient economics and symbolic values vary. Among some fairly straightforward numbers are Augustus' expenditure of 2.5 billion sesterces from funds directly under his control, with public revenues and disbursements for the whole Empire coming to perhaps 500 million annually. The income of a province like Egypt was about 40 million.[2] The largest private fortunes in the first century A.D. amounted to 400 million, while an aqueduct forty-six miles long built over a period of fourteen years under Caligula and Claudius cost 350 million (Pliny *HN* 36.122).[3]

Even if they did compare favorably with such statistics for reliability, though, figures for Caligula's or Nero's spending would still be largely symbolic, meant in the last resort to be taken seriously for what they represent, not for what they are. The distinction made by M. Finley between real statistics absent from ancient culture and the "curious abundance of precise figures" in ancient authors applies to numbers of this kind that add up to political, not statistical, facts.[4] Whatever they actually came to, they had always to be large enough to be thought too large. To the extent that cost was for the most part not an economic measure in the modern sense, there was no particular reason to think of, say, Caligula's heavy expenditures as a reasonable stimulative measure, though that is what they perhaps were by way of reaction to Tiberius' earlier tight-money policy.[5] To celebrate his German expedition (labeled a "farce" by Tacitus: *Germ.* 37.4 and *Hist.* 4.15.2), Caligula "wrote to the procurators with instructions to prepare for a triumph at the least cost but on a scale beyond anything previously done, since everyone's property was at their disposal" (Suet. *Calig.* 47). He may have meant merely that expense to his own or to state funds should be kept at a minimum, but the mad suggestion of frugal extravagance as the directions stand compounds normal imperial excess with Caligula's own specially abnormal ways.

Where conspicuous display is normal in the first place, as it was at Rome, costs may need to be excessive in order to be reasonable, but only so long as they are no more than routinely excessive. That is to say, when excess is normalized, it develops its own normal and abnormal degrees which make up relative pairs, each elusively defining the other. As "the ruling power obtained additional prestige from the very irrationality of the expression," a category of normal anomaly emerged to define what was within the pale and in doing so tended to undermine it by inviting what was beyond.[6] Pliny's estate of 20 million sesterces made him a very wealthy man; the cost of supporting a legion for one year came to around 4 million sesterces in the first century B.C.; and a century later Seneca mentions inaugural dinners at 1 million (*Ep.* 95.41). Perhaps with some exaggeration, he puts one of Caligula's at ten times that much (*Helv.* 10.4), equivalent to the cost of an entire (though unfinished) theater mentioned by Pliny.[7]

The games constituted a special, institutionalized form of this conspicuous consumption at Rome, fed not merely by economic resources but, more dramatically, by copious supplies of blood. In *venationes* the two were inseparable, since supplying animals for slaughter required a major economic enterprise. The raw material needed for human combat was not acquired with the same logistical efficiency nor on the same scale, and games of all kinds were often put on without any bloodshed at all. Nonlethal conspicuous expenditure is typified by Alcibiades' horse racing, which "outdid in numbers of entries the largest cities and was of such quality that he took first, second and third place" (Isoc. *On the Team of Horses* 33–34). The rationale on the quantitative side is display through economic excess, further inflated to the point of irrationality in a story about Mark Antony's promise of money to a friend. After his steward heaped up the whole amount to show how rash he had been, he doubled it (Plut. *Ant.* 4.4). As F. Millar notes, the doublet in Dio which has Nero doing the same thing with a still larger sum (10 million sesterces, 61.5.4) clearly shows the irrelevance of hard numbers.[8] What matters is the principle of excess itself, ready like a blank check to be filled in with any particular quantity, provided only that it is too much.

In accordance with the long-standing code of liberality in ancient society, public expenditures in many instances were symbolic gestures, not economic decisions in the modern sense at all. But "everything relating to economic notions is bound up with a far wider range of ideas that concern the whole field of relationships between men and the relations of men with the gods."[9] The ruinous cost of subsidizing public shows, which led one magistrate to protest by substituting dogs for horses in the chariot race (Dio 61.6.2), helped keep the prestige the shows gained under the emperor's control. Since status was not measured by strictly economic costs in the first place, it could be asserted through conspicuous qualitative as well as quantitative display. This was so, for example, of gifts presented to the emperor and then put on public exhibition by him. A team of hermaphroditic horses and a boy who did everything with his feet because he had no arms or shoulders were amazing for their quality, the bones of people more than nine feet tall were amazing for their size, and a four-headed boy appealed on both scores. Such gifts are "most surprising if also least important in economic terms," because their significance has to do with "the tone of the exercise of monarchy."[10] More specifically, they are a sign of the extraordinary—and therefore potentially bizarre—power of the emperor's position, whose full measure is its capacity to encompass and thereby control anomaly. That perhaps was a factor in the cultivation of pet dwarfs (see Addendum 4). Unusual scale in whatever direction is no less conspicuous a form of anomaly than is excessive expenditure or the scale of violence in the arena, which received a double charge of oddity from wrong size or wrong kind when diminutive gladiators or women gladiators took part.

The sum of 400,000 sesterces which Echion, a clothes dealer described by Petronius, hopes will be spent on a three-day *munus* is amusing because of its implausibility as a hard figure for a real show.[11] It is at the same time a perfectly hard qualitative, typological measure of extravagance.[12] In Livy's phrase, expenditures even on dramatic shows had earlier become "insanity hardly supportable by a whole kingdom" (7.2.13). Restrictions on *munera* under Augustus and Tiberius (e.g., Dio 54.2.4) and efforts to divert funds to more useful projects reflect concern about bringing costs under control.[13] Four-day games around 135 A.D. at Carthage, where prices were relatively low in comparison with Rome, came to 200,000, the cost of large building projects. In the mid–second century some gladiatorial games in Gaul, consisting of thirty-two contests of which eight were fatal, cost perhaps as much as 330,000. Though such expenditures were exceptional, total annual costs for games have been estimated at 90 million during the second century.[14]

The number of participants was no less impressive and escalated relentlessly. At the first gladiatorial show in 264 B.C., 3 pairs of contestants fought; by 174 B.C. there were 37 pairs. Later, even after the size of the show Caesar intended to offer was restricted in some way, he still had 320 pairs, and Agrippa set 700 pairs of criminals against each other (with all being killed). Augustus reckoned 10,000 gladiators just in special shows during his reign; Trajan, about the same number, with an equal number of animals, in a single year. Since games were given on a smaller scale throughout the provinces, the total number must reach into many thousands per year. Quantity came to take on a life of its own in other phases of the games as well. A pool measuring nearly six hundred by four hundred yards for a naval battle staged by Augustus accommodated 2,000–3,000 men, while "Claudius manned warships with 19,000 combatants and surrounded them with rafts to prevent escape. . . . the slope, the coast and hill-tops were thronged with a vast number of spectators. . . . Claudius wore a splendid military cloak. . . . though the fighters were criminals and much blood was spilled, at the end none were killed" (Tac. *Ann.* 12.56.3). Records of individual gladiators' exploits are no less conscious of statistics and have a more than superficial resemblance to the list of scars and trophies acquired in actual campaigns by the one-man legion, L. Siccius Dentatus.[15]

Quantity works together with quality to produce a peculiarly outré effect in the *cena libera,* a copious dinner given to gladiators the night before combat.[16] While providing a last indulgence along with calories needed for the next day's work, the meal was transformed by the prospect of imminent death into a spectacle open to the public and thus affords special insight into the logic behind public consumption of violence. Presumably what attracted the curiosity of those who came to watch was the oddity, the bare thought of such circumstances, or rather the difficulty of knowing what to think about them, similar to the feeling of something deeply amiss aroused by freakish sports of nature put on public display. Norms surrounding death are particularly sensitive and all the more powerful for not being easy to explain, as it is not easy to say why entertainment of combatants before their death is itself good entertainment for spectators who will then be entertained a second time by the combatants' real death on the following day.

The unique dinner mediating between the living and the dead, between normal and abnormal activities, catches from a different angle the incongruity noticed in Seneca's remark that in gladiatorial schools "they fight those they eat with" (*De Ira* 2.8.2–3). Plutarch draws a contrast between those who stuffed themselves at the meal and those who had appetite only for final thoughts about others (*Non Posse Suaviter Vivi* 1099B). His own moralizing aside, he sees that while eating and drinking have lost their normal meaning, they nevertheless are still an obvious thing to do and thus preserve a link to the spectators' own normal world. Like burying a man in his best suit, the situation seems pathetic, tasteless, grotesque, and perfectly natural all at once. If individually many of the spectators felt an *intrusion du pathétique et du sadisme,* as an institution, the vicariously shared last supper previewed the anomaly of mayhem in the arena through a distinctive *Unschuldskomödie* of untimely hospitality inverting the unusual brutality to follow.[17] The same point is made in the *Passio Perpetuae,* where after ridiculing the voyeurism of those who had gathered to watch *(curiositas concurrentium),* one of the martyrs addresses them as "friends today, enemies tomorrow" (17).

Chariot racing, whose religious roots were preserved in the grand procession into the circus, was subject to the same quantitative inflation in obedience to the same axiom of effect through excess and could invite the same infatuation with death. Normal two- or four-horse teams were expanded to six, eight, or even ten, the last by Nero, who also ran camels in place of horses (Suet. *Ner.* 11.1) to add a special touch of qualitative novelty. The logic of this was parodied and exactly reversed when dogs were run to protest the games' extraordinary expense. The twelve races that had become regular by the end of the Republic increased to thirty-four under Caligula and to one hundred under the Flavians. The races then had to be extended into the late evening. Expert drivers reaped huge winnings from victories that could in the course of a career number well over a thousand and whose importance was marked by very careful record keeping, symptomatic of quantitative thinking.[18] A public benefactor left 2 million sesterces for an aqueduct at Bordeaux probably under Tiberius. When Caligula's gift of the same immense sum to a chariot racer is closely followed in Suetonius by rumors of his intention to appoint a favorite racehorse as consul (*Calig.* 55.3), a thematic connection is being made between the extraordinary quantities on which the best games depended for their effect and the irrational politics for which they could be made a convenient symbol.

Even taking into account Dio's remark that numbers in such matters were exaggerated (43.22.4), the scale of animal shows is no less outsized: twenty elephants, six hundred lions, along with other specimens gathered from many places at the time of Pompey; nine thousand wild or tame animals killed by Titus to dedicate the Colosseum; eleven thousand killed later by Trajan.[19] As quality and quantity tended to coincide here, too, the true standard again became oddity: not merely slaughter of animals in immense numbers but of exotic species from exotic places— elephants, ostriches, deer, chamois, bears, crocodiles, hyenas, seals, antelopes, aurochs, panthers, bulls, boars, rhinoceroses, hippopotami.[20]

What is more, every change was rung on every imaginable form of combat, real or burlesque, by day or by night. Besides normal matches between pairs of men, women or dwarfs might take part, people (armed or unarmed) might fight with animals (ordinary or exotic), and animals might fight with other animals, at times roped together (elephants and bulls, bears, crocodiles, or rhinoceroses; lions against tigers, bulls, bears, or crocodiles; bears against pythons or seals). Amid the bewildering succession of shows, details quickly blur, as they must have for the spectators, into a common factor of the bizarre in its own right. Hunts were sandwiched between races in the circus, while staged massacres of wild animals or of unarmed men by hungry animals again took much of their point from exaggeration or inversion of normal hunting. Risk was either greatly increased by reversal of roles for hunter and hunted or mostly eliminated by the arena's highly controlled setting, though real hunting was itself often a cautious affair conducted with beaters, nets, and dogs. Exaggeration, however, came mainly from the provision for killing in abundance, with remorseless expenditure and consumption extended in yet other directions, such as distribution of food through *sportulae* and *visceratio* or by *sparsio* either of prizes or of perfumed water sprayed over the public. On one day Nero staged a hunt, flooded the amphitheater for a naval battle, drained it for gladiators, and flooded it again to give a lavish floating banquet (Dio 62.15.1; cf. 61.9.5). Dio describes a great boat-shaped structure in the arena which held four hundred animals and could suddenly come apart (76.1.4–5).

Mastery of nature took less violent though no less freakish form in elephants trained to dance, sit down daintily to dinner, kneel before the emperor, or write Latin and Greek in the dust with their trunks. When lions caught rabbits in their jaws only to release them unharmed (Mart. *Epigr.* 1.14), the oddly playful menace at which some emperors were especially adept was brought into the arena in the form of oddly veiled violence. The same Caligula who sent a knight at whom he was annoyed to Ptolemy with a sealed message saying, "Don't do anything good or bad to the man I have sent you" (Suet. *Calig.* 55.1), entered feeble animals along with broken-down old gladiators in shows and had amateurs with handicaps engage in mock combat (26.5). Whatever other purposes, such as reducing costs, some of this may have had, one common formal denominator is the double anomaly of violence achieving climactic anticlimax by *not* happening.[21] The hearty *cena libera* plays with the same elements in reverse order by prefacing real terror with a benign social event.

Violence which did, more normally, happen on schedule could even then take the recherché form of mythical horrors staged in real life by condemned men: Laureolus crucified, Attis castrated, Heracles burned alive, Scaevola roasting his own hand to demonstrate Roman resolve.[22] Nero's use of Christians as living torches for an evening garden party belongs with this specifically surreal real violence (Tac. *Ann.* 15.44.4; cf. Juv. 1.155–57). Whatever the exact truth of such reports may be and without discounting an element of sadism, the extreme anomaly in scale and intensity they encapsulate still retained some connection with the defensive response to the possibility of violence deeply embedded in the logic of Roman society and institutionally operative even in the absence of immediate danger.[23] Nero was widely blamed for his treatment of Christians, but Tacitus saw them as outcasts who did pose a threat to public welfare. In his view the issue was principally personal, not systemic cruelty; apart from that, extraordinary violence had a place in the ordinary working of society.[24]

Like divinatory signs, spectacles entail replication and substitution: presentation of a spectacle is re-presentation of an original replicated or imitated in a form more accommodating to the requirements of public security. If the original is something dangerous, substitution permits engagement at arm's length, as happened when combat and death were transformed into a public show that was simultaneously entertaining, owing to distance from serious violence, and potent, owing to serious expenditure of social capital: the elaborate ritual, the frequency with which games were offered, their high valuation as measured by the political approval they could gain, the intensity and scope of bloodshed, human or animal. All of these sustained symbolic economic exchange on a massive scale, as sponsors spent resources in consuming public favor, while the public in turn consumed resources in expending its own favor. The games thus became a classic instance of political transactions at the immediate expense of a third party ("You give me your vote, I give you someone else's money"). At Rome the blood tax, levied on third-party lives, fell within the broad patron/client model for which economic considerations in a narrow sense were secondary. The symbolic largess that had always been a means for exercising power underwent vast inflation as it became a measure of greatly augmented imperial power, now concentrated in the hands of an absolute patron or his agents. Here large-scale physical violence was an especially impressive instrument of display owing to the peculiarly rich perception of wealth, power, and cost through waste that it could uniquely create.

5

Sociology of Public Violence

Like private greed fostering public welfare under the guidance of an invisible economic hand, the visible ("spectacular") violence in the arena was recycled at a deeper level in Roman society, beyond the games' entertainment value for individual spectators. A good deal of attention has been given in recent sociological thought to the role of publicly sanctioned violence, and Clifford Geertz's essay in interpretive sociology on Balinese cockfighting, "Deep Play," can throw some light on how recycling occurred in Rome.[1]

The initial parallel with the arena is the notable brutality of contests in Bali between cocks fitted with razor-sharp spurs. The loser's carcass is often torn limb from limb by its infuriated owner, and the spectators, too, are caught up in passionate empathy with the ritual play, whose complex code expresses social hierarchy. The combat is seen not merely as entertainment but as "blood sacrifice" offered to demons threatening society and carrying cosmological significance, as violence did among the Aztecs. An odd combination of positive and negative elements appears also in the powerful ambivalence between the high value placed on the cock and the repugnance Balinese feel toward any kind of animal behavior.[2]

> In identifying with his cock, the Balinese man is identifying not just with his ideal self . . . but also, and at the same time, with what he fears, hates, and ambivalence being what it is, is fascinated by—"the powers of darkness." . . . In the cockfight, man and beast, good and evil, ego and id, the creative power of aroused masculinity and the destructive power of loosened animality fuse in a bloody drama of hatred, cruelty, violence, and death. . . . This cross-wise doubleness

of an event that, taken as a fact of nature, is rage untrammeled and, taken as a fact of culture, is form perfected, defines the cockfight as a sociological entity. . . . Like any art form—for that, finally, is what we are dealing with—the cockfight renders ordinary, everyday experience comprehensible by presenting it in terms of acts and objects that have had their practical consequences removed and been reduced (or, if you prefer, raised) to the level of sheer appearances, where their meaning can be more powerfully articulated and more exactly perceived. . . . The reason that it is disquieting is that, joining pride to selfhood, self-hood to cocks, and cocks to destruction, it brings to imaginative realization a dimension of Balinese experience normally well obscured from view. . . . . A powerful rendering of life as the Balinese most deeply do not want it (to adapt a phrase [Northrop] Frye has used of Gloucester's blinding) is set in the context of a sample of it as they do in fact have it.[3]

In being at once continuous with and a negation of ordinary life (i.e., being routinized anomaly), the combat epitomizes the liminoid social vertigo feared by the Balinese and felt at Rome as well in connection with warfare. Some fairly specific points of contact with this "bloody drama of hatred, cruelty, violence, and death" come to mind. Boxing, for example, was especially favored in Italy along with bloody combat in the arena.[4] As the most brutal among popular sports, it appealed to the robust taste for violence which the Romans shared with the Etruscans.[5] Boxing naturally lends itself to simple violence, and in the ancient world its object was to inflict damage as directly as possible. Since the head, not the body, was the principal target, the chance for a quick kill (literally, at times) which made rest periods between rounds unnecessary was enhanced by the *caestus* or brass knuckles (small metal dumbbells held in the fist).[6] Under the circumstances, sudden bursts of violence resulted in fearful mutilation of the face. Transformation of brutality into something just barely tolerable in the guise of sport is reflected in black humor turning on the hideous effects of boxing, for example, jokes about a boxer battered beyond recognition even by himself in a mirror or beyond recognition by the authorities, who deny him an inheritance on the grounds of failure to prove his identity (*Greek Anthology* 11.75–78).[7]

The Etruscan game of Pherseu may have involved similarly enriched savagery. One of a pair of contestants, with head covered by a sack and holding a club, defended himself blindly against a savage dog. His task was made still more difficult—and entertaining—by the Pherseu, the second participant, who wore a dark mask and carried a whip or leash for entangling his adversary. The nature of the game, known principally from a few Etruscan wall paintings, is uncertain, but it seems to have been a brutal business providing the double-barreled carnage of gladiatorial combat (similar to that of the *retiarius,* whose weapon was an entangling net) combined with exposure of more or less helpless victims to wild animals. In that case, the Pherseu played the role of a circus master who orchestrated the savaging of a victim, perhaps a condemned criminal, by artful interventions to help keep the action going. Or perhaps better, he was like a toreador combining buffoonery (the masks have been compared with those in comedy) and cruelty (the Pherseu has also been compared to a demon), not by tormenting an animal into maximum violence but a man into maximum terror.[8]

Deep play, at any rate, seems an apt term for what went on in Roman games as well. The title is inspired by Jeremy Bentham, with "deep play" being a game whose stakes are so high that from a utilitarian point of view it is irrational to play it, as public shows at Rome from one point of view were, due to the very high levels of consumption they required. Balinese cockfighting thus symbolizes deeper stakes not subject to superficial rational calculation but instead symbolizing the intractable hazards of life itself. Similarities with games in the Roman arena naturally enough are inexact, but taken together they point to a common process of publicly acknowledging and working through in ritual form dangers that perpetually threaten order.

Relatively abstract, socially axiomized explosions of brutality figure again in the undifferentiated violence from which René Girard derives the ultimate principles of religion and social order. Reciprocal violence in the competition of all against all is bound to destroy society unless it is diverted into a unanimous violence of all against one in order to restore domestic peace. Real internal violence cannot be eliminated but only redirected outward as ritual violence. Like the gladiator, the scapegoat is deeply ambivalent: a feared, marginal figure who yet has a central honored role to play, embodying the familiar two-sidedness of everything "sacred," including gladiatorial combat and the triumph at Rome. As a surrogate for the threat posed by violence, he is formally adopted into society but only to be brutalized into a dangerous outsider.[9] By the same token, gladiators were admired and their status recognized by a formal oath, but this oath bound them absolutely to ruthless discipline as marginal persons.

> The victim is not a substitute for some particularly endangered individual, nor is it offered up to some individual of particularly bloodthirsty temperament. Rather, it is a substitute for all the members of the community, offered up by the members themselves. The

sacrifice serves to protect the entire community from its *own* violence; it prompts the entire community to choose victims outside itself. The elements of dissension scattered throughout the community are drawn to the person of the sacrificial victim and eliminated, at least temporarily, by its sacrifice.[10]

This concept of publicly sanctioned violence as mobilization against the threat of disorder has a general resemblance to the model of publicly sponsored violence in games at Rome as a means for processing disorder. It is true that Girard's violence is internal, while gladiatorial combat especially in its military aspect represented external danger in the first instance. But the distinction is not a rigid one. In the Roman Empire military threats often came from internal civil war, and those killed in the arena could be domestic criminals, while Girard's scapegoat may be marginal because he is foreign. Other points of contact with the gladiatorial games at Rome are closer: the institutionalizing of violence, its intensity and the intense communal emotion it arouses, ritual that is at once mock and real, the importance of collective involvement. What is perhaps most pertinent for our purposes in connection with the social anomaly entailed by incorporation of disorder in public institutions is the pervasive double bind embodied in the scapegoat's ambivalent status. He is a good evil; only by shedding (his) blood can blood guilt be averted; because he is sacred, killing him is criminal, but he is sacred because he is killed. Besides its application to the gladiator's ambivalent status, this double bind roughly parallels the formal contradiction of order reinforced through the gladiatorial games. Moreover, in Girard's view, the element of anomaly gradually emerges in its own right as the religious component recedes: "Games originate in rites that have been divested, to a greater or less degree, of their sacred character." As secularization advances, sacrifice reverts to the presacrificial crisis of raw, purely political violence which ritual violence is supposed to hold at bay. In military form this is what arena games represent. They also embody the added possibility noticed by Seneca that bloodshed in the arena may no longer *rehearse* anything (e.g., courage) but may simply *be* social reality. Thus it will become a dysfunctional institution not controlling but constituting problems.[11]

The efficacy of public violence designed to deflect or absorb external danger comes in large measure from the shock its own abnormality administers. A principle of homeopathy is operative in concentrated doses of violence for responding to crises of all kinds, with concentration taking extensive or intensive, quantitative or qualitative, forms. In divination *piaculum* is "penalty for offense" as well as "offense," and responses (e.g., human sacrifice) may be as "bad" as the danger they seek to avert.[12] Ruthless exorcism of acute danger can be observed in mass political atrocities, too, as unrestrained mob violence becomes a new, inverted order legitimated through quasi-ritual, apotropaic repetition of the old evil by savaging its symbols. Under the stress of fear and hatred, latent patterns of thinking are activated, as they perhaps were in rumors of human sacrifice and cannibalism circulating in connection with Catiline's conspiracy.[13] If the stories were at all true, simple vengeance or terrorism was the most likely immediate motive, but even as mere propaganda, the point they make about the political excess desperate men are capable of applies no less to the extravagant violence of religious reactions in time of crisis. The two are often hard to tell apart. Valerius Maximus tells of a *flamen dialis* turning his political suicide into sacrifice by killing himself at the altar (9.12.5). In the political terror under Sulla, execution carried out at the tomb of a victim of earlier violence deliberately combined religious ritual with political vengeance (Sen. *De Ira* 3.18.1–2; Plut. *Sull.* 32.2), while display of bloody, eyeless heads in the course of partisan violence at Rome may have been influenced by the Gallic custom of collecting the heads of slain enemies. Caesar, too, set up the heads of some mutineers who had been ritually killed (Dio 43.24.4).

Crucifixion was another tool for managing violence through homeopathic counterterror.[14] It was inflicted in extraordinarily agonizing ways, so much so that in hastening death on the cross preliminary torture could actually be an act of mercy. Crucifixion was formally classified as an aggravated penalty and had many variations, for example, crucifixion upside down or with nails through the genitals, generally reserved for lower social orders, especially slaves or criminals, and intended to reaffirm normal public order by breaching it nightmarishly. When carried out on a mass scale, as it was on Spartacus' followers, the combination of extraordinary quality and extraordinary quantity produced a yet more potent means for coping with disorder. The correlation between massive violence and feelings of insecurity which this entails is illustrated by the savage outbreak against the Christians at Lyons in 177. Marcus Aurelius had permitted prisoners condemned to death to be used in place of more expensive gladiators. The substitution was justified in part by the local Gallic custom of human sacrifice, and Christian accounts describe the persecution as a sacrificial-gladiatorial orgy of violence directed against scapegoats and designed to outdo current troubles in kind.[15]

Explaining gladiatorial violence along the lines of social inoculation perhaps receives some indirect support from the increase of brutality in the legal system as bloodshed in the arena gradually became less acceptable, though the correlation is at best loose and there is considerable overlap between the two.[16] Law court and arena are initially linked by the use of games to carry out legal punishment and use of punishment, in turn, to provide public spectacles. One aim of the latter had long been to reinforce social order through an exemplary show of power, while harshness in the courts led to increasing feelings of repression in society at large. To the extent that routine violence has deterrent consequences, the policy was perfectly rational, but severe measures are especially liable to unintended results. During the later Empire, higher levels of violence in the legal system extended to practically every class. Everyone was moving closer to the status of slaves and soldiers, against whom extreme severity had always been permissible because both were marginal groups clearly distinct from the mass of ordinary citizens.[17] R. MacMullen's suggestion that the growing distance between those in authority and all other parts of the populace reduced restraints on official ferocity fits in well with creeping "marginalization" of the general citizenry. Designed brutality spreading beyond the arena into routine legal procedure would have simply brought the anomaly, always inherent in mechanisms for processing violence, closer to the surface. Torture of perfectly respectable people, for example, is a formal reductio ad absurdum of the contradictions in systematized brutality detected by Seneca when he asks spectators at the games why they "deserve" to watch what criminals deserve to suffer (*Ep.* 7.3f). As the Roman public was gradually criminalized, it too "deserved" to suffer what criminals suffered. A town councillor, though protected by his standing, could nevertheless be "strung up for torture and only when he had broken [be] asked the routine question, 'What is your status?'"[18]

6

Social Anomaly and Public Violence

Though the highly refined tools for philosophical analysis available to Seneca and others facilitated acute moral, psychological, and political insight into anger, nothing like a consciously theoretical grasp of violence as an institutional principle developed in ancient thought. Nor did Roman gladiatorial games, more particularly, attract any special attention in their own right. After describing the plebs' preference for bears or boxers over more pretentious displays of mock combat, spoils of war, and kings in chains paraded over the stage, Horace remarks that Democritus, the laughing philosopher, brought back to life would be amused and astonished most of all at the spectators' passion for this sort of thing (*Epist.* 2.1.185–98). As his examples show, unusual violence of one kind or another—sporting, animal, military—was available for every taste, and the factor of anomaly appears, too, when he mentions the appeal of weird creatures like camelopards or white elephants. While Democritus' laughter at human folly carries over into distaste for staged violence on Horace's own part, the issue is incidental to his main purpose and does not represent a deeper assessment of its social role.

Trivial as the thrill of danger aroused by the games Horace has in mind may be, fear was a key component in Roman religion. When Livy defines religious observance as *metus deorum* and says that Numa thought of it as a substitute in Roman society for "fear of the enemy and military discipline" (1.19.4), he is not saying that the aim was to eliminate fear or discipline. Numa did want to reduce preoccupation with warfare, but at Rome reform in that direction had to be content with modest results at best. Livy remarks that the doors of Janus' temple were subsequently closed as a sign of peace only very rarely. The two spheres of religious and military danger are so interwoven that the former is understood by

Livy as an additional medium for dealing with anxiety about public security. Religion *substituted* for fear of external danger by *replicating* it internally in a civic form whose humbling, sobering effect contrasted with reckless aggression (Plut. *Num.* 8.2). Though details are inconsistent, integration of military and civic institutions reappears in Livy's portrait of Numa's successors. The warlike Tullus Hostilius introduced procedures to give foreign relations and especially declarations of war a religious basis, adding internal social fear of the gods to fear of enemy action (1.24.4–9). He is additionally credited with vows to establish the Salian military priesthood and a shrine to Pallor and Pavor (Livy 1.27.7), the latter very clearly again institutionalizing *metus hostium* as *metus deorum*. Domestication of war in the fetial formula is then also attributed to Ancus Marcius, who is specifically said to combine the qualities of Numa and Romulus (Livy 1.32.4). His "oxymoronic" *bellicae caeremoniae* —civilized warfare—restrain Mars by inviting him into society through procedures that change the reality of war only as they repeat it ritually: gods replace human enemies, but both are objects of fear.[1]

The tradition centering on the early kings thus yields a rudimentary sociology of religion which does more justice to the social uses of anxiety—Pallor and Pavor enshrined—than is done by Lucretius' diagnosis of religious obsession. Fear spurs action, and ritual is redundant action which in the form of lethal games alleviated fear of real danger by guaranteeing mastery over harmless substitutes.[2] In chariot racing, a reassuring atmosphere of control for playing out the hazards of victory or defeat was reinforced by a solemn religious procession into the circus through the Porta Pompae and by other rites performed with exactly correct procedure. Gladiatorial games were *munera* rather than *ludi* and apparently not as organically connected with religious ritual as circus or triumphal ceremonies were. All the same, ceremonies surrounding gladiatorial combat, often featured at circus shows, delivered the same message of someone in charge, of things being done as they should be. Though the painted vehicles in which Pliny the Elder says *pugnatores* were "ceremoniously carried to death or at least to carnage" (*HN* 35.49) may not have formed a true *pompa,* they must have looked like one.[3] (The pledge of allegiance or singing of the national anthem at American sports events has the similar aim of creating a larger ritual setting to legitimate and contain the passions shortly to be aroused. In the arena, too, action was solemnified and its climax framed by an organ or small orchestra accompanying combat, much as music on a soundtrack in motion pictures or played at crucial moments during sports events does). Additionally, aside from subliminal legitimating effects from religious ritual, a strong impression of public control and power was created by other features such as display of animals or prisoners and allies from an impressive geographic range, or the assembly of spectators and officials arranged in hierarchical seating order to render social and political solidarity as visible in the arena as crowds centering on the victor in triumphal parades did.

Another facet of Victor Turner's concept of liminoid states, which has already provided some useful clues to institutional violence at Rome, helps give focus to a special dilemma in the logic of efforts to domesticate violence through publicly sponsored substitutes. It was this dilemma that attracted some attention in Roman society and is perhaps part of what Horace's Democritus found absurd about popular entertainment. Violence under public auspices—"official violence," "war games"—is potentially as contradictory as "civil" war, at once "fratricidal" and "civilized." That is why Romans felt reluctance to celebrate victory in civil war (see Addendum 3). Entertainment depending on risk is itself risky; ceremonial or not, ceremonies of violence are themselves violent. As Tacitus noted, some people found real civil war very good entertainment (*Hist.* 1.32.1), and Seneca's realization that spectators could be brutalized at the arena brings out the same contradiction embedded in a major Roman social institution (*Ep.* 7.3f).

Turner sees in liminoid institutions a modification of normally liminal rituals characterized by the typical three stages of suspended normalcy followed by an abnormal liminal phase and return to normalcy. He contends that all ritual taken in its most general form has the structure of "social drama" whose plot is composed of essentially the same three stages transposed onto a more general plane: breach, crisis, and redress/ reconciliation or irremediable schism. Ritual and drama thus come together under the rubric "field of action" or "social arena," the latter being highly suggestive in connection with gladiatorial games.[4] They, too, have ritual aspects, are a social drama within and without the arena, and in a militaristic society admirably illustrate with their condensed, stylized violence the dictum that "ritual is quintessential custom."[5] So far as the three stages of liminal ritual are concerned, the occasion for the games was a *break* in routine fixed in the calendar or added to mark special occasions. The *crisis* took several forms: the uncertainty of life or death played out symbolically in gladiatorial combat, the uncertainty of victory or defeat played out in horse racing. *Redress* lay in the correct, sanctioned violence through which public authority was displayed and reaffirmed; *reconciliation* was achieved by a return to routine activity after the games; *schism*, while occasionally experienced in disruptive civil violence, was not irremediable, as the games for the most part worked effectively.

Crisis, the second of these phases, is the most important, since the first and third represent a normal state of affairs, though in the event of real schism the third stage becomes an arrested, permanent extension of intermediate liminal disorder. The potential dilemma posed by the notion of limited disorder is touched on in an argument of Cicero involving sociological reflection, if not theory, insofar as it is advanced specifically to justify gladiatorial combat. He contends that so long as those taking part are criminals, games provide the best possible support for discipline in enduring "pain and death" (*dolorem et mortem; Tusc.* 2.41). By the same token, occasional participation of respectable people presumably did not necessarily involve *infamia* because a show of bravery was felt to be authentically Roman.[6] The appeal to social utility reappears in Pliny the Younger. The point of his remark on the value of gladiatorial games for arousing bravery and zeal for victory even in criminals and slaves (*Pan.* 33.1) is that, a fortiori, Roman citizens should display a still higher degree of courage.[7]

Several centuries later, when the games came under Christian criticism, pagans returned to this *apologie politico-morale.*[8] Libanius speaks of gladiators "who fell and won" as "worthy of being taken for disciples of the 300 at Thermopylae" (*Oration* 1.5). The *Historia Augusta* mentions two explanations for the Roman custom of staging combat before setting out to war: it was a way either of satiating the goddess Fortuna (Nemesis) or of accustoming troops to violence so they would not panic in real battle (Maximus and Balbinus 8.4–7; cf. Severus 14.11). Though the first of these is historically worthless as a religious reason, taken more generally, it and the second, too, touch on genuine psychological and sociological factors concerning prophylactic rehearsal of violence. Polybius thinks that the Dalmatian war was undertaken in part "out of concern about the softening of Italian troops by peace" (32.13.6–7), and the same line of argument appears in Ennodius, who speaks of gladiatorial combat staged "so that the people who had enjoyed long peace could see in the theater what happened in war" (*Panegyric for Theodoric* p. 284 [Hartel]).[9]

Public carnage is acceptable to Cicero and others, then, because it strengthens public security by forcing people to look danger in the face (cf. *Mil.* 92). But just before the claim about pain and death in the *Tusculans,* he seems to betray disquiet at the possibility that the games' violence may not have quite so bracing an effect when he admits that "to some people gladiatorial shows are cruel and inhuman—and perhaps they are as they are now put on" (2.41). He speaks of his own eagerness to avoid a gladiatorial show, though without saying why (*Att.* 2.1.1). Another letter is more explicit. The hunting shows, Cicero concedes, are splendid, but a sophisticated man has to be bothered when humans are torn apart by animals or animals are run through with spears. A show of elephants was particularly impressive, yet even the crowd had no real pleasure owing to the kinship they felt with the animals (*Fam.* 7.1.3). This last remark brings out two important points: crowd participation in the disturbing as well as triumphant aspects of bloodshed, and the relatively generalized violence, animal or human, which underlay nervous shifts between positive and negative moods. Elsewhere Cicero concedes that though everyone enjoys shows, some pretend not to (*Mur.* 40), presumably because they can think of good reasons why they should not. Even the bloody-minded Claudius could think of such reasons. His numerous gladiatorial shows in which "few animals but many humans died" caused some criticism, and public executions going with them were so frequent that he finally decided that a statue of Augustus overlooking the carnage ought to be removed or hooded (Dio 60.13). After remarking on these contradictory attitudes, Dio adds that Claudius also put to death a lion trained to eat men, though it was very popular, because it provided a sight which he realized was "improper" at Rome.

Another consideration raising questions of sociopathology is brought out by an anecdote in Aulus Gellius about a gladiator who laughed heartily as a doctor was probing his wounds (Gell. *NA* 12.5.13). Evidently feeling uncomfortable with this, Aulus deprecates the machismo as false courage.[10] The anecdote's naïveté nicely spotlights the two sides of gladiatorial combat—individual and social—by pushing gross bravado to the point of masochism, whose disturbing larger social dimension then emerges in light of the gladiator's professional standing. Apart from that, his attitude would be merely a personal quirk, as it indeed is for Aulus, who ignores the social point that someone has to think this way if games are to be put on properly. Without a social setting, the masochism of Aulus' gladiator, who if he was a free man would have sworn a standard oath to endure "burning, binding, beating and death by the sword," matches the sadistic pleasure which the crowd, too, might feel as it watches him being hurt. From this point of view the whole affair seems merely irrational. In point of fact, however, the odd cult of pain is part of the ritual surrounding gladiatorial combat to reaffirm social values inseparable from violence. What makes no sense in Aulus' anecdote makes perfectly good sense when Cicero thinks that it is a means for fostering courage, as Arrachion's death, which by itself is merely grotesque, defines the nature of athletic competition (Paus. 8.40).

Reservations felt by Cicero come out at most indirectly, and the generally low social status of gladiators helped conceal doubts concerning the institution itself by shifting disapproval onto those who did the fighting. We do hear, though, of sharper objections. Dio says that some people took offense on several grounds at the elaborate, massively military gladiatorial shows put on by Caesar: because they showed that war had not sated his thirst for violence, because he was presenting the people with images (*eikones,* "reminders") of real evils they had suffered, and because of their great expense (43.24.1). Though the second of these points has the special unpleasantness of civil war in view, the games also celebrated foreign victories, and so the complaint at least to some extent recognizes the disquieting possibilities in deliberately reenacting real bloodshed, civil or not.

War was itself in many ways a show, made into a *spectaculum,* as Florus remarks, at the appearance of elephants (1.13.8), which by the same token could then turn the arena into a real battlefield. Category confusion is much more unsettling when Tacitus uses *munera* to drive home a point about political irrationality. The lesson is implicit to begin with in the street brawling fomented by Nero in company with soldiers and gladiators (*Ann.* 13.25.3). When the urban rabble becomes involved in civil violence "as though they were at the circus or the games" (*Hist.* 1.32.1, 3.83.1), war is demoted to irresponsible sport (Cic. *Fam.* 8.14.4 recognizes that the game of civil disorder is dangerous to spectators, too). Games, for their part, are promoted to brutal warfare when Vitellius' troops become a *saevum spectaculum* to look at (Tac. *Hist.* 2.88.3) or when he himself presents a *foedum spectaculum* during his own brutal lynching (3.84.5). Another category shift most revealing both for Vitellius himself and for the nature of gladiatorial combat occurs when, after viewing a *munus* put on by Caecina, he eagerly hurries on to visit the battlefield of Bedriacum to see for himself the *foedum* and *atrox spectaculum* of mutilated, rotting corpses (2.70.1).

Like Aulus' gladiator in love with his own pain, Vitellius is a sick man, suffering from raw brutality entirely resistant to social rationalization and yet part of violence in the arena even at its most celebratory and confident. After yet another gladiatorial show given by Valens, Vitellius finally approaches Rome amid a train of troops and corrupt admirers of Nero (Tac. *Hist.* 2.71.1). A broader category of excess then begins to emerge, as overkill is joined by other, more distinctly Neronian forms of extravagance. When Vitellius at last reached the capital, "his sole interest was in squandering money. He built stables for race horses and filled the circus with gladiators and wild animal shows, as though playing with money because he had so much of it" (2.94.3). The leitmotiv, connecting civil war, bloody wartime *munera,* and gratuitous peacetime brutality in one mindless orgy of irrational expenditure and consumption, gives some hint of what Tacitus saw represented in the games. By themselves relatively unimportant as a particular institution *within* Roman society, they assume greater significance when they are seen to be a correlative of the exploding excess and imploding civil violence *of* Roman society.

If sacrifice aims at "gentle violence" which must "never look like murder," it must, at the same time, still be very much like murder.[11] The similarly disturbing dimension of gladiatorial games becomes fully explicit in Seneca's complaint that killing criminals during the noon break in the arena is mere murder: "In the morning men are thrown to the lions and bears, at noon to the spectators. . . . as murderers they deserve death, but do you deserve to watch it?" (*Ep.* 7.3f; cf. 90.45, 95.33). In accordance with current use of mannered rhetoric as an analytic tool for serious social and political criticism, the wordplay in *thrown to* and *deserve* answers to the conceptual anomaly of the games, with *deserve* more specifically implicating spectators themselves in the killing.[12] It is true that Seneca's immediate point is the bad effect of crowds on the moral character of individuals (cf. August. *Confessions* 6.8). The atmosphere at the arena is an example of this, and even then what he objects to is public execution, not serious combat, which he elsewhere values for its lesson of bravery in the face of death (e.g., *Ep.* 30.8).

Lines cannot be drawn too cleanly, however. For in *Epistle 95.33*, when Seneca contrasts current display of a man "brought out naked and unarmed to be a spectacle by dying" with "training for giving and taking wounds which [once] was a disgrace [*nefas*]," the death of helpless people is mentioned climactically as an evil worse even than trained combat, which must itself be ugly enough if there is to be a climax. The remark in *Epistle 7* that Seneca had come for "fun and relaxation which permit human eyes to rest from human blood" again treats some of what went on as unobjectionable. Relatively innocent diversion available at the arena (cf. Sen. *Helv.* 17.1) could include mock combat with blunt weapons, and Seneca adds that in comparison with the butchery at noon, the earlier combat was *misericordia* (*Ep.* 7.3). Still, though the latter did exclude gladiatorial matches, which took place in the afternoon, the situation faced by *bestiarii* "thrown to animals" was itself often nasty, as mosaics and reliefs make plain. The context calls for climax set up by ironic understatement, giving milder forms of arena violence at best a left-handed recommendation: even the morning combat of trained man against animal—itself very brutal—was *misericordia* compared with what happened later.

Seneca's reaction here is a wider application of what he has to say elsewhere about anger. Crowds incensed at gladiators' reluctance to die are like ill-tempered children (*De Ira* 1.2.4–5), and in general people think that the anger they feel at anything from minor to major misfortune is always justified (1.12.3–4). In this second passage, Seneca draws another parallel with children, whose anger in both cases is due to apparent, not real injury or desire to inflict real punishment (1.2.5). Absence of legitimate reasons for violence is a mark also of the *feritas* which is a major political phenomenon (2.5.2; cf. Sen. *Clem.* 2.4.2, where it is called *insania*). Seneca is thinking mainly of individual behavior (hence his vivid descriptions of individuals in the grip of rage: *De Ira* 2.35–36, 3.4.1–3), but as the individuals in question hold power at Rome, their tantrums indeed make peace seem like war (1.12.5). The dynamics of personal anger fits in directly with violence on a larger scale. Like the mood of excited crowds at *munera,* its volatility causes sudden swings to *misericordia* (1.17.4–7), and while good gladiators themselves do not become angry (1.11.2; cf. 2.14.3), spectators do and with a mindless violence that finally has no aim beyond itself. "We flare up at the sight of other people fighting" ("effervescimus ad aliena certamina"; 2.2.5).

If crowds act, ethically, like children, they are still, socially, adults. In the three stages of anger, initial irrational physical reaction is followed by assent, then by relapse into fury. The danger comes from incorporation of the third phase into social behavior (e.g., Sen. *De Ira* 1.2, 3.2). *Munera* are a prize instance of sanctioned mass assent to irrational violence, and in Seneca's *Epistle* 95.30–33 the violence of war is coupled with death in the arena: "What would be punished if done privately, we praise when it is done by people in military uniform. . . . human beings are killed *per lusum ac iocum*" (= *occidere hominem iuvat;* Sen. *Clem.* 1.25.2). Private or communal, anger takes its *meaning* from human intention. Because injury is possible only with intention to harm, only humans can be angry (*De Ira* 1.3, 2.26.4), but anger is always foolish, and its occasionally useful results are no justification for accommodating it in a system of values (1.12.6). As a misguided, suicidal method for dealing with threats, it actually undermines social order, and so Seneca's contention that because anger employed, say, to motivate bravery cannot be controlled, it should never be used at all (1.7–13) is directly pertinent to his critique of violence in the arena (cf. the connections among human and animal savagery, pleasure in violence for its own sake, and ultimate political consequences in *Clem.* 1.25–26).

Like someone dropping in at a modern boxing card, then, in *Epistle* 7 Seneca is contrasting mindless battering of a wholly outmatched fighter with the entertainment afforded by a good but still very bloody match. Though clearly nastier than legitimate combat, execution of condemned criminals was as much a legitimate extension of it as fatally overmatched boxers are still part of the fighting game or as the dead Arrachion was still a winner. Even the exemplary value in displays of courage which

Seneca allows to *munera* vanishes in general bloodlust. The puzzling switch from individual to mass experience and the social dysfunction that accompanies it are driven home by his own return "more inhuman for having been among humans," the punishment which the crowd "deserves" to see and the "bad [publicly sponsored] examples rebounding on those who create them" (7.3 and 5; cf. the play on worthless politicians who "deserve" to suffer for what they do and on society, which does not, Sen. *De Ira* 3.18.2). Group behavior is logically different, though formally very similar, to private behavior. Actions perfectly reasonable when performed by an individual may be quite futile on becoming collective, such as when everyone at a social gathering raises his or her voice in order to be heard better. The rationality of social institutions, accordingly, is difficult to specify, since they do not embody conscious choices pursued through procedures so explicitly as strategies or individual decisions do; they are, rather, choices locked in permanent, complex rituals reflecting implicit social purposes, for better or for worse. Like the gradually increasing noise at a party, the volume of brutality in the arena could have contradictory effects, corporate and individual.

Comparison with Martial on this score is instructive. Like Seneca's letters, his poems on the games catch the anomaly ("wonders") of the arena in epigrammatic wit by exploiting the formal fit between paradoxical show on the one hand, paradoxical expression on the other, with a play on the dual sense of *lusus* and *iocus* (game/joke; e.g., *Epigrams* 1.14) as well as on the confusion between fantasy and reality in the games themselves. Danger, disorder, and abnormality mastered are central themes: nature unnaturally tamed by obedience to imperial authority or a sow giving birth by preposterous Caesarian section when she is hit with a spear (*Spect.* 12–14).[13] Flattery of the emperor, which confines Martial to the amusing aspect of paradoxical public displays, excludes the ugly queerness that Seneca for his part sees. Still, even a lion trained to take its master's hand in its mouth suddenly kills two young arena attendants (Mart. *Epigrams* 2.75), and a line on a tiger made *more* savage by its association with humans (*Spect.* 18) strikes another disturbing rather than admiring note on the nature of public shows by trumping the anomaly in Seneca's "I come home more inhuman for having been among humans."

Martial's propagandistic exploitation of the games as material for flattering poetry is innocent of any theoretical intention. But its treatment of violence in the arena as an auspicious show of political power is in effect a functional explanation, prone, as functionalism frequently is, to overemphasize how systems work and thereby to ignore their contradictions.[14] Dysfunctional aspects are what Seneca sees, his worry being that the brutality of the games remains just that when representatives of the Roman body politic are conditioned to think of deviant violence as a normal part of social order.[15] Applying the model of liminal-states, we can say that gladiatorial combat, once arrested at the middle stage of disorder, becomes a failed, counterproductive ritual. A century later, Marcus Aurelius, too, was so displeased by brutality in the arena that he had gladiatorial combat conducted with blunt weapons, would not watch a lion trained to eat men nor give in to pressure from the crowd to reward its master (Dio 71.29.3–4), and insisted on safety pads after a rope walker had fallen (*Hist. Aug.* 12.12).

Games are typically played in an area—field, board, track, table— marked out as separate and occupied by participants who themselves take on a new identity as they enter. The insulation from the everyday world which this creates is a necessary safety measure when games pose danger to surrounding order. In Rome the safety line was the arena's seating arrangement laid out with elegant precision to mark the encompassing social sphere. The separate, central area was the killing field, in effect an extended prison or disposal area for marginal elements of society: professional gladiators, condemned criminals, slaves, déclassé citizens.[16] Though Cicero casually links *gladiatores* with *perditi homines aut barbari* (*Tusc.* 2.41), the prestige and attention they nevertheless enjoyed were a function of the inverted logic most familiar from the positive/negative poles of *sacer*. In the case of the games, too, a negative factor is at the same time a positive ingredient in the process of disposal as a whole.

A good part of the social message concerning order and disorder carried by the games was recapitulated in the social standing of those who took part. While the Greek *agōn* entailed competitive participant games, the Roman *ludus* was exhibitionist, spectator sport.[17] Since at first, the elite in Greece themselves commonly participated, one effect of the subsequent rise of professional athletes was a shift away from personal involvement. The social meaning of competition, which always had been tied to highly symbolic notions of *arete,* began to be found separately in the games themselves, now viewed more distantly in light of their function within a complex system of values. One practical reason for the change was desire to avoid the risks posed by many sports. Games watched safely from a distance are experienced vicariously and tend to take on more abstract meaning. At the arena "I kill" or "he kills" is replaced by "we kill" when the life or death decision is handed over to the crowd, and "we" win again at the circus when the right color comes in first or in the arena when the right side in a large military reenactment prevails.

Roman mass spectator sport is a prime case in point. What is needed is expendable people to assume the risks which must be run if games are to be played, and especially at Rome, professionalism carried with it marginal social standing. Charioteers and boxers were typically servile or lowborn; gladiators might well be criminals.[18] But the fundamental contrast was worked out in very complex ways. If making a living from trade in gladiators was as bad as pimping, making money from such trade was perfectly respectable. The emperor did so on a large scale. Attitudes toward members of the upper class who competed during the late Republic and earlier Empire were similarly ambivalent.[19] Legal penalties imposed to discourage participation on the part of the elite and the controversy their participation aroused show that games raised nagging questions of propriety. The policy of emperors might be at odds with senatorial views, while laws were no less inconsistent, changed frequently, and were enforced sporadically. Combat with animals posed fewer problems and perhaps seemed less socially risqué because it was a less important element in *munera* than gladiatorial combat itself. The legal code was much concerned with the effect of games on social status, starting with those at the bottom condemned to the beasts or other horrific forms of public execution. Prisoners forced to fight for their lives and slaves sold into the arena could become professionals, as could free men of higher standing who fought under contract. Of the latter, some were escaping from debt; others who took part voluntarily made up a class at the top whose deeply problematic standing was dramatized in the supreme anomaly of an emperor active in the arena or theater.

Though remaining juridically free, citizens who formally took up fighting in the arena became *infames,* close in status to slaves or criminals and thus marginally marginal, so to say. But their loss in standing was nevertheless public gain, insofar as the games' prestige was tied to the participants' skill and status. The meaning of what was happening in the arena naturally varied directly with the social meaning and value of what was put at stake. Most gladiators probably were slaves whose lack of skill or status made their performance nothing more than an ordinary opportunity to see people killed. Good killers, on the other hand, would be found among the much smaller numbers of those with special motivation and training. From that group, mostly free men or freedmen, came the professionals who could best represent the peculiar balance of conflicting values that made the gladiator's admirable but vile death possible. Representation of society itself in the arena by voluntary upper-class combatants could only enhance the entertaining sense of disorientation fostered by the games. Gladiatorial combat thus embodied what C. Barton has called a paradoxical hopeless courage, combining values both lost and won through the empowerment experienced by contestants simultaneously marginal and respectable.[20] Through such people the uneasy combination of order and disorder was transformed into the more radical anomaly—namely, socially accredited social dysfunction—perceived by Seneca and Tacitus.

At the same time and much as in modern society, combat for truly marginal participants was a way of moving up toward the higher status from which respectable participants were slipping. Still, however successfully they managed to cross lines, they were always bound to be exceptions proving the rule. Normal, nonliminoid distinctions between order and disorder, proper and improper, were never wholly effaced. So, while gladiators (along with actors and charioteers) remained disreputable, their indispensable role was recognized through social symbols derived directly from the games' own incongruity: excessive rewards and inordinate popularity ("The Romans love them and punish them"; Tert. *De Spect.* 22.3). Prizes were awarded for what society rejected, since bloodletting in the arena was an aspect of social order by being something against which social order defined itself.

Alarming as this seemed in many quarters, it was largely an extension of the prevailing culture of violence at Rome. If displaying people with physical abnormalities made those who viewed them feel normal, bloodshed could make the public feel powerful, and fear could make them brave, as Cicero and Pliny the Younger claimed. The high tension which made games what they were also made them magnets for trouble during which rioters could "for an hour or two [be] an object of fear to all who cross[ed] their path."[21] Public violence thus constituted what was finally a conservative apotropaic political ceremony channeling aggression in manageable directions. But violence took many other, free-floating forms. Caligula occasionally would force spectators to sit in the broiling sun by rolling up the awnings (Suet. *Calig.* 26.5) or have bystanders thrown into the water at the dedication of a bridge (32.1). According to Dio (59.10.3), Caligula actually fed bystanders to the beasts at one of his shows during a shortage of condemned criminals. The parallel variant in Suetonius tones this last report down with a story about criminals used due to high cost of cattle as food for the beasts (*Calig.* 27.1). Literary events were not without their share of violence, either; losers on one occasion were obliged to lick up what they had written or be beaten with rods or tossed into a river (*Calig.* 20). Some of this had roots in popular traditions of rough-and-tumble sporting abuse.[22] But viewed in the context of a larger crisis of power and authority, it could well seem mere criminal behavior or outright absurdity to critics of the Principate. In the case of Caligula and Nero, that is what it perhaps was intended to be, insofar as (apparent) irrationality has important political uses (see Addendum 5). In any case, more active involvement of the elite, especially under Nero, gave powerful impulse to a rudimentary, highly polemic sociological critique which viewed the anomaly inherent in the logic of institutions for display of power as a contradiction, no longer sustaining but subverting social order.[23]

Participation by the emperor himself was the supreme breach of public norms, and Nero encouraged others who normally would have remained in their seats to join the performance. Old men of consular rank or matrons provided part of the entertainment; a well-known knight rode on an elephant tiptoeing down a tightrope. Conspicuous consumption, its extravagance doubled by random distributions, came into play, too, as party favors of gold and silver coins, jewels, paintings, slaves, animals, and finally ships, islands, or farms were lavished blindly (Suet. *Ner.* 11.2; cf. Dio 61.17.2–18.2). Nero brought amber hundreds of miles down from the Baltic for use in the arena (Pliny *HN.* 37.45; Dio 63.6.1) and awarded a musician and a gladiator symbols of status equal to those of men who had earned triumphs (Suet. *Ner.* 30.2). When Tacitus says that gloves put on by upper-class Romans were used for "boxing instead of military training" (*Ann.* 14.20.4), the complaint about subversion of Roman toughness by Greek sport implicitly justifies the Romans' own sporting violence for its military utility. But that is not to say that violence of any kind was absent from Nero's programs. In a show where he "exhibited" four hundred senators and six hundred knights in the arena, a bull also mounted a wooden cow thought by the audience to contain a real Pasiphae (cf. *Hist. Aug.* Elagabalus 25.4), while an actor playing Icarus plunged to the ground close enough to splatter the emperor with blood (Suet. *Ner.* 12.1–2). Even if these numbers for respectable participants are scaled back and we assume that they engaged only in mock combat, the presence of the upper class still exacted high expenditure of symbolic social capital. More disturbing to critics than old-fashioned brutality or Nero's fondness for unreasonably elaborate equipment was the notional side of such displays. When senators and knights fought, no one died, nor were any of the criminals who also took part killed, but a good portion of the Roman establishment had appeared with them and, like them, had symbolically undergone what they had been spared.

Nero's entertainments seem to have been designed to foster a generally Hellenic style, though what their larger intention might have been is uncertain. Everything from full-scale ideological revolution to nothing more than unconventional personal taste has been proposed, but it is at least clear that as a *cupitor incredibilium* he exploited to the full the principle of excess and anomaly on which public shows as an institution in fact depended.[24] Suetonius is prepared to reckon Nero's games among his "unobjectionable or even praiseworthy acts" by way of contrast to the outright criminal violence of which he was guilty (*Ner.* 19.3). His shows apparently aimed at minimizing gladiatorial combat in favor of artistic competition. Tacitus, on the contrary, sees the genial Greening of Rome during Nero's regime as a destabilization of values no less alarming in its way than arena violence is for Seneca.[25]

Among the public banquets given at Rome to prove that nowhere else could Nero be so happy was one by Tigellinus, served on a floating platform moved gently by boats manned with sexual deviants who were assigned positions "according to age and sexual expertise." Exotic animals had been collected from land and sea, and in Dio's version the festivities, which follow a hunt, sea battle, and gladiatorial combat, end in a mob scene as gladiators copulate with highborn girls before their fathers' eyes and slaves with mistresses as husbands look on, men die in brawls, and women suffocate in the press of people or are abducted. Tacitus describes brothels on the embankments of the lake staffed by well-known women, while opposite them nude prostitutes are posted. After some indecent dancing, "as the sun set, the whole area rang with song and sparkled with lights." Nero, "stained as he was with natural and unnatural vices," capped his own *licentia* a few days later by making and openly consummating a "marriage"—bridal veil and all—with one of his degenerate companions, named (doubtless to much bemused comment) Pythagoras (Tac. *Ann.* 15.37; Dio 62.15).[26]

Because Nero's shows were mainly theatrical, they raised an issue in the first instance of social propriety rather than of violence (*scaena lasciviens*, not *cavea saeviens*). Distinct as theater and arena are in substance, however, they are formally identical in respect to the symbolic norms by which anomaly in the social system is defined to begin with. While Nero's style ran more to conspicuous artistic display than to violence (Suet. *Ner.* 12.1), the one may be as aggressive in intent and subversive in effect as the other. Extravagance is the primary message of the "birds and wild animals sought out in every land and marine creatures brought all the way from the Ocean" for Tigellinus' party (Tac. *Ann.* 15.37.2). Wild land animals are the familiar material of bloodshed in public spectacles (e.g., Dio 68.15.1), and though nothing is said about violence done to them on this occasion, their presence establishes a symbolic link with conspicuous power, as surely as knights and senators even in nonlethal gladiatorial combat do. So far as real violence is concerned, that is amply in evidence in Dio's description. Already during the earlier years of Nero's reign, entertainment had taken a decidedly aggressive turn when he and his cronies breached the most elementary norms of public order by terrorizing the streets of Rome at night (Tac. *Ann.* 13.25; Suet. *Ner.* 26). If havoc was lacking in the arena, it was more than made up outside. Augustus had earlier satisfied his taste for blood in the streets by merely watching street fighters performing safely in the arena (Suet. *Aug.* 45.2).

For Tacitus the common denominator in all of this is anomaly out of hand, as *mores corrupti* spill over from theater and arena into life. That theme is summed up in the anecdote of a naive bodyguard rushing forward to save his emperor when he sees Nero wearing a mask with his own likeness and playing a dramatic role in chains (Suet. *Ner.* 21.3). The point finally is that the young soldier was not mistaken: under Nero and other emperors, theater could be life. Breaches in the wall separating performance from the outside world "flood the game into the spectacle," and that may again be the best explanation for some of the strange stories of violence done to spectators, whatever the specific facts actually were.[27] Exasperating a crowd by deliberately making it uncomfortable seems a singularly risky thing to do; perhaps the trouble began with faulty theater apparatus taken advantage of by Caligula as an opportunity for the bullying he seems to have enjoyed (Suet. *Calig.* 26.5). Dio has an equally dramatic account of the line between theater and politics dissolving under Commodus (72.21.1–2). If the amphitheater was, sociologically, a great public eye, the arena was its object, further kept in focus if awnings shading the seats could be adjusted to spotlight the sun at the center. Rolling the protection back then meant flooding the game into the stands by making the public itself both target of violence and center of action.

Wider social effects of the games at Rome are impossible to measure and probably were no less opaque at the time, in that, like pornography or violence in modern media, they at once contributed to and were an effect of violence, in some respects encouraging it, in others helping to reduce it. After outlining arguments pro and con advanced at the time, Tacitus concedes that one show in the new Neronian manner caused neither scandal nor violence (*Ann.* 14.21.4). Along with arguments for the economic advantage of expenditure on performances, proponents insisted on the valuable opportunity for sharpening literary talent they furnished. Though applying here in the first instance to theatrical performance, wholesome stimulation of competition is similar, as a general proposition about social utility, to the improved military spirit that was supposed to be gained from gladiatorial games.[28] But Tacitus still insists on the *licentia* at work in *laetitia* and attributes it to Nero's personal aberrations while also tracing wider social ramifications. Some people were pressured by financial considerations into taking part, but many others were thrilled at the chance (*Ann.* 14.14.3, 14.15.3). As events gain momentum Tacitus devotes a lurid paragraph to the moral degradation of the "scum" *(conluvies)* active in Nero's theatrical productions (14.15). Next, after suddenly shifting to the overt violence of a vicious riot *(atrox caedes)* that broke out at gladiatorial games outside Rome (14.17), he turns to the debate concerning the wisdom of Nero's innovations (14.20–21). Alarmed moralizing by those convinced that the activities were a bad idea ends with a warning about nighttime orgies (20.5), a possibility shortly realized in Tigellinus' party. Heavy-handed ideological bias and crude sociology aside, this is still exceptionally rich "deep play" in Geertz's sense of the term and a powerful evocation of Roger Caillois' "vertigo": the total dissolution of the work a day world's order invited by carnivals, fairs, or circuses, which in point of fact were major Roman social institutions.[29]

The ultimate consumers of socially sponsored brutality in the arena at Rome were the members of Roman society itself, and broad explanatory paradigms are particularly helpful for sorting out some of the complexities in the very unusual transaction conducted between the two sides. In functional terms, arena games can be understood as a way of accommodating violence to social order. The gross phallus crowned by a respectable matron (August. *De civ. D.* 7.21) and the aggressive behavior of prostitutes during the Floralia were relatively benign levels of the anomaly or dissonance accompanying breached norms. Disjunction was perhaps felt somewhat more strongly and linked to more serious violence when prostitutes took part in mock gladiatorial fighting, and it became more obtrusive still when women of social standing engaged in actual arena combat.[30] Deliberately provocative disjunctions then took on social significance from being, at the same time, festive conjunctions, whose most extreme form—lethal violence as mass entertainment—was connected with what critics like Seneca and Tacitus saw as deeper incoherence. After Tigellinus' party is followed by Nero's perverse marriage, violence engulfs everything. Rome is ravaged by the great fire, and political terror leads up to Nero's own death, itself even in Suetonius' normally bland account a paradigm of deeply anomalous political violence.

Part II

Political Suicide: Were They Pushed, or
Did They Jump?

7

Political Violence and Suicide

The anecdote concerning Arrachion in chapter 1 epitomizes in extreme form the social logic of competitive violence: No pain, no gain. The axiom that success and failure are inseparable is set out not by what happened to Arrachion or to his opponent but by the decision of the judges. Finally, the story is concerned with a system of social values, not with individuals living under it, and the situation on which it turns is constituted by two factors tied to each other reciprocally in a schematized scenario typical of exempla: on the one side, anomaly (in this case, fatal sport violence), on the other, social norms by which the anomaly is assessed and the anecdote given exemplary meaning. Arrachion literally dies trying, and one point his death makes has to do with admirable devotion to the code of competition. Its grotesque circumstances then add a further point about the code itself: winners may also be losers, and losers, winners. Arrachion's fate is at once normal and abnormal, both reassuring and disquieting, like that of the gladiator whose epitaph reads "He died after killing his opponent and winning," or like the robust misery of Aulus Gellius' fighter (Gell. *NA* 12.5.13).[1]

What is more, Arrachion not only dies but kills himself trying, and that is true also of those who committed political suicide at Rome. Their rationale again sprang from ruthless competition and the pressing need it created to accommodate aberrant forms of violence. Tacitus' account of Otho's suicide, for example, is in an important sense another story of a man who dies trying. And it is again the oddity, made all the odder when the suicide is hysterically emulated by some of Otho's troops and accompanied by a very strange omen (*Hist.* 2.50), that gives Tacitus an opening to the dilemmas embedded in Roman politics. He seems to dismiss the truth of reports about a mysterious bird (he calls it a *miraculum*) which, after appearing in a sacred grove, remained undisturbed until it vanished from sight at the very moment of Otho's death. Its unbelievability nonetheless represents the political anomaly of the suicide itself. Tacitus readily grants Otho his personal due given the circumstances, but the circumstances are finally what is deeply anomalous. That point is made by systematic inversion of the things Roman leaders normally do or say: exhort troops, for example, but not to mutiny, as Otho has done earlier, or to surrender, as he now is doing.[2]

Self-sacrifice, too, is a fine thing, but *devotio* in his case also parodies any normal ideas of public service, doubly so and with profound political significance, because, besides being parody, it also makes perfectly good sense and is (again under the circumstances) admirable. The thematic confusion between normal and abnormal, reasonable and unreasonable, explains the emphasis placed not only on Otho's correct style of dying amid disorder but on his curious farewell distribution of gifts. In Tacitus' version, he "distributed money carefully, not as though he was about to die" (*Hist.* 2.48.1); in Plutarch's he "carefully observed what was due and did not act as though squandering other people's money" (*Otho* 17.1). Like his serene self-possession which rationalizes the disturbing moment of suicidal political violence, proper frugality neutralizes his own notorious profligacy.[3] While the significance of the suicide is obvious enough, prudent liberality is a second, largely implicit corollary of the situation's overall logic, rhetorically pleasing but still vaguely inopportune, coming much too late for real political effect, and therefore finally indicative of profound confusion in values.

Though it does not involve suicide, the account of Galba's final moments makes a similar point about incongruity, implicitly through the deep structure of the narrative. In one version mentioned by Tacitus, his last words are quite in character: a plaintive "What did I do wrong?" Suetonius, too, has him trying fecklessly to buy off the troops (*Galba* 20.1), but in another version of his farewell ("Go ahead and strike, if that is in the public interest [*e re publica*]"; Tac. *Hist.* 1.41.2), incompetence and disgraceful abdication are balanced by a supremely dignified farewell word of command. The contrast helps drive home the brutality of his lynching along with its larger political meaning: the emperor is a fool for not understanding the forces at work around him, but when power falls into the hands of a military mob, no one else understands either. Tacitus speculates unkindly that Vinius may have attempted to prevent his own murder in the aftermath of Galba's by protesting that he was not supposed to killed, either in desperate pretense that he was conniving with Otho, the new emperor, or because he really had done so. According to a second report, he was too terrified to say anything at all, memorable or not (*Hist.* 1.42). Vitellius' last words to an abusive tribune—"not without class" even by Tacitus' unforgiving standards—are in the same way un-witting political truth, touching directly on and yet incongruously out of touch with the circumstances: "Still, I *was* your commander" (*Hist.* 3.85). A man who had himself been a living freakish "portent" (3.56.2) man-ages to recall, but in no way restores, Roman norms for a moment at the end as he dies. What is more, the state itself is actually in question, as "most people pitied the fate of the Principate more than the fate of Vitellius" (3.58.2). Other emperors renounced power or had it taken away; Vitellius faces the extreme incongruity of not being able to give power away, and Tacitus remarks on how odd it all is (3.68; cf. Suet. *Vit.* 15).

The logic around which these stories are built shaped a highly com-plex and important aspect of Roman political life. The suicide or death of emperors embodies the same political futility that makes Tacitus doubtful about suicidal resistance to them as often no more than "aggres-sion and empty display [*inani iactatione*] of freedom inviting reputation—and execution" (*Agr.* 42.3). If suicide is an admission of failure no matter how stylishly it is done, the emperor's suicide is a mirror image both of suicide by his opponents and of his own assassination at their hands, insofar as the latter is no less a sign of failure in the political system as a whole. In fact, assassination and suicide effectively coincide when Ger-manicus' threat (or offer) to kill himself is accepted by one of the troops: "Here, take my sword; it's sharper!" (Tac. *Ann.* 1.35.5). We can credit Tacitus with an eye for more than drama here, though there is plenty of that in the scene, which formally parodies both elegant suicide such as Otho's and suicide carried out with the aid of a helpful bystander. Like the celebrated quip about the consulship of "Julius and Caesar," the jest is politically disturbing because the amusing nonsense is read directly from the situation. It seems quite impossible to tell what anyone's proper role under the circumstances is, including that of Germanicus, as ambig-uous a figure as Otho, to say nothing of Tiberius lurking behind the scene.

What is strange is that suicide may well be the right, perhaps the only, thing to do. If violence in the arena was disorder focused inside a danger zone surrounded by a larger social order, in suicide it was con-fined to selected targets whose elimination could prevent wider political disruption. The correspondence, of course, was not nearly so clean as that, but Tacitus does use both to represent political incongruity more generally. Gladiatorial violence at times seems indistinguishable from civil war, while suicide can be treated as a calamity signaled by omens, another index of something amiss on a large scale in Roman society.

Besides the bird marking Otho's death, as Thrasea Paetus kills himself he says to the quaestor who has brought the death order, "Look, young man—and may the gods avert the omen—you were born in an age that requires toughness" (Tac. *Ann.* 16.35). The ominous calamity in question is the need for the desperate integrity which the quaestor is witnessing in Thrasea's suicide and which in fact was needed again when Thrasea's son-in-law, Helvidius Priscus, was subsequently executed.

Enforced suicide was not an institution in the same sense that either public shows or divination were. It had for the most part no legal standing, officials were involved only to the extent of forcing performance, and it was a ritual only in the sense that all more or less sanctioned social behavior is. But since it embodied violence no less plainly than gladiatorial combat did and had become common enough in Roman politics to bring with itself a loose set of rules, it can count at least as an ad hoc institution, expressive of longer-term arrangements in political power.[4] As a rational choice, suicide was subject to rules governing games played against other rational agents, while making ample room at the same time for the nonutilitarian symbolic considerations which take rational choices beyond narrow self-interest but stop short of irrationality.

Suicide is universally a way of escaping the intolerable consequences of military defeat or political failure in public life. At Rome long before the imperial period, Appius Claudius is said to have killed himself to avoid humiliating defeat in a struggle with the plebs (Livy 3.58.6), and his death was given out as due to natural causes (Dion. Hal. 9.54.4–5) to prevent his enemies from scoring political points at the admission of failure. The right to choose suicide in place of execution, too, is recorded at the time of the Gracchi (App. *BCiv.* 1.3.26). During the late Republic, as intense political competition that had always been the mainspring of Roman life began to run out of control, personal danger escalated along with the level of civil violence. Since competitors were now all Romans, in a game with mostly unwritten rules the focus in political meaning of suicide began to sharpen.

The death into which Antony was "forced" by Octavian (Suet. *Aug.* 17.4) was part of a complex, three-sided internal political endgame in which suicide played a decisive role (Dio 51.10–15.1; Plut. *Ant.* 76–86). Cleopatra had formed a Club of Partners in Death with Antony. After testing the efficacy of poisons (Plut. *Ant.* 71.3–5), she began to use threats of suicide to strengthen her hold over him. Once he had killed himself, her life (and wealth) again became a bargaining chip, this time with Octavian, and finally a means to lull Octavian into permitting an opportunity for Cleopatra's own suicide. Uncertainty about how death had actually happened, loyalty between man and woman, and political points to be scored by moves made with one's own life all duplicate strategies in use under the Principate. During the earlier Empire, the adoption of suicide by the elite made it a somewhat more normal peacetime option, since losing had always been painful, but losing unconditionally and permanently to one's equals seemed intolerable to many.[5] With political self-assertion for most members of the upper class now sharply restricted, suicide became not solely a gesture of personal despair or defiance but something imposed by the political system and—as virtue made of necessity—a way to assert political freedom by dying "more at the desire than on the decision of enemies" (Vell. Pat. 2.22.4). This unusual, hybrid passive activism is a factor in Tacitus' keen interest in how Roman aristocrats met death.

If suicide, then, was not an institution, it was shaped by institutional values. Not only did it enjoy some legal recognition even in the case of slaves, but careful provision was made for specific rights attaching to it. Sanctions applied solely in the event of a connection with other crimes, and here a peculiar relationship between life and death makes itself felt. Suicide to block escape from the consequence of crime committed during life (on the principle *crimen extinguitur mortalitate*) was itself declared criminal, and to assure that as the ultimate act in life, death would not cancel all other illegal acts, the escape hatch was closed by a second principle that suicide could be treated as both admission of guilt (*conscientia criminis*) and sentence on oneself, the latter in effect making suicide into substitute execution, as political suicide more informally was. In any other circumstances it incurred no penalties and enjoyed official recognition when carried out for such reasons as debt (*pudor aeris alieni; Dig.* 49.14.45.2) or to make a personal statement (*iactatio;* 28.3.6.7). The second is associated with the death of philosophers, but Tacitus uses the same term for more general political gestures (*Agr.* 42.3) to which philosophy was often closely linked at Rome, while *pudor* due to disabling debt was a common reason for loss of social status. *Iactatio* was roughly a positive, *pudor* a negative, motive; the two corresponded respectively to more aggressive and more defensive moves. By largely excluding moral considerations and minimizing restrictions, Roman law maximized the sphere in which suicide could be exercised as a political right and to that extent invited its use.

Though enforced suicide was treated very gingerly in the code, political suicide as such was part of the larger system of values operative also in cases having nothing to do directly with politics. When Caninius Rebilus kills himself to escape the woes of old age though no one had thought he was tough enough to do so (Tac. *Ann.* 13.30.2), the point his death makes is a personal one about courage. It is carried out for a purely private reason and is straightforwardly admirable by way of contrast to, say, the suicide that inspired an unkind quip about an "accident" which the deceased had had with his sword (Quint. *Inst.* 6.3.69), comparable today to wondering whether a man dead by his own hand knew that the gun was loaded. The complex, often contradictory currents running through the circumstances and motives of suicide made it choice material for a rich typology in many different registers.

Domitius, who takes poison in despair only to vomit it up in panic at the thought of dying, gratefully frees his doctor when he learns that he had given him a weak potion, expecting his patient's change of mind all along (Suet. *Ner.* 2.3; in a version complimentary to this relative of Nero, Seneca focuses on Domitius' escape from death, *Ben.* 3.24). It is not clear whether the motive for suicide was private or not, but its nice cynicism turns the story into a highly revealing epitome of a world scarcely distinguishable from the world of declamation: lost hope, desperate resolve, suicide, panic, last-minute reprieve, along with a good measure of hypocrisy and bluff. Cato's death, the classic instance of exemplary political suicide, is at the same time highly self-centered, while another exemplary death mentioned by Dio is purely altruistic (46.53.3). A soldier despondent at falling into enemy hands and on the point of execution is noticed by a fellow prisoner who had come to respect him during earlier service together. The best stiffener he can think of for his old comrade's morale is to kill himself in his sight. Velleius similarly tells of an Etruscan seer caught up in political terror and, after urging a friend who had also been taken into custody to "do as I do," dashing his head on the prison doorpost (2.7.2; cf. Sen. *Ep.* 77.14). Arria's celebrated "Paete, non dolet" (Pliny *Ep.* 3.16.6) comes typologically close to these examples in its focus on purely personal integrity, while taking place in circumstances as political as those of Cato's. The extensive Cato literature together with the prominence of such nuances in the historical tradition shows how important the moral-political logic of suicide was at the time.[6]

8

Political Game Rules

In view of their predominantly political motivation, the many anecdotes about suicide can usefully be thought of as hinging on an intricate set of game rules. A study of political suicide at Rome in fact may well be a modest exercise along the line of what is now called game theory. If the term is anachronistic, the idea is not. Every group has rules for governing behavior; game theory tries to identify and assess the various strategies possible within their limits.

The case of Tiberius' daughter-in-law is an instructive starting point (Suet. *Tib.* 53). Attempted suicide was an initial move on her part, countered first with enforced survival, while the ensuing standoff was then resolved either through successful suicide (itself in turn trumped by Tiberius' subsequent claim of clemency for not having treated her like an ordinary criminal) or through actual execution disguised as suicide. After losing an eye during a beating administered at Tiberius' order, Agrippina resolved on suicide by starvation but was kept alive through forced feeding, probably because suicide that could be taken as defiant self-assertion would count against his prestige, as submission would not. According to Tacitus, she did kill herself, "unless she was starved so that her death would look like suicide" (*Ann.* 6.25.1), the latter presumably being staged, if that was what was done, to look like submission or admission of guilt instead of plain execution, which would come too close to murder.[1] In Suetonius, too, she finally succeeds in killing herself, and Tiberius' gambit then is to claim credit for not having had her strangled like an ordinary criminal, using not what he did but what he might have done as a standard for political meaning.

Though commonly employed as a rigorous, largely mathematical methodology in areas such as military and diplomatic strategy or economics, on a smaller scale and in looser form game theory of a sort has long been a tool of historical and political analysis.[2] Modern game theory favors "scenarios"—typical situations or theoretical case histories—to exemplify strategies. So, as a matter of method, did Thucydides, with his set speeches written in an analytic style to bring out permanent, abstract axioms underlying behavior. Narrative of events is the game; speeches are embryonic game theory designed to spell out moves imposed by the game (*ta deonta;* Thuc. 1.22). Greek culture in general was inclined to paradigmatic ways of thinking. Earlier still, Herodotus' account of the logic of economic choice in the Babylonian sale of brides (1.196) is a good instance of the specifically quizzical patterns game analysis often brings to light.[3] Plato, who favors formal mathematical diagrams for setting out the structure of things, includes in book 8 of the *Republic* character sketches showing how psycho-political types as a rule behave. Aristotle's heavily analytic style of thinking and writing leads him in the *Politics* to isolate formal schemata of power with special attention to antinomies. Applied to ethics, the Peripatetic method produced genuine scenarios of its own in Aristotle and in Theophrastus' *Characters.* In more refined guise, Sallust's or Tacitus' thumbnail obituaries, fixing the essential shape of a whole career in a few crisp phrases, are later examples, as are the strange death scenes of emperors or the *sententiae* and anecdotes figuring prominently in Roman historiography and literature more generally.

It is true that anecdotes are not austere formulae but dramatic moral *exempla.* Still, game theory itself takes on narrative realism from scenarios, and inasmuch as anecdotes were used with the intention of condensing essential truths operative in particular situations, they can usefully be compared with formal axioms on several scores. Both are concerned with deeper patterns of behavior, both employ nonfactual thought experiments, and both disclose tendencies that may be largely implicit. On this last point, the situation in cases of suicide was much like that of Diodorus Siculus' "semi-laws" of war (30.18.2): while violating law, war still has informal lawlike rules of its own, such as the sanctity of heralds or the inviolability of truces.

Hidden rules, moreover, are often counterintuitive as well, and that, too, attracted a good deal of attention in ancient thought, becoming in epigrammatic Silver Latin not merely a principle of paradoxical expression but also a distinctive, conspiratorial way of thinking about hidden inner workings, preeminently in politics. Gift exchange in ancient society, for example, was a pervasive ritual (game) governed by a complex, subtle set of rules appearing in various guises: the relation between patron and client, elections, grants of imperial clemency, or the donative cum bribery cementing relations between army and general. The systemic anomalies which go with social institutions tend to be salient either at places where it is convenient to veil power, as it was in gift giving, or where coordination between ends and means breaks down. Abstract, analytic patterns became a habit of thought in discussions of the intricacies of gifts: "The one who does not return a favor is grateful, the one who does, is not" (Sen. *Ben.* 4.21.3; cf. the contorted contrasts describing an amazing case of slaves' loyalty to their mistress in 3.23.4 or a father's mercy for a son in Sen. *Clem.* 1.15.2). If the rule that no good deed goes unpunished is too sweeping, at Rome some certainly did not (*possint laudata puniri; Clem.* 1.2.1). And so even innocent people, Seneca notes somewhat nervously, may need clemency, for since mercy is an exercise of power through other means, when power becomes absolute, innocence is beside the point. In the same way, as we have seen, paradoxical expression was a natural corollary of paradoxical thinking about gladiatorial violence. Gladiators are people Romans love to hate (Tert. *De Spect.* 22.3) because of the contraries they hold together in uneasy, potentially dysfunctional tension.[4]

A classic case of full-blown dysfunction is enshrined in the title of Joseph Heller's satirical novel, *Catch-22,* which has recently been dignified by admission into the dictionary as a common noun. The "catch" is a somewhat more baffling version of circular opposites like those in gift exchange: if a pilot wants to fly combat missions, he is regarded as crazy and therefore eligible for medical exemption from flying combat missions, but only on request, and a request proves his sanity, so he must fly combat missions.[5] This, too, has a crisp, aphoristic sound. It is a rule governing behavior and a queer one. Two facets of political suicide at Rome in particular are worthy of exploration in light of these intricate formal patterns: the rules underlying instances reported principally in Seneca, Tacitus, Suetonius, and Dio Cassius, and connections between the political logic at work in them and the larger institutional anomaly in the Principate, culminating in a Roman catch-22 to the effect that "I have to kill myself in self-defense, because the emperor is going to kill me in self-defense."

Other things such as frequency, methods, and the effect of philosophy on motivation had an important part in suicide at Rome. But beyond these relatively specific factors were broader considerations that made a particular case of, say, Stoic resistance into a move which counted politically (to revert to the language of games). So far as the potentially irrational behavior it may exhibit is concerned, suicide often does raise questions of intelligibility quite apart from political meanings it can have. Lucretius (3.79–82) noted that people commit suicide because they are afraid of dying, an odd circular situation with distinctly quizzical features formally similar, for example, to resigning a game of chess in order to avoid defeat or, for that matter, killing oneself to avoid being executed. Political suicide could in fact be a powerful last move, hence Caesar's anger at Cato's suicide (Dio 43.12) or Tiberius' chagrin when someone kills himself before he can strike ("Why, he escaped me!" Suet. *Tib.* 61.5; cf. the case of Cremutius Cordus, Sen. *Ad Marciam* 22.7). But if it was a good last move, it was also a terminal one, affording opportunity for self-assertion only of a very unusual kind. The paradoxical notion of "enforced freedom" which it entails is touched on by Sallust's remark that in destroying their property and then themselves by fire, the inhabitants of Thala "paid of their own free will the penalty they feared from the enemy" (*Iug.* 76.6). Under the circumstances, suicidal freedom of action is at once vacuous and real, and in the case of Rome, too, questions of whether those who committed suicide were pushed or jumped becomes a genuinely complicated matter when the chief accomplishment of a political career may have been killing oneself.[6] "Due to the endless series of disasters things had reached the point where virtue was thought to be nothing else but dying nobly" (Dio 60.16.7), hence Lucan's or Seneca's peculiarly hectic ideas about political virtue.

Facing imminent arrest, Scipio stabbed himself, and when his enemies inquired about him, his reply was "Imperator bene se habet" ("The general is doing just fine," Sen. *Ep.* 24.9–10; cf. Val. Max. 3.2.13). Seneca sees this as vindication of personal integrity. But Scipio is no philosopher; his remark is a political move and one with the ambivalence that any move has when it is made once the game is lost. The same bon mot has a different setting in Tacitus. When Nero, suspected of having poisoned Burrus, paid him a sick call, the dying man's only remark was "Ego me bene habeo" ("*I'm* just fine," Tac. *Ann.* 14.51.1; cf. Vitellius' equally self-possessed, futile, and revealing "Still, I *was* your commander!" Tac. *Hist.* 3.85). Like Scipio, Burrus preserves a soldier's dignity to the end, and though suicide is not a factor, death as an occasion for protest still is. The very currency of these portable typological scenarios for suicide, murder, or plain death is evidence of the extent to which death could be thought of as a formal, relatively abstract political move dictated by rules of etiquette governing relationships in Roman political life.

Since bloodshed in the arena was institutionalized and confined mostly to participants of marginal social standing, its dysfunctional aspects were detected only by those inclined to look with a critical eye to begin with. Political suicide, in contrast, had much less institutional status, though it did directly affect the highest levels of society. Its uncertain circumstances—not legal, yet not exactly illegal or criminal either—further reinforced by the highly dramatic situations it created, made suicide an exceptionally revealing example of the reach and intensity of violence in the political system at Rome. While the violence of *munera* was secondhand, external, and diffuse, that of suicide was firsthand, internal, and focused. Suicide fell mainly outside formal laws, and its political function was shaped by involuted implicit rules of the kind that governed gift exchange, where meeting obligations could be an insult, or clemency, where restraint could be aggression.

9

The Tactics of Political Suicide

The first and central axiom in the political logic of forced suicide is the emperor's power, all the more effective for being partially indirect, like the devious authority of someone who can order a window closed merely by saying that it is open or can give orders by making requests, as Mucianus does when he "gently suggests and asks" the Senate not to rake up inconvenient old political troubles (Tac. *Hist.* 4.44.1). Clemency is no less useful on this score, in that power great enough to work quietly—or not to have to work at all—is as politically elegant as were the shows where power was flaunted by lions trained to catch rabbits and then let them go unharmed.[1] The signal sent by Tiberius' refusal to permit the spendthrift brother of the future emperor Galba to stand for a province was enough to make him commit suicide, and two relatives of Sejanus acted on the *signum mortis* when priesthoods promised to them while Sejanus was still alive were assigned to others (Tac. *Ann.* 6.40.2; Suet. *Galba* 3.4; cf. Dio 59.20.3, 60.11.8). Though Thrasea was not forced to kill himself until later, by telescoping the first sign of Nero's displeasure into an "indication of imminent death" (*Ann.* 15.23.4, 16.24, 16.35), Tacitus brings out a conjunction that is perfectly real on one political plane by means of another that is factually false (cf. *Ann.* 13.22.2 with 14.22 and 59 [Plautus]).

Insofar as it is not mere chronology but insight into causes and connections, historical perspective is bound to foreshorten events, though not so dramatically as this. In another case the moves are condensed further still into a supremely spare exchange: "Hello, Caesar!" "Goodbye, Fulvius." Fulvius then commits suicide along with his wife (Plut. *De garr.* 508A). This perhaps falls just within the bounds of *ludibrium* plausible in Roman politics; the motif of instantly effective unspoken power, with suicide replaced by ad hoc lynching, becomes parody when a hench-man of Caligula responds to greetings from a group of senators and the one to whom he angrily replies, "You're greeting me—you who hate the emperor?" is torn to pieces on the spot by the others (Dio 59.26.2).

Names in a notebook titled *Pugio* were marked down for enforced suicide by Caligula, the dagger being more discreet, as handguns are in comparison with military rifles. Names in a second notebook titled *Gladius* were scheduled for execution (Suet. *Calig.* 49.3), a demonstra-tion of overt power, while imprisonment and exile in their varying de-grees of severity provided more nuanced methods for eliminating players from the field. Members of the elite enjoyed some immunity from legal penalties, but procedures were vague enough to permit any number of strategies, and all restraints were overridden when the emperor believed that he faced serious danger. Enforced suicide was thus parasitic on the law in a special way; being both indirect and extralegal, it constituted a hybrid self-execution which, conveniently for the emperor, could be thought of as both criminal-free and victimless. It is referred to only once in the *Digest,* when governors are denied the right to authorize choice of death, though it had been allowed in rescripts (48.19.8.1). While suicide in protest for political reasons is not specifically recognized, it might at times have qualified as a case of *iactatio* or *pudor.*

Though details are often uncertain, when the circumstances of par-ticular cases are taken all together they make up a fair representation of the rules under which suicide occurred. After introducing the dual sui-cide of Labeo and his wife to illustrate "the continuing carnage" at Rome, Tacitus remarks that besides being a way to avoid execution, speedy suicide commonly had the payoff *(pretium)* of preserving prop-erty and burial rights. Only then does he turn to the facts of the case by mentioning charges brought against Labeo, but without clearly indicat-ing whether they were true or false. Then he returns to the rationale of suicide by adding that Tiberius publicly explained his own actions in order to deflect responsibility (*Ann.* 6.29).[2] Apart from what the facts were and apart from Tacitus' or Tiberius' estimate of them, the general rules themselves are plain enough: move by the emperor, countermove aimed at mitigating its effect, and counter-countermove, here a letter sent to the Senate justifying the initial move.

Evidently a frequent topic of conversation in Rome was whether the deceased had been a victim of suicide, forced or voluntary, had been executed (Tac. *Ann.* 3.16.1, 6.23.1, 25.1; Tac. *Hist.* 3.54.3; Dio 58.11.7), or had actually died a natural death (*Ann.* 2.42.3, 6.10.3, 12.52.2, 14.47.1). Accounts by the historians may be no less unclear in this respect, at times saying nothing about guilt or about innocence either.[3] The terminology of execution could overlap with that of suicide when the distinction did not seem important or was taken for granted, or when the facts were not certain. Suetonius applies *animadversum in auctores* to Scaurus and Cremutius Cordus (*Tib.* 61.3), who committed suicide, according to Tacitus (*Ann.* 4.35.4, 6.29), while the suicide of Iulus Antonius mentioned by Velleius Paterculus (2.100.4) is not evident from Tacitus or Dio (Tac. *Ann.* 4.44.3; Dio 55.10.15). The *mors opportuna* of Piso (*Ann.* 4.21.2) is more likely to have been natural death, as was that of Agricola, *felix* for "his distinguished life as well as timely death" (*opportunitate mortis;* Tac. *Agr.* 45.3). A certain ambiguity, however, may attach to the phrase owing to the different meanings it had from the emperor's or the dead man's point of view, and after mentioning rumors of murder, Tacitus adds a remark about no one believing that if Domitian had truly felt regret, he would have been so eager to learn of Agricola's death (43). In *Annals* 6.10.2 the phrase *aguntur ad mortem* leaves unclear whether the victims were executed or forced into suicide, and so does the passive *abscinduntur venae* in the account of Vestinus' death in *Annals* 15.68–69 (attributed directly to Nero by Suetonius; *Ner.* 35.1).

Caligula exploited the gray area by continuing to extend social invitations to people he had executed and then claiming that they had in the meantime committed suicide (Suet. *Calig.* 26.2). Claudius did not even think of asking how his wife had actually died when told that Messalina was dead (Tac. *Ann.* 11.38), and it might have been difficult to say in her case, since as she was trying unsuccessfully to kill herself under duress, a tribune did the job for her.[4] In Suetonius, Claudius does wonder where she is, presumably having forgotten that he has ordered her execution (*Claud.* 39.1). Though this version dramatizes his absentmindedness, the wider political background of both accounts is the fact that such questions could arise all too routinely under the Principate.

The distinction between execution and suicide is further blurred by surrogates, like the tribune sent to Messalina, who took over the victim's proper role as agent of his or her own death, just as a cooperative victim, as self-executioner, took over a role the emperor preferred not to play. At a final meal, after Libo had received the fatal order, he directed his slaves to kill him (to commit suicide for him, as it were; Tac. *Ann.* 2.31; cf. Pliny *Ep.* 8.14.12; Dio 47.49.2). When they refused, the occasion quickly turned nightmarish. Amid mounting panic, the lights went out, and in the darkness, dramatically seen by Tacitus as Hades on earth, Libo finally managed to kill himself in abject terror.[5] Vestinus has more success in inducing his doctor to cut his veins and carry him into a hot bath (Tac. *Ann.* 15.69.2); Seneca, too, is given poison by his doctor and taken to the bath (15.64); and Ostorius, on receiving the emperor's order, cuts his veins and, as that proves too slow, has a slave hold the dagger steady so that he can himself push it into his own throat (16.15.2).

One dramatic measure of Nero's political isolation at the end is that he can find neither friend nor enemy—neither suicide by proxy nor execution—to grant him death (Suet. *Ner.* 47). It is tempting to imagine an earlier enigmatic oracular prediction that he "would come to a wretched end though in danger neither from friends nor enemies," in the style of prophecies such as the one that rivals would fall into Severus' hands "neither alive nor dead" (*Hist. Aug.* Pescennius Niger 9.5; *Hist. Aug.* Clodius Albinus 9.2–4). Suetonius' highly colored account of Nero's death is a fine example of how anecdotal narrative details function as miniscenarios playing out rules of behavior. In point of fact, Nero could readily have been accommodated by friends or enemies: the latter were hot on his trail, and as they closed in, his secretary finally did help him cut his throat (Suet. *Ner.* 49). But authentic or not, it is all meant to come together in a death dramatizing the deeply strange moves being made in the political game at Rome. Tacitus'even keener interest in death scenes similarly reflects the peculiar political significance that last acts had come to have, and it must have seemed profoundly right that Nero, too, was forced to kill himself and then made a bad job of it.[6]

The political shock of execution, conveniently reduced by enforced suicide in private, could be reintensified by suicide deliberately performed in public. Protest was a factor along with personal despair in the suicide of the knight Samius at his expensive advocate's home on discovering that the advocate was conniving with the other side (Tac. *Ann.* 11.52). That is true again in instances of suicide in the Senate or elsewhere before others (Tac. *Ann.* 5.7, 6.40.1; Dio 58.21.4, 58.4.6; Suet. *Tib.* 61.4). Gestures of opposition like this called for counterdisplays of authority to make defiant suicide seem less free because it would count as having occurred under some degree of official control. Suetonius mentions attempted suicides bandaged up and hustled off to prison only half alive (*Tib.* 61.4; cf. Tac. *Ann.* 6.48.3; Dio 58.27.4). After taking poison in the Senate, Vibulenus Agrippa was rushed off to prison for hanging but proved to be already dead (Tac. *Ann.* 6.40.1). Some room was left for maneuvering about what counted as suicide in the first place, and since suicide could assure property rights, these frantic measures were an attempt on the part of the authorities to have their cake and eat it too by securing death without needing to trade anything in return. In the case of Agrippa, Tacitus' further suggestion of efforts to hang a corpse ("His neck was stretched in a noose, though he was already dead") creates an impression of absurdity, while at the same time disclosing the real agent of death behind suicide. What is more, unseemly squabbling about rules which give the emperor every advantage anyway helps shift emphasis from the suicide to the symbolic game itself, where the historians want it to be.

As an equivalent to execution, suicide under duress was a decisive exercise of power on the emperor's part, while also being, as a substitute for it, a concession to the victim's standing and thus part of a formal trade-off, however one-sided it was in substance. The code under which Augustus rejected Antony's overtures for a truce and "forced him to die" (Suet. *Aug.* 17.4) carried over into peacetime when those who had been condemned in court were granted the right to "choose" and then carry out the manner of their death (*liberum mortis arbitrium;* Tac. *Ann.* 11.3.1, 16.33.2; Suet. *Dom.* 11.3). The privilege, commonly extended to members of the upper class (and to a freedman of Augustus; Suet. *Aug.* 67.2) in deference to their status, helped reduce damage done to the emperor's own status by lending execution legitimacy. In a case handled cleanly for all parties concerned, one conspirator was immediately executed to remove a direct threat to Vespasian, while another who was condemned later after trial in the Senate cut his own throat (Dio 66.16.3–4). Historians were interested in political ramifications, but a case mentioned by Tacitus mostly for its personal newsworthiness is an instance of suicide replacing execution because of social privilege extending through an elaborate personal chain of command. When Plautius Silvanus, who had thrown his wife out of a window, could give only a very confused account of what had happened, he was quietly sent a dagger by his grandmother, whose friendship with Augusta indicated that the hint came from the emperor himself (Tac. *Ann.* 4.22).

Exile or choice of how one was to die could be spoken of as "permitted" (Tac. *Ann.* 11.3.1, 16.11.3, 15.71.4), and honorable burial along with a valid testament was a "reward" for suicide (6.29.1). By conceding a right to die with dignity, the emperor recognized the claims of his victims while still denying them, since the concession he was under some constraint to make limited his exercise of authority only symbolically. And even that symbolism did little to conceal the display of power in cases where he faced no serious threat. When Caligula's young cousin, on receiving an order for suicide, has to ask where he should aim the sword (Philo *Leg.* 30–31), the situation just manages to fit in at the outer margin of the system, where something uncomfortably close to murder is still an understandably prudent use of power and permits Gemellus to die like a good little Roman. The death of Drusus from enforced starvation, on the other hand, went too far. Tiberius' direct involvement precluded any buffering of responsibility, while his official report of the pathetic details so jeopardized the rules under which violence was rationalized that the Senate's normally sham horror at the victim's sham guilt became genuine revulsion at the public flaunting of power (Tac. *Ann.* 6.24–25; Suet. *Tib.* 54). The suicide of a woman Tiberius had harassed for rejecting his sexual advances similarly became an occasion for public disapproval directed at him by the theater crowd (Suet. *Tib.* 45).

Imposed suicide allowed degrees of duress to be varied at will. If power was to be made plain, death could be forced so quickly as to deny real choice of method or time and thus make suicide tantamount to execution (Tac. *Ann.* 6.18.1 and 15.60.1 describe cases of outright, abrupt execution; Suet. *Ner.* 37.2 details something, called medical treatment by Nero, between summary execution and suicide; Tac. *Ann.* 15.69.2 is an instance of hasty suicide). Execution was veiled, on the other hand, by more deliberate *liberum mortis arbitrium* and by the legal rights to burial or property which it normally carried, but pressure was still present, since here again desire to assure that privileges would in fact be honored encouraged quick action before formal proceedings had gone too far.

Suicide was thus a complex coefficient of political prerogatives. For the victim it could be an opportunity for damaging the emperor's reputation. While pretending grief, Tiberius also felt the need to complain that the manner of Piso's death was a reproach to himself (Tac. *Ann.* 3.16.2) because of the *invidia* it had caused (cf. 6.26.1, 6.29.2, 12.8.1, for instances of suicide that increased *invidia* against the emperor). It is not clear that Piso intended his death to be a gesture of protest, but suicide could easily do harm under the circumstances because of its equivalence to execution, and rumors indeed circulated that Piso had not killed himself but was actually executed (3.16.1). Still, suicide under duress and execution were not the same, and from the official point of view the former combined concession to the victim's status with indirect, quasi-legitimate exercise of the emperor's power, hence Tiberius' concern to spell out charges in a letter to the Senate after Labeo's suicide (6.29.2). Suicide that looked like execution needed justification. Earlier a mixture of "*invidia* and appeals" addressed to Tiberius after Silanus had given up any effort to defend himself apparently contributed to a sentence of exile milder than execution or enforced suicide and further mitigated by the emperor (3.67–69). If self-importance was not the philosopher Euphrates' motive for requesting Hadrian's permission to drink hemlock, he may have wanted to avoid misunderstanding along this line and with it possible embarrassment for the emperor (Dio 69.8.3). It was doubtless *invidia* that provided the leverage for evening up scores when the accuser of a man driven to suicide by Agrippina was expelled from the Senate (Tac. *Ann.* 12.59.2; in 14.12.3–4 *invidia* occasioned by executions and banishments which Agrippina had engineered is turned against her by Nero).

Dio remarks that Tiberius saw in suicide a way to "avoid the appearance of having killed his victims himself," and Dio's own conviction that it is actually worse to force a man to kill himself than to execute him is largely at variance with the political system he describes. In a similar vein, Tiberius forced the Senate to handle indictments "so that he could avoid responsibility (as it seemed) while the senate would convict itself of injustice" (58.15–16), and Dio reports a rumor that Tiberius stayed away from Rome to avoid the shame of being present at false sentencings (58.24.2). If the Senate itself could not be saddled with guilt, various legal maneuvers were available for permitting the emperor to evade formal responsibility.[7] Domitian followed the same rationale, "arranging that not a few died by their own hands in one way or another so they would seem to have died voluntarily and not by necessity" (Dio 67.3.4; cf. Tac. *Ann.* 6.25.1).

Nero's bungled strangling, then divorce, banishment, and murder of Octavia were so widely condemned that he finally felt obliged to bribe someone to confess adultery with her (Suet. *Ner.* 35.2). All of these moves were necessary because in a competitive society like Rome (Tac. *Ann.* 15.73.1, 4.54.2) public opinion still exerted some restraining influence. It is a theme in Seneca's appeal to the young Nero (*Clem.* 1.8.1, 1.9.6, 1.15.5, 1.18.3, 1.21.1 and 4), and Tacitus occasionally alludes to fairly widespread resentment at the fate of some victims of infighting at Rome (*Ann.* 3.11, 14.60–63). If power is thought of as money circulating in a political economy, suicide exemplifies the ambivalent relationship between debtor and creditor. Each of the parties was hostage to the other, and to protect his own political capital the emperor had to ensure the credit of enemies by permitting them to cash in the value of status. Refusal to do so—e.g., Nero's threat to get rid of the entire Senate once and for all (Suet. *Ner.* 37.3, 43.1)—meant bankrupting the whole system.

We see things from a rare official angle in Velleius Paterculus' remark that Iulus Antonius, after being spared by Augustus, "was himself the avenger [by suicide] of the crime he had committed" in violating the imperial household (2.100.4; cf. the apparently guilty suicide of Cornelius Gallus, "driven to death" by hostility on all sides after falling from Augustus' personal favor, Suet. *Aug.* 66.2). So deeply did Augustus feel Julia's guilt that when Phoebe, one of her servants, committed suicide to avoid punishment, he remarked that he would rather be her father than Julia's (Dio 55.10.16; Suet. *Aug.* 65.2). If the emperor seems to be in the right, suicide carries no *invidia* for him and counts as a fully justified equivalent of execution. Torquatus Silanus thus plays into Nero's hands when, despairing of a legal defense, he permits his suicide to be used as presumptive proof of guilt (Tac. *Ann.* 15.35). That is how Nero tried to handle the murder of his mother, too (Dio 61.143; Suet. *Ner.* 34.3; Tac. *Ann.* 14.7.6, 10.3), and it may be why Caligula pretended that his victims had killed themselves (Suet. *Calig.* 26.2). Caligula also voided wills of those who died without naming him heir if there were reports that they had intended to do so, and when as a result perfect strangers were terrified into putting him in their wills, he accused them of playing tricks by continuing to live and sent poisoned confections to many of them (38.2). It is not clear whether this is supposed to be attempted murder designed to look like guilty suicide or a broad hint that real suicide was in order.

In one version of Drusus' death current at the time, the possibilities of ambiguous responsibility are handled with extraordinary adroitness. A taste for the special intricacies of what might be termed incipient crime fiction seems in part to explain why Tacitus "does not want to leave the report unmentioned," though he says he does not believe it (*Ann.* 4.10). It is, in fact, a very good story. In order at the last moment to add a new wrinkle to his plan for poisoning Drusus, Sejanus warns Tiberius not to accept any drink offered him at dinner with his son. When a cup is then in fact offered, he passes it on untasted to Drusus, who drinks it without hesitation. Under the circumstances, Drusus' subsequent death can very well be taken, not as an obvious sign of innocence, but as an indication of guilt whose consequences he could escape only by suicide. (Tacitus is sceptical on just this point, Tiberius not being a man to go along so easily in such a matter.) Whatever the actual facts may have been, the logic of suicide made it natural to think of Drusus's death politically as an involved three-phase murder, suicide, and murder at one remove disguised as suicide. By pretending to save one of his victims (Tiberius), the true murderer (Sejanus) induces him to eliminate the other (Drusus) and thereby himself become the apparent murderer by being duped into what is, in fact, meant as self-defense while also causing what looks like guilty suicide. Taken together, the two phases of murder and suicide reciprocally make up a reductio ad absurdum in which the real victim appears as the guilty party, the apparently guilty party (Tiberius) as the apparently intended victim, while the actual guilty party remains unseen behind his two actual victims.[8] So far as the code of suicide presupposed by Sejanus' plan goes, when Drusus drinks from the poisoned cup, he seems to be accepting what amounts to execution at the hands of Tiberius for treason, while Tiberius for his part is conceding him the right of suicide in place of execution.

Extraordinary as even the idea of such a case is, its involutions taken in conjunction with official concern about *invidia* suggest how difficult the problem of public relations surrounding suicide must often have been.[9] Suetonius reports that Seleucus, one of the "Greek companions" especially enjoyed by Tiberius, was first exiled, then driven to suicide, for having asked the emperor's staff about his current reading in order to come prepared for the questions Tiberius would put at dinner (*Tib.* 56). In Tacitus, Pompeius Macer and his son kill themselves owing to Tiberius' displeasure at the association of Macer's father with Pompey and the divine honors he received from the Greeks (*Ann.* 6.18.2). Both stories illustrate the petty jockeying for position and shifting political alliances tied to family connections that made it difficult to determine real motives, to say nothing of facts. If Silanus, Caligula's father-in-law, really did avoid joining him on a stormy sea trip in order to seize Rome in case the ship went down (Suet. *Calig.* 23.3), then it was not unreasonable to force him to commit suicide. Inquiries put by Libo to a soothsayer about the prospect of wealth sufficient to pave part of the Appian Way, if they were not simply the actions of a demented man, could reasonably be seen as an effort to prepare a power base (Tac. *Ann.* 2.27–31), all the more so since extravagant expenditure was an axiom of political ambition. No less preposterous rumors of Dido's vast treasure attracted serious interest in even higher circles (Suet. *Ner.* 31.4). Another member of Tiberius' circle, asked about the odd Greek he used, was sent into exile for sneering at Tiberius' earlier stay on Doric-speaking Rhodes (Suet. *Tib.* 56).

As they stand, such pretexts for action seem wholly frivolous or implausible; Tiberius would perfectly well have recognized Doric when he heard it, and the idea perhaps is that he did, but wanted the answer as a typically outrageous excuse. Official records, moreover, may have remained incomplete when suicide occurred quickly, and some of the charges were perhaps no more than an initial smear to set the victim up for more serious accusations, if they were needed later. But the uncertainty surrounding many cases must also be due not so much to deficient or malicious sources as to the genuine ambiguity and elusive personal factors which were among the advantages for the emperor of resorting to enforced suicide. The true cause of Scaurus' suicide, namely Macro's hatred, is discovered by Tacitus only behind accusations of adultery and anti-Tiberian poetry (*Ann.* 6.29.3–4). Political situations are ultimately what political cultures make of them, and the one at Rome saw suicide as a way of reducing and diffusing the effect of violence by filtering responsibility through layers of political gossip.

"It is generally agreed that Gnaeus Lentulus Augur, a very wealthy man, was driven to despair of his life through fear and anxiety and to make Tiberius his sole heir" (Suet. *Tib.* 49.1). The facts of this case, which were perhaps more fully known at the time, are largely a matter of conjecture as they stand in Suetonius. In the first place, they may describe not suicide at all but the death of an elderly man without the will to live any longer. Moreover, although the event is grouped by Suetonius with other examples of greed, in Tacitus' view greed was not one of Tiberius' faults (*Ann.* 3.18.1). If the death was suicide, as seems likely, the decision could have been a purely personal one. Still, Lentulus' fear does strongly suggest political considerations of some sort, and if there were any, they would make his suicide a species of compulsory/voluntary death in the face of an unfocused threat, not exactly forced but not free either. The possibility of political pressure, in any case, brings with it a full range of strategies. The legacy, for example, might have been designed by Lentulus to turn suicide into *invidia* against Tiberius by signaling its involuntary nature on the principle that "only a bad emperor is made heir by a good father" (Tac. *Agr.* 43.4).

Even genuinely voluntary suicide owing to *taedium vitae* could be politically sensitive, since under the circumstances moves were sometimes bound to be seen where none were being made. That is why it could be in the emperor's interest to forestall the kind of invidious effect which Suetonius' report has here by preventing suicide (Suet. *Aug.* 53.3; Tac. *Ann.* 6.26.1) or to forestall charges of greed by disclaiming interest in legacies (Suet. *Aug.* 66.4; Tac. *Ann.* 2.48.2). If Tiberius had any responsibility for Lentulus' death, it could be doubly masked by the suicide and the legacy but equally unmasked by both, depending on the reading given to each. As a relationship of domination and submission with numerous implicit and explicit facets, suicide endowed interpretation itself with great potential as a political move.

In disposal of legacies, political power assumed a specifically monetary form in which the dialectic of compulsion and freedom was veiled by formal exchanges, again leading to a good deal of incongruity all around. Wills became death as well as life insurance policies, and in Tacitus' version of Seneca's break with Nero, bargaining political power or life itself means bargaining wealth. Like clemency, politicized wealth comes with tangled strings attached. Seneca wants to return what Nero has given him because he wants to escape impending trouble, while Nero refuses to take back what Seneca has received because of the damage his prestige will suffer (Tac. *Ann.* 14.53–56). The abortive transaction is explicitly governed by rules of monetarized gift exchange: "We have both fulfilled our obligations—you as much as a ruler can give to a friend, I what a friend can take from his ruler" (14.54.1). The elaborate sham deal seems fair to both sides but in fact never is, and here, too, the etiquette of wealth and patronage is soon replaced by that of naked power (15.61–63). Seneca's initial denial of complicity in a conspiracy is reported to Nero (the game begins with potential winners and losers), who wants to know only whether he appears to be thinking about "voluntary death" (power, not innocence or guilt, is the issue). Upon learning that Seneca has shown no sign of fear or despair (thus denying the emperor's power), Nero issues an explicit death sentence (the decisive move through display of power), which Seneca then carries out in a theatrical suicide (the final compromise between imperial and private prerogatives to determine winners and losers and confirm the playability of the game for both parties). Seneca in a sense has both committed suicide and been executed, while Nero has not executed anyone and yet has asserted authority.

In Tacitus' account, Seneca manages to take, rather than to be granted, the right of suicide. But it was a game that the emperor for the most part was bound to win (hence the feebly euphemistic term *necessitas* for suicide; e.g., Tac. *Ann.* 6.23.1), and his opponents were keenly alive to the inherent contradiction, epitomized by several Tacitean oxymora about "voluntary suicide in the face of imminent condemnation" (4.19.4). Libo is terrified into what Tiberius liked to call "voluntary death" (2.31.3); Poppaea, too, is "terrified by fear of prison into voluntary death" (11.2); and Nero, the son of Germanicus, was thought "to have been driven to voluntary death" (Suet. *Tib.* 54.2). The language perhaps echoes a bitter quip circulating in Rome (cf. Lucan's "No one is forced to die willingly"; 4.484). As the supreme assertion of personal autonomy, genuine *mors voluntaria* was uniquely suitable for conveying reverse political meanings under the Principate. The absentminded Claudius was himself a secondary victim of euphemistic code language (*Ann.* 11.2–3.1). When Asiaticus' liquidation was being engineered, an appeal on his part for the right of suicide was apparently faked in order to exploit the implicit admission of guilt. Claudius intended the approval he then gave to be a genuine favor, supposing that both the request and the admission were authentic.[10] Once the guilty party had made the proper move, it was the emperor's turn to make his, but in this case guilt, appeal, and clemency alike were all fraudulent, and the apparently voluntary suicide was in fact plain execution, a sequence rivaling the circumstances of Drusus' death.

As a deferential gesture from the emperor's side, permitted suicide had other tactical uses as well. For one thing, it might win the welfare of loved ones in return for the victim's life. Plautus rejected the advice of those urging him to resist the political pressure he was under and decided instead to accept execution passively, "perhaps because he thought that the emperor would be more lenient to his wife and children whom he loved" (Tac. *Ann.* 14.59.1). Though not actually suicide, this comes very close formally to the case of Piso, who also rejected the idea of resistance and, when the soldiers arrived, opened his veins after leaving a will flattering Nero, "from love of his wife" (15.59.5). Otho similarly thinks that his own "quick death [by suicide] will earn [*mereri*] the victor's clemency" (Tac. *Hist.* 2.48.2), and a good deal of bartering with lives of family members apparently went on. Under Galba, Tigellinus exercised a claim on Vinius because he had saved Vinius' daughter, not out of genuine clemency but to have private obligations ready as a hedge against falling from favor (1.72). After Vitellius threatens Otho's brother and his son in the event that his own mother or children are harmed, fear restrains Otho from taking any action against them, and Vitellius then wins credit for clemency (1.75.2, 2.47.2). Later, out of concern for his own relatives, Vitellius, in turn, did nothing to Domitian (3.59.3). Along with loved ones, property, too, became part of the equation. In discussing the repercussions of Sejanus' fall, Dio says that many committed suicide either to avoid imprisonment and execution or to permit children to inherit property.[11] He sees in the latter provision a deliberate "invitation to suicide on the part of Tiberius" (Dio 58.15; cf. Tac. *Ann.* 6.29).

If part of the advantage enjoyed by the emperor is that suicide reduces his responsibility, the situation can be turned against him by replacing enforced suicide with forced execution. On receiving the order to cut his arteries, one of Nero's victims first demonstrates personal courage by willingness to do so (cf. Dio 58.4.6), then insists that the soldier complete "his glorious mission," and in fact has to be executed (Tac. *Ann.* 16.9.2; cf. the Roman prisoner of war who stabs his guard in the eye to goad him into killing him, Frontin. *Str.* 4.5.16; Florus 1.35.5). What is more, by putting up resistance with his bare hands, Nero's victim manages to "fall more in anger than in fear and as though amid battle with wounds in front"—an exact equivalent to defiant suicide that would be reported with great relish at Rome by those who kept score. As the execution (murder) implicit in suicide is made explicit, a point is scored against the emperor, and the same political logic turning suicide into protest the emperor may want to prevent now by inversion equally turns refusal of suicide into protest that the victim may want to make. In the former, suicide is a point directly for the opposition; in the latter, execution is a point directly against the emperor. (A rough modern equivalent of this tactic is refusing to move from the path of tanks during street demonstrations.) Those are the alternative strategies Seneca has in mind when he discusses the pros and cons of anticipating execution by suicide or making the executioner carry the order out (*Ep.* 70.8f).

As is natural in this reciprocal system, a similar deflationary effect can be achieved when those with power take threats to commit suicide at face value, transform them into offers, and accept them. Or the emperor may refuse to respond to provocation, as Vespasian does when he declines to be forced by the Cynic Demetrius' insolence into executing him. As it passed around among those who mattered at Rome, his contemptuous joke about "not killing barking dogs" (Dio 66.13) would have gone some way to counter any impression of weakness that his restraint might create. Two other Cynics, on the other hand, did manage to provoke a forceful reaction (whipping and execution; 66.15.5), while harsh response and jest are combined in an anecdote concerning the formidable Tiberius. Stung by what he saw as slander, he imposed suicide, quipping that the poet who had cast him in the role of the bloody-minded Atreus would himself be made to play the role of Ajax (58.24.3–5). The jest was meant to count as a deft touch of *ludibrium,* camouflaging power by giving it a show of geniality. People whose social reality included live crucifixion in the arena could only acknowledge the ingenuity of forcing a playwright to play a fatal stage role in earnest. Nero, too, ignored or played down insults directed at him (Suet. *Ner.* 39.3), and after a typically moralistic explanation for the policy (Nero had no sense of shame anyway), Suetonius allows that indifference was a good tactical move because an angry response is what made attacks count in the first place. Thick skin is a rule of state again urged by Dio's Maecenas, because sensitivity suggests guilt (Dio 52.31.5–8), while Livia assures Augustus that it is safer to ignore ugly rumors, since anger causes fear, hatred, and finally genuine danger (55.19). Like foiling a bank robbery by refusing to take the demand for money seriously, not playing the game at all can be the best possible move.[12]

Much is often made by the historians of the distinction between suicide before and after trial or conviction. Preemptive suicide would do nothing to reduce the legitimacy of official action against those who were in fact guilty (e.g., Plancina; Tac. *Ann.* 6.26.3). For the innocent, though, it avoids unmerited trouble and humiliation (Suet. *Tib.* 61.4; Dio 58.15; Tac. *Ann.* 4.28.2, 12.59.2) or assures property rights going with voluntary death. A senator threatened with legal action for having complained that the Senate thought one way and voted another killed himself before being brought to trial (Dio 59.18.5). The report reveals that humiliation was not principally a matter of personal aggravation but of lost political status, and that is the explanation of an apparent contradiction noted by Pliny the Younger (*Ep.* 3.9.5). It seems reasonable that a guilty person would commit suicide to escape certain conviction, but unreasonable that he would be bothered by shame at being convicted if he was willing to commit the crime in the first place. The answer is that chagrin has nothing to do with feelings of guilt but instead concerns loss of status in case of conviction. In the event of real innocence, preemptive suicide, in addition to preserving legal rights, may count as an act of protest and as such is a relatively aggressive countermove—aggressive, of course, only in a system which made no more than passive measures available for opposition to the emperor, short of assassination.

In a culture where physical violence wore so many masks, the Stoic ideal of personal freedom worked to replace assassination with a peculiar aggressive suicide, counting as a hostile act but one directed against oneself. That is the political, psychological, and moral displacement detected by Seneca's keen sense of anomaly in the most celebrated of all political suicides: at the end, he remarks, Cato killed himself "not so much angry at Caesar as at himself" (*Ep.* 24.8). If an inner sense of guilt or impotence could make suicide a form of self-punishment, the social system in which it was carried out made its external theatrical form an act of political violence.[13] The latter, moreover, was tied to internal personal motivation of another kind. A good part of the impact which Cato's suicide made came from philosophical idealization of the just man's absolute rational control and moral autonomy that moved suicide from something permitted toward something wielded as an ethical weapon. As a result, the external *necessitas* in view of which philosophy had traditionally allowed suicide took on a more specific political meaning from the duress, also called *necessitas,* applied by the emperor. In politicizing philosophy, politics was itself in turn given a philosophical dimension, especially so in connection with Stoic opposition and the *mors ambitiosa* it inspired.

Suicide was ordinarily carried out by such methods as cutting veins, taking poison, and stabbing or starving oneself. Several of these permit time for reconsideration (Suet. *Vit.* 2.3, perhaps parodied by Petronius, Tac. *Ann.* 16.19; cf. Suet. *Ner.* 2.3) or an appeal (Tac. *Ann.* 6.9.2) that would give some leverage to the victim in what might now be a game of political chicken (manipulative suicide nowadays employs an overdose of sleeping pills). The emperor had scored a point, suicide had been carried out symbolically, and so room was open for making additional points with last-minute clemency. Under arrest for complicity in Sejanus' conspiracy, Publius Vitellius, after cutting his wrists, allowed himself to be bandaged up and died later of disease. According to Suetonius, he interrupted suicide at the request of friends, who perhaps were playing for time (*Vit.* 2.3). In Tacitus' version, once having abandoned "hope and fear," he ends his life in deep mental depression after (by?) cutting his wrists (*Ann.* 5.8.2). Nerva, a close friend of Tiberius, was not inviting mercy when he resolved to die by starvation, but he used the opportunity instead to protest current policy by rejecting the emperor's pleas that he remain alive. Though he was under no pressure, the leverage his action could still exert is clear from Tiberius' acknowledgment of the *invidia* brought on himself by such a death (Tac. *Ann.* 6.26.1), and Dio says that some changes in policy were made (58.21.4–5). Leverage stemmed from the damage done by repudiation of the emperor's personal authority, which depended on the kind of obedience Augustus won when he dissuaded a senator largely unknown to him from starving himself to death because of blindness (Suet. *Aug.* 53.3). When Vibius Marsus remained alive but only "as though he were starving himself" (Tac. *Ann.* 6.48), he may have been trying to gain time, and Tiberius' death did in fact save his life.[14] Food became a weapon in the emperor's hands, too, through forced feeding to block suicide or a minimal diet during arrest "not to prevent flight but to prevent death" (Dio 58.3.4–5).

If suicide was a political language, what it said could be given added point through unusual, rhetorical gestures, such as breaking one's neck with a chain in prison (Tac. *Ann.* 6.14.1) or strangulation with one's own breast band (15.57.2). Valerius Maximus, who is particularly impressed by Portia's death through suffocation from fumes of smoldering coals held in her mouth, compares that very unusual method favorably with that of her father (4.6.5). Seneca's preoccupation with the whole subject of suicide leads him to mention several no less exotic ad hoc methods: placing one's head in the wheel of a moving wagon or, most astonishing of all, choking oneself on the Roman equivalent of toilet paper (sponges in latrines, *Ep.* 70.19f; cf. the similar improvisation with a handkerchief in Val. Max. 9.12.7). Both were carried out by men without social standing, but if their deaths did not by themselves count politically, the second case in particular is made by Seneca into a tour de force of symbolism with a specific political point.[15] Though cited to show that even the lowest of humans are always free to die, it is understood by Seneca in connection with his own political life and the lives of people like him. Such a suicide, he says, "was an insult to death" (*Ep.* 70.20), although if it actually happened, it was in all likelihood more an act of despair than of heroism, as suicide doubtless often was (Tac. *Ann.* 2.24.2, 4.28.2, 45.2, 50.1, 14.37.2).

The parallel story of Epicharis' equally shocking suicide by means of her own breast band after severe torture also takes on greater political point when Tacitus remarks on the contrast between her fidelity and the cowardice of others in the conspiracy (*Ann.* 15.57.2). Though she is a marginal player, the countermove her defiance represents is essential to the system (cf. the defiance, though without suicide, of other women under torture in *Ann.* 14.60). Cases of dramatic public suicide such as those by people who had been ruined at Caligula's rigged auctions (Suet. *Calig.* 38.4) perhaps involved equal measures of plain despair and defiance.[16] The defiance conveyed by Silanus' death was a good deal subtler.

Forced into suicide (Suet. *Claud.* 29.2) on a false charge of incest, he may have chosen to die on the very day of Claudius' incestuous marriage to Agrippina "to increase the reproach." The new bride, at any rate, restored Seneca to favor "to counter the bad public impression" (Tac. *Ann.* 12.8.1).

In their personal as well as political application, Seneca's reflections on suicide have direct connections with another form of violence. It must frequently have occurred to members of the elite as they watched games that what was expected from gladiators might well be expected from them. In that way, too, sanitized though it was, violence in the arena could spill into life. The cult of unflinching death in the arena was practically identical to the cult of unflinching political suicide current in some circles and described in highly theatrical terms by Tacitus, Seneca, and Lucan. If gladiators who die willingly are admired while those showing fear are hated (Sen. *Tranq.* 11.4) and if *vivere est militare* (Sen. *Ep.* 96.5), everyone ought to accept death bravely once it is inevitable, as gladiators do (*Ep.* 30.8). This line of thought reproduces, on a personal level, and radicalizes the social logic of public violence, which carries out its positive function in a specifically negative way. The gratifying public sense of security in *munera* comes from watching supreme danger, and achieving freedom means accepting death (*Ep.* 26.10; cf. 61.2). That is exactly the rationale for suicide as well, hence the political lesson in the pathetic deaths even of slaves and prisoners, to say nothing of Sempronius Gracchus offering his neck to the executioner (Tac. *Ann.* 1.53.5) or Galba his throat to the mob (Tac. *Hist.* 1.41.2). In the former case, the ideological dimension is brought out by Tacitus' remark that Sempronius' death was worthy of a family tradition from which his own life had degenerated. Like qualified recognition of gladiators' courage, this transmutes a particular instance of dying into a more manageable idea of death. In the case of Galba, the ideological message lies in the absurdity of a head of state—the supreme embodiment of social order—submitting to assassination.

Vitellius' blind suspicion of what the centurion Agrestis has to report induces Agrestis to offer startling proof of good faith by killing himself on the spot (Tac. *Hist.* 3.54.3; cf. Dio 46.51.3). Tacitus adds that in another version Agrestis was executed.[17] In a puzzlingly parallel case recounted by Suetonius and Dio (Suet. *Otho* 10; Dio 64.11), a soldier charged with lying or desertion when he reported the defeat at Bedriacum committed suicide in front of Otho. Feelings run high in combat, and the centurion could well have acted not to register protest but in disgust or despair. Suetonius, whose own father was with the army at the time, explicitly remarks on the exemplary effect of the other suicide on

Otho, who promptly decided to follow suit (cf. the case in Dio 46.53.3). As his death, in turn, led to further suicides among his soldiers "from grief" (Suet. *Otho* 12.2), the event was receiving broader political interpretation through a domino effect in which behavior intended to be exemplary leads to mass hysteria (a result familiar from similar incidents among Japanese troops and officers in World War II). Even if for Agrestis himself the gesture was nothing more than despair at official stupidity during a crisis, it would naturally be connected with the larger code of suicide by others, as the deaths even of obscure people are by Seneca.

Diffuse protest against political conditions in general is at work again as Arruntius contemplates a depressing array of good reasons for killing himself. Though able to survive the corrupt Tiberius, who was himself on the point of death, he would do so only to endure his totally ignorant successor, Caligula, himself in the care of the scoundrel Macro, who, after being chosen to get rid of Sejanus, committed more crimes than he did (Tac. *Ann.* 6.48.2; Dio 58.27.4; cf. the suicide of Vitellius' mother "from weariness at the present and fear of the future," Suet. *Vit.* 14.5). The political point of the game is preserved, though with its logic inverted, in another case mentioned by Pliny the Younger which clearly was meant as a gesture of protest. In the strict privacy of a sickroom and after looking about carefully, a friend of Pliny's confided that he was clinging to life despite painful gout "to outlive that crook [Domitian] by at least one day" (*Ep.* 1.12.8).

Cato's death is the paradigmatic case of suicide as a move to protest repression coupled with a second move anticipating the countermove of *clementia* (Dio 43.10f). Knowing that Caesar would spare him in order to gain credit for clemency, by committing suicide he preempted not execution but pardon to unmask the equivalence of clemency and power which constituted a crucial principle as well as a crucial anomaly in political logic at Rome. This results in a distinctive criss-cross pattern: "I [Caesar] begrudge you [Cato] your death, because you begrudged me saving your life" (Plut. *Cat. Min.* 72.2; cf. Plut. *Sayings of Romans* Caesar 13; Val. Max. 5.1.10). Even after Cato's death, a claim by Caesar that he had intended to offer pardon carries no weight, since suicide itself now blocks that move, too, as effectively as it blocks execution.

Cato's unshakable resolve is further highlighted by variations on the theme of aided suicide. Sometimes companions intervene to restrain him (cf. Plut. *Ant.* 69.2; Plut. *C. Gracch.* 16.4; Florus 2.13.72), and when his weapon is taken away he angrily or wittily demands it back ("My servants are betraying me!"; Plut. *Cat. Min.* 68–70; App. *BCiv.* 2.14.98), pointing out that he can kill himself in more ways than one. Seneca (*Prov.* 2.10) seizes on this to contrast Cato's death with the mutual suicides of

Juba and Petreius by remarking that Cato would no more ask another man for death than for life. Whereas Vocula was stopped from killing himself by slaves and freedmen only to be executed by his enemies (Tac. *Hist.* 4.59.1), Cato avoided the still greater irony of *not* being executed by Caesar and thereby placed himself in a liminoid political space where he could neither be killed nor saved (Sen. *Ep.* 24.6; contrast Nero's dilemma, Suet. *Ner.* 47). The same tactic in more popular guise figures again in an anecdote of Plutarch (*Caes.* 16.9): turning down an offer of pardon from Scipio, a captured soldier of Caesar kills himself with the remark that Caesar's men offer and do not accept clemency.

The fate of loved ones or relatives was a valuable card which could also be taken from the emperor's hands by the suicide of everyone concerned in order to preclude the threat of clemency for survivors. After Caecina Paetus was arrested under Claudius, his wife, Arria, stabbed herself to strengthen his resolve, then pulled the dagger out and handed it to him with a remark that became a celebrated epigram of resistance: "Paetus, it doesn't really hurt" ("Paete, non dolet," Pliny *Ep.* 3.16.6; cf. Dio 60.16.6; Plut. *Brut.* 13.3–6). She in fact refused to survive him and had earlier confronted a woman who had chosen to give evidence instead of dying with her husband: "I should listen to you who are still alive, though your husband died in your arms?" Noticing that relatives were keeping close watch for fear of her intentions, she leaped from a chair, dashed her head against the wall, and, after recovering her wits, recalled that "I told you I would find a hard way to die if you keep me from an easy one." Pliny expresses some reservations about this strategy. He remarks that Arria had "eternal glory before her eyes," and Tacitus is still more explicit about the danger of counterfinality in the politics of self-righteous weakness, treating some suicides as mere self-centered theater (*Agr.* 42.3–4: *ambitiosa mors*). Victimhood provides leverage against power, but only when it is not itself too obviously manipulative and repressive.

Simultaneous suicide of husband and wife or close relatives, especially when one partner was plainly innocent, was closely related to the strategy of countering enforced suicide through cool, indifferent acceptance.[18] If suicide really does seem voluntary, its value as a sign of the emperor's authority is reduced; conversely, when it is refused, the execution he is forced to carry out reduces the legitimacy of his power by dramatizing its reality. The possibility of misunderstanding or false claims which went with such gestures, however, could only add to the already substantial ambiguities of suicide. Suicide in common could be an admission of guilt (as it perhaps is in Dio 59.18.5), but when one partner elected freely to die with the other, the common deaths would inevitably become a powerful political symbol of loyalty beyond the emperor's reach.

Tacitus' description of Seneca's death is noteworthy for its coverage of many of the formal possibilities presented by such situations: loyalty to political friends and the more intimate relationship with a spouse; the wife's resolve to die with her husband; his fear for her vulnerability if she lives on, though Paulina was in no danger from Nero, who knew that sparing her life would help minimize his reputation for cruelty; the symbolic solidarity of husband and wife sealed by simultaneous wounds. Other, more competitive aspects of political gamesmanship appear as well. Seneca makes a point of his readiness to concede Paulina a greater share of fame even than his own, and Tacitus mentions a rumor "among people who thought the worst" that so long as Nero seemed hostile she wanted to make a virtue of necessity by gaining the fame of dying with her husband (*Ann.* 15.64.2). As soon as hope of survival appeared, life proved more attractive. The pallor from which, according to Tacitus, Paulina never recovered because of her ordeal, must have reinforced for others as well the memory of Seneca she faithfully cherished, though her own survival was at the same time a reminder of Nero's clemency.

A hint of room for bargaining comes up again in another case. So long as her husband had hope for acquittal, Plancina was determined to share his fate. Once pardoned herself, however, she began to put distance between the two of them, and he immediately understood what her attitude meant (Tac. *Ann.* 3.15.1). Driven by bitterness, Pollitta, the wife of one of Nero's victims, went around unkempt from perpetual grief and ate enough food only to stay alive, in a kind of symbolic suicide elsewhere described by Seneca as borderline "unwillingness to live, inability to die" in connection with Marcia's excessive mourning for a son (*Ad Marciam* 3.3). To save her father, now also in danger, Pollitta besieged the emperor with hysterical personal appeals. When he remained unmoved, the father refused to compromise his integrity by naming Nero primary heir and together with his daughter and another relative committed suicide (Tac. *Ann.* 16.10). Multiple, family suicide is thus the last stage in an aggressive campaign of protest through traditional public signs of personal squalor (cf. Dion. Hal. 8.39.4; App. *BCiv.* 1.8.67, 2.3.15), of abuse (she "wept like a woman, screamed like a man" at Nero; Tac. *Ann.* 16.10.4) and voluntary semistarvation, using food in yet another way as a weapon. Aside from its psychological plausibility, the combination of threat and appeal, anger and despair, dramatizes the way in which weakness can become an instrument of offensive action. The importance of social relationships further magnified the impact of suicide concentrated in certain families whose tradition of political activity stretched back into Roman history. The idea both of family history and solidarity is dramatized by Tacitus with a few theatrical touches as victims from three generations die together, gazing on each other after using the same dagger in the same room (*Ann.* 16.11.2). In another case, family solidarity is heavy-handedly violated by lictors, who forcibly prevent a father and daughter from embracing (16.32.1).

On being assured by Caligula that he was scheduled for execution, Canus expressed deep gratitude, though Seneca is not certain what he meant. Perhaps it was an insult to show that under Caligula death was a favor; perhaps it parodied the need to be grateful for anything the emperor did; perhaps death truly was a release. In any event, when the summons ten days later interrupted a game of checkers, as Canus left to be executed, he demanded that his opponent not claim to have been winning. The anecdote's political meaning is not affected by the fact that death in this case is not due to suicide, and Seneca himself thinks of Canus' unruffled attitude as a tactical move in a game: though he played checkers *(lusisse),* he refused to play seriously *(inlusit)* the game that Caligula wanted him to play (Sen. *Tranq.* 14.4–7). Coolness reinforced with the aid of philosophical detachment is a theme of some remarks of Epictetus on reducing the impact of official penalties by total indifference (1.1.29–32). The proper response to exile or confiscation of property is simply to follow whatever normal activity is still permitted. It is a sign of weakness to worry even about the difference between death and exile. Epictetus apparently thinks that exile could actually be worse for people so caught up in competition that accepting disqualification from political life (e.g., Tac. *Ann.* 1.53.2) seems more humiliating than being executed.

Petronius' stylishly contemptuous behavior during his last hours is another variant (Tac. *Ann.* 16.19). After being detained at Cumae in political limbo to preclude effective resistance, he "abandoned both hope and fear." Then from time to time opening and closing his veins in parody of the serious uses to which these gestures were ordinarily put, he enjoyed trivial amusements in place of discussions on immortality and indulged in brief naps "so that his forced death would appear to be natural." Finally, to this denial of Nero's power by untroubled acceptance of death, he added defiant assertion of his own freedom by replacing the obligatory will flattering the emperor with a detailed list of his crimes.

Suicide, then, is a countermove against the emperor if it can be made to count as a truly free act: "Surely taking punishment so easily is escaping punishment" (Val. Max. 3.2 ext. 6). Given the highly personal nature of elite Roman society, an index of style was bound to be a factor in the political as well as moral meaning of death. To the extent that moves were symbolic, they were liable to devaluation, as Nero understood when he countered gibes by seeming not to feel them (Suet. *Ner.* 39.3). Before killing himself, Asiaticus makes certain that some prize trees will not be damaged by heat from his pyre, "such coolness did he feel at the end" (Tac. *Ann.* 11.3.2). Upon being charged with *maiestas* and cowardice, Gaius Fufius Geminus stabbed himself "to show how a man dies" and proved at least the second charge wrong by displaying the wound to the officer who had come to enforce the sentence (Dio 58.4.6). When the consul Vestinus kills himself, "fearing nothing or pretending not to," the slight paradox points to the moral-political stance that was as important for public opinion as inner intention (Tac. *Ann.* 15.69.2; cf. Lucan's theatrical death, 15.70).

In one risky, rarely used counterpart to this move, the emperor could himself face death coolly to solidify his position by flirting with assassination ("Kill me if you will": Dio 59.25.8, 68.3.3, 15.4–6, 16.1(2), 76.14.5–6; Suet. *Calig.* 15.4; Suet. *Vespasian* 14). On the one hand, such invitations to murder are high-minded forms of political *devotio*. Caesar claimed that he preferred death to living in fear, Titus that he would rather be killed than kill (Suet. *Tit.* 9.1); a policy of clemency designed to reduce hostility through gestures of trust could in fact be suicidal (Vell. Pat. 2.57.1). In a self-deprecatory variant, Antoninus Pius refused to pursue inquiry into a conspiracy on the grounds that he did not want to find out how many people hated him in case more were involved (Pseudo-Aur. Vict. *Epit.* 15.6). On the other hand, as emperors normally played from strength, insouciance could have the force of an insincere threat to resign: others can be coerced by daring them to act against oneself so long as they cannot. Pressure was applied more subtly still by Portia on Brutus, when after wounding herself with a knife she threatened suicide unless he revealed his political plans (Dio 44.13). The wound, intended to win his confidence in her ability to endure the torture which would follow a failed plot, could not help adding force to the threat of suicide as well: "It is better for me to die than to live, if you distrust me." In Valerius Maximus her trial stab proves that she can commit suicide if Brutus' conspiracy fails (3.2.15); in Plutarch there is no threat, and Portia in fact faints as the tension mounts (*Brut.* 13.3.6, 15.4). Arria's similar gesture is encouragement rather than threat.

Threatened suicide is useful, though again risky, in crises of military authority or morale, where it taps aspects of *devotio* combined with blackmail. Germanicus was not the only one to use it that way. In Tacitus' *Histories* 3.10.4, an officer, drawing his sword, threatens to die either at his troops' hands or his own, in the former case forcing them to murder him, very much as opponents of the emperor do when they refuse to commit suicide on order. Pompey, too, threatens suicide if troops will not let him relinquish his command (Plut. *Pomp.* 13.2; contrast the soldiers who threaten to murder someone if he does not *take* command, Addendum 5). Avidius Cassius put down a mutiny by appearing dressed only in a loincloth and challenging his troops to kill him (*Hist. Aug.* 4.7; cf. the barehanded Silanus, Tac. *Ann.* 16.9.2), Scipio's symbolic willingness to die was similarly leverage for quelling a rebellion (Livy 28.27.9–10), as was, in a different fashion, the story of Coriolanus' mother's threat to commit suicide (Plut. *Cor.* 35.3; Dion. Hal. 8.53.2).[19]

A more common direct countermove available to the emperor was devaluating dramatic suicide through a claim that pardon would have been offered anyway (Tac. *Ann.* 2.31.2).[20] After one of his victims had been pressured into suicide, Nero, "as was his custom," said that he had intended to pardon him, guilty though he was (15.35.3). On another occasion he favored a capital charge specifically to win praise by later interceding to prevent execution (14.48–49). In a speech dealing with some accusations currently under discussion, a speaker in the Senate brings up Tiberius' complaints about people who forestall clemency through suicide (3.50.2). Loss of an opportunity to exercise authority indirectly by graciously not exercising it was as annoying to Tiberius as was removal of a symbol of royalty which kept Caesar from gaining honor for refusing honor he really wanted (Suet. *Iul.* 79.1). The tactic is used with unusual finesse by Tiberius in handling the dual suicide of Labeo and his wife (Tac. *Ann.* 6.29). Treating Labeo's death as a trick to cover guilt by shifting blame to the emperor, Tiberius says that he himself had done no more than formally terminate their friendship. After insisting that Labeo was in fact guilty, he adds that his wife had been in no danger, though actually no less guilty. The onus is thus shifted back onto both victims, so that the suicide of both is equivalent to justified capital punishment, while one is neatly also made recipient of clemency offered too late.[21]

Since calm acceptance makes suicide voluntary in one sense (as an act of defiance against the emperor), while belated clemency makes it voluntary in another (as not his responsibility, after all), suicide which the emperor (claims that he) did not want could count as a score for both sides. That was the standoff which Cato's repudiation of clemency aimed at preventing, and the bewildering array of move, countermove, and counter-countermove, of fact and conjecture, in all of this was controlled by political logic which could soon reach the edge of incoherence, though opaque intentions were exactly what made both suicide and clemency useful instruments. Complaints about the Senate's "slavery" were true enough in the very specific sense that clemency on the emperor's part was ultimately the same compound of fear and incentive used to control potential resistance among slaves.[22] The threat of exile, for example, worked in principle against the elite at Rome much as the perpetual threat that slave families might be broken up by sale of one or more of their members did. Strategies of control in slavery accordingly in some ways also account for how power was exercised under the Principate: "Masters [emperors] reinforced the system of relatively generous treatment with a constant counterpoint of violence in order to secure their ends. Together the generosities and climate of fear which can be seen to surround servile [senatorial] life help to explain the survival over time of the Roman slavery [imperial] system."[23]

Several cases of outright execution help bring out some of the complexities in a system that drew the line separating execution from suicide at best uncertainly and rendered clemency systematically ambivalent. Learning that through an error in name the wrong person had been executed, Caligula decided that it did not really matter, since the victim deserved death anyway (Suet. *Calig.* 30.1; Dio 59.22.4). And on discovering that someone he had executed for his wealth was in fact a poor man, Caligula exclaimed, "Why, he tricked me! And for no reason at all! He could still be alive!" (Dio 59.18.5). The apparently unnecessary deaths in each of these situations involve retrospective judgments; the second is formally analogous to clemency frustrated by premature suicide and recurs in a parallel incident under Nero. While examining a victim's head that had been brought to him, he exclaimed, "I didn't realize his nose was so big!" Though it may have simply been a casual bit of *ludibrium,* Dio thinks that the remark was made "as though he would have spared him, if he had known" (62.14.1). In the official view, the first of these cases is mistaken but still justified; the second and third are just mistakes, one (apparently) genuine, the other pretended. So far as a victim of premature suicide is concerned, he is as dead as victims of plain error are. At the same time, ex post facto pardon through belated clemency is more reasonable than jocular admission of error or ex post facto condemnation of a victim of plain error. On occasion, official claims of intended clemency must have been sincere. Yet the disturbing similarity of all of these situations and the frivolous attitude toward fatal mistakes bring out the incongruity lurking at every turn. Suicide which forecloses genuinely intended mercy is in a sense a mistake on the victim's part. The victim is, however, no less a victim if he or she has in effect been bluffed into unnecessary death. According to Suetonius, bluff was in fact deliberately used to drive Tiberius' grandson Nero to suicide by a police official who showed up with instruments of execution as though under orders of the Senate (Suet. *Tib.* 54.2; for suicide from terror at false charges, see Tac. *Ann.* 4.28.2; for a consul-elect terrified by a threat from Augustus into leaping to his death, see Suet. *Aug.* 27.3).

The case of Fulcinius Trio is another instance of lethal move and countermove (Tac. *Ann.* 6.38; Dio 58.25). After deciding to take his own life before the work of his accusers was complete, he drew up a will expressing contempt for Tiberius, calling the emperor, among other things, a senile idiot. His heirs naturally were eager to suppress that section, but Tiberius insisted that it be read in order to demonstrate his own toleration of free speech and perhaps also to learn the truth at any cost. The normal strategy on both sides is thus reversed. Once the victim is out of the way, tolerance (like clemency) can be a useful gambit for those with real power; by the same token, once condemnation is certain, defiant candor can be a good move for victims otherwise compelled to be circumspect. The "Codicilli" slandering senators and priests (Tac. *Ann.* 14.50.1) were probably satirical political pieces cast in the form of fawning or frank addenda to wills. The antagonists are locked in circular logic: the price of free speech is suicide, the price of a reputation for tolerance is free speech, and free speech is then used to damage the emperor's reputation. Caligula's gagging of victims to prevent them from making any noise as they die is a monstrously *unfair* tactic (Sen. *De Ira* 3.19.3).

10

Political Anomaly and Suicide

The importance for Tacitus or Seneca of all of the twists and turns in political suicide at Rome lies ultimately in the systemic political anomaly of which they are symptomatic. *Clementia* is a special case in point and one worth particular attention in connection with suicide. Both were naturally spoken of in the language of gaming or something close to it and "counted" in ways that varied widely with the side of the table at which players sat.[1] Both, moreover, entailed paradoxes springing from a give-and-take transaction through which each party sought to reach accommodation with an unequal relationship. Like gift giving, of which it was in fact a supreme instance, clemency had perversely inverse effects, being so dangerous to recipients in some circumstances that they might feel driven to drastic action against a benefactor or, in the case of suicide, against themselves, as Cato did in response to Caesar's charity.

Vaunting the death of opponents was liable to prove counterproductive during civil war, first because while inspiring fear it could also inspire resentment. In any case, recalling those who had died at their own hand might well score a propaganda point only by way of acknowledging that a point had been well played on the other side. Caesar accordingly preferred indirect shows of power through clemency, "the new way of winning to protect ourselves through mercy and generosity" (*nova ratio vincendi ut misericordia et liberalitate nos muniamus;* Cic. *Att.* 9.7C), whereas to his opponents it was merely a "tricky move" (*insidiosa;* 8.16) to please people frightened by Pompey's open anger.[2]

If Caesar's own words make his intention of coming out ahead plain enough, they also suggest a defensive way of going about it, and the analysis worked out in Dio 55.14–21 under the guise of advice Livia gives to Augustus does in fact treat clemency as a move imposed by the *limits*

116

of power (cf. Sen. *Clem.* 1.9). Conscious of the many dilemmas facing those in authority and losing sleep particularly over the possibility of conspiracy, Augustus realizes that executions will not really increase his safety, while letting the guilty off merely encourages others (Dio 55.14.1–3). The problem is compounded by Livia's decidedly jaundiced view of human nature. Even good rulers are bound to be hated, since people's natural bent for disorder is immune to persuasion or force (55.14.4–8, 55.16.3), and Augustus himself gloomily adds that the greatest danger actually comes from friends ("solitude is frightening—and so is company"; 55.15.6). Since danger from some, then, is inevitable, but it is unfair to penalize the guiltless, and since self-defense or preemptive action damages one's reputation (55.16.4), Livia's idea is to reserve execution strictly for incorrigible enemies (55.18.1). In all other cases, self-defense should take the form of clemency (55.14.8, 55.16.4f).

She then proceeds to balance her pessimistic assessment of the hazards of power with equally extreme optimism about restraint, which wins goodwill and respect all around (Dio 55.16.5), though there is still something less than complete trust in her talk of "guarding subjects so they cannot take wrong action even if they want to." Clemency is safe because measured public humiliation can bring troublemakers to their senses, and it helps avoid the general belief that official executions are never justified (55.18.3–6, 55.19.2–3). Drastic action against some creates self-defensive fear, not goodwill in others (55.21.2): "If you punish all crimes as they deserve, before you know it you will have wiped out most of the human race" (55.20.4; cf. Sen. *De Ira* 2.31.8 and, less drastically, 2.9.4: a wise man who becomes angry at every wrong he sees will go mad). Livia thus minimizes the fear (Dio 55.18.3) or resentment which clemency, too, can arouse and prefers to stress the positive response it is supposed to invite. But the deep ambiguity of power relationships mediated by clemency comes through in a remark, put in appropriately contorted Greek, to the effect that it is weakness which has a way of extorting concessions from strength under cover of goodwill: clemency works because its recipients "figure that a man who has been wronged but does not retaliate can be counted on, provided he is not wronged again, to go to any length to do further favors to the party in the wrong" (55.21.3). Seen in this way, clemency seems a curiously defensive move, if not a sign of weakness in response to an implicit threat posed by power itself to its holder.

Though focusing less exclusively on clemency, Maecenas' speech in Dio 52 takes a similar, soft Machiavellian line. The stage is set for a wide-ranging formal analysis of political logic (including gain/loss calculations, e.g., in 52.10–11) by Agrippa's remark that to avoid irrational *(alogos)* action what is needed is careful deliberation (52.3.3). The entire discussion is, in fact, an elaborate study of the pitfalls of power and touches frequently on the uses of clemency.

Both speakers accept the unavoidable hostility felt by ambitious subjects which presents their ruler with the dilemma of choosing between restrictions unfair to them and freedom dangerous to himself (Dio 52.8.1–8, 52.17.2). One of Agrippa's justification for "democracy," by which he means the old republican oligarchy, is its ability to avoid just that problem. In arguing for monarchy, Maecenas has to take Livia's optimistic view of clemency. It can cause a change of mind in those who are hostile and who might be turned into desperate men by repression. People are won over when they see that they are not only not being wronged but actually receiving favor (52.34.8–11), and Maecenas closes with the sanguine assurance, "Believe me when I say that you [Augustus] will never be hated or plotted against" (52.39.4). Restraint in the use of power to do everything ought to be proportional to desire to do nothing except what is right. This idealism is then glossed more realistically as "doing what people will like you for," and Maecenas concedes that people never fully express their thoughts to the powers that be, who must therefore judge them "from what they are likely to be thinking" (52.38.1–4). Estimation of risks by the politician is thus moved onto a theoretical, paradigmatic level much like that on which historians, who often have to write about what is likely to have been true, find themselves.

Maecenas does not deny that the overt threats which are bound to occur must be dealt with rigorously, though even then harsh judgments should be conspicuously moderated by the ruler to make conspirators' guilt convincing (Dio 52.31.9). No one really believes that those with power exercise it fairly, hence the value of allowing others to take part in—or, more cynically, implicating them in—official actions (52.7.4, 52.31.4). In all its guises, clemency is a surrogate for freedom, and as advocate for the latter, Agrippa takes a sceptical view of the reception clemency is likely to receive. In a more candid statement of what Livia has to say about the extortion endured self-defensively by those who have power, he complains that since people's appetite for entitlements is boundless, not only is a monarch expected to provide everything, but the hostility of those who fail to get what they want is greater than the gratitude of those who do (52.12.2–4).[3] Clemency is thus drawn into the seemingly endless, self-defeating paradoxes of gift exchange.

It is not surprising, then, that official magnanimity might finally be devious self-interest. Pliny the Elder lauds Caesar for burning captured letters of his enemies unread (*HN* 7.93–94; cf. Dio 72.7.4, 78.21.1). Caligula made similar gestures of ignoring evidence but kept his options open by burning only copies of incriminating letters (Suet. *Calig.* 15.4, 30.2). Suetonius devotes a chapter to Tiberius' moderate reaction to criticism ("if you open that window [of becoming angry], you will be doing nothing else"; Suet. *Tib.* 28), in accordance with Augustus' advice (Suet. *Aug.* 51). Getting rid of evidence and tolerating criticism could, in fact, just as well be strategic ignorance designed not quite so charitably to spare enemies as to spare oneself the need to act on information it seems safer or more convenient to ignore, a move familiar to any Roman politician who had refused to accept unwelcome signs in divination.[4] "It is not a good thing to see and hear everything" (Sen. *De Ira* 3.11.1). Under the Empire, clemency had so hardened from subtle, if risky, policy into a formal resource of the system that displaying power by concealing it could become material for political theater: in one of Domitian's shows lions were trained to catch rabbits, then gently release them unharmed (Mart. 1.6, 14, 22, 48, 60, 104). In so ceremonially sensitive a society as Rome, the subliminal message about unexercised imperial power detected by Martial in such performances can hardly have been entirely a product of his own imagination.

Even when it was perfectly sincere, then, clemency posed delicate questions of political etiquette which several emperors attempted to forestall by pledging not to execute senators (e.g., Dio 68.2.3 [Nerva], 68.5.2 [Trajan], 69.2.4 [Hadrian]; *Hist. Aug.* Severus 7.5). When one senator was found guilty of parricide, Antoninus Pius faced an awkward situation but managed to carry out the obligatory death penalty indirectly by exiling him to a deserted island (*Hist. Aug.* 8.10; cf. Dio 78.21). The rationale is that of burying Vestal Virgins alive to get around executing them. Marcus Aurelius similarly "allowed rather than ordered" the death of Cassius and regretted even that, since he, too, was reluctant to execute senators (*Hist. Aug.* 26.10). When Cassius' head was brought to him, he expressed dismay at no longer being able to grant clemency (*Hist. Aug.* Avidius Cassius 8.1; in Dio 71.26.1 he worries that Cassius will kill himself or be killed before he can be offered clemency). Bad emperors said the same kinds of things, for well meant or not, in being a display of power, clemency entailed the contradiction at work also in forced voluntary suicide and had close connections with it.

Never being just mercy, but power veiled as mercy, clemency had implicitly to be its own opposite if it was to be effective. To underscore how admirable and rare clemency is, Seneca must be painfully frank about the power it represents (*Clem.* 1.1.2, 1.19.1, 1.5.4). "The man who owes his life to another has lost it" ("perdidit enim vitam qui debet") and lives on as though on display in someone else's triumphal procession (1.21.2). Sallust is no less blunt: "Even if he is merciful and good [*clemens et bonus*], a man with more power is feared because he *can* be bad [*licet esse malo*]" (Sallust[?] *Oration to Caesar* 1.4). Dio (75.2.2) mentions a senator who, after sponsoring the decree in which Severus pledged restraint, became one of his first victims.[5] This is the background for the odd mixture of sense and nonsense, candor and hypocrisy, in Vitellius' tearful suggestion that, owing to his previous services, Asiaticus, who is being railroaded, be offered a choice of death. When Claudius "seconded that proposal for clemency" (Tac. *Ann.* 11.3.1), *clementia* was all iron fist and no velvet glove. Tacitus makes the same point just as wryly, when Tiberius, (more or less) regretting a hasty execution, arranges in the future for a cooling-off period before condemnation is carried out. Despite this formal provision for clemency, though, "the senate was not free to change its mind and Tiberius never did" (Tac. *Ann.* 3.51.2). Tiberius evidently reacted to accusations of *inclementia* with still more *inclementia* (4.42.3) because he saw *clementia* as weakness, though a streak of sheer contrariness was perhaps a factor as well (2.38.1).

The scene with Asiaticus combines sheer farce with satire, in that his life is not spared at all (cf. the promise of clemency—not carried out—for a man on the way to execution; Amm. Marc. 29.3.7). In Dio he is incriminated through the identification of a bald man by a witness who knows no more than that Asiaticus is bald, too (60.29.5). Caught in this maze, he rejects the "favor" *(beneficium)* of a (relatively) gentle end through starvation and opens his arteries instead, perhaps to make clear that he was a victim of violence. The double switch of clemency serving as a mask to make the power behind it transparent operates in the opposite direction when Caesar justifies cutting some prisoners' hands off on the grounds that, since his clemency is well known, he can be unforgiving without seeming to be vicious (*BGall.* 8.44). Brutality revealing restraint serves as exception proving the rule. The Senate enters into this spirit of clemency when the (ironic) proposal is made to replace a more severe penalty with exile and loss of property on the grounds that the guilty party, kept live, will suffer more. Exile thus counts equally as an example of public clemency and cruelty (Tac. *Ann.* 14.48.4; Caesar takes the same line in Sall. *Cat.* 51.20). The cult of clemency which the Senate established for Gaius after one of his particularly threatening outbursts, on the other hand, was probably a matter of serious wishful thinking rather than of irony (Dio 59.16.10), though it is easy to see how hopelessly opaque intentions could quickly become.

If Caesar wanted to think that he could get away with being ruthless because it was obvious that he was not, clemency normally worked the other way around, with power being too obvious to need proving (Sen. *Clem.* 1.21.1)—that is to say, to need *further* proof, as is shown by a passage in Aurelius Victor (*Caes.* 20.10–13). It is reasonable to grant clemency if someone pleads that he opposed you under duress and did not really want to do so. It may be more prudent, though, to show mercy only after first ruthlessly getting rid of any hope of clemency that might encourage opposition. Once power is in place, restraint can be one of its modes. That was a leading axiom of Roman imperialism, and its military origins made clemency in domestic politics doubly galling. Not surprisingly, it recommended itself to Adolf Hitler, who also saw the possibility that clemency might be an idea whose time can never come because it is feasible only when it is either unnecessary or impossible: "In actual fact the pacifistic-humane idea is perfectly all right perhaps when the highest type of man has previously conquered and subjected the world to an extent that makes him the sole ruler of this earth. Then this idea lacks the power of producing evil effects in exact proportion as its practical application becomes rare and finally impossible. Therefore, first struggle and then we shall see what can be done."[6]

Here is Livia's paradox again. You can dispense with strength only when you have not dispensed with it, and since you cannot dispense with it because you are vulnerable, the only hope for ever dispensing with it is not to dispense with it until your security is assured. Conversely, if clemency is granted, it may well have to be granted for self-preservation and thus not really be granted but extorted. In order to secure friendship, Vespasian gave the consulship to someone who had been pointed out to him as a special threat. The gesture was as much favor as clemency, but there is no great difference between the two, and if this shows, as Suetonius claims, that Vespasian never was driven to kill anyone out of fear (*Vespasian* 14), it also shows how he could be motivated by what amounts to defensive and proleptic, if not exactly anxious, clemency. The opposite possibility of belated clemency is doubly odd in the event of suicide, for as power has already been exercised (suicide carried out), it is no longer possible to veil the violence, and so proclamation of clemency is a double bluff (like Petronius' "vices or imitations of vices"; Tac. *Ann.* 16.18.2). Procedural incongruity is taken a step further along this line in the case of Lucius Vetus, who had committed suicide with two close relatives. After burial, the three were formally condemned, and Nero then intervened to grant them permission to choose their manner of death. Like tardy pardon, tardy permission was an attempt to cut political losses incurred from the deaths (16.10f). That is intelligible enough but still so incoherent that Tacitus views the proffered permission as a mere joke *(ludibria)* on a level with the absurd timing (again labeled *ludibria*) in the Senate's expulsion of two members officially denounced in a letter from Nero which neglected to mention that they had already been executed (14.59).

Institutional incoherence is a theme once more in Seneca's account of a complaint against Cremutius Cordus for attempting suicide (*Ad Marciam* 22.7). As a target of official displeasure and facing probable condemnation, he was under pressure ultimately to commit suicide (he did in fact starve himself; Tac. *Ann.* 4.35.4). As a result, he found himself in a trap: "If he wanted to live, he had to ask Sejanus, if he wanted to die, he had to ask his daughter, and both were inexorable." The actual facts are unclear. His property may have been about to escape confiscation through normal suspension of penalties in the event of death before condemnation. His enemies, accordingly, were put in the position of wanting him dead—but not yet. Seneca, though, is not interested in legal niceties; the wry remark that "to prevent him from doing what they had forced him to do a complaint was entered that Cordus was dying" ("queruntur mori Cordum ut interpellent quod coegerant") underscores the absurdity.[7] Going to court makes perfectly good sense if execution or forced death counts as a show of power in a way that voluntary death does not. All the same, Cordus' enemies were going to court also because "they were losing a person they were trying to get rid of." Beyond its considerable catch-22 rhetorical effect, the abrupt double take triggered by queer language of this kind in Seneca or Tacitus is designed to catch the queer, circular way of thinking about politics necessary under the Principate. The attempted execution of a dead man mentioned by Tacitus in *Annals* 6.40 makes a similar point.

What the fragile logic of political suicide finally points to, then, is a pervasive double bind in Roman politics. If his subjects have to cap a successful career by killing themselves, the emperor's position has strange dilemmas of its own, too. As Domitian complains, he can prove that he faces genuine conspiracies only by getting himself assassinated (Suet. *Dom.* 21; *Hist. Aug. Avidius Cassius* 2.5; cf. the centurion Agrestis' suicide to prove good faith, Tac. *Hist.* 3.54.3). In much the same vein, Seneca warns Nero that he can eliminate everyone but his successor, since anyone gotten rid of for that reason is bound to be the wrong man (Dio 61.18.3; *Hist. Aug. Avidius Cassius* 2.2; Livy 40.9.1: crimes are not taken seriously until they are committed).

Personal malice and public policy being as tightly interwoven as they were at Rome, real or imagined maneuvering to score symbolic points could be detected everywhere, for example, in the claim that Tiberius had Plancina executed only after Agrippina was dead, not because he did not hate her; he did hate her, but he did not want to please Agrippina, who also hated her (Dio 58.22.5). One-on-one political violence was governed by a complex set of interlocking moves further complicated by a fundamental aspect of all rational competition: good moves may be bad, since an opponent, also knowing that they are good, plans to make them a mistake. Agrippina would have been well advised to patch up her quarrel with Plancina. Petty point-scoring had less serious consequences when Pollio ended a quarrel with Timagenes only because Augustus had begun one (Sen. *De Ira* 3.23.8). Even in staying out of trouble by avoiding powerful people, one needed to avoid *seeming* to avoid them, as that could mean trouble, too (Sen. *Ep.* 14.8).

Execution, to begin with, was concealed under the guise of enforced suicide, whose advantage for the emperor could then be countered by refusal or by compliance carried out as an act of protest, itself once again countered by an offer of posthumous clemency, which in turn could be forestalled by suicide committed expressly to preclude pardon. Power thus meant having the last word in a particularly literal sense (cf. "Hello, Caesar!" "Goodbye, Fulvius!"; Plut. *De garr.* 508A), and straightforward execution was perhaps carried out in some cases because the alternative seemed to invite too much trouble. Taken together, the various combinations arrange themselves in a payoff matrix of sorts whose significance as political protocol extends well beyond the particular moves it calls for (figure 1).

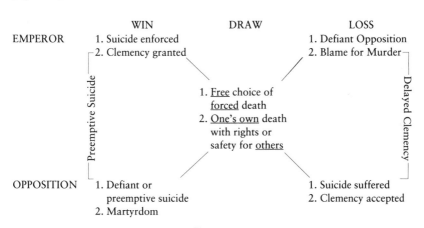

	WIN	DRAW	LOSS
EMPEROR	1. Suicide enforced 2. Clemency granted	1. Free choice of forced death 2. One's own death with rights or safety for others	1. Defiant Opposition 2. Blame for Murder
OPPOSITION	1. Defiant or preemptive suicide 2. Martyrdom		1. Suicide suffered 2. Clemency accepted

left axis: Preemptive Suicide — right axis: Delayed Clemency

Figure 1

While political matches could be played as winner-take-all games of brute power excluding any cooperation, more typically they were complex bargaining contests calling for rational strategies coordinated with, as well as opposed to, decisions made by others. Winning means asserting status; losing is having it diminished. The former is defined for both sides in the left vertical column of the figure, the latter on the right; wins and losses for each side lie on the horizontal axes; the correlation of victory for one party with defeat for the other extends along the diagonals. The emperor scores when he forces suicide or acceptance of clemency, the second of these moves being all the more effective on the principle that the recipient of a gift is placed in the weaker position. On the other hand, he loses insofar as victims die defiantly or their death is perceived to be without justification. Seneca's death was *caedes*—both "murder" because it was undeserved and "execution" because he refused suicide until receiving a formal order (Tac. *Ann.* 15.60–61). Points scored or lost by the opposition are the reverse, scored when suicide is seen as an invidious gesture of protest or as mere murder committed by the emperor, lost through undistinguished death or submission to clemency. The alternatives, accordingly, are by no means mutually exclusive. Even political martyrs have in fact been gotten rid of; defiance for its part may be a wasted move, as Tacitus knew; and forced suicide to some extent is always apt to be a damaging as well as real show of power.

Real games depend on reciprocity. Both sides must have a chance to win, and so at least a pretense of mutual respect is indispensable: when the opponent is worthy of praise, losing to him is softened and winning becomes all the sweeter. So far as political life is not actually a game, though, reciprocity entails a good deal less graciousness, hence the "contradiction" in a remark of Seneca apropos of Cato: "Mors illos consecrat quorum exitum et qui timent laudant" (*Prov.* 2.12). On the one hand, Cato's death, rather than the dead man himself, is feared because suicide is a political weapon; at the same time, it can be praised in that he poses no real threat, and it must be praised in that political games require common values.

Each move takes its value from the relation it has with other moves. By itself, enforcement of suicide is plain victory for the emperor, plain defeat for his victims, but its value is further enhanced by what it is not, namely straight-out execution. When they are linked diagonally, the win/loss columns of both parties meet to form an intermediate draw avoiding the either/or outcome of a pure zero-sum game. If winning is assigned the value of 1 and losing the value of 0, the intermediate position is still a one-sided outcome, leaving the emperor with more and his victims with less than ½ but preserving sufficient balance to keep the system as a whole playable. Semantically, this central area of accommodation is marked out by "enforced voluntary death" or "enforced freedom," reflecting the more fundamental political oxymoron of "voluntary slavery" embedded in the structure of the Principate (Tac. *Hist.* 4.2.2; Tac. *Ann.* 1.2.1, 7.1, 3.65.3, 14.13.2). When Tacitus (*Ann.* 16.9.1) mentions the case of someone neither executed nor forced into suicide but sent into exile to wait for imminent death from advanced age, the category of "natural death permitted" would again count as a draw to the emperor's advantage, since he achieves what he wants without violence while making an appropriate concession to appearances.

Substituting numbers for wins (1) and losses (0) and with negative or positive signs representing presence or absence of physical violence as it affects each player, we have a new formulation (see figure 2).

	WIN	DRAW	LOSS
EMPEROR	1. +1		1. +0
	2. +1		2. +0
		1. } emperor +$\frac{2}{3}$	
		2. } opposition −$\frac{1}{3}$	
OPPOSITION	1. −1		1. −0
	2. −1		2. +0

Figure 2

For the authorities, suicide enforced is indirect exercise of physical coercion, and clemency granted is its direct suspension; for the victim, suicide is the direct consequence of coercion, clemency the direct consequence of its suspension. The unequal nature of the game is evinced by the negative or null value of every outcome on the horizontal win/loss axis of the opposition, for whom compulsion is unavailable. Its victories are all won at the cost of violent death (1 but negative), and survival is still bought at the price of submission to clemency (positive but 0). By way of contrast, even when the emperor's reputation suffers damage from his use of power (0), he retains the advantage of wielding it indirectly (+). In draws, while both parties score, he again enjoys the advantage ($\frac{2}{3}$ against $\frac{1}{3}$), and though violence is employed (−) it is accompanied by gracious concessions (+).

Victory can be snatched from the emperor (down the left vertical) by preemptive suicide, while posthumous clemency shifts loss away from the emperor (down the right vertical) unless it is blocked by prior rejection, a move that is indeed decisive though only to the extent that conceding but refusing to count defeat is. Falling outside the rules are, for the emperor, unrestricted violence or his own suicide, the former being inadmissibly overt, the latter inadmissibly passive. The first possibility is posed by Caligula's realization that he could do anything to anybody (Suet. *Calig.* 29.1) or by his plan to move from Rome to Antium, then to Alexandria, after wiping out the leadership of the Senate and knights (49.2). This is destruction of the political symbiosis between ruler and ruled which Seneca describes in utopian terms (*Clem.* 1.3–4, 13–16) because he is aware of its actual fragility (1.7.3, 8.5). So far as suicide by the emperor is concerned, apart from the death of Otho and to some extent of Nero, that move is rare. It is suggested by a foreign observer of the Roman scene (Suet. *Tib.* 66) and hyperbolically by Caligula (Suet. *Calig.* 56.1). Titus, too, was said to have sworn that he would rather die than kill and to have flirted with assassination apparently confident in his popularity (Suet. *Tit.* 9.1), though Suetonius reports that before taking power he was widely hated for bloody-mindedness (6.2). The panic-prone Claudius once thought of abdication (Suet. *Claud.* 36) which stands to exile as suicide stands to assassination, and so did Nero when his power had slipped away (Suet. *Ner.* 47.2; an earlier insincere threat [34.1] was a mere tactical move within the system). For the opposition, too, naked violence directed by the emperor against themselves is inadmissible (though effective, of course), while the game is brought to an end in the opposite sense when they assassinate him.

The middle area of compromise—where a draw of sorts could be achieved and a bargain struck in the economy of violence—makes a vital contribution to the system's stability (see Addendum 8). It is worth examining in light of another formal game-theoretical model focusing more narrowly on calculation of gain and loss. Under the Republic *libertas* meant freedom to do; under the Principate it had diminished into negative freedom from being done to or, somewhat more positively, freedom to express some opinions and permission to do some things.[8] This left the emperor with the whip hand, and his optimism about his position along with the opposition's pessimism about theirs must have been founded on what, in more formal modern terms, have been called "maximax" and "minimax" assessments, identifying, respectively, the best and least bad outcomes of a situation.[9] Each of these possibilities is, at the same time, one of the facets of *clementia*: what the emperor can do as seen from his point of view and what he refrains from doing as seen from the opposition's much less sanguine point of view. "Because Caesar can do anything, there are many things he cannot do" (Sen. *De Consolatione ad Polybium* 7.2; Dio 52.38.1).

Clementia was a major feature of propaganda for autocracy on the part of Caesar and his immediate successors, with Augustus in particular seeing that the political issue centered on loss or gain of power or, rather, on assessments of losses and gains, and that people are more resistant to incurring losses than to forgoing gains (Dio 55. 14–21). The keener feeling of deprivation at losing something you have than at failing to get it in the first place (Thuc. 2.62.3; cf. Xen. *Cyr.* 7.5.82) is a defensive, conservative reaction that applies more broadly to political power and took on special importance under the Principate. Credit agencies still prefer to speak of cash discounts for those who do not use charge cards rather than of surcharges on those who do.[10] The political discount pocketed by the emperor was the real power he wielded and the very limited pro forma share he had to concede. After a time, as Tacitus observes, there were few left who remembered enough about the Republic even to feel cheated (Tac. *Ann.* 1.3.7), and so most were content to think of the surcharge they were paying—the power and freedom taken from them—not as something they were giving up but as something they were merely not getting that was due anyway to the emperor for assuming responsibility.

Inapplicable as quantitative terms are in many ways to the political situation at Rome, formal models for estimating gain or loss in order to weigh one against the other can sharpen and formalize some of its features, particularly those concerned with assessments involving status, property, or life constantly being forced on both sides. "The accounts [of power] add up only when they are audited by one person" (Tac. *Ann.* 1.6.3) because many transactions must be off the books. But the actual exercise of power required everyone to make calculations, and because suicide was not an institution, its rules were immanent in the immediate logic of circumstances. Though choices were not made in complete ignorance of possible outcomes, which for the most part were predictable given the unequal distribution of power, relative utility still took some careful figuring. In counting on the best possible outcome, the emperor could afford to be an optimist, whereas his opponents, in choosing the best of the worst possible results, had to be pessimists. Expectations beyond maximax and minimax points are irrational confidence or irrational pessimism, and deeply pessimistic estimates of the political situation were bound to play a role in suicide at Rome, for example, in the decision that surviving Tiberius only to live under Caligula was unprofitable. So far as excess confidence is concerned, that comes up, as we have seen, in Caligula's reckoning that "he could do anything to anybody" (Suet. *Calig.* 29.1; cf. 32.3; Mart. 7.21.3–4) or that everybody's property was at his disposal (Suet. *Calig.* 47; cf. Suet. *Ner.* 32.4; Dio 77.10.4: "Nobody but me [Caracalla] should have money"). The best possible minimax face, on the other hand, was put on the Senate's position by Pliny the Younger's gratitude at being free because the emperor had told him to be (*Pan.* 66.4) or by a knight's assurance to Tiberius that "it is not our business to evaluate whom you promote above others and why; the gods have given you supreme power, what is left to us is the distinction of obedience" (Tac. *Ann.* 6.8.4).

There was space, besides, for any number of other compromises, extending from temporary efforts at real power sharing under some emperors through the Tacitean rule that good men can serve even under bad rulers to various nuances of exile or confiscation. As negotiations over time led to implicit trading norms, a wide range of possibilities opened up: clear choices, conditional choices, mutual solutions, no solutions. Having the most to lose, the Senate was forced to accept solutions favorable to the emperor, who could count on being hurt less than his rivals by failure to reach accommodation. Nothing like third-party arbitration was available to introduce other factors, and though self-interest imposed enough restraint on both sides to make bargaining possible, negotiations were at best one-sided and could easily slide into a pure conflict game or one posing dysfunctional dilemmas rather than choices. Suicide in a sense attempted to turn dilemma into choice, though one inevitably entailing the contradiction of "enforced voluntary suicide." In the extreme situation of a game played with decisions on each side no longer affecting the other, pessimism or optimism naturally tends to become irrational.[11]

Reluctant admission by Tacitus and others that no realistic alternative was available to this complex array of mixed, cooperative, and conflict games amounted to recognition of a common interest in preserving the system on the part of both sides. Under the circumstances, though, accommodation often ran along self-defeating loops of the sort frequently formed when tacit cooperation fails. Correct moves depend on divining the other party's intention by inferences made from the larger situation. But if two people are cut off during a telephone conversation and each assumes that the other will call back at once, both will wait, and no call goes through; if each assumes that, since this is so, the other will wait, both call at once, and again no call gets through. When, in addition to difficulties of this kind arising from the nature of cooperative relationships, coordinated decisions have to be reached amid profound mistrust, the opportunity for miscalculation becomes almost limitless: "If a man knocks at a door and says he will stab himself on the porch unless given $10, he is more likely to get the $10 if his eyes are bloodshot."[12]

At Rome the emperor's "bloodshot eyes"—the ugly faces Caligula practiced in front of a mirror, the better to intimidate people (Suet. *Calig.* 50.1)—were a history of real or threatened autocratic violence; the opposition's were wealth, status, or honor, all grounds for the worst suspicions on his part. Wealth and status afforded means for conspiracy; honor furnished motive and could more particularly encourage the tactic of strength through weakness, for example, burning one's bridges in the conviction that since only honor was left, everything had to be dared. As we have seen, clemency offered one way to forestall that possibility, but the logic of preemptive strikes can just as readily take over, and so what appears in Tacitus or Suetonius as gradual revelation of the emperor's bad intentions all along may, in fact, have been increasingly aggressive self-defense on his part.

The treatment of the ambiguous deaths of several emperors by assassination or suicide in Tacitus takes its political significance from the final breakdown of these already precarious rules, as happened catastrophically in A.D. 69, when emperors were taken out of the game through several dramatically bad moves. Nero presents a particularly interesting case. Earlier, when he held authority, in forcing suicide or granting clemency he had wielded power in the normal manner within the system, whose progressive disintegration, by way of contrast, was marked by instances of inadmissible brutality or outright murder, preeminently that of his mother. The same political point is made by reports—true or not— of his plans for indiscriminate violence: executing generals, governors, everyone in exile everywhere, poisoning the whole Senate at dinner, burning Rome, and turning wild animals loose on the populace (Suet. *Ner.* 43.1, 37.3; Dio 61.11.1 [whatever Nero *could* do was right], 62.16; contrast Sen. *De Consolatione ad Polybium* 7.2 [because Caesar can do anything, there are many things he cannot do]). In reflecting that "no *princeps* had realized what he could do" (Suet. *Ner.* 37.3), he was in effect contemplating not victory but an end to the game once and for all, and his own equally aberrant death corresponds, then, at the other end of the spectrum, to these extravagantly optimistic as well as destructive notions of power. He faces lynching, assassination by his enemies (or rather execution, as he had been formally condemned by the Senate), or plain suicide at his own hands or with the help of someone else who was willing to die first as an example, and he finally suffers hybrid mercy killing cum suicide at the hands of a faithful servant.

The broader, systemic political implications of this wild improvisation with elementary rules of power has a touch of sheer farce as well, intended by the hostile historical tradition to be true to the system if unfair to Nero. Having abandoned his ferocious plans for vengeance because they could not work, he decides to appear unarmed before the troops in Gaul and— just cry. They will, he believes, be shamed into loyalty and follow him in hymns of victory, which he ought right now be composing (Suet. *Ner.* 43.2). Vitellius' difficulties reveal the same dysfunction in game rules, though he has only one option—abdication—which he tries futilely to use three times. Twice he changes his mind, he is turned down by everyone a third time (Suet. *Vit.* 15), and finally he is lynched.

Apart from drastic systemic breakdown of this kind, the several calculated grades of exile and of other penalties available in the routine relationship between the two parties permitted the game to be played for lower stakes and with increased odds for a draw of sorts. Even the harshest exile takes an opponent off the board without liquidating him or her and leaves open the possibility of reinstatement.[13] Whatever form it takes, the possibility of compromise holding the alternatives together in a precarious balance springs largely from the single system of values in fact shared by both sides.

> It is striking how interchangeable and ambiguous were the attitudes of the different groups in the aristocracy. . . . The emperor himself often cultivated the literature that nerved his subjects to speak out, the astrology that they pursued at the risk of capital punishment, and the rhetorical exercises that extolled tyrannicide. Literature, astrology, and rhetoric, like their practioners, were sources of possible danger to the throne. They were also characteristic to the Roman establishment. Add the old families, political marriages, and Stoicism. The operation of these latter factors, too, in the circles of the emperor's enemies, is obvious.[14]

The common set of values, however, looked quite different from the playing field's shifting perspectives, vividly dramatized by the theme of emperors friendly one moment, murderous the next. Interpretive rules for various circumstances of suicide made up a loose ideology spelled out most consciously and fully in the philosophical wing of opposition to imperial power. Some of the political activism it encouraged seemed of scant value to Tacitus, owing to its self-righteous vanity and poor judgment (e.g., the "untimely wisdom" of Musonius Rufus' "tiresome and ridiculous" peace protest; Tac. *Hist.* 3.81.1). But he was also concerned about a more insidious depoliticization due to the breakdown in cooperation which went with exhibitionist opposition. Cooperation meant submission to the emperor, and Tacitus betrays some personal sensitivity about the fine line between collaboration and reasonable cooperation, like that of Agricola, needed to keep the system going. Since the Principate was inevitable, cooperation was indispensable, and so the danger in aggressive rejection of collaboration was that inviting a demonstration of the emperor's power might very well also confirm it.

Depoliticization in this sense of contributing to collapse of the Principate's playability is detectable in Musonius' more politically sophisticated pupil, Epictetus. After Helvidius Priscus is ordered not to attend the Senate by Vespasian, he insists that he has the right to do so as long as he is a member. Epictetus then sketches a steady escalation in the conflict between prerogatives on each side: "But you may not speak / Then don't ask my opinion on anything / But I must do so / Then I must give it freely / But I will kill you / Then your part is to exile or kill, mine to go or die calmly" (Arr. *Epict. Diss.* 1.2.19–22). In claiming that such gestures are "paradigmatically" valuable, Epictetus contrasts Priscus with a senator who on receiving the same order would thank Caesar for the exemption and thus not have to be kept away at all, because he could be counted on to remain silent. Like clemency, repression is most effective when it is unnecessary. In this scenario, it is collaboration on the part of compliant senators that kills political dialogue, while it is kept going, on the other hand, between Priscus and the emperor. But if the emperor is pushed into drastic action, the hard-line confrontation, based on nonnegotiable inner rectitude, which Priscus seeks subverts the system, too (cf. Dio 66.13.2–3): where freedom of speech is necessary it may also be ineffective. Subversion can, of course, be an effective move within the rules of the game; inviting execution by refusing to commit suicide on order reveals suicide for the execution it really is. But Tacitus saw an equal danger from intransigence devoid of larger political significance.[15]

Realistic assessment of the rules under which the Principate operated is the point of an anecdote about Corbulo, whose military prestige posed an (imagined) threat which apparently led Nero to order outright execution. Before it could be carried out, Corbulo killed himself. His last words *(axios)*, appropriately laconic for a tough soldier, seem to be an admission that he deserved to lose: "I have it coming!" Such are the rules of a game that should never be played by coming to an emperor like Nero unarmed (Dio 63.17.6).[16]

Irrespective of any formal models or matrices, both of which are at best highly schematized, rules in the first instance are best known intuitively by those who must play under them. As in any two-handed competitive game, political choices at Rome proceeded reciprocally through a closed range of possibilities, driven at times, however, by a paranoid logic of fear which frequently informs the narrative of ancient historians and gives it its primary political meaning.

In reflecting on Otho's conspiracy, Tacitus notes that owing to heavy debts his only hope lay in political disorder and that he was in any event goaded on by hatred of Galba and envy of Piso. This is a familiar enough combination of political and personal factors, but Tacitus goes on to some far more interesting remarks. "Otho was pretending fear, too, in order to increase his ambition [*fingebat et metum, quo magis concupisceret*]. He had been dangerous to Nero and could not [under Galba or Piso] expect the honor of another exile to Lusitania. A potential rival was always suspected and hated by those in power. That had hurt him under the old emperor [Galba] and would do so even more under the young one [Piso], aggressive by nature and made resentful by a long exile. Otho (Piso would say) could be killed" (Tac. *Hist.* 1.21.1). As Poppaea Sabina's

lover, Otho had stood in Nero's way and was gotten rid of by appoint-
ment to office in Lusitania. The "honor" was therefore in actual fact yet
another nuance of exile to clear the way for Nero's marriage to Poppaea,
so that in disposing of pretense on that score, Otho's irony recognizes
that the next game will not be played to a quasi-draw but will be a final
win/loss proposition.

His own "pretense" of fear may mean that he was justifying his
ambitious plans to others by talking of the personal danger he faced, as
Brutus and Cassius did when they "pretended to fear violence from
Antony in order to increase dislike of him" (Vell. Pat. 2.62.3). But the
phrasing of Tacitus' account could equally well represent what Otho was
telling himself. In that case, he would not have been deceiving himself
with unreal fear so much as psyching himself up to action by running
through mental simulations of real danger. That special sense of *fingo* is
part of the meaning of *fingebant simul credebantque*—"were talking
themselves into really believing"—in Tacitus' *Annals* 5.10.2. In any case—
self-justification or auto-suggestion, calculated or honest—things become
real in good measure as they are thought to be so.[17] When Otho thinks of
himself as a threat to Piso, he also has to think of Piso's hostility as
justified, and then the fear Otho feels (emphasized in Plut. *Galba* 24.3) is
real, while being pretended, too, in that it can be used to win support
from others or as a genuine enabling factor in the scenario he conjures up
for himself. As Otho's own motives become inextricably interwoven with
Piso's, he finally can tell himself, honestly as well as dishonestly, "I have
to kill him in self-defense, because he is about to (and should, if he is
wise) kill me in self-defense."[18] He knows that Piso must be killed because he knows (and is afraid) that "Otho can be killed." Stark political
reality is pinned down by the stark simplicity of both thought and expression in the crisp, doubly objective third-person indirect discourse of
occidi Othonem posse. Although what conspirators intend to do is not so
purely self-defensive as they like to make themselves believe, it is, after
all, self-defensive to the extent that survival—pushing instead of being
pushed—always is.[19]

Just such a dialectic of submerged intentions and possibilities is
played out in the variant accounts of a confrontation between Nero and
Julius Montanus. The emperor's position carried with it certain ill-
defined sexual prerogatives. In Suetonius' version (*Ner.* 26.2), Montanus
nearly beats Nero to death for having pawed his wife, while in Tacitus
(*Ann.* 13.25.2), the incident begins from a chance street meeting during
which Nero attacks Montanus, who at first goes unpunished because
Nero thinks that he acted in ignorance. However, on receiving an apology for the self-defense, according to Dio, Nero remarks, "So he *did*

know he was hitting Nero." Then "Montanus committed suicide" (Dio 61.9.3–4). In Tacitus, where Montanus is "forced to die," Nero again takes the apology as reproach, that is, as implying resistance against the emperor's power to do as he wants, much as trying to repay a gift would. The whole affair amounts to a very strange form of the King in Disguise mingling with his subjects to learn what they think of him (cf. the stories of Augustus prompted by divine signs to beg on the streets in disguise; Dio 54.35.3). Someone who had unintentionally struck Cato in the baths and later apologized was dismissively assured by him that he did not even recall the blow (De Ira 2.32.2–3). Here potentially serious moves in a game are reduced to a meaningless incident by treatment on the one side as an accident, on the other as unnecessary apology. Cato's purely philosophical restraint aside, if the man had no special social standing, he was not a player at all, could make no moves, and therefore was incapable of offering a real insult (cf. the insult to Caligula that did not count because it was made by a Gallic shoemaker in Dio 59.26.8; part of Claudius' ineptitude was that he could be so easily insulted with impunity, Suet. Claud. 15.4).

The potential for circular logic in such patterns of political violence has been much discussed in connection with the rationale of preemptive strikes in modern game theory. The dilemma is the familiar one of two people approaching a revolving door from opposite directions. They may pass smoothly or, if they read each other's intention incorrectly, stand frozen in indecision or collide like two armies in Livy, neither of which wanted to fight and would have gone off in opposite directions but joined battle because each thought the other would advance if it retreated (10.36.3). One or the other of the last two moves is certain to be made as soon as the logic of tacit coordination goes awry: "I am going to the left because I think he thinks I think that he thinks . . ." Tacit coordination of an unusually complex kind is what the Principate called for and what often failed.

The logic of political suicide at Rome has even more curious aspects: not only "I have to kill *myself* in self-defense because he is about to kill me [in self-defense]" but, to foreclose unwelcome offers of clemency, "I have to kill *myself* in self-defense because he *won't* kill me [in self-defense]." (*Self-defense* needs bracketing insofar as neither emperor nor opposition recognized that it could be a genuine motive of the other.) Suicide was, on the one hand, a familiar tactic based on the reasonable axioms that death may at times be preferable to life and that death at one's own hands may be preferable to death at the hands of one's enemies. Still, shaped as it was by the tangled relationship between emperor and members of an elite unable to come to terms with loss of status, it also became a sign of deeper anomaly at work in the system, a *normally* anomalous course of action whose political significance, like that of bloodshed in the arena, as a routine political move came exactly from its routine abnormality. Tacitus allows only that some good moves are possible in bad games of this kind or, in J. Kany's phrase, admires individual suicides but deplores suicide as such.[20]

Suicide to escape public loss of status, which had long been part of the shame culture at Rome, came into special vogue during the late Republic and early Empire. Both were periods of disorder as the old disintegrated and something new began to emerge. In the Republic, however, suicide was not so much part of the system as a sign of its failure, whereas it was integral to the Principate and thus a sign of systemic contradiction.[21] In the former it was a last resort in despair at anarchic violence (e.g., App. *BCiv.* 4.4.26), in the latter, a last resort in despair at official policy (e.g., Tac. *Ann.* 5.8.2).

Were they pushed or did they jump? In criminal investigations the paradox of "neither" opens up interesting possibilities (e.g., that the body has been moved from elsewhere). By virtue of a peculiar balance of power in Roman politics, the paradox there is "both." Since victimhood, too, could count politically, those who committed suicide were pushed into jumping, or in the case of clemency scorned, they jumped because no one would push them.[22]

The aim of rules is to make games playable by establishing the possibility of moves, with all possibilities together constituting the strategic range within which any particular tactical moves are actually made. Reports of political suicide at Rome span everything from bare accounts leaving unclear whether suicide in fact occurred to entire sequences of move and countermove. In the former, uncertainty may itself be a political fact and not solely a matter of historical ignorance, inasmuch as rendering responsibility ambiguous was a major aim of both sides. Though the collection of cases in the works of the historians is fragmentary, it is also sufficiently rich to permit reconstruction of the rules of engagement more generally. In political competition, playability means overall political stability, and even if that is possible only on an uneven playing field, as it was at Rome, in games of survival there is no alternative to continued play. Under the circumstances, while not ceasing to be a game, political suicide did cease in some respects to be a rational game and brought into sharp focus an aspect of the Principate that was simultaneously functional and dysfunctional.

Epilogue

Owing to the complexity of social reality, alternative meanings emerge at any number of points along the spectrum extending between the domains of what is private, individual, and psychological and what is public, communal, and abstract.[1] In some respects the two poles are entirely autonomous: legal systems, as systems, are impersonal procedures having nothing to do with the feelings or intentions of individuals. At the same time, though Justice wears a blindfold and holds her balance level, social institutions are unintelligible apart from living agents and their conscious aims. While illicit drug use in modern societies can be understood at very general levels such as the dynamics of free markets, patterns of social stratification, or, more abstractly still, long-term trends in cultural values, its reality lies equally in the immediate escape it provides for some, the immediate gain for others. The impersonal economic relationship of drug seller as entrepreneur to addict as customer and their relationship as individuals are not incommensurate because one or the other is false but because the focus of each is different.

In Rome, at that end of the spectrum where immediate intentions of individuals are salient, for spectators *munera* meant entertainment; for sponsors they meant the costs and rewards of status. For those active in politics, suicide meant the personal hazards of competition. If explanation is simple and straightforward at this level, there is still ample room for a good many differing attitudes and assumptions, some of which in fact helped select what went into the historical tradition to begin with. Judgments about the personal behavior of one or another emperor at *munera* and about the contemptible or admirable death of a senator frequently determined Tacitus' choice of material.

At the other end of the spectrum, less overt but much broader patterns come into view. Here political suicide was regulated by the logic of internal domestic needs involving violence on a small scale and governed by loose conventions to accommodate the flexibility required for political action. So long as power among competitors during the Republic remained more or less in balance, suicide fell beyond rather than within the system, but once the emperor had won a decisively superior position, it was incorporated as a (quasi-)routine alternative.

Munera were a somewhat different proposition. Dealing with essentially external threats from man or beast, they were public and corporate in nature and therefore more heavily ritualized. By way of contrast to the *intro*jection of violence through political suicide, bloodshed in the arena was a more positive, fully socialized *pro*jection of power and *ex*pulsion of danger. As danger is marginalized in the person of the victim, violence is set apart ritually to be viewed as spectacle. *Munera* were rituals in a fairly strong sense of the word. Ritual, of which theatricality is a defining property, typically appears where social order is breached, and it eliminates anomaly by coming to terms with it—"entertaining" it—through stylized mimicry and rehearsal. On the old rule of eye for eye, tooth for tooth, ritual assures equilibrium by reproducing danger and treating it, so to say, as a sensitive spot in the body politic that needs "worrying." By inflicting pain to lessen pain, bloody games, like tragic drama, were effective because the attraction their repellent features exerted also brought relief. Pain, that is to say, presupposes gain and is pointless in its absence; few societies will enjoy harrowing enactments of some of their own worst fears without a surplus of reassurance in return. At the same time, there is a need to be harrowed, because in a violent world gain implies pain as the price exacted when vital interests are at issue.

The result is a combination of good and bad violence, each painfully and gainfully doubling as the other. The form this took at Rome is an unusually transparent instance of the integrating effect that euphoria induced by mass violence can have on "public opinion," defined broadly as social control which aims at protecting group interests through psychological and physical sanctions. While *munera* placed a heavy premium on the latter, their logic still depended on what violence meant, and in that regard they too constitute a form of public opinion whose effect in fact ended only when "the dead member drop [ped] from the social body."[2] Aside from instances when suicide was performed theatrically by way of protest, ritual repetition and mass emotion played no part in political suicide, whose aim was precisely to make trouble as undramatic and unobtrusive as possible. Embodying purely internal violence as it did, it remained for the most part a restricted, semiprivate game.

The spectrum running from concrete to abstract can also be seen as a scale along which the multiple contexts of social reality are distributed, with meaning determined by whichever context holds the center of attention and with other contexts bringing other meanings into view. The contextual dimension of public bloodshed is graphically illustrated by a mosaic from Rome that sets *munera* apart as spectacles twice over, first in its own re-presentation of combat in the arena, which itself, additionally, re-presents real violence. Various meanings are defined in reference to spatial contexts assigning a place to everything and putting everything in its place. In the bottom portion of a sharply delineated square, two gladiators labeled "Maternus" and "Habilis" face off under a caption reading "As they fought, Symachius provided [or thrust] the sword" ("Quibus pugnantibus Symachius ferrum misit").[3] The gladiators, the death sign (Θ) affixed to Maternus' name, and the caption all place combat in the context of an uncomplicated, instantly accessible social reality. In the upper section, Habilis is at the point of killing the prone Maternus; on the left, an official looks at the coup de grâce while pivoting toward the unseen stands. The scene is accompanied by the captions "We see this" ("Haec videmus") and "Symachius, good man!" ("Symachi, homo felix"), both apparently statements made by the invisible spectators. If the word *neco* attached to the official means "I kill [Maternus]," if Symachius is both the editor to whom the official is turning and the person claiming to be the killer through the agency of Habilis, then the simple, photolike reality takes on larger social meaning from the surrounding implicit context. For while *Haec videmus* still sees things at the obvious level of entertainment being enjoyed by spectators at *munera* and then by those who see the mosaic, the acclamation carries a wider symbolism of power centering on the unseen but notionally present editor, whose sponsorship of immediately entertaining violence is explained by various broader economic, political, and social contexts to which gestures point and captions refer. In relation to these settings beyond the arena and the mosaic, *munera* come also to mean wealth, popular favor, and authority over life or death, the last two being placed in yet another context of meaning whenever sponsors transferred "I kill" to the crowd. Then "I kill" was transformed into "You kill," and that, in turn, became a special moment of social solidarity and shared power through conferral of authority to say "We kill." The essentially social character of competition, especially at Rome, is enshrined in the derivation of *agōn* from the root idea of a "gathering" or "meeting." Serious games played before no one seem pointless, hence the importance of attendance as well as performance statistics in modern times, of elaborate seating arrangements and public subsidies in Roman society.

The matrix of specific tactical moves corresponding to the logic of political suicide at Rome constitutes a similar set of contexts with a rich variety of meanings determined by what is said or done, where and how it is said or done, and who is involved. In mosaic representation, *neco* could very well signal the invisible presence of the imperial impresario.

Violence was a brute fact of political life but one not easy to rationalize. Even when used in legitimate self-defense, Seneca holds that it must be inflicted without *ira* in an odd nonviolent violence (e.g., *De Ira* 1.16.5–7, 19.2), and the clemency which alone can eliminate it is ultimately motivated by self-interest. He is aware of the disparity between definitions and reality (*Clem.* 2.7.4). The line separating clemency from routine justice or severity from cruelty is often unclear, and the link of clemency to violence that comes out in Augustus' early career (1.11–12) is not entirely offset by his later restraint in dealing with a youthful would-be assassin (1.9). One can fantasize about the young Nero's opportunity never to use violence at all, but the political logic of clemency leaves open the possibility that he can and must. The *De clementia* may well be unfinished because the fact that he did proved too much even for Seneca's considerable powers of dialectic synthesis.

Seen at the systemic end of the spectrum of Roman society, arena games and political suicide were two distinct packages for retailing wholesale violence or—in the language of social logic—two of the species in which the genus violence was made specific, each defining functions in accordance with its own distinctive rationale and the distinctive kinds of potential dysfunction that went with it.

Addenda
Notes
Selected Bibliography
Indexes

Addendum 1: Legal Antinomy

"Those who had fled out of fear were later afraid of having been afraid" (Tac. *Ann.* 4.70.2); "the solution that had been found had the very opposite effect [than the one meant to influence the behavior of debtors and creditors]" (6.17.2); "the tax [on buyers of slaves] was remitted uselessly, since the merchants who were supposed to pay it merely added it to the price" (13.31.2). While critics of the Principate were sensitive to contradictions, they viewed them principally as material for bringing out moral incoherence to good rhetorical effect. That is the point made by the first of Tacitus' paradoxes. The other two highlight contradictions in the sphere of law and economic policy, whose dilemmas attracted attention for the evidence of dysfunction they could be made to furnish, fairly or not, at a deeper systemic level.

Seneca remarks that it is always easy for one false witness to discredit other true witnesses, while political bias makes judges apt to acquit a man because of dislike for those supporting him, despite a strong case to the contrary (*Ben.* 6.8.2–3; cf. Tac. *Hist.* 2.10.2: the best defense for the accused was dislike for the accuser). Changing circumstances, too, readily lead to bad laws or bad application of good ones. Livy records a measure proposed at an earlier stage of Roman history specifically to punish those who did not mutiny in order to whitewash those who did (7.41.48). That is the kind of incoherence which became a focus of what seemed wrong with the Principate. When people justly convicted of bribery under Nero were later pardoned, the original charge was strengthened retroactively to treason so as to justify pardon on the grounds that treason had often been a *false* charge under Nero. The result, Tacitus complains, was to render a perfectly sound law against bribery useless by misuse of another sound one against treason (*Hist.* 1.77.3).

Along with his normal disgust at civil violence, there is perhaps an additional, deeper point to Tacitus' remark that since the army sacking Cremona included men from many different places with wholly different customs, "no crime was illegal" (*Hist.* 3.33.2). Beyond the touch of conventional rhetorical hyperbole, this readily brings to mind more serious reflections about the nature of law and order, for example, that the incoherence into which Roman society had slipped in a sense *did* decriminalize crime. The effect is much like that in the deeper second thought of Tacitus' complaint that "you would think people liked

141

Nero's performances—and maybe they *did*" (*Ann.* 16.4.4). The proscriptions gave rise to a similarly puzzling legal loop formed when criminal behavior *is* the law, for in a revolutionary situation it did make strange sense that people killed in error should be put belatedly on the list as though they were still alive, so their deaths could be regularized (App. *BCiv.* 4.2.7; Plut. *Sull.* 32.2; cf. offers of clemency or choice of method for suicide extended by the emperor—posthumously).

"Since demanding interest and making it usurious is unknown [in Germany], [ignorance of usury is preserved, and usury itself] is avoided [*servatur*] better than if it were forbidden" (Tac. *Germ.* 26.1). If this is "a rather absurd remark," it is so by design and only in a very special sense.[1] The extreme compression in *servatur,* combining positive and negative meanings, marks the intrinsic antinomy in law as such and its relation to morality touched on earlier by Tacitus in the *Germania* (19: "plus ibi boni mores valent quam alibi bonae leges") or in the equally "absurd" epigram about Rome, "earlier troubled by crime, now by laws" (Tac. *Ann.* 3.25.1; cf. 3.27.2 on accumulation of contradictory laws). Insofar as laws are a sign as well as a cause of something amiss, their absence may afford more protection than their presence, and the same paradox is the subject of an analysis of sumptuary legislation (*Ann.* 3.52–54), fittingly made by Tiberius, who in many ways embodies deeply intractable aspects of government for Tacitus. The antinomy lies in the impossible choices to be made when solutions are themselves problems. Tiberius reflects that people who demand effective laws complain about repression as soon as the laws are passed; as a body in bad shape needs (but cannot endure) tough measures (cf. Livy, pref. 9), once attitudes have become part of the problem, the vicious circle (*corruptus simul et corruptor,* Tac. *Ann.* 54.1; *colere et coli,* 55.2) is practically impenetrable. It is better therefore not to legislate behavior at all, "because if you want to do what is not yet forbidden, you may fear [that if you do it] you will be forbidden; but if you do it with impunity, neither fear nor shame is left" (Tac. *Ann.* 54.2). Innate caution, that is to say, keeps people from doing everything they might do, but once they know that they can, there is no reason for restraint. Law entails enforcement, and if that fails, the law in effect invites what it forbids. Like St. Paul, Tacitus' Tiberius sees that regulation may succeed only in revealing how bad people are.[2]

The same legal issue comes up in a passage of Dio suggesting bafflement about how to cope with conflicting tendencies at work in Roman society (56.25.7). Since some knights had taken up fighting as gladiators in defiance of the disenfranchisement it entailed, the penalty was removed in the hope that either decriminalization or the greater penalty of possible death in the arena would have a deterrent effect. On the principle again that laws may actually stimulate the behavior they try to discourage, it was perhaps hoped that a deterrent effect in the first alternative would come from a sense of shame induced by the absence of legal penalty. So far as the grimmer, more realistic second case is concerned, lethal self-correction according to Dio was in fact effective, owing to the participants' suicidal urge, nourished by public passion, including the emperor's, for combat.[3]

Nero gave large sums of money to friends, who were then required after his fall to return 90 percent. Though little was left, and some were without any tangible property at all because they had squandered everything, forced auctions of what could be recovered did at least ensure that those enriched by Nero would now be as poor as those from whom he had stolen (Tac. *Hist.* 1.20). Some time later, the remainder of what had been raised by auction and not turned over to the treasury was awarded to people recalled from exile, but as most of the liquidated property had again already been spent, this time by the government, the award was practically worthless (1.90). The point of these relatively unimportant details in the context of a major political crisis lies in the pattern of futility they form, underscored by the delayed reaction created through a narrative gap between the two passages. The small remainder of wealth unjustly received and then irresponsibly consumed by others is liquidated, justly enough, but only to create a second, equally impoverished group. Once recovered, even this small amount is mostly spent by the state, whose worthless reparation to recalled exiles leaves yet one more set of losers.

In less serious cases, legal gridlock easily yields absurdity. If the charge that a head of Tiberius had been placed on a statue of Augustus (Tac. *Ann.* 1.74.4) posed the dilemma of offending Tiberius if it was taken off or Augustus if it was left on, then Tiberius' angry outburst was directed at the whole impossible situation, as the strange opening lines in a letter sent to the Senate may also have been, though Tacitus and Suetonius take them as a sign of moral collapse: "I'll be damned more than I am damned if I know what to write or how to write or what not to write to you" (Tac. *Ann.* 6.6.1; Suet. *Tib.* 67.1).[4]

Addendum 2: Orgiastic Violence

Political violence at the end of the Republic, particularly during the proscriptions, became a staple of historiographic rhetoric, with Marius' blood frenzy setting records only to be bettered by Sulla and those who came after him (Dio 30–35.102.10–12; Diod. Sic. 38–39.4; Plut. *Mar.* 43–44; App. *BCiv.* 1.8.71–75). Foreign enemies, too, were butchered on a lavish scale, either in battlefield slaughter or in terroristic public executions, with the same aim of intimidation that ferocity in civil war had. An exceptionally brutal instance is the treatment of forty-five hundred prisoners who were tied in groups of thirty to stakes in the Forum, beaten, then cut on the tendon at the back of the neck, dragged outside the city (still living?) like broken dolls, and left to the dogs and birds (Dion. Hal. 20.16.2). Exaggeration aside, it appears that in the grip of what Livy terms "sweet rage" *(dulcedo irae)* the Romans would on occasion kill humans and animals alike in captured cities (Livy 9.14.11–13, 28.20.6–7, cf. 41.18.3–4 [where first everything alive is killed, then everything else is smashed; cf. Suet. *Iul.* 75.3; Polyb. 10.15.5]). The Germanic custom of annihilating entire defeated armies down to the last man and destroying all of the booty (Tac. *Ann.* 13.57.2; cf. Orosius *History* 5.16) seems to have been a more strongly sacrificial version of excess violence on principle, so to say (cf. Thuc. 7.29.4).

In descriptions of mutilation during mob action or desperate combat, the historians often mention not only gouging of eyes but biting or "eating" (Polyb. 15.33.5–10; Diod. Sic. 27.4.4; Livy 22.51.9; Tac. *Hist.* 4.42.2; Dio 59.29.7, 68.32.1, cf. 71.4.1). Sulla had heads brought to him to "devour" with his eyes, since he would not venture actually to use his teeth (Val. Max. 9.2.1). If the turn of phrase is rhetorical, there is no reason to dismiss the reality it dramatizes. A connection between eating and violence comes up again when Antony is said to have kept Cicero's head in sight of his dining table (App. *BCiv.* 4.4.20; cf. Sen. *Ep.* 83.25), perhaps for reasons having something to do with the Italian practice of including gladiatorial matches in entertainment at banquets. Cannibalistic rage appears also in accounts of Vitellius' and Otho's brutality (Suet. *Vit.* 14.2; Tac. *Hist.* 1.44.1), and Dio himself does not hesitate to talk of his own "desire to eat the emperor's flesh" (58.17.1; Sen. *De Ira* 3.4.2; Sen. *Clem.* 1.25.1).[1]

Stories of exotic brutality in earlier Roman history occasionally sound like those told later about the emperors. After more stakes had been put up than condemned men could be found, bystanders were grabbed at random to make up the difference (Dio 30–35.104.6; cf. 59.10.3), while Lucius Flamininus had a prisoner killed at a banquet merely to entertain a boy favorite or a mistress who had never seen a man die (Plut. *Flam.* 18.2–5; Plut. *Cat. Mai.* 17.2–4; cf. Livy 39.42.5–43). Valerius Maximus has a separate category for atrocity (9.2).[2]

On a purely psychological level, such binges can be understood as expending unused emotional firepower or, perhaps better, as running a victory lap: after the hypertension of acute danger in combat, killing at leisure helps wind down angry fear and permits those who have survived to enjoy the luxury of participating in death with impunity (as gladiatorial shows permitted vicarious participation in equally "spectacular" violence).[3] In discussing the dehumanizing effect of atrocities at some length, Polybius speaks of the uncontrollable, self-sustaining escalation which accompanied them (1.79.4–81.11, 82.2, 86.6–7), and Dio remarks that the man who kills thinks for a moment that he is immortal (the victim isn't thinking anything; 47.44.4). Polybius, however, says little about why escalation occurs, and Dio has what he regards as normal combat in mind. The psychopathology of violence is of much greater prominence in Seneca, who distinguishes atrocity *(feritas)* from anger proper *(De Ira* 2.5). The latter leads to atrocity when it is gratuitous (2.33, 3.14–21) or seizes entire groups in mindless violence (1.2.3, 3.2.2–6; cf. Tac. *Hist.* 3.84.2–3). Though dealing most directly with the moral and psychological dimensions of anger, Seneca is in fact concerned with violence more generally, inasmuch as the behavior of angry autocrats is apt to be public behavior. Unlimited power, moreover, is often tied to unlimited luxury, which, in turn, fosters the unreasonable *ira* (2.25.4, 3.40.2–5; Sen. *Ep.* 47.19, 95.32), whose excessive violence combined with conspicuous expenditure of wealth comes to expression publicly in the arena as well. In Seneca's *De clementia* 2.4, *crudelitas* is excessive but still rational violence directed against crime, whereas *feritas* is insanity, violence for its own sake, without reason and with no profit *(compendium)* in view.

Amplified violence is a theme again in accounts of mass suicide. Juba had a great pyre built on which he planned to immolate himself, his family, and some fellow citizens (Pseudo-Caesar *African War* 91); in another instance suicide along with destruction of property on a pyre is carried out after a luxurious banquet (Livy 26.13; cf. Sall. *Iug.* 76.6). As symbolic acts of arson in conjunction with suicide, funeral pyres express the external aggression that may accompany self-destruction (cf. Diod. Sic. 2.27.2, 38–39.2.2 [killing oneself by burning a house down], 25.17). This blend of destructive rage and defiance is no less intense in individuals like Caecilius Agricola, who went home after he had been condemned, drank his fill of cool wine, smashed all his expensive drinking cups, and then cut his arteries (Dio 76.5.6; cf. Suet. *Ner.* 47.1; Pliny *HN* 37.29). In various societies mass suicide frequently took on horrendous proportions, embracing the death of leaders along with wives, children, and citizens at large (App. *Hisp.* 6.33; App. *BCiv.* 1.10.94, 2.10.64; Florus 1.34.15, 1.38.17, 2.33.50; Amm. Marc. 24.4.25; Diod. Sic. 25.17; Livy 26.13–14, 28.23.2–3; Plut. *Mar.* 27.2–3; Plut. *Brut.* 31.2–4; Plut. *Sull.* 14.4). Perhaps the oddest case is the decision of the Abydians, sealed by a curse on those who backed out, to kill their wives and children and then fight to the death. Though Philip captured the city before the plan could be carried out fully, so astonished was he by the defenders' continuing death frenzy that he granted a three-day period of grace, as it were, for those who still wanted to kill themselves. Many, including whole families, did so (Polyb. 16.31–34; cf. Livy 21.14.1, 31.17.4–18.9). It is unclear to Tacitus whether a freedman of Agrippina who killed himself when she died acted "through love or fear" (*Ann.* 14.9.2), and complex currents of guilt, despair, fear, defiance, and humiliation must have been at work also in mass killings of the kind carried out by Britons against wives and children, "as though in pity" (Tac. *Agr.* 38.1).[4]

In suicide by contagion among troops at the death of an emperor or general (e.g., Plut. *Otho* 15.3, 17.4–5 [where they are affected by *perimanēs erōs*]), the impulse is further strengthened by oaths of devotion to a leader (e.g., Dio 53.20.2–4). Vows not to survive the emperor made by individuals to divert danger from him when he was ill (Suet. *Calig.* 14.2, 27.2) together with their military counterparts, vows to die with one's commander (Plut. *Sert.* 14.4–5; Plut. *Crass.* 29.7; Caes. *BGall.* 3.22; Amm. Marc. 21.5.10), were more formal versions of *devotio*, which itself in one account assumes the strange form of a suicidal *request* for decimation by shamefaced troops (Plut. *Ant.* 44.3).

Though some of these cases represent sheer hysteria, others have a deliberate political rationale. Some suicides were acts of defiance, while massive violence against defeated enemies had an obvious deterrent effect. During the proscriptions terror came close to public policy, as often happens during revolution. Officially posting the names of condemned persons under the forms of normal bureaucratic procedure was without precedent (Dio 30–35.109; Plut. *Sull.* 30–32; Florus 2.9.25), but it soon became an even worse unprecedented precedent in later upheavals, when proscription had been transformed into deliberate policy (Dio 47.3–6; App. *BCiv.* 4.3–6, on the often grotesque situations arising from licensed brutality).[5]

Whatever guise it took, spectacular violence—in the original sense of "violence meant to be seen"—was in part driven by the same intention to engage public attention through escalating scale and intensity that played a central role in the arena. Violence was meant to be seen because it was meant to convey a message; to ensure that it did, it had to be conspicuous, and in functioning as a semantic marker, incongruity by way of excess was as essential to the meaning of public violence as queer signs were to divination. "The marvellousness [unbelievability] of an event, however, does not unfit it for use in communication. If you want to send a message, you must ensure that its recipient realises a message is being sent. Often enough you and the recipient will have some established convention so that he will know in advance where to be looking. But if not, you will have to make your message eye-catching and spectacular for it to catch his attention. You must, in short, aim to produce *miratio*."[6] A jangling emergency bell, though primarily warning of another disturbance, does so by itself first being disturbing.

Violent responses, too, are effective because their frightfulness shows something *terribly* powerful and terribly *drastic* being done. Need for drastic action, which may lead to the selection of surprising targets, explains tendencies to suicidal behavior. Suicide itself is the most extreme response to the threat of violence and can be displaced onto precious, normally sacrosanct objects whose voluntary destruction is an outlet for anger. In a more recent instance from San Salvador, during a severe drought in 1884 the town council decreed that if rain did not appear within eight days, no one would go to mass or say prayers; that in another eight days, all churches would be burned and rosaries destroyed; that in still another eight, all priests and nuns would be beheaded. In addition, "for the present, permission is given for the commission of all sorts of sin in order that the Supreme Creator may understand with whom he has to deal."[7]

Intense violence, then, including the variety encountered in the arena, meant what it meant by doing most spectacularly, emphatically, or absurdly what it did. The gap between message and action was bridged in part psychologically through the magical thinking, particularly potent in performance of public ritual, by which one's own actions seem to compel those of others.[8] Sociologically, the efficacy of games is perhaps better explained via performative acts and statements which immediately *do* what they are or say. As the validity of "I now pronounce you husband and wife" lies in the social system defining marriage, so the efficacy of public violence in the arena sprang from its own ceremonial authority and specifically from its high intensity. In this connection, S. J. Tambiah has proposed redefining the notion of sympathetic magic as "persuasively analogical" ritual which does not cause or predict but encourages results.[9] The "analogical transfer of qualities" effected in *munera,* then, would be achieved through the stylized shouting and body language of highly excited crowds, especially when they held power of life or death over combatants.

What *munera* did, performatively, was to define and legitimate public violence against outsiders, and the specifically psychological effect of this is J. Elster's mass, quasi-magical consciousness that groups have of their own (omnipotent) authority, which may well have been reinforced for some of those present by murky feelings about real (magical) effects of the passions they felt. By indeed destroying marginal people in a most direct way, brutality in the arena would readily appear to deal convincingly with threats to public security on other, more symbolic and persuasive levels.

Addendum 3: The Ambivalent Triumph

"Very great power is never secure" (Tac. *Hist.* 2.92.1), and so displaying even its unquestioned forms had special hazards. In taking advantage of a triumph to deter further opposition, Caesar paraded pictures of various opponents committing suicide, but the fear this caused also aroused potentially dangerous resentment (App. *BCiv.* 2.15.101; cf. Dio 43.24.1). Since the implicit threat to others posed by triumphal displays during civil war was apt to renew the original danger whose removal was being celebrated, such triumphs were handled with great circumspection. Mucianus was careful to use his success in foreign campaigns as a pretext for celebrating victory in civil strife (Tac. *Hist.* 4.4.2), while Tiberius, in turning down the idea of dedicating a temple to Mars Ultor with a new altar of Vengeance, remarked that foreign victories are to be celebrated, civil losses concealed (Tac. *Ann.* 3.18.2; cf. Cic. *Phil.* 14.22–23; Dio 51.19.5; Val. Max. 2.8.7). Pretense, however, was not easy to maintain, especially since true feelings traditionally came out at times of celebration. Thus the loss implicit in victory during civil war was turned into an awkward jest about Realpolitik in a chant of Caesar's troops: "If you do right, you will be punished; if you do wrong, you will be king" (Dio 43.20.3). In a variant from earlier Roman history extending the dilemma to war as such, the younger generation refused to recognize the success of a general who had his son executed for breaches in discipline (Manlius: Val. Max. 9.3.4; Livy 8.12.1), and the issue appears in another guise in the ongoing discussion of Horatius' execution (or murder) of his sister and the behavior of their father, who had not only joined in condemning her but also celebrated a triumph (Dion. Hal. 3.21.10, 22.3–10; cf. Torquatus: Dio 7 Zonaras 7.26).

Anticipating the pity aroused by Perseus' children and the death of the victorious Paulus' own sons, Plutarch focuses on the disturbing sight and harsh sound of captured weapons in the parade and on the unpleasantly martial, rather than civic, trumpet blast (*Aem.* 32.4, 33.1). Elsewhere Plutarch distinguishes the specifically bloody victory celebrated by triumphs from the peaceful ovation marking successful negotiations (*Marc.* 22), a distinction confirmed by Aulus Gellius (Gell. *NA* 5.6.21–23). An award of one or the other was influenced by political alliances or considerations of prestige, with unworthy enemies such as pirates or slaves meriting only an ovation. But the cost of victory was also a crucial factor reflecting the ambivalence of war itself. A triumph might be denied either because the cost of victory had been too high or because it was not high enough. In the former event victory seems shocking, in the latter disappointing, and both together reveal the dilemma that achievement in war is bound to cost too much. If the cost is low, success merits only an ovation. But a triumph means that success was expensive, a general rule acknowledged by Paulus' diversion of the heavy costs of victory onto himself through the moral equivalent of *devotio* (Val. Max. 5.10.2), so that the loser (Perseus) still had his children after Paulus' own had died (Livy 45.40.7–41.12; Plut. *Aem.* 35–36; Sen. *Ad Marciam* 13.3; Dio 20 Zonaras 9.24; Diod. Sic. 31.11). Camillus gets off much more lightly when he merely stumbles after offering a prayer for minimal consequences to himself and to Rome, though the mishap was later taken as an omen of his own condemnation and the fall of Rome (Livy 5.21.14–16; Val. Max. 1.5.2; Dion. Hal. 12.14.2; Plut. *Cam.* 5.5–7; cf. Frontin. *Str.* 4.5.14).

At bottom, the problem these stories address is one that reappears in divination: experience teaches us not to trust even our most masterful moments, whose uncertainty is measured by capricious oracles, riddling signs, and vague suspicions about divine malice. Any feelings of extraordinary power that might have been inspired by ill-defined ideas about a triumphator's divine status would also have been reminders of ordinary human vulnerability.[1] Not confidence but fear of the evil eye *(invidia)* is at work in Camillus' prayer that coming disaster be limited in scope, "if [my success] seems too much to any god or man." When his triumph did seem to show excessive confidence, public anxiety was duly aroused (Livy 5.23.5–6). Vaguely religious instincts along these lines perhaps still played some part in more narrowly political considerations of the kind that Pompey had in mind when he deprecated a triumph even for foreign conquests in view of the fear that had been caused by the power of Marius and Sulla (Dio 37.20.6).

Apotropaic features had a role in normal triumphs, and counterweighting of a sense of achievement was even more in evidence at public funerals, naturally a time for mourning as well as praising a man who had once been a triumphator but now was dead. In Dio's eyewitness account of Pertinax's funeral, the ceremony surrounding the wax effigy of the deceased dressed in triumphal clothing dramatically illustrates the complex interplay between life and death, strength and weakness (75.4–5.5). When Augustus' body, too, was hidden in a coffin placed beneath his wax image, again dressed in victor's garb, emphasis lay on success and life, but something less reassuring came out as recipients threw triumphal awards received during his regime on the pyre (Dio 56.34.1, 42.2). Earlier, at the funeral combat honoring Agrippa, Augustus alone had worn white, and everyone else had worn black (Dio 55.8.5). Dressed though his image still was in triumphal symbols, Augustus, too, was now dead. Recognition of dependence on achievements by the surrender of triumphal awards acknowledges the fragility even of supreme human power, here discarded in retrospective ritual, as its symbols were lost prospectively in death portents such as the inscription torn from a triumphal statue during a storm and deposited on a tomb (Suet. *Dom.* 15.2).[2]

Already during the triumph itself, prudent, if not exactly anxious, honor was paid also to the gods for success (Livy 28.9.7, 37.59.1, 38.44.10). Mars' impartiality was as much threat as promise (42.14.4), hence the troubled thoughts prompted by a departing consul about the uncertainty of wár and the possibility that victory would go to the other side (42.49). It is at the moment of supreme triumph over Carthage that Scipio pronounced a *memento mori* on Rome (Polyb. 38.22; App. *Pun.* 19.132).

The same ambivalence, transmitted from war and triumph to combat in the arena, was then enshrined in Nemesis' connection with the amphitheater. After surveying various proposals, M. Hornum concludes that as goddess of punishment for wrongdoing, she represents the power of the state demonstrated in *munera*. While this is what she could mean to public officials, a different view was taken by participants, for whom, against the background of life or death put at stake again and again, the bringer of vengeance might suggest the capriciousness of success.[3] If administrators, then, saw a divine patron of law and order, individuals were concerned more directly though a good deal less confidently with survival, and soldiers' private dedications to Nemesis in legionary amphitheaters permit some conjecture about this personal dimension. The dedication to Nemesis by a trooper on his discharge may well be not only "gratitude for a successful career," as Hornum suggests, but also gratitude for survival of dangers epitomized in arena games. Hazards of combat and the fickleness of Fate, at any rate, are the final message on the stele of a gladiator who, having died in his eighth match, advises those still alive "not to have faith in Nemesis—that is how I was deceived." The vision that led to another dedication by a centurion in the amphitheater was perhaps an anxiety dream; in Artemidorus, as Hornum notes, the dream appearance of Nemesis is ominous when it occurs before important undertakings.[4]

Display of genuine success in triumphs lent itself readily to propagandistic shows of false success, which invited exposure as an attempt to deny or conceal the real trouble that triumphs in fact dealt with, and at a real price. Tacitus portrays a touch of hysteria in the *esplosione di folle festività* by which Nero reassured both himself and the public after his mother's death.[5] The psychoanalytic axiom that prohibition implies desire to do what is prohibited finds a political analogue in shows of power overcompensating for fear of weakness. Celebrations for Nero's escape from Agrippina are characterized by Tacitus as a rich mixture of fear and hypocrisy on the public's part, with guilt in addition on Nero's own (*Ann.* 14.10, 13.2). Anxiety, not confidence, is again betrayed by portents reported at the time (12.2), and games given after the great fire had several defensive aims: to distract public attention (cf. Dio 54.17.5), to address guilt and fear by calling on the gods, and to provide therapeutic violence against Christians (Tac. *Ann.* 15.44–47). The anxiety and anger this injected into the occasion, however, were so misdirected that they led to pity for Nero's victims, and lack of confidence in the regime then further deepened when an attempted breakout of gladiators gave rise to terrified public preoccupation with revolution, much talk of Spartacus, and reports of more gloomy portents. It is true that the atmosphere of hectic celebration as it is described in the *Annals* reflects Tacitus' own estimate of anxieties that may well not have been so obvious or widespread. His remark that what once was a sign of public success now was one of public calamity (14.64.3) is more epigrammatic judgment than report, but there seems to be no reason to discount entirely the consciousness of disorder which Roman institutions could fuel as well as allay and which seems to have colored public displays more deeply than usual at the time. Discovery of the Pisonian conspiracy again called for augmented games (*Ann.* 15.74.1) as much to minimize further danger through a show of force as to celebrate escape from it. A temple was vowed defensively to Salus and the weapon intended for use against the emperor dedicated hopefully to Jupiter the Avenger.

Caligula and Domitian were accused of celebrating triumphs unjustified or tricked out so shamelessly with false signs of success that the emperor's real vulnerability seemed to constitute the primary motive. Fake prisoners of war (Suet. *Calig.* 45, 47; Tac. *Agr.* 39.1), for example, could represent anything from anxious propaganda to wishful thinking.[6] An elaborate triumph of Gallienus sought to "confirm what was pretended" (Aur. Vict. *Caes.* 33.15; *Hist. Aug. Gallieni Duo* 9.1: "With this parade the fool believed that he was deceiving the Roman people"). Though he was in a dangerous position, it is not clear that the show of power was intended to create a false impression, and that notion may be hindsight on the part of the historians, for whom a connection between triumph and weakness, however, seemed plausible. The sense of danger ordinarily only implicit amid feelings of confidence at authentic triumphs was so overt on this occasion that it inspired cynical jesting about the emperor's failures, as wits in the crowd had earlier called Domitian's false triumphs "funeral celebrations" because of their high cost (Dio 67.9.6; cf. Pliny *Pan.* 16.3).

Expressions of disenchantment with military glory in poetry are a somewhat different, though related case (Hor. *Odes* 1.35.4: *superbos vertere funeribus triumphos;* Prop. 3.5.15: *victor cum victis pariter miscebitur umbris: / consule cum Mario, capte Jugurtha, sedes* [compare the paradox of the victorious but dead athlete or gladiator]; Ov. *Am.* 1.15.4; Prop. 2.15.45, 3.18.17; Verg. *Aen.* 2.504, 10.500–505; Luc. 1.12). To emphasize this aspect of power for his own purposes, Virgil, after barely touching on the Trojans' victory and the confidence it produces in book 11 (13–21), devotes the rest of the book overwhelmingly to the cost of war. Aeneas' own mind is "bewildered by death" (3), and the funeral rites (replacing the illusory *exspectatique triumphi,* 54) along with the intense grief that accompanies them and the disaster awaiting the victorious Greeks after Troy fell (252–80) are all driven home. Such disturbing sentiments do not represent official attitudes; but neither do official attitudes represent everything that military victory meant in Roman society, while reservations do reflect recognition of the heavy cost and transience of military success.[7]

As victory and defeat, success and failure, define each other uneasily, exulting in triumph entails exulting in danger, and the unstable relationship is perhaps the background for Caligula's exultation, not in danger but in disaster. His regime, he complained, was "threatened by oblivion because of its prosperity," since it had not been made notable for any public calamity such as military or natural disasters, accidents, famine, plague, fire, or earthquake (Suet. *Calig.* 31). Demented ferocity or ferocious wit aside, Caligula knew what every reporter or historian knows: news is bad news (cf. Herostratus, the man who burned down the temple of Ephesian Artemis solely to become famous for arson; Val. Max. 8.14. ext. 5). Like those who watch or celebrate triumphs, people who hear news are survivors, they hope to remain so, and their appreciation for survival is in proportion to the degree of danger. For the same reason, rumors, the most common form of news, are generally disturbing, and bad omens, too—yet another form of news in the ancient world—were compelling in a way that good ones were not. Caligula's remark is meant by Suetonius to demonstrate monstrously petulant boredom, but disaster as a matter of fact does rivet attention, and war in particular has seemed to be one of the most compelling of dangers to many besides Romans. "For millennia humans of every station have sought to escape—no matter where—daily repetition of the same thing. It is true that one can seek change, flight and escape in private relations, in love and friendship or in personal conflict. But only the great adventure, a general moratorium of daily routine [*Moratorium des Alltags*], can bring a total revolution in life and in the order governing everyday rules: conflagrations, floods, earthquakes and other natural catastrophes and finally the curse brought on by men themselves: war—religious, ideological, national, social or however it is grounded and justified."[8]

Caligula's boredom represents at his own level the disappointment felt, at theirs, by fans at the arena or by generals denied triumph because not enough blood had been shed. His conception of noteworthy achievement is (typically) perverse, because the historically important "action" he longs for is mainly simple external violence devoid of intrinsic social significance. It is not even clear that he was fretting about lost chances for massive relief efforts mounted on occasion by emperors. Accommodation with social order, on the other hand, gives institutional violence a highly complex, ambivalent character which makes the interplay of opposites in triumphal ceremonies or arena combat difficult to understand.

T. Mitchell's examination of the sociology of bullfighting is of special interest in this connection, since the greater accessibility of *la fiesta de toros,* which has been a prominent feature in Spanish culture for centuries, helps throw light on the distinctive ambivalence of violence in *munera* as well. There is no evidence for historical derivation of one from the other, and because bullfighting has no intrinsic military component either, formal similarities to gladiatorial combat are remote. Similarity to *venationes,* on the other hand, is much closer, and though *manliness* perhaps better catches what is at stake in Spanish blood sport than does *bravery,* irrespective of the special forms that public violence takes in different cultures, the social psychology or sociopathology at work in the appeal of *gladiator, bestiarius,* and *matador* is much the same. This psychological facet falls under the last of three categories distinguished by Mitchell: belief, ritual action, and emotion. In respect to lethal games, emotion is the entertainment they afford not through mere diversion from humdrum life but by offering "ecstatic" entry into an alternative world.[9]

The elusiveness of what such escape means is due to its partially dysfunctional nature. Like all absolutes, all-absorbing passion for danger in the bullring does not admit of further explanation while at the same time finding one in (abnormal) passion for honor. Supercharged violence, which for the unsympathetic outsider seems mindless risk, for the devotee is also stylized risk and therefore a vehicle of something more than pure danger. Viewed sociologically as a spectator sport, then, gripping rehearsal of military danger in gladiatorial combat is a counterpart to the "safe [but harrowing] substitute for the real things" created by intense shared experience at bullfights. To fulfill its social function, the "pit of passion" provided by both institutions legitimates through compelling mass participation what is otherwise forbidden as well as frightening— an effect exploited for more subtle political and moral ends by the pressure Nero put on the Roman nobility to take part in his not-quite-right shows. The disgust felt by those who reject bloody games is actually shared by aficionados, who are devotees precisely because of their interest in the forbidden. The former are repelled because they are simply viewers, as Seneca at times was in the arena; the latter are attracted because they are also voyeurs. As a general proposition, interludes take their meaning from the routines they interrupt; as disgust inter- rupts and complements attraction, so fear complements and is presupposed by the sense of power aroused during *munera* and triumphs.[10]

The logic of such institutions is thus determined by the dual impulses they tap. The sadomasochistic appeal of bullring violence is liable to engender faintly hysterical instability in the spectators' response. In the sympathy for elephants showed by the crowd during a show of Pompey's, feelings normally reserved for humans suddenly veered to the animals, just as, in Spain, the normal relationship between human and animal, victor and victim, dramatically switched when a brave bull, credited with the deaths of twenty-one horses, was spared at the last minute by public demand. Suicidal urges accompanying masochistic exaltation would have appeared at Rome chiefly in those who chose to fight and were therefore motivated by something more than a desire to survive danger they could not avoid. Like compulsive gamblers who in the last resort want to lose or for whom losing at least makes no difference, players and devotees of blood sport may view losing everything as a way of winning (as Caligula in a sense did in wishing for natural disasters to make his regime interesting). A striking parallel between bullring and arena emerges in just this murky area where extreme situa- tions receive extraordinary rationalization. Mitchell cites the case of a matador "lacking in taurine skill [and] also lacking in fear, [for which] he had become the idol of the masses." In his last performance, though badly hurt, he continued and finally "saw his bull drop dead as he was being carried off to the infirmary where he died himself twenty minutes later. The public deified him overnight."[11]

This is the inherent contradiction brought out in the story of Arrachion or in epitaphs of gladiators who lost their lives in winning; the religious dimension of Arrachion's imagined entry into the abode of the Blessed reappears, too, in the vaguely religious background, bolstering both legitimacy and transcendence, created by bullfights held on the feast days of saints. In the frenzy of absolute combat, comparable to Roman martial *furor* or to what the Indo-European ber- serker felt, a matador described by Hemingway knelt to bite one of the bull's horns. The social meaning (Mitchell's "belief") of such unusual behavior centers on a supreme sense of honor *(verguenza torera, pundonor)* embodied in the fighter and taken to a fever pitch as the issue of life or death—survival of the fittest—comes to depend on a precarious balance between supreme skill and luck or between manliness at its best and cowardice at its worst.[12] The part played by the emperor in *munera* during the Empire gave a more communal and political turn to what was at stake. The coup de gràce accordingly was delivered under controlled circumstances after the issue had been decided, whereas the moment of truth for the matador can still be a moment of great danger. It is probably too much to see the interplay of skill and luck in lethal games as an allegory of free will and fate, but the latter two in point of fact are daily facts of human experience recognized by everyone at some level of consciousness, and the alternatives they represent are what make serious games absorbing.[13]

Addendum 4: Political Monstrosity

In many cultures "freak shows" are an important psychological and social medium for dealing with the threatening Other. Encountered as undeniably real, freaks are deeply disturbing, yet if they can also be made to seem ludicrous and entertaining ("sports of nature"), as abnormality is acknowledged and safely assigned a place of its own they become deeply reassuring. What matters is classification, not authenticity; fake monsters may be as effective in this regard as real ones.[1]

According to Suetonius, Augustus "would relax by playing dice, marbles or nuts with attractive little boys whom he had looked for throughout the empire. For he was repelled by dwarfs, cripples and all such creatures as offensive jokes [*ludibria*] of nature and bad omens" (*Aug.* 83). Normal little people are pleasant diversion (presumably from normal big ones), while physical abnormality is bad joke and bad omen at once, particularly for someone "deeply disturbed by *ostenta*," as Augustus was (92). Not wanting to impose his own taste on the public, he put on display a youth of respectable family less than two feet tall, weighing seventeen pounds, who had a very powerful voice (43.3). This is evidently plain theater connected with a fifty-cubit snake mentioned by Suetonius. The public was being treated to a sideshow whose appeal lay in its exorcising latent fear of abnormality through controlled public spectacles confirming the normalcy of everyone else. Where divination is believed to work, abnormality will naturally be entertaining in a peculiarly rich sense. Sideshows in effect become manmade divination in which the need for reassuring rituals of control is met all the more efficiently as society manufactures portents and then administers to itself the shock they deliver. Public display of oddities for entertainment thus fits in easily with entertaining displays of abnormal violence in the arena, where reassurance of another kind is offered. Pompey placed representations of unusual motherhood in his theater (Pliny *HN* 7.34–35), Severus Alexander made dwarfs and fools available to the public (*Hist. Aug.* 34.2), and both Strabo (15.1.73) and Dio (54.9.8) mention a gift to Augustus of a boy or man without shoulders who used his feet in place of arms. In addition to size, the uncanny impression of simultaneous youth and age that dwarfs make would have been as notionally disturbing as the infantile senility of the tiny but immensely aged Cumaean Sibyl was.[2]

Suetonius has a second story: Domitian had a habit of attending gladiatorial shows in the company of a "small boy dressed in scarlet with an ominously small or misshapen head [*parvo portentosoque capite*]. The two were frequently seen talking together, at times about serious matters of state" (*Dom.* 4.2). The abnormal size of Domitian's confidant, probably one of the house jesters in vogue at Rome, was again a socially sanctioned, amusing departure from normalcy.[3] Like people who fought in the arena, dwarfs were marginal figures, not dangerous but strange enough to create a sense of powerful incongruity which could take sinister political forms (in fact, dwarfs were used in the arena for special effects). When yet another dwarf at one of Tiberius' banquets wanted to know why a certain person charged with treason was still alive, Tiberius remonstrated with him for the insolent breach of propriety—and then shortly wrote to the Senate asking the same question (Suet. *Tib.* 61.6; cf. Dio 48.44.3; Hdn. 1.17.3; cf. Vatinius, "deformed in body and ready with offensive jests," Tac. *Ann.* 15.34.2). The queer thing such figures are *seen* to be and the out-of-order things they *say* become a sign of what the emperor's incongruous political power allows him to *do*.

The anecdote about Domitian is another instance of the bizarre behavior of bad emperors, and when it is left standing by Suetonius without explanation, we realize that pointless political absurdity could be a matter of course under the Principate. The dwarf's "portentously" hideous head then turns him into a disturbing omen, in fact into a "bad omen" of the kind that disgusted Augustus, and Suetonius' reference elsewhere to Caligula as "monstrous" (*Calig.* 22.1) or the application of "portentous" to the unfortunate Claudius by his mother (Suet. *Claud.* 3.2) has the same force. What political statement Domitian himself might have wanted to make by associating ostentatiously with the dwarf is not so clear. Perhaps it was one of the insolent gestures through which emperors displayed their power to break any norm they chose in moments of political theater. If that is so, besides being public freak show and omen, Domitian's little companion was also an instance of distinctively Roman *ludibrium*.

But it was not exclusively Roman, since curiously similar displays have occurred in recent times when their meaning was more accessible. Like the effect of surrounding oneself with obviously inferior people, the contrast with physical abnormality is liable to problematize as well as reinforce superiority. Though the ambivalent effect is difficult to measure from one society to another because of varying attitudes toward the abnormal, a powerful sense of incongruity in status is clear from the meeting between the full-size duke of Wellington and Tom Thumb, shrewdly titled "The General" by P. T. Barnum. The arrival of another imposing Barnum midget, "Commodore" Nutt, at the White House warranted interruption of a cabinet meeting during the troubled times of the Civil War, and after introductions had been made all around, the visitor traded jests with Lincoln. Tom Thumb, too, was officially received in Washington after his marriage in a fashionable New York church attended by the cream of American society. He had earlier won attention from the nobility in England, including Queen Victoria, on whose lap he was received. Barnum spoke of Tom's own "intense love of the ridiculous," and the subversive potential of such juxtapositions, which leave uncertain exactly whose stature is being measured, was noted at the time by

British critics, as it had been in Rome. One critic wrote in *Punch,* "Barnum solemnly declared . . . that his only object in taking the unhappy monstrosity to Europe was to humble crowned heads by exposing their folly and weakness, and to show them to the New World slavering over a loathsome dwarf, and enriching him with a colossal fortune." Writers at *Fraser's,* too, admitted that "by first winning approval of the elite Barnum's midget at once attacked us in our weak point—our reverence for respectability" but did not question why Tom Thumb was fascinating to tastemakers in the first place.[4]

Aside from their suggestion of insanity, reports of banquets to which Elagabalus invited eight bald, one-eyed, or otherwise handicapped people (*Hist. Aug.* 29.3) reflect the idea that nonaccountable power is best displayed through unaccountable behavior, as do the two hunchbacks smeared with mustard sauce and then displayed on a silver platter by Commodus (*Hist. Aug.* 11.2). Unresolved juxtaposition of incongruous elements—in effect, riddle without solution—is the formal principle by which surrealism defines reality itself as nonsense. "What is yellow, has four legs, two heads, and weighs 500 pounds?" (two 250-pound canaries) is not a true riddle but a surreal "catch" joke. The consciousness of what might be called terminal anomaly that was a factor in the vogue of the grotesque under some emperors is at work especially in anecdotes about lunatic behavior in high places apparently defying any sort of rationalization (e.g., Caligula braining a fellow officiant instead of the animal victim [Suet. *Calig.* 32.3] or calling a high-level night meeting because he wanted to dance [*Calig.* 54.2]).[5]

Addendum 5: Political Game Moves

Most game theory is normative, specifying what players should do, not describing what they actually do. Owing to their interest in exempla, ancient historians were inclined to think predominantly of moral norms and to pay less attention to the political reasonableness even of objectionable behavior imposed by circumstances. It is true that Dio sees in the elaborate incoherence of Tiberius' attitude toward Sejanus a strategy designed to paralyze reaction (58.6.4), and Tacitus realizes that Tiberius' reluctance to assume power could have been a clever way to lure senators into betraying their true feelings (*Ann.* 1.7.7), a ploy called *impudentissimus mimus* by Suetonius (*Tib.* 24.1). But such moves are principally taken as evidence for personal dishonesty. Everything Tiberius does seems sinister and devious, and he acts that way because what is done by the people he deals with seems sinister and devious to him. The practical consequences of that pattern for candor and trust were plain enough, its theoretical dimensions less so. Considerations of genuine pathology aside, some of the emperors' apparently unreasonable behavior must have been a strategy for leverage in a difficult situation. "It is not a universal advantage in situations of conflict to be inalienably and manifestly rational in decision and motivation," writes T. Schelling.[1] Valerius Maximus (7.4.5) has a military application of the rule: after Metellus marched his troops around Spain at random until no one knew what he was up to, he pounced on a city that he had been unable to take and that had become careless.

Unaccountable behavior may be a method of circumventing rules fostered by the rules themselves. J. Elster writes,

> When a person guided by a code of honour [e.g., for gaining vengeance] has a quarrel with one who is exclusively motivated by rational considerations, the first will often have his way. But in a quarrel between two persons guided by the code, both may do worse than if they had agreed to let the legal system or the council of elders resolve their conflict. . . . For this reason, mafiosi seem to do better for themselves in the United States, where they can exploit the rationality of ordinary people (or of other criminals), than in Sicily, where they meet people who share their values. . . . One cannot rationally decide to behave irrationally, even when one knows that it would

be in one's interest to do so. One can try to appear irrational without really being irrational, but in practice the real thing is usually more convincing.[2]

It is impossible to tell where the line at Rome ran. Both parties were guided by the same code, and both did indeed do worse than they might have, not least because the council of elders was one party to the conflict, not a third party or mediator.

Even when it misreads possibilities along this line, the hostile historical tradition still provides ample raw material for a game-theoretical reading of power's being deployed in devious ways from positions of (apparent) strength or (apparent) weakness.[3] A more familiar tactic than deliberately erratic behavior for getting one's way is threatening to resign on the grounds that one cannot get one's way. The most spectacular and successful example in Roman history is the secession of the plebs (e.g., Plut. *Coriolanus* 6). It may be a hazardous move. In a case mentioned by Ammianus Marcellinus, a proprefect who threatens to resign succeeds only in bringing himself into danger and, after failing to solve the problem more directly by assassination, commits suicide (14.5.7–8). Consideration given briefly to abdication by Claudius, who sometimes was not quite certain whether he actually was or even should be emperor (Tac. *Ann.* 11.31.1; Suet. *Claud.* 35.2), is attributed not to tactical considerations but to fear (Dio 60.15.4), whereas in Suetonius, Nero deliberately tries to lessen his mother's influence by pretending to have abdication in mind and thereby bring *invidia* on her (*Ner.* 34.1).

The gambit naturally is riskier when indispensability is used to prepare for, rather than to confirm, power. Velleius treats Tiberius' retirement to Rhodes as high-minded concern about the effect of his own prestige on the younger heirs-apparent (Vell. Pat. 2.99.2), while Dio (55.9.7) and Tacitus (*Ann.* 1.53.1, 6.51.2) treat it as exile due partly to complications from his relationship with Julia. Among the reasons mentioned by Suetonius is one with a more specifically tactical aim: if Tiberius could avoid being taken for granted as a player on the political scene at Rome, he would be in a better position to exploit opportunities when they came along. When Augustus in fact became ill, Tiberius paused on the way to Rhodes, but he had to set out again despite unfavorable winds to scotch rumors about his real intentions (*Tib.* 10–11). In view of Poppaea's position at Rome as First Tart (*principale scortum;* Tac. *Hist.* 1.13.3), her rare public appearances and then only with partly veiled face "so as not to become too common a sight or because it flattered her" were an application of the same strategy (on distance lending enchantment, see Tac. *Hist.* 2.83.1; on the value of not becoming old news, see Livy 35.10.6).

A cluster of other moves, closely related to resignation or withdrawal through their common strategy of backing into power, come up from time to time in the writings of the historians. Reluctance to take power, for example, is a less aggressive way to achieve the same effect that threatening to resign has. Wanting the title *rex,* Caesar refused to accept it in order to show that he did in fact want it (by plainly inviting others to press it on him), as became clear when those who enforced his ban on its use were accused of starting rumors that he did want it and therefore were removed so he could accede reluctantly to demands which now would indeed be pressed on him (App. *BCiv.* 2.16.108). Under Tiberius, Junius Blaesus refused the proconsulate—but not so strongly that he could not be persuaded to take it (Tac. *Ann.* 3.35.3). Tiberius himself was talked into power, in the view of some, honestly (Vell. Pat. 2.124.2), but even if his reservations about taking office after Augustus' death were perfectly candid, they were interpreted at the time as tactical retreat for strategic advance. Tacitus remarks that Tiberius' talk of republican restoration appeared bitterly amusing to some (*Ann.* 4.9.1) because it was taken as an insincere move. His aversion to accepting power looked like a maneuver to pressure the Senate into granting him—and thus really augmenting—power he already had (*Ann.* 1.7 and 11; Suet. *Tib.* 24). If Tiberius was motivated by fear, his offer to share power could have been perfectly honest, but when Suetonius says that he used various strategies to delay immediate threats from Germanicus and others (Suet. *Tib.* 25), it is clear that his fear is supposed to be fear of losing power, not of the dangers posed by having it. Disparity between fact and appearance in such matters was a natural occasion for irony, intended or not. Caesar wanted power to act as he saw fit granted formally by the Senate, though he was already exercising it owing to his victory (Dio 42.20.1), and he expressed gratitude when it was granted (46.47.1; cf. the mocking request by the Parthians for what they had already taken from Rome, Tac. *Ann.* 15.25.1).

Readiness to take on difficult jobs is a more direct move and for that reason actually a good deal more subtle than resignation or reluctance, since its overtness is likely to disarm suspicion. Augustus' indispensability is tied to the interest others have in letting someone else bear the burdens of office (Dio 56.39.5), an apparent imposition elsewhere clearly recognized as a way for ambitious people to achieve power (43.18.3). Tarquin, too, was supposed to have gained influence by doing hard jobs, leaving easy ones and praise to others (Dio 2.9.2–4; cf. Dion. Hal. 10.58.3). The genuine talent and devotion this strategy requires often make those who employ it sinister figures; Sejanus is a notable example (Vell. Pat. 2.127–28). One of Pompey's speeches in Dio (36.25–26) shows him carefully appearing not to want what he did want in order to avoid arousing jealous opposition (36.24.6, 36.45.1), as Otho did from Laco and Icelus because they favored not just someone else but anyone other than him (Tac. *Hist.* 1.13.2). The immediate result was a proposal that Pompey be forced to take power, though his anger at the tasks loaded onto him offended even his friends for its pretense (Plut. *Pomp.* 30.5–6). Caesar, too, in justifying aggression against the Germans, told his officers that aggrandizement requires painful effort, which then merely attracts jealous hostility from those who enjoy its advantages (Dio 38.39–40; cf. 43.18.3). Once power had been won, Augustus camouflaged it under stern duty in the same way by reserving for himself key provinces, on the grounds that ruling them was more demanding, and gave easier ones to the Senate (Dio 53.12).

Insofar as refusing or resigning power in order to solidify a position works only when power is there to begin with, the move amounts to a curious variant of *clementia,* effective for being taken as much as an implicit threat as an offer. During the earlier Principate, proposals to restore republican government had the effect of veiling the necessity—and, more subtly, the threat and reality—of imperial power. Suetonius represents Augustus as reluctant to abandon power out of fear not only for himself but also for Rome (*Aug.* 28.1), and in Dio his position is so strong that he can turn power—which he fully intends to hold despite its risks (53.8.6, 9.3)—into proof that an offer he makes to retire must be genuinely disinterested (53.6.3–4). The argument is a tour de force, pushing clemency (53.4.1–2, 7.2) to the point not merely of refraining from exercise of power but of abandoning it altogether in order to force the Senate to press it upon him (53.7.4; in 53.11 various involuted strategies at work in Augustus' public stance are traced with the utmost analytic precision). The offer was rejected, and acceptance of an offer to share power made later by Tiberius was again shown to be impermissible under the rules of the Principate. For the emperor would then have to give the game away by displaying his real monopoly of power, and the opposition was in fact forced to retreat in embarrassment (Dio 57.2.5–7; Tac. *Ann.* 1.12).

Emperors are embarrassed when their offer to the Senate is accepted; its offers of titles to good emperors, on the other hand, may be modestly refused or deferred (e.g., *Hist. Aug.* Marcus Antoninus 9.1–4), and the game is then entirely inverted once more when a bad emperor (Commodus) accepts titles *(Pius, Felix)* offered by the Senate—but in mockery (*Hist. Aug.* 8.1 and 9). An offer of resignation may be turned down for several reasons: to keep someone's service, to demonstrate control, to stifle protest. The first is the Senate's motive vis-à-vis Augustus; the last two are Nero's when Seneca tries to withdraw from public life.

Refusing power became part of conventional political ritual to help paper over the naked force and ambition through which succession was actually effected. Chances for misunderstanding and confusion on all sides were high. When Maximinus, for example, "either not knowing what was going on or himself the secret planner," was offered the crown by his troops, he first refused, but on being threatened with death, he "accepted the honor" (Hdn. 6.8.5–6; Amm. Marc. 20.4.17, 20.8.10; Livy 7.39.14; Plut. *Galba* 10.2; Tac. *Hist.* 2.51 [escape by a back door]). Devious move and countermove could finally make it impossible even for those involved to know exactly where power lay. To coerce Gordian into office, the strategy of "assume power or die" is formally spelled out by one of the players in Herodian's version. At first thinking mistakenly that men who had burst into his room with drawn swords meant to kill him, Gordian soon learned that he was indeed in danger, faced with choosing between a present and clear threat of death or future, uncertain, but encouraging prospects if he joined the rebellion (7.5.3–6; *Hist. Aug.* Gordiani Tres 8.6). The force of the demand is further bolstered when the intruders claim to be no less ready to die themselves than to kill him, since one desperate act calls for another. That move utilizes an implicit threat of suicide to create a classic instance of bridge burning, with the reluctant nominee—as much deprived of alternatives as his nominators are—simultaneously co-opted into the group and threatened by it, in greater danger from his supporters than from potential enemies.

Caesar found it much easier to avoid the trap of being coerced into dependence on others. After strengthening his own position by expressing readiness to die rather than submit to pressure from mutinous troops, he weakened their leverage by treating the threat they posed as unconvincing because they had as much to lose as he did (Dio 41.26–34). Threats of assassination against candidates unwilling to take power thus contrast with invitations to assassination (or threats to resign, such as Augustus') by emperors to confirm power they actually have, while the threat to Caesar and the counterthreat or bluff by him combine elements from both. When political suicide is factored into these gambits, violence done to oneself inverts violence done to the emperor, and that, in turn, is reversed into an odd self-assassination when it is the emperor who kills himself, as Otho does. These interlocking and paired alternative moves are represented by the weapons themselves in the claims that a senator had brought a sword into the Senate house and that poison had been found in his own home (Tac. *Ann.* 4.21.2). Assassination is linked to suicide insofar as poison could just as well have been intended for suicide as for an attempt on the emperor, and that may have been one reason why the accusation was rejected as too crude (*atrocius*).[4] Though Tiberius' firm hold on power allowed him to reject a proposal for a bodyguard composed of armed senators, in claiming that his life would not be worth very much if it had to be protected that way, he played derisively on a familiar theme, and part of the joke may have been in the possibility, ironically left unmentioned, of danger the guard itself would pose to his security (Tac. *Ann.* 6.2).

The tactic of exerting leverage through indispensability is applied in a very odd way in the rumor, rejected by Suetonius, that Augustus selected Tiberius because with such a successor he himself was bound someday to seem a better man (Suet. *Tib.* 21.2; Dio 56.45.3, 58.23.4, 59.5.1 [the move had some success]). Talk about Tiberius having Drusus attend gladiatorial shows so his delight in violence would become common knowledge (Tac. *Ann.* 1.76) involves the same general idea, itself then reversed when a father is suspected of eliminating a widely admired son out of fear at the unflattering contrast once he becomes his successor (Livy 35.15.4).

The distinction between force and threat of force which comes into play in such moves is the most crucial tactical consideration of all, as political games are played best when only threats are needed (Suet. *Tib.* 37.4). To paint his lurid picture of official brutality (e.g., the *immensa strages* of *Annals* 6.19.2), Tacitus tends to conflate the two by depicting fear as virtually a physical fact. Since executions were actually relatively few in number, the general climate of anxiety seems to have been a sufficient deterrent, and in a poorly defined political system where the threat of extreme action could be mostly bluff, there was room as well as need for any number of alternative moves.

Addendum 6: Clemency

Gift giving and clemency alike are methods of exercising power, with clemency being a comparatively negative way of doing so by *not* taking something (life or property) rather than granting it. Since clemency created a strong impression of what had been lost, that is, freedom, it exemplifies the principle of loss aversion and was all the more resented for concealing the loss behind a show of goodwill. What one got had first been taken away and then given back on loan, with interest due in the form of grateful compliance. The logic of clemency and gift exchange unfolds along much the same lines to generate the same antinomies. As veiled exercise of power, each reverses meanings and intentions and makes what is otherwise an elementary relationship deeply problematic, so much so, in fact, that the correct response may seem to be rejection, even when the offer is survival.

Several of the advantages clemency confers on the party who extends it turn up repeatedly in the quasi-theoretical deliberations, complete with formal speeches, recorded by the historians. Though bits and pieces are widely scattered, they belong to a complex reciprocal system all of whose parts presuppose and imply each other. Clemency is advisable because it takes account of the changes in fortune which may turn giver into receiver and because it invites additional support by making submission easy. It is safer because people pushed into a corner can be very dangerous (Polyb. 9.28.4; 29.20; Livy 45.8.6; Diod. Sic. 23.15.1–3, 27.15.3, 27.17.3; 31.3; 33.18; Sallust[?] *Oration to Caesar* 3; App. *BCiv.* 5.5.44, 2.6.38; App. *Pun.* 8.51, 9.57, 9.59, 12.85; Dion. Hal. 2.35.3, 4.58.3, 6.19.1–2; Dio 43.16.3–4; Pseudo-Caesar *African War* 92; Onasander *Strategikos* 35.4, 38.1–5, 42.19). Paradoxically, though, the danger it also poses comes directly from the security it is meant to provide. Clemency was indeed what brought it about that Caesar, who had said that he would rather die than live in fear, was assassinated (Vell. Pat. 2.57.1; cf. Cic. *Att.* 14.22.1; Tac. *Hist.* 3.66). When Augustus spares the Egyptians because they will be useful to him but offers as a pretext the honor he wants to show to Alexander and Serapis (Dio 51.16.3), the pretext is necessary in part to avoid any appearance of weakness.

Third-party mediators may need to use indirect methods for diverting violence, but when they are powerful enough it can simply be stopped (Sen. *De Ira* 3.39–40), because power so great that it need not be used still can be used and vice versa. If the essential reality of clemency, too, is not mercy but restraint by a

163

superior in using his power to take vengeance on an inferior (Sen. *Clem.* 2.3.1), he must make sure that he is seen to have power. Then if "having power [*arbitrium*] of life or death over an enemy who once was one's equal is complete vengeance," (1.21.2) clemency *is* vengeance, and what is granted is also kept. In *clementia liberum arbitrium habet* (2.7.3), the phrases "is free to be lenient" and "has absolute power" may be mutual text and subtext. If "he who owes his life loses it," clemency does not spare its victim. It means "triumphing over one's own victory" only so far as the victor caps success by finding nothing worth taking from the loser (1.21).

Caesar's two-part order to spare Italians but kill their allies in order to terrorize others (App. *BCiv.* 2.11.74 and 80) separates the alternative possibilities of power ordinarily combined in clemency and thereby reveals its true nature in cross-section. In much the same way, an unexpressed third alternative—that Rome uses irresistible power—is what gives force to both parts of the choice it offers rivals: "Either surrender unconditionally or defeat us" (Polyb. 15.8.14, 36.5.1–5). On rare occasions when the tables were turned, Rome itself faced the alternatives of acknowledging superior power by accepting either clemency or destruction (App. *Sam.* 4.3–4).

After Cannae, the Romans decided that since clemency even toward their own people in Hannibal's hands would be a dangerous sign of weakness, severity would be doubly unnerving to him (App. *Hann.* 5.28). The policy of never negotiating from anything but a plainly superior position was designed to remove the pressure of real negotiation by forcing the other side into reliance on nonnegotiable Roman good faith. But that, too, could leave open possibilities of leverage. The Aetolians surrendered in the belief that, as helpless suppliants immune from violence, they would be free to take advantage of any opportunities which might come along and thus would not be helpless at all but in a position to exact concessions (Livy 36.27.8). The Roman view, on the other hand, was that clemency presupposed the Senate's own total discretion, whose limits Rome was under no obligation to define because there were none (Livy 37.1.5–6). Leniency for Carthage similarly hinged on unconditional surrender, as only then would concessions be favors, not treaty provisions. For if negotiations are an extension of war by other means, a treaty would allow Carthage to continue violations as though still engaged in an equal contest with Rome under rules binding on both sides. True clemency, on the contrary, has the absolute force of a free favor rather than a quid pro quo settlement (App. *Pun.* 9.64).[1]

The danger of presumption or misunderstanding in power plays made without power comes up in personal relationships as well. Caesar's clemency was taken as evidence by Plancus of his own virtue when he confused what Caesar forgave with what he approved (Vell. Pat. 2.83.2), and Caesar's associates were actually pleased to see his clemency taken advantage of, presumably because they disapproved of it, though he was in fact guided by shrewd calculation (Pseudo-Caesar *Alexandrian War* 24). Eumenes declined to request a favor at the Senate's invitation so as to pressure the Romans into making one themselves and being generous about it (Polyb. 21.18.5–10). Though this was not exactly clemency, since Eumenes was an ally, it brings the logic of clemency into play insofar as he was attempting to exert leverage from an inferior position. In Livy's version (37.52.6–10, 54.15–17) manipulation of *indulgentia* and *modestia* by the two sides, each employing "labyrinthine politeness" *(inexplicabilis facilitas)*, finally leads the annoyed Senate to demand that Eumenes commit himself. The issue is his claim and that of the Rhodians to power in Asia Minor, with the conflict being mediated by Rome, whose obligation both sides see as a means to turn their own weakness into strength. On another occasion the Romans' strategy was to separate the positive and negative facets of clemency, as Caesar did with his "spare-kill" order. Two envoys whipsawed the Rhodians by dividing between themselves the complementary roles of tough and sympathetic negotiators (Livy 45.10.7–15).

The demand for unconditional surrender, however, runs the risk of under-cutting opposition to continued fighting within the enemy's camp and thus stiffens resistance by burning his bridges for him. The Romans, who saw the danger of putting people into corners, obtained the best of both worlds by de-manding surrender but building a reputation for using absolute power with restraint once they had it. Appian's Augustus realizes that submission may actu-ally still bring added leverage to those who submit. For if continued resistance by the weaker side leads to bargaining, then so long as the adversarial relationship holds, the stronger party retains power which may well be lost through the ob-ligations of clemency imposed on the victor by surrender (App. *BCiv.* 5.5.45).

In Tacitus' looser formulation of this extraordinarily complicated situation, peace is advantageous to the defeated, only glorious to the victor (*Hist.* 3.70.3), who in fact may discover that he is obligated not merely to grant clemency but, additionally, for the opportunity to do so. Thus to win a reputation for clemency Otho spares the opposition leader, Marius Celsus, who counters by using his loyalty to the deposed Galba as the basis "for actually making a claim on Otho." Only someone from the enemy camp can be granted clemency, and Celsus makes a virtue out of being that man, unlike Eumenes, who tries unsuccessfully to act as though he were. Tacitus says that the genuine loyalty which subsequently devel-oped between the two was a pleasant surprise to everyone (*Hist.* 1.71; cf. Tac. *Ann.* 12.36–37) and then characteristically adds a touch of further incongruity to the incident by remarking that the troops were now admiring the same qualities in Celsus which they had just been hating. He goes on in the next section (*Hist.* 1.72) to recount how the wholly worthless Tigellinus had been protected from the anger—again incongruous—of both those who hated and those who loved Nero, finally escaping through a claim he had on Vinius for saving his daughter, which Tigellinus had done, not out of true clemency but as an insurance policy.

Byzantine calculations of self-interest aside, clemency may have another, broader motivation. Spirals of violence can be halted only if one party at some stage is prepared to swallow injury.[2] Cicero's appeal in Dio for letting bygones be bygones after Caesar's assassination combines a standard warning about the uncertainty of events (44.27) with reference not to a spiral but to a cycle *(kyklos)* of violence into which even neutrals are pulled (44.29.1).

Seneca develops the same line of argument combining high-minded restraint with self-interest. Vengeance entails not only immediate danger to oneself (people are apt to break their own knuckles punching someone, *De Ira* 3.28.3; "if it is safe, forgive," *Clem.* 1.20.2) but also the longer-term threat of self-perpetuating violence (e.g., the anger causing not only fear in others but also hatred, which, in turn, causes danger to oneself; *De Ira* 2.11.1). A more subtle cause of escalation is fear of losing face, as in the self-justifying obstinacy of those who know their anger is unjustified (3.29.2). This is *fuite en avant* driven by a compulsive increase in stakes to avoid losing rather than to win. Such a trap, Seneca often insists, can only be escaped by not joining the game in the first place out of a sense of one's own vulnerability.[3]

Ultio is an ugly word, *talio* is not much better, and since competition to beat or be beaten is intrinsically bad (*De Ira* 2.32.1), Seneca recommends ignoring insults. It is the sign of a great man, but an aggressive aspect to forbearance comes out as well in the remark that "the most contemptuous kind of *ultio* is to make someone seem not worth getting even with" (2.32.3, 3.25.3–4; Sen. *Clem.* 1.21.3). Not giving pleasure to enemies by becoming angry (Sen. *De Ira* 3.40.1) is a rule that anyone, weak or strong, can understand, but claiming that eagerness for revenge is a sign of resentment (3.5.8) is apt itself to seem a sign of impotence if it is an excuse for doing nothing. On the one hand, clemency's passivity is supposed to foster general goodwill; on the other hand, more realistically, it means withdrawing into the security of private life. Seneca manages to support both views with a doctrine of universal human imperfection. If the whole race is guilty, then no individual is particularly so, and everyone deserves indulgence, for which Seneca finds no end of excuses (2.30–31.5, 3.11–12, 3.24–29, 36.4). The wise man should avoid anger altogether because evil is so widespread that he would have to be in a state of perpetual rage (danger) and in any case would be a hypocrite, as he is guilty, too (2.6.3–2.10, 2.28, 3.28.1).

This philosophical line is a corollary of the somewhat less high-minded political awareness that when just about everyone is implicated in a system, nobody is guilty of anything. Self-serving charity aside, if life is a jungle, it is simply safer to practice clemency by going along, looking the other way, or staying clear of the public competition from which violence arises. But now clemency is something negative, a tactic as much rooted in resignation as in mercy, though still feebly aggressive insofar as revenge can be enjoyed by reflecting that one's enemies, no matter how powerful, will someday be dead (Sen. *De Ira* 3.42–43) or someday be put down by somebody else (Sen. *Constant.* 17.4). Another polite reason for backing down is *magnanimitas* (*Constant.* 11.1; coupled with *clementia,* Sen. *Clem.* 1.5.3; cf. *magnitudo,* Sen. *De Ira* 3.40.1). But while contemptuously bribing a porter for admission to an important house (*Constant.* 14.2) could be a matter of preserving dignity, it can no less be a prudent way of avoiding confrontation with the master (e.g., 19.2). Though Seneca can speak eloquently of submitting to the demands uncompromising virtue imposes ("let infamy come, so long as we don't deserve it"; *De Ira* 3.41.1), *libertas* does not simply mean "not putting up with anything" we think wrong (*Constant.* 19.2). In fact, transformed into philosophic detachment, it helps rationalize the compromises with just about anything that may be needed for survival.[4]

While granting, then, that failure to avenge oneself—that is, clemency—risks contempt and that therefore individuals are more or less forced to seek vengeance (Sen. *De Ira* 2.11.1, 2.33.1; Sen. *Clem.* 1.7.3–4, 8.1 and 6; Sen. *Ep.* 14.10: not stepping on others may make them think they can step on you), Seneca also holds that insults from those with more power must be borne with something resembling inverse clemency (*De Ira* 2.33). In recounting several horrendous anecdotes about abuse of power in 3.14–21, he concedes that though helpless victims ought to have reacted, failure to do so at least proves that anger can be suppressed. Returning to the question of an alternative to submission, he first pursues, not active resistance, but suicide: "So long as things do not seem so intolerable as to drive us from life, we must get rid of anger" (3.16.1). Only then does he pick up the thought of vengeance by warning rulers of the dangers their own *ira* poses from its victims. Not much room is left for self-defense, if conflict with equals has to be avoided as too risky, with superiors as foolish and with inferiors as degrading (2.34.1). Though a powerful thirst for vengeance permeates Roman society, those who can indulge anger and those who must swallow it are equally caught up in the danger it brings. Both are engaged in "war," and since "the man who has offended you is either stronger or weaker, if weaker, spare him, if stronger, spare yourself" (3.5.6–8; the dangers of revenge are ultimately part of the double paradox of sparing oneself by sparing others and punishing oneself by punishing others, see Sen. *Clem.* 1.5.1, 1.10.3). Seneca has already spoken of submission or clemency as positive preemptive restraint replacing negative preemptive attack: "Rivalry falls away as soon as it is abandoned by one side; only two can fight. . . . he is the best man who steps back first. Then the loser wins. . . . [Otherwise] when you want to withdraw, it is too late" (*De Ira* 2.34.5). That is the logic of clemency's benign public side, which behind its facade is always devious: voluntary restraint or necessary retreat are still extensions of rivalry by other means. "See to it that your enemies don't enjoy your anger" (3.40.1; Sen. *Constant.* 17.4).[5]

Addendum 7: Loss Aversion

The speeches in Herodian, normally trite, include one much more interesting specimen concerned with something that comes very close to the principle of loss aversion and is appropriately cast in economic terms. The speaker is the parsimonious Pertinax, who is faced with financial difficulties owing to Commodus' extravagance (2.3.7–10). Hope for a better future, he says, is correlative to regret for past disappointment, but the latter is in fact much harder to forget than are happy memories immediately consumed along with the enjoyment itself. Some political consequences follow from the longer-lasting effect of painful events. The pleasure of liberty (while we are enjoying it), for example, is less than the pain of slavery (when we remember liberty we have lost), and while we take actual enjoyment of property for granted, we never forget its loss. So far, unpleasant memory of past troubles has been illustrated with pain felt at losses, and losses figure again in what follows. Public prosperity, Pertinax goes on to say, is much less gratifying to individuals than their own success is, and so reductions in consumption necessary for the general welfare strike people as an unreasonable decline in their standard of living, since it is hard to admit that if everyone is to receive a share, public resources have to be used sparingly. It is not entirely clear how these remarks hang together, but if Pertinax means that a decrease in our income is painful when we think that something is being taken away from us, his point would seem to be that it is better, instead, to think of something we simply fail to get, not of possessions we are entitled to have and resent losing. If, in addition, he is making the second point that we remember with resentment the loss of something we think we are entitled to, his remarks touch on the barrier to change caused by self-interest, which makes any alteration in the status quo appear to be unfair deprivation.

Similar ideas about the preferability of birds in hand come up in connection with the quasi-economic trade-offs of clemency (Dio 52.12.2–4). Those who receive favors show little gratitude because that could be an admission of unworthiness, and since they regard the favor as their due, no gratitude is called for in any case; those who do not get what they want are hostile, because they feel robbed of what is (as they see it) theirs, and so if they are not angry, they would be admitting that they do not deserve to have anything. This last is a shrewd insight into the politics of discontent, which seeks to use anger itself as evidence for the justice of claims being made. One of Plutarch's political axioms lays down the rule that common people feel more resentment at rich citizens who give nothing of their own wealth than at the poor who actually steal from the public (*Precepts of Statecraft* 822A). From one point of view, this reverses loss aversion, inasmuch as people feel more keenly what they are not getting than what is being taken from them. At the same time, they also regard what they are not getting so strongly as their own that the failure of the rich to give seems greater deprivation than being stolen from by the poor. The real calculus in this case, though, ultimately is not so much concerned with loss or gain but with attitudes about social obligation.

Another version of the principle occurs in Dionysius of Halicarnassus 5.67.1–2. Since concessions merely breed additional demands, the desires of the lower class are best checked from the very start. Once appetite gains strength, it can be crushed only with difficulty, for greater anger is felt by people at being deprived of what they have already been granted than at not getting what they want (cf. 8.75.2). Concessions, that is to say, are readily taken to be entitlements, as contributions from the wealthy are in Plutarch, and entitlements become springboards for more grants (cf. *facit quidem avidos nimia felicitas;* Sen. *Clem.* 1.1.7). After commenting on the difference between subtracting and not adding (Sen. *De Ira* 3.28.4), Seneca links the tendency to discount what has been granted and to feel resentment about what has not with competitive jealousy for what others have (3.31).[1] Because of greed for what we want, we do not think of what we have gotten (Sen. *Ep.* 81.28: "cogitamus non quid impetratum sed quid petendum sit"); in the language of bookkeeping, "Your accounts are wrong; you list expenses high, income low" ("falsas rationes conficis; data magno aestumas, accepta parvo," Sen. *De Ira* 3.31.3; cf. Sen. *Ben.* 3.3). The gratitude, too, of those who get what they want is less than the anger of those who do not, because the former think that it is their due, the latter that they have been deprived of what is theirs. Attention to what we possess is the point again of some moralizing in Dionysius of Halicarnassus: "It is right to demand (back) our own property, while not desiring that of others" (8.8.3), and "it is shameful to lose what we have through desire for what we do not" (8.13.2). Loss aversion is radicalized into self-denial in Seneca's *De tranquillitate animi* 8.2: "One must reflect how much less painful it is not to have something than to lose it." Better even than being content with what one has is being content with nothing.

The admonitory tone of these passages makes the point that people are all too often intent on what is *not* theirs. Dissatisfaction may stop with negative begrudging of things to others but can just as easily assume another familiar, more aggressive political form. As fear gives way to greed or ingratitude, what we have seems less satisfactory than the prospect of gaining more, and risk seeking comes into play. The contrast between the calculus of loss aversion and that of aggressive acquisition figures in a formal discussion of imperialism in Dio Cassius, who sets the two views off sharply from each other. For the loss-averse man, peace creates and preserves wealth, war expends and destroys it; for the risk taker, peace destroys first what war wins, then peace itself, whereas war preserves possessions in addition to winning those of others (13.55.1–3). The caution in the

first of these policies guided Augustus' attitude toward expansion of the Empire
(Tac. *Ann.* 1.3.6), while Caesar, in rationalizing aggression against the Germans,
saw things quite differently (Dio 38.36–40.3). Individuals may well be inclined to
play it safe (as Cicero did, according to Plutarch, by calculating dangers too
carefully; *Brut.* 12.2), but in the case of states, even if what they have were
entirely secure, aggression would be the better policy as a matter of principle. In
point of fact, though, nations always do face danger; those which remain defensive risk losing what they have, while those waging preemptive war keep their
property and add that of others (cf. Dio 48.8.2–3: "One side wanted to take the
property of others, the other wanted to keep what it had"; Tac. *Ann.* 15.1.4:
"Private citizens keep what they have, political glory involves fighting for the
possessions of others"). The zero-sum social Darwinism expressed in these sentiments can readily lead to internal conflict once external resistance has been
eliminated. The decisive direction of Caesar's own career was in fact out from
Rome to Gaul and Britain, then back to the center, a pattern enshrined in the
widespread theory of Roman ambition imploding on itself after external danger
had vanished.

Much of this is commonplace moral sentiment or involves risk/reward calculations that figure in practically any situation: it is only commonsensical to go
ahead if failure is not too expensive, to stop if it is (Dion. Hal. 8.27.2–3). Still,
calculations and especially the effect they have on forming operational styles
easily escape notice. Loss aversion produces engineers and administrators, risk
attraction produces entrepreneurs, inventors, explorers (and revolutionaries).
One of the things that makes Catiline so disturbing a figure in Sallust is that when
a man conjoins "appetite for the property of others to profligacy with his own,"
risk attraction runs amok to produce aimless acquisition of power (Sall. *Cat.* 5.4;
cf. Tac. *Hist.* 1.52.2, 2.86.2 [*raptor, largitor*]; Dio 51.15.2; Pliny *Pan.* 27.3–4). If
what belongs to others becomes Catiline's when he takes it and if he spends what
is his own, too, income *is* outgo as everything is sucked into a process of compulsive consumption and expenditure much like that attributed later to bad emperors. In the language of political management, Empire succeeded Republic at
Rome when a cautious corporate board split into warring groups, some led by
reckless gamblers, who were themselves, in turn, succeeded by monopolists presiding over a relatively stable system.

The delicate balance between ambition and restraint that is a central theme
in the *Agricola* comes up repeatedly elsewhere in Tacitus. Risk taking and risk
avoiding invite embodiment in classic types. The former gets generally unfavorable portraits highlighting pathological ruthlessness, restlessness, or criminal intent (Tac. *Hist.* 2.86.2: "a very bad man in peace, in war not so bad to have
around" [*pace pessimus, bello non spernendus*]; 4.49.1). It is finally danger itself,
not its rewards, that drives Cornelius Fuscus, who had earlier left the senatorial
order because he wanted peace and quiet (*Hist.* 2.86.2–3). Risk seeking is commonly made into a virtue by pleading necessity. Compulsive gamblers plunge
most heavily to recover heavy losses, and experiments attest that the same situation receives risk averse or risk seeking responses depending on how dangerous it
is perceived to be. A less risky course of action saving the lives of two hundred out

of six hundred people is selected by a large majority, but when the choice is restated as requiring the certain death of four hundred, a large majority prefers the more risky course.[2]

The dictum that nothing is safer than haste in crises when action counts more than planning (Tac. *Hist.* 1.62.1; cf. 1.38.2) is well illustrated by Antonius Primus, the Roman George Patton, *acerrimus belli concitator,* who is everywhere at once on the battlefield and able to sweep away even cautious men with fire-eating calls to combat (*Hist.* 3.2–3; 17). The rule that it may actually be safer to run risks takes a more cynical form when people find war preferable because their position in peacetime is questionable (4.49.1: *in pace suspecto tutius bellum*). The *promptus* or *audax* (1.48.4; cf. Sen. *De Ira* 3.41) often contrasts with the lazy, cowardly, or prudent man, and in weighing risks against rewards (*metus* against *fortuna,* 2.80.1) the prudent Vespasian reflects that in private life a man can decide how much he wants to get, whereas aiming for the top means gaining or losing everything (2.74.2). Merely thinking seriously about power is dangerous, and practically everyone had become unaware of their aversion to risk under the Principate (Tac. *Ann.* 1.2.1: current safe ways are preferred to the old dangerous ones; Tac. *Ann.* 1.3.7; Tac. *Dial.* 36–41: tame political rhetoric; Tac. *Germ.* 14.2). The *cunctator* Suetonius Paulus is another risk averse man who would rather be smart than lucky and believes that victory begins only where the possibility of defeat stops (*Hist.* 2.25.2), whereas the impulsive Cerialis was successful "because luck [*fortuna*] helped where skill [*artes*] was absent" (5.21.3).[3]

Addendum 8: Degrees of Penalty

By itself or in combination with other penalties, exile was exceptionally suitable for providing just the right level of discomfort to be inflicted in various circumstances (Dio 56.27.2–3). The general correlation between status and penalty on which the political semantics of punishment rested is illustrated by the public execution of a prominent freedman on the one hand, the apparent exile and secret murder of Laco in the aftermath of Galba's fall on the other (Tac. *Hist.* 1.46.5). In the former, execution and public humiliation go together; in the latter, execution and exile at first are mutually exclusive alternatives which subsequently come together as one conceals the other. Carefully calculated *beneficia* dispensed by the emperor constitute the corresponding set of positive status markers.

Penalties stood in roughly ascending order of severity:

1. Secret surveillance (Tac. *Ann.* 16.10.2)
2. Open surveillance (Tac. *Ann.* 6.14.2)
3. Restriction to Rome and nearby territory in a novel reverse *relegatio* (Suet. *Claud.* 23.2)
4. Restriction to Italy and nearby territory (Dio 52.42.6). The "forgotten" assignments which kept appointees from leaving for their offices were perhaps unofficial forms of this
5. Easy exile from Italy without a guard (Tac. *Hist.* 1.88.1) or under the guise of foreign study (Tac. *Ann.* 4.44.3)
6. Exile, with each additional slave accompanied by an additional guard (Dio 59.8.8)
7. Exile and loss of property (Tac. *Ann.* 16.33.1)
8. Exile, loss of property and office (Tac. *Ann.* 15.71)
9. Exile to an island, occasionally chosen for its harshness (Tac. *Ann.* 4.30), with interdiction of fire and water (6.30.1)
10. Expulsion from the Senate, exile and return to Rome under arrest (Tac. *Ann.* 6.3.3)
11. Strict custody followed by execution (Tac. *Ann.* 13.1.3)
12. Exile followed by execution en route or later (Dio 59.18.3) or by forced suicide (Tac. *Ann.* 16.17.2; Suet. *Calig.* 29.1: "I have swords as well as islands")
13. Death during either a genuine or "official" attempt at escape (Tac. *Ann.* 2.67.3)

Deportatio, which was the most severe form of *exilium,* involved restriction to specific places, such as an island; *relegatio* could be close to *deportatio* but usually entailed less onerous exclusion from a particular place. Ranked penalties were negative mirror images of a social hierarchy in which people were classified by privilege. The social game, accordingly, was played not with men of equal value (like checkers) but with men of varying rank and power (like chess pieces). *Existimatio* (social standing) could be gradually diminished and finally entirely lost along with loss of freedom (*Dig.* 50.13.5); then no move was possible, and the player had been taken out of the game (e.g., Tac. *Ann.* 14.22.3). Besides achieving that aim immediately and without violence, an exile that was lengthy could also make the victim's death obscure (*Ann.* 1.53.2).

The system of gradation opened room for everything from serious penalties such as denial of the right to make a will in the case of those banned from fire and water to the relatively petty humiliation of restricting the level of consumption (no more than twenty slaves), passing over certain names in public reading of the roster of knights (Suet. *Calig.* 16.2), or forcing knights to read, silently and in public, a report on their misdeeds (Dio 56.27.2–3, 57.22.5; Suet. *Aug.* 39). Claudius devised an intermediate variant on formal censure by removing the *nota* but allowing the erasure to show (Suet. *Claud.* 16.1).

Detention to prevent both escape and suicide (Livy 39.19.2) recorded for the late Republic may have been only a temporary measure; later those who crossed the emperor could be kept in a more calculatedly sinister limbo between life and death under house arrest (Dio 58.3.4) or subjected to systematic *ludibrium* in place of execution to dramatize loss of status and power (54.15.4–6). Besides toying with victims—brought in, not dead or alive, but neither dead nor alive—denial of either death or decent life obliterated political identity by putting the victim in a null class to suffer living *damnatio memoriae,* not entirely forgotten, but not remembered either (cf. Otho's pathetic farewell to his nephew "to not wholly forget or too much remember" that Otho had been his uncle; Tac. *Hist.* 2.48.2). Caligula's reply to an appeal for death from a prisoner was a joke along the same line: "You call that *living?*" (Sen. *Ep.* 77.18), and Tiberius refused execution to another "because we are not friends yet" (Suet. *Tib.* 61.5).[1]

An especially refined form of *clementia* splitting the difference between being "permitted" to die (commit suicide) in a manner of one's own choosing and dying a natural death was permission to die naturally from old age or disease (Dio 59.19.8; Tac. *Ann.* 16.9.1, with exile). Here true intention—genuine mercy (Sen. *Clem.* 1.1.4), desire to avoid responsibility, contemptuous show of power?—is exceptionally hard to pin down. The first two are given an unusual twist when popular demand for Tigellinus' death is denied by Galba on the ground that since he is terminally ill, killing him would be tyrannical (Plut. *Galba* 17.4). The political power game being played with life and death comes to light in the sequel. By way of "mocking the frustrated crowd," after offering thanks (*sōtēria*) to the gods for what now is both shrewd escape and marvelous medical recovery, Tigellinus proceeds to plunge back into political life.

Like defiant suicide, the vulnerability of old age could be wielded as an offensive weapon owing to the immunity it provided for plain talk (Tac. *Ann.*

13.42.2: *extrema senecta liber*). It had uses for the emperor, too; unable to free Publius Celer from a charge, Nero delayed taking action, and Celer finally died of old age (13.33.1). In voluntary exile, dangers of free speech were avoided by the opposite expedient of eliminating the need to say anything at all through *secessio* from political life or, rather, by turning silence itself into a free statement. Thrasea's enemies were much annoyed by his threat to exile himself (16.22.2, 16.28.3), and Lucius Piso's threat of withdrawal induced Tiberius to ask him to change his mind (2.34.1). The political value of voluntary withdrawal stands to enforced exile as suicide in protest stands to execution, hence the "exile and death pronounced on himself" by Cato (Sen. *Ep.* 104.33). Exile is made to seem both voluntary and enforced when Silanus, who earlier had realized that exile was indicated *(demonstrari)* by Augustus' repudiation of friendship, was allowed to return by Tiberius. While papering over the facts by transforming his exile into apparently voluntary absence with a bland reference to Silanus'"trip" *(peregrinatio)*, Tiberius also allowed Augustus' personal disapproval to remain in effect so that Silanus could stay in Rome but receive no honors (*Ann.* 3.24.3–4). During the Republic, after a man facing the death penalty had been given an opportunity to go into "voluntary" exile before being found guilty, he was formally denied fire and water, and if he returned he could then be killed with impunity.[2]

Notes

Introduction

1. These examples come from K. Bringmann, "Topoi in der taciteischen Germania," in *Beiträge zum Verständnis der Germania des Tacitus,* Teil 1, Abhandlungen der Akademie der Wissenschaften in Göttingen, ed. H. Jankuhn and D. Timpe (Göttingen: Vandenhoeck und Ruprecht, 1989), 72–78. Cf. A. Lund, "Kritischer Forschungsbericht zu 'Germania' des Tacitus," in *ANRW* II.33.3 (Berlin: De Gruyter, 1991), 2211; and idem, "Gesamtinterpretation der 'Germania' des Tacitus," in *ANRW* II.33.3, 1868–69. Bringmann uses the term *axiom;* Lund speaks of *stereotype.* I also use *norm* in a relatively loose way as an equivalent of *axiom, rule,* or *principle* to include both prescriptive and descriptive factors, both what is right and what is fact. For a narrower view of social norms as unconditional requirements rooted in public opinion ("the done thing") distinct from tradition, moral, legal, and private norms, or rational outcome-oriented calculation, see J. Elster, *The Cement of Society* (Cambridge: Cambridge University Press, 1989), 97–115. Even in Elster's definition, social norms may include other motivations such as self-interest (106), and they define anomaly by "focussing and coordinating expectations" (105). Anomaly, that is to say, is the unexpected, the exception or violation which any rule entails.

The case for relatively abstract and universal cross-cultural structures is argued in D. Little, *Varieties of Social Explanation* (Boulder, Colo.: Westview, 1991), 148–50. The broader social rationale of several Roman institutions has received some attention in recent studies: J. North, "Diviners and Divination at Rome," in *Pagan Priests,* ed. M. Beard and J. North (London: Duckworth, 1990), 61–71; P. Veyne, *Bread and Circuses,* trans. B. Pearce (London: Penguin, 1990), 221–22, 235–36. After discussing two functional theories—that divination served as an objective way to reach decisions free from partisan interests and that it aided morale during crises—North proposes a third model, one more specific to Roman culture, that emphasizes the correspondence between divination and location of political power. Like the fragmented authority which preserved balance among members of the oligarchy in the Republic, divination was widely available to the ruling elite. When power later became concentrated in a few hands, individual diviners emerged in association with individual magnates. As North remarks (65), there are various ways of looking at the same data. While his own correlation between religious and political authority works well on *Roman* divination, it is less effective in explaining Roman *divination,* which as a feature of society more generally is bound to have a more abstract rationale. Multiple explanations are possible because facts group themselves, kaleidoscopically, at different levels of generality: the concrete political level, which involves distribution of authority at Rome, chosen by North, and higher levels, where broader functional explanations come into play.

Under the Republic, particularly in its late phase, when upper-class solidarity was decaying, *munera* were given by individuals to gain popular favor during elections. The entertainment provided by games and the advantage enjoyed by their sponsors are again aspects of a fundamental political principle, in this case of what Veyne terms "euergetism" governing the relationship between rulers and ruled: shows won political favor because they were entertaining. But this does nothing to explain why extreme, stylized public brutality was so pleasing. If we are not satisfied to dismiss that as a quirk of the Roman character, then another, quite different axiom tied to violence rather than to internal political exchange of entitlements comes into view. Gladiatorial combat itself had an essentially military character, was connected with formal military triumphs as well as with more general displays of (coercive) power by ambitious strongmen, and gradually assimilated yet more massive bloodshed through public slaughter of animals. All of this suggests that, besides affording a useful quid pro quo in the particular circumstances of Roman politics, *munera* also embodied an axiom operating on a more general psychological and social level that was related to violence itself. The "intelligible spectacle," distinguished by Roland Barthes from the "sadistic spectacle" in modern wrestling and identified with its deeper social meaning, comes close to the notion of a relatively abstract logic underlying *munera;* see Barthes, "The World of Wrestling," in *Mythologies,* trans. A. Lavers (New York: Hill and Wang, 1972), 20.

2. Wasting food during a famine was a standard way for cities under siege to spread disinformation (Dio 15 Zonaras 9.2; Frontin. *Str.* 3.15.1–3; Val. Max. 7.4.3; Livy 5.48.4, 23.19.13–14). The Romans, on the other hand, turned down funds offered by allies to prove that they actually did not need help (Livy 36.4.9). A cynical Caesarian version of constituted reality is recorded in Suetonius' *Divus Iulius* 77: "The omens will be more favorable when I want them to be." The principle is stated as a very general proposition by Varro: "As painter is prior to picture and craftsman to product, so societies are prior to what they institute"; *M. Terenti Varronis Antiquitatum Rerum Divinarum Libri I XIV XV XVI,* ed. R. Agahd, Jahrbücher für Klassische Philologie, suppl. 24, I.4.

3. "[To] depreciate Tacitus as a sour debunker is to miss the subtlety, the sheer virtuosity of his psychological insight. His Augustus is a gigantic fraud, but not simply a fraud; he deceives men not solely for his own profit, but largely for theirs. The social process pursues its devious course behind the arcana that a shrewd government has set up"; P. Gay, *Style in History* (New York: Basic Books, 1974), 29.

The distinction sometimes drawn between normative and pragmatic rules is useful for describing how political reality was (re)created during the transition from Republic to Principate. Normative rules are explicit, publicly acknowledged norms; pragmatic rules are implicit norms arising at the margin of political life and consisting of what is desirable for self-interest or necessary for survival. Despite their marginal character, they too constitute genuine rules, because "men employ stratagems which are not pronounced upon in the normative rules. They also follow [other] pragmatic rules which permit them to make calculated breaches of the normative rules. . . . The situation seems to tremble on the brink of disorder and disintegration, yet . . . there is an overall order and regularity"; F. G. Bailey, *Stratagems and Spoils* (New York: Schocken Books, 1969), 109. Pragmatic rules are particularly important when new forms of power emerge. "As their use becomes more widespread, more blatant and obtrusive," Bailey wrote, "so the point of crisis approaches, when either they must be normatively legitimized or suppressed. . . . Hence the ratio of normative to pragmatic rules can be taken as an indicator of potential instability. The ratio is not, of course, the *cause* of this instability; it is a sign only. The cause is a maladjustment between the normative structure and its environment" (189). This is an admirable commentary on Roman politics. Initially Caesar and his immediate successors hid the increasingly dominant ratio of pragmatic rules behind the appearance of normative republican rules that were in fact being replaced. "The names of the offices were the same [under Augustus] . . . but few were left who had seen the Republic. The nature of the state had changed and all the old honorable character was gone" (Tac. *Ann.* 1.3.6f); Tiberius "covered new [pragmatic] crimes with old [normative] words" (4.19.2). A revolutionary crisis emerged when the new code was openly legitimated, and those who understood Roman politics as a longer-term decline in values were aware that the transformation of pragmatic into normative rules was a symptom, not the cause.

Because subjective and objective factors are hard to disentangle, stipulating socially what is real is no simple matter. Self-definition may be the next thing to self-deception, and confusion between the two becomes a central theme in Tacitus' picture of how Roman society worked. While some "put on faces" *(vultus mutantur)* pretending that Nero's matricide was a great public boon, the *facies* (scene) of the crime could not be changed, and so Nero himself was not able to bear looking on it (Tac. *Ann.* 14.10). Keyed to the play on *vultus/facies* (public appearance), the leitmotiv is denial of reality—both external political and internal moral reality, both on the part of Nero and of others. His guilty conscience is seen by Tacitus as an interiorized version of the dismaying external signs he was also reported to have heard (sounding trumpets, voices mourning at Agrippina's tomb), while official declarations of thanksgiving fold together legal reality (political truth is what political power says it is), legal fiction (much of what it says is make-believe,) and sheer unreality. *Simulatio* and *dissimulatio* are the two sides of the process, the former replacing with illusion the reality denied by the latter.

All of this is given a typically ethical spin by Tacitus: everyone is a hypocrite. But ethical considerations aside, the situation is also an excellent example of what in dissonance theory is termed "changed knowledge." What everyone is trying to do is to reach accommodation with unpleasant facts, and two principal alternatives for doing that are changes in behavior and strategies of denial. "The existence of dissonance being psychologically uncomfortable, [it] will motivate the person to try to reduce the dissonance and achieve consonance. . . . By the term cognition . . . , I mean any knowledge, opinion, or belief about the environment, about oneself, or about one's behavior"; L. Festinger, *A Theory of Cognitive Dissonance* (Evanston, Ill.: Row Peterson, 1957), 3. Reduction is effected through either changed cognition (e.g., admitting that smoking is bad and quitting) or changed knowledge (denying or forgetting that smoking is bad; Festinger 6, 155, 158).

Applied to Roman society, this model says that political cognition was changed through active cooperation with the Principate, while knowledge was changed by denying that the Republic had been superseded. The latter is the familiar tactic of strategic ignorance: the telescope to Nelson's blind eye, the telephone left off the hook, Marcus Aurelius burning unopened evidence of treason to avoid being forced to take distasteful steps (Amm. Marc. 21.16.11). Deactivating the system by declaring a moratorium on further reports of signs (Livy 34.55.4), sacrificing with head veiled, and traveling in a closed litter to avoid seeing anything you don't want to see (Cic. *Div.* 2.77) are examples from divination. Augustus' confiscation of unauthorized oracles circulating publicly and careful authentification even of books in state keeping (Suet. *Aug.* 31.1; Tac. *Ann.* 6.12; cf. Livy 25.1.6–12) or the control of information to prevent panic (Livy 22.55; Caes. *BGall.* 6.20.1–2) aim at inducing ignorance in others. Social dissonance can be reduced on a large scale by mobilizing public consensus, hence the importance of signs officially accepted and interpreted by the Senate, with the state in effect standing for all the other people whose agreement helps reduce dissonance felt by individuals (Festinger 177–259). Dissonance theory recognizes that individuals and societies as often as not fail to resolve contradictions, and that is what interested historians of the Principate. If unpleasant political tensions could be reduced in Neronian Rome through sheer hypocrisy, the urge to gloss over inconsistency more subtly through ambiguous language (Festinger 14–17) is illustrated by the contradictory realities behind talk of "clemency" or of "voluntary enforced death" in political suicide. Dissonance theory is discussed by H. S. Versnel, who emphasizes incompatibility among beliefs persisting in all areas of life; Versnel, *Ter Unus* (Leiden: Brill, 1990), 1–38.

4. In Dio (8 Zonaras 7.26), Postumius claims that since the Roman army had acted under duress in surrendering and the duress was applied through trickery rather than bravery, the agreement was not binding. This extraordinary reasoning left the Senate as puzzled as ever, but it did finally reject the pledge. See N. Rosenstein, "*Imperatores Victi*: The Case of C. Hostilius Mancinus," *Classical Antiquity* 5 (1986): 230–52, on the legal and political complexities. Another conceptual problem raised by the situation is related to the central dilemma of *clementia*. The Samnites are advised by an aged statesman both to destroy the Roman army and to release it. The statesman explains the oraclelike contradiction (Livy 9.3.8) as a decision either to ensure Roman friendship by showing mercy or to guarantee Roman military weakness by showing none. Compromise, judged by him to combine the worst of both policies, is what ensued: the Roman army survived,

not grateful but eager for revenge. The ethical muddle is brought out again in the sly rationalizing of capitulation by one of the Roman officers: "If we can endure death to save our country, why not shame?" (4.15).

5. Cf. A. Watson, *The Law of Persons in the Later Roman Republic* (Oxford: Clarendon, 1967), 77–101. Child exposure, especially of defective infants, and disinheritance are symbolic substitutes for outright killing.

6. The first quotation is taken from D. Daube, *Roman Law: Linguistic, Social, and Philosophical Aspects* (Edinburgh: Edinburgh University Press, 1969), 75, the second from J. Crook, "Patria potestas," *Classical Quarterly* 17 (1967): 119–20. Death forestalled the problem in most cases, since fathers were rarely alive when their sons held high office; R. Saller, "*Patria potestas* and the Stereotype of the Roman Family," *Change and Continuity* 1 (1986): 7–22. Another game at Rome for playing out the strategy of political connections through family relationships is the subject of M. Corbier, "Divorce and Adoption as Roman Familial Strategies," in *Marriage, Divorce, and Children in Ancient Rome,* ed. B. Rawson (Oxford: Clarendon, 1991), 47–78. So abstract could moves become that a woman might be divorced and remarried while still pregnant, the fetus being quite irrelevant to what the exchange meant politically. On the very unusual, semitheoretical relationships possible through adoption, see Corbier 67.

Unusual legal punctilio made such situations more likely to occur in Roman society. In another striking instance, again involving authority, the consuls, after first being invited to a banquet in honor of a triumphator, would be asked not to attend to avoid problems of precedence (Plut. *Quaest. Rom.* 80; Val. Max. 2.8.6). On reality controlled through control of signs, see H. D. Jocelyn, "The Roman Nobility and the Religion of the Republican State," *Journal of Religious History* 4 (1966): 101–4. Jocelyn also points out that the (semi)magical link between act and consequence helped immunize Roman religion against rationalistic criticism, since its reality lay in immediate sociopolitical results, not in more vulnerable connections with a second, divine world. Though social arrangements normally seem self-evident, when a difficult choice has to be made, their subjective, constituted nature becomes noticeable, and questions of legitimacy are unavoidable. But dilemmas are not so readily felt when those who must make hard decisions focus attention on practical aims. Cynical scepticism on the part of Romans, accordingly, should not be overestimated; public religion just did work as it was supposed to, and so practitioners had little reason not to be serious about it. Even when the religious rationale for divination in particular was questioned, the political logic of the practice remained largely untouched, though if J. Linderski is correct in suggesting that "when the gods started talking the language of Caesar, [Cicero] preferred not to believe in their enunciation," then *De Divinatione* may reflect a more drastic breakdown in the legitimacy of divination; Linderski, "Cicero and Roman Divination," *La Parola del Passato* 37 (1982): 37–38. For a survey of politically constitutive religious rules, see E. Rawson, "Religion and Politics in the Late Second Century B.C. at Rome," *Phoenix* 28 (1974): 193–212; on Greece, see R. Parker, "Greek States and Oracles," *History of Political Thought* 6 (1985): 298–326.

7. E. Bruch, "Political Ideology, Propaganda, and Public Law of the Romans: Ius Imaginum and Consecratio Imperatorum," *Seminar: Annual Extraordinary Number of the Jurist* 7 (1949): 5. Annulment of reality is a major topic in D. Daube, "Greek and Roman Reflections on Impossible Laws," *Natural Law Forum* 12 (1967): 1–84. Erasing the past through *abolitio memoriae* (Daube 53–57) is in principle similar to the Roman response to the Caudine Forks debacle. While divination aimed at erasing history in the perfectly ordinary sense of avoiding future trouble, the response to guilt among the Vestals could involve much more strenuous efforts at making conceptually impossible people disappear. Like Postumius, a fallen Vestal was in limbo. She was neither virgin nor normal woman, her death by starvation was not outright execution but not suicide either, and her history could be canceled retrospectively through suppression of her name; F. Münzer, "Die römischen Vestalinnen bis zur Kaiserzeit," *Philologos* 92 (1937): 216–22.

8. The constitutional paradoxes of *patria potestas* are discussed in Y. Thomas, "Vitae necisque potestas," in *Du châtiment dans la cité,* Collection de l'Ecole Française de Rome 79 (Rome: Ecole Française de Rome, 1984), 525–45. Its social consequences are examined in M. Bettini, *Anthropology and Roman Culture,* trans. J. Van Sickle (Baltimore: Johns Hopkins University Press, 1991), 3–13. The status of *impuberes* comes up in *Digest* 1.6.4 and 50.16.195.2 (cited in Thomas 530n64); though under a tutor until puberty, in principle they possess *potestas* and are *sui iuris.* For self-defeating logic more generally in the legal sphere, see Daube on reductio ad absurdum as a principle of legal thought (*Roman Law* 176–94, esp. 180). The special contradiction of *summum ius summa iniuria* naturally attracted the attention of Seneca, who notes that penalties applied too rigorously and frequently diminish their own deterrent shock effect by working to normalize crime and thus undermine public order as they reveal to the public how widespread disorder is (*Clem.* 1.22.2, 23.2, 24.1). See M. Ducos, "Les Problèmes de droit dans l'oeuvre de Tacite," in *ANRW* II.33.4 (Berlin: De Gruyter, 1991), 3235–36.

Delation was another area fertile in legal dilemmas. The consequences of denying informers a reward if the accused committed suicide before the end of the trial might seem to be that "the clearer the proof of a man's guilt, the more likely he was to escape by suicide, so that the stronger the evidence, the less the motive for a prosecution"; F. Marsh, *The Reign of Tiberius* (New York: Barnes and Noble, 1931), 171. This would not actually have happened if the Senate had continued an investigation after suicide so the person who had provided genuine evidence of guilt could receive a reward; see E. Koestermann, "Die Majestätsprozesse unter Tiberius," *Historia* 4 (1955): 85 n31. Cf. Dio 57.15.4–5. But the paradox does nevertheless represent a genuine logical possibility when suicide is both a way out for defendants, guilty or not, and a way to avoid execution, justified or not, for the prosecution. Tiberius' veto of the proposal to withhold rewards in cases of suicide on the grounds that safeguards against the abuse of law are apt to destroy its use makes perfectly good sense but also oddly reverses the rule *abusus non tollit usum*: abuse in a sense *is* use. Tacitus' own comment is that "informers, who are never properly deterred by penalties, now were being encouraged by rewards" (*Ann.* 4.30.2). Cf. Suet. *Dom.* 9.3: "If you do not punish delators, you create them."

On the illegality of a patriotic act and other anomalies in laws on suicide, see below, chap. 9, n. 13. M. Finley comments on the "classificatory monstrosity" of *liber homo bona fide serviens* created by the tangled social standing of a free person who believes that he or she is a slave; Finley, *The Ancient Economy,* 2d ed. (London: Hogarth, 1985), 65. See Addendum 1.

9. For a general discussion of counterfinality, that is, means inconsistent with their own ends, especially the distinction between mistaken individual judgment and rational but self-defeating collective action, see J. Elster, *Logic and Society* (New York: Wiley, 1978), 106–18.

When riddling oracles are held up as evidence of its uselessness, divination is being treated as an "information system"; see R. Lane Fox, *Pagans and Christians* (New York: Knopf, 1987), 212, 228. The transmission of opaque messages is the supreme counterfinality: "Interpreter needs interpreter and oracle must be referred to oracle" (Cic. *Div.* 2.115). Apparently impenetrable oracles in fact can be accommodated by the logic of divination insofar as the special communications problem they pose of having too many meanings or none at all marks the limits of human knowledge, not contradiction in the system. In the situation at the Caudine Forks it is the legal rules of warfare that work at cross-purposes to problematize another facet of social reality. The questionable trade-offs in this case between what is expedient and what is honorable and the incoherence of the relationship between the two has a modern parallel in an incident from World War II. After escaping during the fall of Singapore, Australian general H. Gordon Bennett was received without enthusiasm by the general staff in Melbourne, and a subsequent inquiry concluded that his departure was irregular because at the time he had not yet been a prisoner of war but was no longer a combatant either. To bolster its claim that the escape, normally a soldier's duty, was improper, the report held that even the Australian government could not have given him "permission" to escape once the supreme commander on the spot (British general Percival) had agreed to surrender. See L. Wigmore, *The Japanese Thrust* (Adelaide: Griffin, 1957), 384, 650–52.

"A Roman captured in a proper war ceased to be a citizen and at once became a foreign slave. If he returned to Rome in a way that was creditable to him, he regained his citizenship"; A. Watson, *International Law in Archaic Rome* (Baltimore: Johns Hopkins University Press, 1993), 42 (cf. 37–43 for the Caudine Forks case). On formalism as a special characteristic of Roman law and for further examples of "second-best" accommodation to legal dilemmas, see A. Watson, *The State, Law, and Religion* (Athens: University of Georgia Press, 1992), 64–70.

10. Other terms used by B. Whorf for core patterns are *meaning, configuration, rapport, thought world, habitual thought,* and *metaphysics.* Whorf, *Language, Thought, and Reality,* ed. J. B. Carroll (Cambridge, Mass.: MIT Press, 1956), 58, 67, 72, 74, 81, 89–92, 147, 258.

11. On theories that myth and ritual alike are patterned by paramount biological requirements of survival, see H. S. Versnel, "What's Sauce for the Goose Is Sauce for the Gander: Myth and Ritual, Old and New," in *Approaches to Greek*

Myth, ed. L. Edmunds (Baltimore: Johns Hopkins University Press, 1990), 60–62. If the end is security, the means are reestablishment of control. "Ritual represents the creation of a controlled environment whose artificiality stands for the norm violated by the actual state of affairs"; J. Z. Smith, *Imagining Religion* (Chicago: University of Chicago Press, 1982), 63. In this view, hunting ritual in which animals are killed in a wholly proper though unrealistic way is not sympathetic magic but a "perfect hunt with all the variables controlled" (64). Thus, so far as bloodshed in the arena was another ritual of control, *venationes* were perfect (entertaining), unrealistic, and entirely safe hunts. Ritual accordingly appears at weak spots: "Religious ritual and legal ceremony . . . confront problems and contradictions of the social process. . . . they are concerned with breaches of regular norm-governed relationships"; V. Turner, *Process, Performance, and Pilgrimage* (New Delhi: Concept, 1979), 88. "One often finds in human cultures that structural contradictions, asymmetries, and anomalies are overlaid by layers of myth, ritual, and symbol, which stress the axiomatic value of key structural principles with regard to the very situations where these appear to be most inoperative"; V. Turner, *The Ritual Process* (Chicago: Aldine, 1969), 47.

12. R. Bastide, "La Connaissance de l'evénément," in *Perspectives de la sociologie contemporaine: Hommage à Georges Gurvitch* (Paris: PUF, 1968), 165–66.

13. J. Tainter, *The Collapse of Complex Societies* (Cambridge: Cambridge University Press, 1988), 194.

Chapter 1. Public Spectacles as Broken Routine

1. Medical aspects of the stories are discussed in R. Brophy III, "Deaths in the Pan-Hellenic Games: Arrachion and Creugas," *American Journal of Philology* 99 (1978): 363–90. An instance of both competitors' dying mentioned by Philo (*Quod omnis probus liber sit;* 17.110–13) is treated in R. Brophy III and M. Brophy, "Deaths in the Pan-Hellenic Games II," *American Journal of Philology* 106 (1985): 194–97. When neither wins in another case, both are declared victors (see below, chap. 10, n. 1). Africanus' list of victors includes brief mention of legendary feats of speed or strength and of other special circumstances; Arrachion's posthumous victory is recorded among them, as is that of another winner who strangled his opponent in wrestling. Cf. J. Juthner, *Philostratos: Über Gymnastik* (1909; Amsterdam: Grüner, 1962), 62. Because death in the course of wrestling, boxing, or the *pancratium* had occurred during a quest for honor, it was not actionable under Roman law and was pertinent only to the freeborn (*Dig.* 9.2.7.4).

The affinity between athletics and the exceptional takes many forms. Record keeping, used also for gladiatorial contests, naturally tends to define sport by reference to extreme cases, though in a qualitative manner ("first," "best of his time") rather than the quantitative, statistical manner typical of modern culture. Recording only the winner and ignoring everyone else leads to a binary system reflecting the conception of competition as a simple zero-sum, win-lose proposition. Epitaphs, though, may name the deceased's killer (L. Robert, *Les Gladiateurs dans l'Orient grec* [Amsterdam: Hakkert, 1971], 232)—with (199, no.

214) or even without (95, no. 34) any mention of his own successes—and include the name of his avenger (95, no. 34; 146, no. 107). The five examples of which Arrachion is one are introduced in Philostratus' *On Gymnastics* by a paragraph on the military uses of athletic competition at Sparta (19). Two others besides Arrachion repeat the theme of victory or death. One contestant is inspired by a message from his trainer to his mother: "Believe it if you hear that your son is dead; don't, if you hear that he has lost"; another is stirred by a trainer's willingness to pledge his own life as surety under a law requiring that losers be executed (234). Extremely violent incidents that come up frequently in the lives of athletes (e.g., Heracles or the boxer Cleomedes; Paus. 6.9.6–8) mark their border status between human and divine and are patterned on stories of heroes; see J. Fontenrose, "The Hero as Athlete," *California Studies in Classical Antiquity* 1 (1968): 73–104; and J. Mikalson, *Honor Thy Gods* (Chapel Hill: University of North Carolina Press, 1991), 31. The problem of assigning a place in the social order to the physical violence of which heroes are capable is a particular instance of their generally ambivalent position, and the intense violence of competition that put real athletes in the same marginal position raised conceptual difficulties which received attention from fifth-century Sophists. See, e.g., Antiphon's *Tetralogies* (cf. Plut. *Per.* 36.3). On the religious dimension in Philostratus' version, see below, chap. 3, n. 23. A bibliographical survey of recent work on *munera* can be found in chap. 3, n. 1, below.

2. For judicious remarks on maintaining a balance between secular and religious facets of sport, modern as well as ancient, see J.-P. Thuillier, *Les Jeux athlétiques dans la civilisation étrusque,* Bibliothèque des Ecoles Françaises d'Athènes et de Rome 256 (Rome: Ecole Française de Rome, 1985), 416–17. On residual magical blood-power in gladiatorial games and *venationes,* see J. Bayet, "Le Suicide mutuel dans la mentalité des Romains," in *Croyances et rites dans la Rome antique* (Paris: Payot, 1971), 139. Some could still find the games deeply "pleasurable" in late antiquity, perhaps in defensive reaction to Christian criticism of their violence. See E. Merten, *Zwei Herrscherfeste in der Historia Augusta,* Antiquitas 4.5 (Bonn: Habelt, 1968), 78; and A. Chastagnol, *Trois Etudes sur la Vita Cari,* Antiquitas 4.12 (Bonn: Habelt, 1976), 75–80.

3. Thuillier, *Les Jeux athlétiques* 702.

4. Some brief remarks on ritual as a symbolic, cognitive system appear in S. R. F. Price, *Rituals and Power* (Cambridge: Cambridge University Press, 1984), 8–11. Cf. H. Penner, "Rationality, Ritual, and Science," in *Religion, Science, and Magic,* ed. J. Neusner, E. Frerichs, and P. Flesher (New York: Oxford University Press, 1989), 17; and J. Skorupski, *Symbol and Theory* (Cambridge: Cambridge University Press, 1976).

5. L. Friedlaender, *Sittengeschichte Roms,* 10th ed., vol. 2 (Leipzig: Hirzel, 1922), 53. Cf. C. Weber, *Panem et circenses* (Dusseldorf: Econ, 1983), 17: "Begierig sogen die Betrachter des grausamen Geschehens dieses aus Blutgier, Sadismus, Massenpsychose und pervertierten Unterhaltungsbedürfnis gemischte Gift in sich auf."

6. P. Veyne, ed., *From Pagan Rome to Byzantium,* vol. 1 of *A History of Private Life* (Cambridge, Mass.: Belknap, 1987), 202.

7. Virgil borrowed from the gladiatorial death ethic for the coup de grace delivered to Mezentius ("Deliberately accepting the sword thrust into his throat, he pours out his life on the armor in a gush of blood"; *Aen.* 10.907–8). Cf. P. Hardie, *Virgil's Aeneid: Cosmos and Imperium* (Oxford: Clarendon, 1986), 152–54. Stylized violence went with replacement of normal military accoutrements by stylized equipment; see G. Ville, "La Guerre et le munus," in *Problèmes de la guerre à Rome* (Paris: Mouton, 1969), 192–93.

8. S. Oakley, "Single Combat in the Roman Republic," *Classical Quarterly* 79 (1985): 392–410. The rarity of team sports in ancient society perhaps tended to foster strongly personal reactions in spectators toward the contestants. In the opening section of *De Ira* 2(2–4), Seneca emphasizes physical empathy—e.g., the urge to yawn when we see others yawning (cf. *Clem.* 2.6.4)—including reactions triggered by threats (*comminatio, ictus*) which make us blink or fear for our bodily safety in other ways. Thus *tristitia* at the sight of a make-believe shipwreck is due to consciousness of our own vulnerability. Cf. Ov. *Ars Am.* 1.164 (*tristis harena*). Seneca's remark about reactions "disturbing minds that do not want to be disturbed" (*De Ira* 2.2.5) underscores the power of raw impulse and also aptly characterizes the dissonant impulses which some public institutions arouse in order to allay. Anger proper occurs in the next stage, as reason joins in the reaction, while the last phase is a wholly irrational demand for furious action (2.3.5–4.1). Since anger (aggression) is sandwiched between impulses below and beyond reason, Seneca is naturally conscious of the dangerous side to communal violence of all kinds.

9. C. Barton, "The Scandal of the Arena," *Representations* 27 (1989): 8.

10. This point is made by James Boswell in "On Executions"; see Boswell, *The Hypochondriack,* vol. 2, ed. M. Bailey (Stanford, Calif.: Stanford University Press, 1928), 276–85. After explaining the attraction of "spectacles of cruelty," to which he was himself addicted, as caused by a combination of pleasure at one's own safety while others are in peril with a desire to be "moved," he goes on to say, "Of all publick spectacles, that of a capital execution draws the greatest number of spectators. And I must confess that I myself am never absent from any of them. Nor can I accuse myself of being more hard hearted than other people. On the contrary, I am persuaded that nobody feels more sincerely for the distresses of his fellow-creatures than I do, or would do more to relieve them. When I first attended executions, I was shocked to the greatest degree. I was in a manner convulsed with pity and terror, and for several days, but especially nights after, I was in a very dismal situation. Still, however, I persisted in attending them, and by degrees my sensibility abated; so that I now can see one with great composure, and my mind is not afterwards haunted with frightful thoughts: though for a while a certain degree of gloom remains upon it. I can account for this curiosity in a philosophical manner, when I consider that death is the most aweful object before every man, who ever directs his thoughts seriously towards futurity; and that it is very natural that we should be anxious to see people in that situation which affects us so much. It is true indeed that none of us, who go to see an execution have any idea that we are to be executed, and few of us needs be under any apprehension whatever of meeting with that fate. But dying publickly at

Tyburn, and dying privately in one's bed, are only different modes of the same thing. They are both death; they are both that wonderous, that alarming scene of quitting all that we have ever seen, heard, or known and at once passing into a state of being totally unknown to us, and in which we cannot tell what may be our situation. Therefore it is that I feel an irresistible impulse to be present at every execution, as I there behold the various effects of the near approach of death, according to the various tempers of the unhappy sufferers, and by studying them I learn to quiet and fortify my own mind."

The effect of public death is given an individual, philosophical turn here. Penal execution was only a minor part of the games at Rome, though it is the main target of Seneca's criticism in *Epistles* 7. Boswell, too, is aware of an immediate deterrent social effect ("We are sure society could not exist without such a right"; 276) as well as a broader defensive effect insofar as sobering reflections about death itself are widespread. On the same topic, Johnson remarked to him that most people never think of death because fear of it is so natural that "the whole of life is but keeping away thought of it" (279n8). Though this recognizes a lack of concern on the part of those for whom public violence is merely entertaining, it also recognizes fear of death as a repressed factor. Boswell's own recommendation that "the faces of those who are hanged should not be covered, as in Britain, but exposed, as is the custom upon the continent, that the distortions may be seen" (283) helps throw a slightly different light on the story about Claudius' eagerness to sit where he could watch the faces of gladiators as they died (Suet. *Claud.* 34.1). Suetonius seems to take it as a disgusting revelation of character, since Claudius had apparently himself denied *missio,* but it may have reflected a more normal aspect of the intense personal absorption in danger which Goffman calls "getting a piece of the action." See E. Goffman, *Interaction Ritual* (Chicago: Aldine, 1967), 149–270.

Some survivals of the rationale for gladiatorial violence operative in the public brutality of more recent times are discussed in M. Foucault, *Discipline and Punish,* trans. A. Sheridan (New York: Pantheon, 1977): replication of criminal violence by quantifying pain and making it formally proportional to the crime (34); repairing breaches in public order through theatrical, purposely excessive penalties (47–51; for atrocity as a positive idea, see 55–56); connections with warfare (57). The intensity of emotions aroused during public executions often led to reversals of the kind described by Boswell, as disgust became pity or awe, the victim was glorified, and rioting ensued (Foucault 50, 59–65). The "element of challenge and of jousting in the ceremony of public execution" (51) is an even closer approximation to the entertainment provided by gladiatorial combat. The dual aim of terrorizing the public into obedience while inducing it to join in inflicting punishment—e.g., through mistreatment of the criminal (58–59)—parallels the dual function of the games as deterrent display of power and occasion for public self-identification with the use of power to eliminate undesirables, for example, through the crowd's right to decide whether a gladiator is spared or not. Cf. Athenagoras, *Embassy* 35.

The powerful, somewhat unfocused violence associated especially with execution or sacrifice of prisoners at funeral rites is discussed in D. Hughes, *Human*

Sacrifice in Ancient Greece (London: Routledge, 1991), 6–7, 54–56. Destructive sacrifices not utilized (e.g., eaten) but gotten rid of mark close encounters with death and express grief felt as anger toward others or oneself. Grief, of course, was not prominent among the emotions let loose by death in the arena, though anger of a sort was, and so occasionally was fear or pity.

11. V. Abt, J. Smith, and E. Christiansen, *The Business of Risk* (Lawrence: University Press of Kansas, 1985), 20; on compulsive gambling, see 122–26. In "Where the Action Is" (*Interaction Ritual* 149–270), E. Goffman examines the many guises which risk taking, viz. "action," assumes. His analysis of how "character" (214–39) is defined through popular expectations of right behavior under pressure—particularly a cool, "game" way of dying by criminals (229–33)—is especially suggestive in connection with standards of professional behavior for gladiators at Rome.

The survey of major sociological theories of gambling by Abt, Smith, and Christiansen (16–26) brings up other parallels with arena games. A (largely illusory) opportunity of sharing in power and wealth is offered to ordinary people by gambling (21); games, likewise, helped create an impression that Roman society as a whole was receiving a share of imperial power to which it was entitled. Highly egalitarian odds in some forms of gambling, notably public lotteries, similarly reinforce a political message about the availability of wealth to everyone (21–22); at Rome, public appetite, already catered to through generous *munera* "owed" by those in power, was further satisfied by popular participation in blind, lotterylike distributions *(sparsiones)* in conjunction with games. In modern society, gambling mimics respectable economic activity such as investing (22); similarly, combat in the arena borrowed respectability from the warfare it imitated. The contradiction between widespread disagreement in modern societies about whether gambling is a good or a bad thing (25) and its immense growth in the public sphere (26) parallel the expansion of *munera* at Rome despite reservations about gladiators.

12. T. Mitchell, *Blood Sport* (Philadelphia: University of Pennsylvania Press, 1991), 56–74, See Addendum 3.

13. Details can be found in B. Brundage, *The Jade Steps* (Salt Lake City: University of Utah Press, 1985), 89–90, 155–78. On Mayan culture, see L. Schele and M. Miller, *The Blood of Kings* (New York: Braziller, 1986), 111, 209–40.

14. J. Broda, D. Carrasco, and E. Moctezuma, *The Great Temple of Tenochtitlan* (Berkeley: University of California Press, 1987), 65; G. Conrad and A. Demarest, *Religion and Empire* (Cambridge: Cambridge University Press, 1984), 59, 216; E. Boone, ed., *Ritual Human Sacrifice in MesoAmerica* (Washington, D.C.: Dumbarton Oaks, 1984), 43–44. The latter study has some remarks on mass carnage in other cultures (221), on its entertainment value in Mexican society (57), and on the connections between sport, death, and the underworld (119–27; see Brundage, *Jade Steps* 140–44). In Mayan sport, severed ball-heads could be replaced by living victims trussed into the shape of a ball before being killed. "Captives were forced to play the ballgame in a court; the defeated captives were taken to a temple and bound into the form of a ball; in the finale, they were rolled down the stairway to their deaths" (Schele and Miller, *Blood of Kings*

249). In another parallel pointing to similar religious roots, Mayan idols' mouths were smeared with blood drained from the chests of sacrificial victims (Brundage 164), and at Rome, blood taken from gladiators was poured perhaps into the mouth of a statue of Jupiter. A more general ideological parallel is the sheer scale of human sacrifice as a vehicle for exercising power from the center over peripheral regions in Mexico (Broda, Carrasco, and Moctezuma 154–56) and control of costly games from Rome to assert central imperial authority.

15. C. Duverger, *L'Esprit du jeu chez les Aztèques* (Paris: Mouton, 1978), fig. 25, compared with Thuillier, *Les Jeux athlétiques* 124, 210 *(fig. 28)*. Also Duverger 143, 199.

16. Conrad and Demarest, *Religion and Empire* 59–60.

17. Duverger, *L'Esprit* 92–93, 123–28. Aztec gods depended for their existence on (human) sacrifice in an unusually direct way: see J.-P. Vernant, "Theorie générale du sacrifice et mise a mort dans la *thysia* grecque," in *Le Sacrifice dans l'antiquité,* Entretiens sur l'Antiquité Classique 27 (Geneva: Fondation Hardt, 1981), 12 n1.

18. On "taming" death in Aztec ritual, see Duverger, *L'Esprit* 131, 145.

19. Ibid., 133–34; on defeat implicit in victory, see 180, 277 ("Le somptueux manifeste la puissance. Mais la pompe ne saurait faire oublier la sourde et terrifiante anxiété du peuple mexicain"). On the unusual scale of human sacrifice and its link to anxiety, see Brundage, *Jade Steps* 42, 67, 171; animals, too, were ritually slaughtered (194).

20. Duverger, *L'Esprit* 126–28, 134–55, 204–6, 261–74. See Conrad and Demarest, *Religion and Empire,* chaps. 2 and 5, on the ultimate contradiction in a system of life-giving death analogous to the antinomy of antisocial social games at Rome.

Chapter 2. Games and Liminoid Ritual

1. Turner, *Process, Performance* 36–59; idem, *Ritual Process* 36–52; idem, "Comments and Conclusions," in *The Reversible World,* ed. B. Babcock (Ithaca, N.Y.: Cornell University Press, 1978), 287. The liminal is "that which is neither this nor that, and yet is both"; V. Turner, *Forest of Symbols* (Ithaca, N.Y.: Cornell University Press, 1967), 99. Gennep's original scheme has three phases: separation from normalcy, a marginal or liminal condition, and reaggregation. In nonritual, liminoid transpositions, these appear more generally as abandonment of normal criteria in speech, physical appearance, or behavior; formal oddity (riddles, anatomical freaks); and resolution into normal meaning (riddles solved, freaks eliminated).

2. A. van Gennep, *The Rites of Passage,* trans. M. Vizedom and G. Caffee (Chicago: University of Chicago Press, 1960), 191–92.

3. Ibid., 113. On gladiatorial games as *fantastiques rites de passage,* see M. Clavel-Lévêque, *L'Empire en jeux* (Paris: CNRS, 1984), 75; on their role as *rituels d'intégration* more generally, see 10, 84. Although gladiators as a class are subject to final expulsion, combat in the arena, from the individual gladiator's own perspective, includes a third phase of return. Having survived the ordeal, the

successful fighter returns to his own world, and in cases of manumission or grants of citizenship after an impressive series of victories, he is accepted in the larger society as well. I owe this point to Richard Saller. In divination the sequence danger/response/restoration involves ritual expulsion ("extermination" in the original sense) of intrusive elements such as monstrous births.

4. T. Mitchell, *Violence and Piety in Spanish Folklore* (Philadelphia: University of Pennsylvania Press, 1988), 94.

5. Gennep, *Rites of Passage,* chap. 8.

6. Ibid., 148, 164.

7. Clavel-Lévêque, *L'Empire en jeux* 11n8. The arena becomes representational space in mosaics as the viewer, who takes the crowd's place, looks at participants themselves looking away toward an invisible editor, whose implied presence manifests itself in visible control over the life or death of defeated fighters. See S. Brown, "Death as Decoration: Scenes from the Arena on Roman Domestic Mosaics," in *Pornography and Representation in Greece and Rome,* ed. A. Richlin (New York: Oxford University Press, 1992), 205–7. Only at Rome and then only when the emperor was in attendance would the social macrocosm be complete; elsewhere a lesser, microcosmic spectacle of unity was to be seen. Presiding over games from a special seat, the emperor embodied the same culmination of social order that appeared in reliefs showing him as paradigmatic sacrificer. See R. Gordon, "The Veil of Power: Emperors, Sacrifices, and Benefactors," in *Pagan Priests,* ed. M. Beard and J. North (London: Duckworth, 1990), 201–31. On the visual impact of monuments and festivals, see A. Rouvert, "Tacite et les monuments," in *ANRW* II.33.4 (Berlin: De Gruyter, 1991), 3057.

8. On political messages coded in professional wrestling, see B. Lincoln, *Discourse and the Construction of Society* (Oxford: Oxford University Press, 1989), 148–59; and Barthes, "World of Wrestling" 15–25.

9. M. Douglas, *Purity and Danger* (New York: Praeger, 1966), 35.

Chapter 3. Gladiatorial Combat

1. Tert. *De Spect.* 12; Auson. *Eclogues* 23.33–36. On the development of gladiatorical combat from sacrifice to game, see I. Weiler, *Der Sport bei den Völkern der Alten Welt* (Darmstadt: Wissenschaftliche Buchgesellschaft, 1981), 228–32; on the multiple function of games, see 244. The distinction between ritual killing and sacrifice is discussed in Hughes, *Human Sacrifice* 1–3. General treatments of arena games can be found in *Dictionnaire des antiquités grecques et romains,* s.v. "gladiator" and "venatio"; *PW,* suppl. 3, s.v. "gladiatores"; Friedlaender, *Sittengeschichte Roms* 1–112; G. Ville, *La Gladiature en Occident des origines à la mort de Domitien,* Bibliothèque des Ecoles Françaises d'Athènes et de Rome 245 (Rome: Ecole Française de Rome, 1981); D. Nardoni, *I gladiatori romani* (Rome: Edizioni Italiane di Letterature e Scienze, 1989); J. P. V. D. Balsdon, *Life and Leisure in Ancient Rome* (New York: McGraw-Hill, 1969), 288–302; R. Auguet, *Cruelty and Civilization* (London: Allen and Unwin, 1972); M. Grant, *Gladiators* (London: Weidenfeld and Nicolson, 1967); T. Wiedemann, *Emperors and Gladiators* (London: Routledge, 1992); Weber, *Panem et circenses;*

M. Clavel-Lévêque, "Rituels de mort et consommation de gladiateurs," in *Hommages à Lucien Lerat I*, Annales Littéraires de l'Université de Besançon 29, ed. H. Walter (Paris: Belles Lettres, 1984), 189–208; Veyne, *Bread and Circuses* 208–14, 221–22, 354, 398–419; C. Barton, *The Sorrows of the Ancient Romans* (Princeton, N.J.: Princeton University Press, 1993); M. Sassi, *Il linguaggio gladiatorio* (Bologna: Patron, 1992); and Robert, *Les Gladiateurs*. An annotated collection of passages concerned with Roman games in general is available in S. Barthelemy and D. Gourevitch, *Les Loisirs des Romains* (Paris: Société d'Edition d'Enseignement Superieur, 1975), 156–255. J.-C. Golvin and C. Landes, *Amphitheatres et gladiateurs* (Paris: CNRS, 1990), has numerous illustrations.

2. For this and some of the following points, see Ville, *La Gladiature* 282–86, 276–77, 303, 308–12. As ties with funerals were broken and games could be given for any number of reasons or for none in particular (78–88, 158, 169, 172, 201, 204), they came to represent violence in the abstract (on the increase of pure violence, see 15–16, 423–24). H. S. Versnel argues that human death in the arena may in fact have retained strong sacrificial connections even under the Empire; see Versnel, *Inconsistencies in Greek and Roman Religion*, vol. 2 (Leiden: Brill, 1993), 210–17.

A similar shift toward the abstract appears in divination. While some of the signs grouped together by Livy (e.g., 22.1.8–15, 27.11.1–6) were probably in fact individually expiated, groups of signs may occasionally have been dealt with all at once. The latter procedure, which is consonant with the preference for generic over individual forms in Roman social organization, additionally suggests a relatively abstract *procuratio* not directed at specific signs but serving as an omnibus response to all signs that occur during some period of time. See *PW* 23.2, 2294, s.v. "prodigium"; M. Beard, "Priesthood in the Roman Republic," in *Pagan Priests*, ed. M. Beard and J. North (London: Duckworth, 1990), 31; and North, "Diviners and Divination" 54. After a certain quantity of disorder had been put on record, so to speak, the books were squared when the Senate took action on prodigies seen during the previous year and reported all at once to it by the consul. This is an administratively efficient procedure reckoning as much with danger as such as with any particular threat. On apotropaic measures directed against abstract threats, see C. Faraone, *Talismans and Trojan Horses* (New York: Oxford University Press, 1992), 42. The flexibility of vows made with a proviso for fulfillment at any time or place (Livy 36.2.5, 22.10.1–6) presumably was justified by thinking of the danger in question abstractly; one *ver sacrum* was delayed for twenty-one years (Livy 33.44.2). As ritual loses specific concrete meaning, it tends to become symbolic and abstract: it was sufficient to declare war by throwing a spear into a small piece of enemy territory located at Rome, another military unit could substitute in a triumph for the victorious army still away on campaign, and ritual marches around Rome were staged at a few symbolic places. See H. Scullard, *Festivals and Ceremonies of the Roman Republic* (Ithaca, N.Y.: Cornell University Press, 1981), 146, 214, 125.

3. Tert. *Adv. Marcionem* 1.27.5; Ville, *La Gladiature* 467. For a collection of passages from Christian literature, see Ville 273–97. The nude swimming in flooded orchestras denounced later by John Chrysostom as Aqua-Follies, in a

strong moral sense of the term, combined theatrical entertainment with the athletic and technological marvels of the arena; see G. Traversari, *Gli spettacoli in
acqua nel teatro Tardo-Antico* (Rome: Bretschneider, 1960), 46–48. Though
public shows were most often presented in theaters, chariot racing was viewed by
a far larger number of people; Balsdon, *Life and Leisure* 268.

4. At Olympia athletes themselves might consult an oracle to help with the
severe pressures of competition. See Philostr. *Heroicus* 52–58; *Greek Anthology*
11.161, 163. The second of these epigrams is actually a joke about expecting very
much relief from that source: the answer is "You will win, unless you lose." Cf.
Cic. *Div.* 2. 144 for a parodic interpretation of athletes' anxiety dreams.

5. M. Clavel-Lévêque, "L'Espace des jeux dans le monde romain," in *ANRW*
II.16.3 (Berlin: De Gruyter, 1986): "Ces expériences, dans le champ réduit de l'aire
de jeu, les spectateurs peuvent les vivre 'comme exorcisme ou comme exercise.'
. . . L'expérience ludique . . . fait vivre par procuration des émotions et des
pulsions que la vie quotidienne réprime . . . [the games] apparaissent comme
exercise de maîtrise sur un objet d'essai, plus petit et plus facile à manier, et manié
par d'autres, quand il est plus dangereux" (2468). Through sublimation they
provided "satisfactions substitutives à des renonciations aux désirs primitifs"
(2464). As a liminoid mode they represent a subjunctive, rather than an indicative, time and place where hopes and fears can be dealt with more freely.

6. J. Goldstein, ed., *Sports, Games, and Play* (Hillsdale, N.J.: Halsted Press,
1979), esp. 185f, 247f. Cf. Fox, *Pagans and Christians* 65, on the anger that was
felt by Romans to be a special problem in their society. It helped solidify political
alliances, but only by fostering a highly aggressive sense of group membership
and competition against personal enemies. Such a cultural climate might well be a
necessary, though not sufficient, factor for making bloody combat in the arena
acceptable. The stimulating effect of competition is what L. Fiedler calls, in
connection with pornography, "watering [rather than purging] the emotions";
Fiedler, "Towards a Definition of Popular Culture," in *Superculture: American
Popular Culture and Europe,* ed. C. Bigsby (Bowling Green, Ohio: Bowling Green
State University Press, 1975), 40–41.

7. R. Caldwell, *The Origin of the Gods* (Oxford: Oxford University Press,
1989), 8. Caldwell is referring specifically to Burkert's definition, which in its
focus on violence is especially applicable to the games, both human combat and
hunting. "Anxiety is involved in many human rituals, and one might be tempted
to make this the definition of religious ritual. . . . many religious rituals seem
intentionally, and artificially, to produce the atmosphere of awe, using all the
registers of darkness, fire, blood, and death. What happens, then, is a concentration and shift of anxiety from reality to a symbolic sphere, and this makes it
possible to handle anxiety to some extent. . . . Religious ritual, by producing
anxiety, manages to control it. . . . Even feelings of pollution and guilt become
manageable, as highly artificial taboos are set up with expiatory ritual in the
background to make up for each transgression. And as anxiety tends to draw a
group together, group solidarity is all the more established by the experience and
performance of anxiety overcome"; W. Burkert, *Homo necans,* trans. P. Bing
(Berkeley: University of California Press, 1983), 50. This restates, from another

point of view, Seneca's point about the overwhelming influence exercised by crowds on individuals at the arena (below, chap. 6). Cf. Burkert's remarks on the conjunction of anxiety with rage in the violence of sacrifice: Burkert, "Glaube und Verhalten," in *Le Sacrifice dans l'antiquité*, Entretiens sur l'Antiquité Classique 27 (Geneva: Fondation Hardt, 1981), 112–15. Human sacrifice is the desperate and vicarious act of a man "fighting like a cornered rat" (115)—exactly what was wanted vicariously from gladiators.

8. On the disturbing presence of gladiators in Roman society, see K. Bradley, *Slavery and Rebellion in the Roman World, 140 B.C.–70 B.C.* (Bloomington: Indiana University Press, 1989), 84–90; O. Kiefer, "Der Römer und die Grausamkeit," in *Kulturgeschichte Roms* (Berlin: Aretz, 1933), 67, 96 (with reference to Stekel in connection with the idea of the will to power); and Grant, *Gladiators* 114. "There might well be present, or develop in certain individuals, a special 'killing instinct,' a unique and thrilling experience, an experience of power, of breakthrough, of triumph," writes W. Burkert in R. G. Hamerton-Kelly, ed., *Violent Origins* (Stanford, Calif.: Stanford University Press, 1987), 170. Killing gladiators or slaves is a symbolic exercise of power over everyone who could be dangerous to society (Clavel-Lévêque, "L'Espace des jeux" 2426f). "The purpose of the most brutal and apparently archaic rituals is not merely to relax taboos and have a nice 'recreation' in the limited modern sense, but literally to re-create the community by reenacting a process of community disintegration and regeneration" (R. Girard in *Violent Origins* 127). See J. Huizinga, *Homo ludens*, trans. R. F. C. Hull (New York: Harper and Row, 1970), 77, on games as (magic) control over events. See also Ville, *La Gladiature* 457, 462–64. K. Hopkins, in *Death and Renewal* (Cambridge: Cambridge University Press, 1983), 29, notes that games create order through fear, substitute for the thrill of war, and assuage fear of death. Sartre has an interesting discussion of laughter (which is a natural by-product of entertainment) as a defense mechanism for ejecting outsiders who violate the rules of a group; see J.-P. Sartre, *The Family Idiot: Gustave Flaubert, 1821–1857*, trans. C. Cosman, vol. 2 (Chicago: University of Chicago Press, 1987), 153–66. On laughter as aggressive display of teeth, see Burkert, *Homo necans* 24.

In light of gladiators' status as expendable outsiders, a scene described by Dio (72.21.1–2) is remarkably revealing. Commodus stands in the arena before the seats of the senators, saying not a word but grinning, in one hand the severed head of an ostrich, in the other a bloody sword. Violence plays out here in a rich set of opposites—senate/emperor, human/animal, center/periphery, performer/spectator—which leave uncertain how power is being used and where danger or security is. Dio adds that he and his fellow senators kept themselves from bursting out in laughter by chewing leaves from the laurel they were wearing to avoid inflaming Commodus further. The laughter, surely anxious as well as amused despite Dio's claim that it was not caused by any distress *(lypē)* they felt, brings out the volatility of the forces put into play in the atmosphere of the arena. (A counterpart to this scene outside the arena and with the figure of authority in danger occurs in Germanicus' strange confrontation with mutinous troops [Tac. *Ann.* 1.35.5].) The uncertain boundary in *munera* between human political violence and animal violence lies behind metaphors such as Valens "raging with frenzy as though trained to do harm like a beast in the arena" (Amm. Marc. 29.1.27); see R. MacMullen, *Changes in the Roman Empire* (Princeton, N.J.: Princeton University Press, 1990), 92–93. In a jesting reverse metaphor, one of Valentinian's pet bears, trained for viciousness, was nicknamed Innocentia and finally set free in reward for "burying [in herself] many victims"; J. Matthews, *The Roman Empire of Ammianus* (London: Duckworth, 1989), 260. On less perverse nicknames for animals and on gladiators' names drawn from myth, see Robert, *Les Gladiateurs* 191, 299 (Eteocles sets up a memorial to his brother, Polyneices [211, no. 245]; Achillia fights Amazon [188, no. 184]).

9. "Rituals . . . may well disclose . . . what it is that primarily bothers a society, what are the problems that threaten its cohesion"; W. Doty, *Mythography* (University: University of Alabama Press, 1986), 88. K. Coleman, in "Fatal Charades: Roman Executions Staged as Mythological Enactments," *Journal of Roman Studies* 80 (1990): 72–73, suggests "correlation between a disaster-ridden reign and the mounting of an exotic extravaganza in the arena." On publicly reassuring threats of punishment to slaves in Plautus, see H. Parker, "Crucially Funny," *Transactions and Proceedings of the American Philological Association* 119 (1989): 233–40. Condemnation of Christians to the arena in the course of persecution was at times due to genuinely defensive fear, confirmed by oracles, that the gods were angry at the Christians' atheism; see Fox, *Pagans and Christians* 426, 486.

10. On this view of the temple's place in the Augustan system and the requirement that barbarian leaders take an oath of obedience there (Suet. *Aug.* 21.2), see J. Croon, "Die Ideologie des Mars Kultes unter dem Principat und ihre Vorgeschichte," in *ANRW* II.17.1 (Berlin: De Gruyter, 1981), 246–75. Croon also notes that despite the strength of Augustus' position, only the violence which Mars embodied permitted the god to safeguard the Empire's security (274). Croon remarks on the irony that later emperors, who also made propaganda out of Mars in his aspect as conserver and peacemaker, had to spend a great deal of time on war (272).

11. K. Latte, *Römische Religionsgeschichte*, 2d ed., Handbuch der Altertumswissenschaft 5.1 (Munich: Beck, 1967), 119–20. See above, chap. 2, on the expulsion of the gladiator.

12. On the character of Mars and Quirinus, see G. Dumezil, *Archaic Roman Religion*, vol. 1, trans. P. Krapp (Chicago: University of Chicago Press, 1970), 209, 259–62. Dedications to Iuventas—symbol of Rome's vigorous but vulnerable youth—during the Hannibalic crisis combined anxiety and confidence; see Scullard, *Festivals* 208. The analogous protective but destructive hero (Achilles, Heracles, Ajax, Horatius) is another case in point. Mars was typically ambivalent or neutral (*caecus*, Luc. 7.111; *communis*, Sen. *De Ira* 1.12.5), and when his negative potential was the object of cult, he was seen as protector-defender rather than victor; see V. Rosivach, "Mars, the Lustral God," *Latomus* 42 (1983): 509–21. If the triumphator is "he who raises the apotropaic cry, 'Io, triumphe,'" in moments of great danger, he is precisely triumphator and not (yet) victor; see G. Radke, *Zur Entwicklung der Gottesvorstellung und der Gottesverehrung in Rom* (Darmstadt: Wissenschaftliche Buchgesellschaft, 1987), 209–10. On the ambivalent

public image of soldiers, see J.-M. Carrie, "The Soldiers," in *The Romans*, ed. A. Giardina, trans. L. Cochrane (Chicago: University of Chicago Press, 1993), 116–17; and N. Dixon, *On the Psychology of Military Incompetence* (London: Cape, 1976), 202.

Fortuna shows the same pattern. While it tends to be *good* luck and Roman expressions of confidence especially in military matters are common (Latte, *Römische Religionsgeschichte* 178–79), optimism in the nature of the case is a matter of degree relative to grounds for pessimism and often serves as propagandistic image-making to strengthen tough-mindedness in the face of insecurity. Cf. fortuna's connection with *Spes*. The powerful negative component in *religio* was bound at best to create optimism of the kind felt by a doctor before a hazardous operation or by the conspirators who reportedly took a dagger from the temple of Fortuna (Tac. *Ann.* 15.53.2). *Fortuna melior* (Latte 179) is more obviously wishful thinking, blind chance seems prominent in *Fors Fortuna* (*PW* 7.1, s.v. "Fortuna," 18), and Cicero mentions an altar to *mala Fortuna* (*Nat. D.* 3.25.63). For *Fortuna dubia, casualis,* or *brevis,* see *PW* 7.1.30. Additionally, Hellenistic ideas about *Tyche* influenced Roman attitudes. Livy prefaces a catalog of military blunders with a remark about Fortuna blinding people to prevent them from frustrating her purposes (5.37–38); cf. "Surely fortune is always the decisive factor, causing success and failure to everything on the basis of its own whim rather than of true merit or facts" (Sall. *Cat.* 8.1).

Purification was probably the original core of triumphal ritual, performed regularly each year in conjunction not so much with victory as with the danger entailed by warfare itself. On the other hand, the self-indulgent magnificence of later triumphs reflecting influence from Hellenistic kingship emphasized power—for example, by parading and killing captives—while celebration of a triumph only on special occasions recognized the victor's personal accomplishment; see M. Lemosse, "Les Eléments techniques de l'ancien triomphe romain et le problème de son origin," in *ANRW* I.2 (Berlin: De Gruyter, 1972), 444–48. Analogously, the cult of Victory, too, registered alternative views of military success, as either assigned by autonomous capricious Chance or earned by the victor's own *virtus*. When the second of these predominated or the charismatic leader was believed to enjoy permanent divine favor, the hazards of chance were minimized, and then irresistible universal power became the principal message of propaganda; see J. Fears, "The Theology of Victory at Rome," in *ANRW* II.17.2 (Berlin: De Gruyter, 1981), 745–49, 780–82. But confidence in the power of individuals or the state does not exclude strong awareness of the costs and uncertainties of victory and requires constant confirming especially in times of crisis (Fears 815). However genuinely pacific Roman intentions were, *iustitia, pax, concordia,* or *securitas* were always contingent on "der bewaffnete Weltsfriede"; see H. Stier, "Augustusfriede und römische Klassik," in *ANRW* II.2 (Berlin: De Gruyter, 1975), 21–23.

Signs served a similar dual function, foreshadowing success when properly dealt with yet always marking the uncertain rhythm of war. Like alarming medical symptoms, they may temporarily be false alarms but sooner or later come true. See D. Levene, *Religion in Livy* (Leiden: Brill, 1993), 108–9. On the reciprocity of positive and negative in divination and in the triumph, the latter including measures to avert the danger of *Fortuna a tergo gloriae carnifex* (Pliny *HN* 28.39), see T. Köves-Zulauf, *Reden und Schweigen,* Studia et Testimonia 12 (Munich: Fink, 1972), 65, 121–49, 287.

13. W. Harris, *War and Imperialism in Republican Rome, 327–70 B.C.* (Oxford: Clarendon, 1979), 35.

14. For a discussion of theories concerning the triumph in general, see H. S. Versnel, *Triumphus* (Leiden: Brill, 1970); procedural details are collected in *PW* 7.1, s.v. "triumphus," 493–511.

15. Versnel describes links to New Year's festivals (*Triumphus* 201–303); cf. Wiedemann, *Emperors and Gladiators* 47, for similar connections in the case of *munera*. The combination of positive and negative energy (e.g., in *spolia opima*) is treated in Versnel 78, 312, 379. Cf. Addendum 3.

If *munera* incorporated a pattern of order and disorder, triumph and danger, reacting on each other, then festivals *(feriae)* and games *(ludi)*, in which *munera* were frequently included, showed a similar polar contrast. Besides fixed *(stativae)* festivals, there were movable *(conceptivae)* festivals, whose date could be adjusted to circumstances, and emergency *(imperativae)* festivals given in response to crises (Macrob. *Sat.* 1.16.4–6). The latter were operationally much like *procuratio*, answering unexpected oblative signs in divination, and in fact festivals or games were commonly established to help avert danger. In the case of imminent military danger, anxiety-ridden defensive festivals constituted, from a formal point of view, an antitype to the triumph, in which negative elements were subordinate to celebration of success. Thus the cult of (Bona) Mens, founded after the battle at Trasimene apparently as a reminder of the consequences of bad military judgment, did for society at large what the slave's warning did for the triumphator. A sense of insecurity made itself felt in the religious calendar at many places, in unlucky days of military catastrophe, in obscure festivals with purificatory or apotropaic aims (Regifugium, Poplifugia; see Scullard, *Festivals* 81, 106, 148, 159), and in festivals that included unusually brutal episodes that were probably apotropaic in origin (foxes burned alive or dogs crucified; Scullard 103, 170). When Caesar had some mutineers ritually decapitated and their heads fixed near the Regia, he may have been tapping an obscure ritual in which fear and confidence were made to work together by similar treatment of a horse's head to stimulate military vigor (Dio 43.24.4; Scullard 193–94). At the Fordicidia, when the ashes of a cow's fetus torn from its mother and burned were kept for later use as fertilizer in the fields, the fertility that both phases of the action had ultimately in view was enhanced through polar gestures of life-taking brutality and life-giving nourishment. In dealing with death directly, negative and positive possibilities were sharply separated between two distinct festivals for departed spirits, the Parentalia affording friendly contact, the Lemuria sinister contact with the dead. In the arena death was entertaining because it was encountered both ways at once.

16. *Munera* given *pro salute* for the emperor had immediate political motives (Ville, *La Gladiature,* 160–64, 208–11) but sprang from concern about warding or buying off danger (Suet. *Calig.* 14.2, 27.2; Dio 59.8.3) through grateful (and

nervous) celebration of power. More immediate danger to the emperor's life was countered by more drastic suicidal *devotio* on the part of individuals (Versnel, *Inconsistencies* 219–27). *Supplicatio,* too, performed in response to troubled circumstances, had defensive *(obsecratio)* and assertive *(gratulatio)* facets. Faced by ominous signs, Nero anxiously offered "what he called festivals for his safety" (Dio 61.18.3). It is true that on a later occasion his entry into Rome was marked by what seems to have been a highly confident, parodic triumph celebrating artistic rather than military prowess (Suet. *Ner.* 25.1–2; Dio 63.20); cf. M. Morford, "Nero's Patronage and Participation in the Arts," in *ANRW* II.32.3 (Berlin: De Gruyter, 1985), 2026. Perhaps his reputation for contempt of *religio* (Suet. *Ner.* 56) stemmed from such gestures. The return from Greece, however, is also linked by Dio with a "frightening" personal warning about conspiracy at home (63.19.1), and if the two were connected, the triumph may be another example of a defensive reaction as unrealistic as other ostensibly confident actions Nero took toward the end of his regime. For the connection between assertive vengeance and defensive self-protection, i.e., between triumph and danger, in Roman legal tradition, see A. Lintott, *Violence in Republican Rome* (Oxford: Clarendon, 1968), 49–50.

17. Burkert, *Homo necans* 23, 26: "Ritual [is] a behavioral pattern that has its primary function—present in its unritualized model—but which persists in a new function, that of communication . . . , [which] can also be one-sided [as well as reciprocal], as, for example, when a threatening gesture is answered by ritual submission, which thus yields a hierarchy. . . . A religious rite is almost always 'serious': some danger is evoked arousing anxiety, which then heightens attention and lifts the subsequent proceedings out of the colorful stream of daily experience. . . . By far the greatest impression is made by what terrifies, and it is just this that makes aggressive rituals so significant." "When another dies, the frightening confrontation with death and the pleasurable shock of survival leaves a deep impression" (ibid. 50). This principle, especially relevant to the arena, helps bring out the force of Tacitus' comparison of mutual slaughter by sixty thousand barbarians to a marvelous, deeply gratifying spectacle watched in complete safety by the Romans (*Germ.* 33). Representations on monuments often focus on the coup de grâce; vital anatomy is shown unprotected, perhaps because fatal injury seemed preferable to mutilation; and natural death or death by accident or disease was worth mentioning on epitaphs because gladiators normally died violently (Robert, *Les Gladiateurs* 120–22, 69, 233, 293). For the contrary, terrifying intrusion of arenalike carnage into real life, see chap. 6. Those fighting in the arena are foreign and (ultimately) dead, while those watching are citizens who live on. The contrast is the same as that between blood spilt *(cruor)* and blood in the veins *(sanguis),* the former being cognate with *crudelitas,* the idea from which gladiatorial combat in fact took its social purpose; see J. Maurin, "Les Barbares aux arènes," *Ktema* 9 (1984): 102–11.

On "consensual pageantry" binding ancient society together, see Fox, *Pagans and Christians* 81; on festivals like the Saturnalia as a means to legitimate order through limited disorder and not merely as occasions for venting lower-class anger, see J. N. Bremmer, ed., *Interpretations of Greek Mythology* (Totowa,

N.J.: Barnes and Noble, 1986), 138. Legitimacy and solidarity would both be enhanced by the thought that death in the arena was an extension of ritualized capital punishment; cf. Burkert 46n46.

N. Luhmann's distinction between risk on the one side, danger on the other, applies to the different modes of experiencing violence at the arena. Danger comes from external objective threats, risk from the consequences of human decisions. In these terms, the gladiator's risk represents society's danger. See Luhmann, *Risk: A Sociological Theory,* trans. R. Barrett (Berlin: De Gruyter, 1993), 18–31, 200.

Joyce Carol Oates touches on similar symbolic aspects of modern boxing in *On Boxing* (Garden City, N.Y.: Doubleday, 1987). Referees, who are the official representatives of society within the ring with authority to control violence and determine the victor, were also present at some ancient combat sports. At Rome the presiding official, especially the emperor, held an analogous position, though the spectators could exercise more direct control over victory and defeat than they do now in boxing (47–50). For pictorial representation of the victor's symbolic look away from the loser toward the invisible editor to mark the last phase of combat, see Brown, "Death as Decoration." In one mosaic (204–5), if the word *neco* is spoken by the editor and means "I kill," he is specifically claiming authority over life and death. In modern society, while other sports also permit the crowd to share in a communal triumph, boxing reverts to the "murderous infancy of the race" and does so in a special area, the ring, governed by primitive rules (Oates 19). For the equally primitive notion that potency can be transferred to the fan (fanatic?) through contact with the fighter's sweat (108), compare the immensely strong Maximinus, who collected and exhibited his sweat in quart-size jars (*Hist. Aug.* 4.3) The crowd's frenzy at peaks of violence marks its eagerness to share in primal victory over the opponent, the Other whose social incarnation beyond the ring may reflect tensions in modern society (e.g., white resentment at successful black boxers), as gladiators' social marginality and mobility did in ancient society (Oates 62–69).

18. Clavel-Lévêque, *L'Empire en jeux* 71. On ritual as a game (with reference to Lévi-Strauss) and its distancing effect, see S. Tambiah, *Culture, Thought, and Social Action* (Cambridge, Mass.: Harvard University Press, 1985), 128–46; on "learning to learn," see 132. The notion of ritually fixed games throws light on a puzzling passage in Tacitus (*Germ.* 10.6). Before entering battle, one tribe would match a prisoner of war in combat against one of its own members, with the outcome indicating the outcome of the battle. Individual combat linked to mass warfare is common enough (Livy 1.24, 7.10/26, 8.7), but here it seems to be only a preliminary sign (cf. Procop. *Goth.* 5.20) to indicate the right rather than the might on each side. As it stands, Tacitus' account requires that one side fight even though its representative has already been defeated, but provided that the prisoner is matched against a superior opponent, the match becomes safe rehearsal, and a favorable sign is more or less assured.

19. For a general discussion of the relation between combat sport and war, see M. Poliakoff, *Combat Sports in the Ancient World* (New Haven, Conn.: Yale University Press, 1987), 89–115. Different ethnic styles of gladiatorial combat

probably had a military background; see Clavel-Lévêque, "Rituels" 195. On the assimilation of gladiator to soldier, see Barton, "Scandal" 3n18; and Hardie, *Virgil's Aeneid*, 152–54. Gladiatorial combat was in fact used specifically to enhance military morale, as bullfighting in Spain more recently has been. In the 1940s, the day before departing for the Russian front, the Spanish Blue Division attended a special bullfight in the Plaza de Toros in Madrid, where two famous matadors "each [sought] to impress the soldiers by their prowess. Never were [they] more magnificent as they demonstrated artistry and courage before a crowd whose passions were aroused by the deadly *mano a mano*. . . . This was the memory that the soldiers would take with them"; G. Kleinfeld and L. Tambs, *Hitler's Spanish Legion* (Carbondale, Ill.: Southern Illinois University Press, 1979), 23. Cf. Mitchell, *Blood Sport* 13 (sporting violence before military induction), 146–47 (the martial character of bullring music, e.g., the bugle call corresponding to a trumpet blast in the Roman arena).

20. On Roman militarism, see K. Hopkins, *Conquerors and Slaves* (Cambridge: Cambridge University Press, 1978), 25–37; Harris, *War and Imperialism* 9–53; G. Woolf, "Roman Peace," in *War and Society in the Roman World*, ed. J. Rich and G. Shipley (London: Routledge, 1993), 183; and H. Sidebottom, "Philosophers' Attitudes to War," in Rich and Shipley, 260. On persistent, though reduced experience of disorder in the Empire, see Woolf 188–89; on military incompetence of the Roman crowd under the Principate, see Tac. *Ann.* 1.46.1, 3.40.3; Tac. *Hist.* 3.58.1, 82.1. On general indifference to human life in Roman society, see Y. Grisé, *Le Suicide dans la Rome antique* (Montreal: Bellarmine, 1982), 186–88; and Lintott, *Violence* 35–51. The "expediency" which in Lintott's view explains Roman cruelty is another way of describing a relatively abstract, impersonal social logic for handling endemic violence; cf. Tac. *Ann.* 14.44.4, on decimation and mass execution of many slaves for the crimes of one. "Every large-scale example [omne magnum exemplum] is unjust to a degree, since public welfare is bought at the price of individuals" (cited in Lintott 42). Examples *are* "examples" because of their larger axiomatic truth often overriding particular facts. That is part of the rationale for bloodshed in the arena too. See below, chap. 9, n. 13.

After surveying foreign policy during the Republic, Harris concludes that the Romans went to war predominantly for reasons of expansion, not self-defense, though aggression and fear were interwoven and motives are at best difficult to fix (163–254). Confidence in military prospects at the level of policy, however, does not mean that war was unproblematic. Absence of craving for peace (35) is consistent with awareness of the risks in warfare, and even in triumphant displays of power, a sense of danger is bound to remain active at a psychological level close to the roots of behavior from which ritual springs, as gladiatorial combat did in playing out the threat as well as the promise of violence. Harris observes that the justice or justification of war was determined largely by its outcome: victory shows whose side the gods are on, and so correct declaration of war involved not proper reasons but proper procedures. Psychologically, then, the magical elements in fetial war ritual helped steer results in the "right" direction (170–71) and by bolstering confidence reduced anxiety, much as favorable signs did. However ready the Romans were to fight, though, the ritual undergirding war incorporated consciousness of the danger that war always entailed. Besides fetial prayers for expansion of Roman power (118–22), there were more anxious, defensive vows for preservation of the status quo (Livy 22.9.10), to say nothing of the many cautionary details in triumphs. See J. Rich, "Fear, Greed, and Glory," in Rich and Shipley 63.

21. On displacement of war by combat sport, see Poliakoff, *Combat Sports*. Participation in *munera* rather than normal military service is treated as a problem in Dio 75.2.5 perhaps due to its economic effect, but Commodus' passion for appearing in the arena seemed shameful because his weapons were not being used against real enemies (Hdn. 1.15.7). Some interesting remarks on arena games as a substitute for war can be found in J. Pearson, *Arena* (London: Thames and Hudson, 1973), 150–53. Public participation was not entirely vicarious. After hunts were completed, spectators might be invited into the arena to claim dead animals, which they probably did with the same excitement felt by modern fans storming the field after play concludes (*Hist. Aug.* Gordiani Tres 3.8; Probus 19.2). The violence which could easily accompany this was at times kept in check through assignment of booty by lot, but blind distribution of prizes itself occasioned disorder, according to Herodian, sometimes with fatalities (5.6.9–10). Perhaps distributions were made separately to men and women (Dio 69.8.2) to reduce injuries. When harmless animals were let loose, the crowd could itself do the hunting: *Dictionnaire des antiquités grecques et romains*, s.v. "venatio," 705.

22. J. Humphrey, *Roman Circuses* (Berkeley: University of California Press, 1986), 11, 256, 258. On symbols of political-military victory in the circus, see 94, 262, 269, 638 (victorious emperor parallel to victorious charioteer). Images of the gods in attendance to watch proceedings (82) would reinforce the sense of a larger setting for what was happening. See Clavel-Lévêque, *L'Empire en jeux* 93–100, on the cult of victory.

23. *Stuffy* is Balsdon's term (*Life and Leisure* 320). The violence linking artistic and sporting events reappears in the behavior of modern rock concert and soccer audiences; see Coleman, "Fatal Charades" 68, on hysteria on and off the stage in mimes. E. Rawson, in "Chariot-Racing in the Roman Republic," *Papers of the British School at Rome* 49 (1981): 8, remarks on a shift of interest from owners to (competing) charioteers or from horses to (competing) colors. Syme speculates that the image of a charioteer found on another man's tomb "perhaps perpetuates what [the dead man] adored while still on earth; and the victorious charioteer might serve as a good omen or psychopomp on the last journey. It will be permissible to evoke the fantasies of those who are infatuated with the heroes of sport or speed, or who identify themselves with popular idols in the performing arts, in any age"; R. Syme, "Scorpus the Charioteer," *American Journal of Ancient History* 2 (1977): 87. That is to say, the athlete's glory could have connections with the religious dimension of heroization which gave meaning to life itself. On the title *paradoxos* ("marvel!") bestowed for unusual achievement, see Robert, *Les Gladiateurs* 250–52. A link of this kind was possible because of the abstract, generic nature of public competition. Being highly malleable, it had no particular purpose, without, however, being purposeless, and therefore could be

shaped into any number of things. Seneca remarks that the anger of people at gladiators for their reluctance to die is spurious, since they have no real idea what they are angry about (*De Ira* 1.2.4–5).

24. Athenaeus has a section on gladiatorial combat and other forms of violent party entertainment especially among Italian peoples (4.153F–155F). Armed war dances were popular, and what began as sham combat could become fatal in ways that again involved suicidal impulses, if not exactly suicide. After the player in a game of chicken had put his head in a noose, a round stone on which he stood was kicked away, and he had to cut himself free with a knife. For affinity between arena and banquet, see C. Saylor, "Funeral Games: The Significance of Games in the *Cena Trimalchionis*," *Latomus* 46 (1987): 593–602; Brown, "Death as Decoration" 188, 197; E. Gowers, *The Loaded Table* (Oxford: Clarendon, 1993), 27, 37–48; and below, chap. 4.

25. On seating arrangements, see T. Bollinger, *Theatralis licentia* (Winterthur, Switz.: Schellenberg, 1969), 1–24; Clavel-Lévêque, *L'Empire en jeux* 154–73; J. Kolendo, "La Répartition des places aux spectacles et la stratification sociale dans l'Empire Romain," *Ktema* 6 (1981): 301–15; and C. Edwards, *The Politics of Immorality in Ancient Rome* (Cambridge: Cambridge University Press, 1993), 110–19. On social hierarchy schematized in mosaic representations of great hunts, see Clavel-Lévêque 82–83. Every group in society from highest to lowest was represented; see E. Rawson, "*Discrimina ordinum*: The Lex Julia Theatralis," *Papers of the British School at Rome* 55 (1987): 83–114. At the top was the emperor, whose family increasingly became the focus of public festivals in which ceremonies of victory took on special importance as victory itself became one of his own abstract, intrinsic qualities; see M. Salzman, *On Roman Time* (Berkeley: University of California Press, 1990), 138, 144–46, 179–83, 187. Eight out of ten gladiatorial games, along with cults of deities devoted to warfare, were concentrated in December as part of the imperial cult, and costs of the display were still high in the later Empire.

26. Clavel-Lévêque, "L'Espace des jeux," esp. 2408–25, 2431–38, 2451–62, 2482–98, 2529–44. On the anomalous political position of the urban poor in Rome, pacified by bread and circuses because they were a potentially dangerous group situated between slaves who worked and the elite who did not, see P. Lekas, *Marx on Classical Antiquity* (New York: St. Martin's, 1988), 125–29. The need met by bread was obvious enough; the one met by games brought more complex relationships to light, especially in the easy move from violence safely within the arena to dangerous violence beyond.

27. Friedlaender, *Sittengeschichte Roms* 75. See Clavel-Lévêque, "Rituels" 201, and *L'Empire en jeux* 75, on allegory in the arena. Carefully calculated arena architecture, guaranteeing the visibility of what happens down at the center of action to assure its sensuous impact on spectators, is discussed in Golvin and Landes, *Amphithéatres* 48.

28. Cf. Friedlaender, *Sittengeschichte Roms* 53.

29. Balsdon, *Life and Leisure* 256. On the contrasting logic of zoo and circus (i.e., order/disorder), see P. Bouissac, *Circus and Culture* (Bloomington: Indiana University Press, 1976), 103, 109–22. On the *logique du rite* in sacrifice more

generally as a way of encountering the sacred safely by diverting fatal divine power onto an animal, see Vernant, "Theorie générale du sacrifice" 5.

30. J. Aymard, *Essai sur les chasses romaines,* Bibliothèque des Ecoles Françaises d'Athènes et de Rome 171 (Paris, 1951), 469–481; on the history of animal shows at Rome, see 54–85.

31. Ibid., 91–98, 483–502, 62, 57, 77–79, 503–22, 190.

Chapter 4. Extravagant Expenditure, Conspicuous Consumption

1. Statistics on the games can be found in Friedlaender, *Sittengeschichte Roms* 51; on the large number of days set aside for games, see Weiler, *Der Sport* 242. A 120-foot-high portrait of Nero on linen (Pliny *HN* 35.51) and the Domus Aurea with his colossal statue are other instances of purely quantified excess. On architectural luxury, see Edwards, *Politics of Immorality* 137–72. Columns supporting nothing at all (Sen. *Ep.* 86.6–7) epitomize useless display. On Dio's disapproving emphasis on the cost and scale of games, see R. Newbold, "Cassius Dio and the Games," *L'Antiquité Classique* 44 (1975): 589–604. Gladiatorial games therefore are ritual also in the specific sense that, in Burkert's definition, ritual employs exaggeration to achieve a demonstrative effect (i.e., it is "showy") and thus to create public communication; see Hughes, *Human Sacrifice* 1–2. That is what makes an anecdote in Dio more than merely freakish. One of Tiberius' powerful friends invited a neighbor he wanted to intimidate to stay with him for two days, then razed his empty house on the first day and replaced it with a much better one on the second (Dio 58.22.2).

"In the political bestiary next to Machiavelli's lion and fox there is place for the peacock" (Veyne, *Bread and Circuses* 385). Pompey's plan to irritate his enemies by entering Rome on a chariot drawn by four elephants was foiled because the gate was too small (Plut. *Pomp.* 14.4); Aemilius Paulus' 120 cattle (Plut. *Aem.* 33.1) were outdone by Antiochus' 1,000 (Polyb. 30.25.12; Merten, *Zwei Herrscherfeste* 63–64); and Dio tells of a successful Roman general who insisted on riding to dinner on an elephant (49.7.6). Fatted cattle, gilded horns, the handsomest captives, the rarest or the biggest animals, all betray the simple logic of excess underlying even the most pretentious public ceremonies. Rules of transformation on the system's abstract level permit substituting Pompey's elephants, which were in fact too big for the gates of Rome, with Constantius, who made himself seem taller than he was by habitually stooping when he passed under a high gate (Amm. Marc. 16.10.10).

Dixon's remarks (*Military Incompetence* 180–88) on "supernormal or larger than life stimuli," such as specialized military dress and gestures, by which responses are aroused in ritual have some pertinence to the heavily stylized military costumes in the arena. The response that stimuli aim at is a strengthened sense of confidence, and traditional military "bull-shit" is just such exaggerated ritual designed to inspire feelings of control in the face of "death and unconstrained disorder" (185). The exaggeration, however, reveals as well as reduces anxiety; troops who largely ignore correct procedures to focus on survival once they are in real battle will compulsively go through ritual weapon checks as they approach combat. Finding themselves in danger which was in a sense unreal or offered no hope of survival, gladiators were expected to follow correct procedures to the end, and the entertainment which that provides, as Dixon observes, becomes real military disaster when parade ground ritual is extended to the battlefield in a supreme attempt to maintain control amid chaos. All of this suggests how ritual exaggeration in the arena could help mediate the real and the imaginary by representing both through real but stylized havoc.

Some of Dixon's speculative suggestions along this line on the peculiar ambivalence of military ritual may derive support from and throw light on the mysterious phrase "Ave imperator, morituri te salutant" (Suet. *Claud.* 21.6). "[Thus] the military salute effectively combines the threat of a raised arm with the reassurance of the open hand in which no weapon could be concealed. A similar admixture of contrary motives occurs in the practice of presenting arms. The trigger is turned towards the 'enemy', but the gun remains firmly in the possession of the presenter" (Dixon 182). Particularly if the salute involved raising weapons which in the hands of marginal people also posed danger, the combatants would be simultaneously threatening and renouncing violence, the latter both through the salute and the acknowledgment of a death sentence, especially if the group who saluted Claudius with these words was made up of criminals, as Dio says (60.33.3). Compare Commodus' "salute" to senators (Dio 72.21.1–2; above, chap. 3, n. 8).

It is hard to see why or how the phrase came to be used on this occasion, if it was not a regular formula. On the other hand, if it was something that Claudius might expect to hear, it would more naturally serve in its role as a feed line for repartee portraying his invincible gaucherie. The third person *salutant* in Suetonius has a certain formal, distancing effect (but Dio has the first person), and the interpretation given to his response by the fighters seems to be a maneuver within rules governing clemency in the arena. Below, chap. 10, n.1.

2. F. Millar, *The Emperor in the Roman World* (Ithaca, N.Y.: Cornell University Press, 1977), 191; for a full discussion, see 133–201. See also T. Frank, *An Economic Survey of Ancient Rome*, vol. 5 (Baltimore: Johns Hopkins University Press, 1940), 607.

3. R. Duncan-Jones, *The Economy of the Roman Empire* (Cambridge: Cambridge University Press, 1974), 343–44. Tacitus counts 200 or 300 million sesterces as great wealth (*Dial.* 8.2).

4. Finley, *Ancient Economy* 35–36. The theme of freakishly quantified excess reaches its climax in *Historia Augusta* Elagabalus 18–33, whose author admits that, while anecdotes about the scale of Elagabalus' luxury are worth reporting, those about his sexual monstrosities are not (18.4), and even some of the former are "beyond belief" (30.8).

5. On the contradiction between reserved Roman and freehanded Greek attitudes reaching crisis proportions under Nero, see M. Cavallaro, *Spese e spettacoli*, Antiquitas 34 (Bonn: Habelt, 1984), 34, 67–71, 166, 172. While the cost of games increased overall during Julio-Claudian times, Augustus, Claudius, and especially Tiberius made some attempt to check its growth. Caligula and Nero encouraged it (161–92, esp. 187–92). See M. Griffin, *Nero* (London: Batsford,

1984), 197–207, on "the problem of finance" more generally. Roman extravagance was quick to take advantage of Roman religious scruple that required
repetition of festivals in the case of even minor errors (Dio 60.6.4–5, 12.51).

The wider social ramifications of economics are reflected in the virtual
identity of real money and game tokens distributed as political largess (Griffin
142), whose symbolic reality (like that of credit cards and other forms of debt in
modern economies) could create a perception of prosperity by standing for a
vague promise of more. For some remarks on deficit spending and Keynesian
economic theory in this connection, see Griffin 116. The stimulation administered
by the former can be seen as destructive in the long run, and that is how critics
viewed the games, despite some shorter-term beneficial economic consequences,
including the encouragement of innovative technology. S. Mrozek, in "L'Evolution des prix en Italie au début de l'Empire Romain," *La Parola del Passato* 3
(1978): 273–80, discusses inflation in the price of luxury goods due to changing
values during the late Republic and early Empire. So far as random scattering of
prizes is concerned, together with the disorder that might occur, it could seem to
have a subversive, egalitarian character in representing transfer of power to the
people and irresponsible waste of resources (Dio 59.9.6–7). While wanting to
destroy the Senate for not voting him divine honors, Caligula (instead?) scattered
coins to the people, some of whom were killed in the resulting brawl (59.25.5).
Nero's throwing of tokens to the populace also led to concern about wild expenditure (61.18.2), as did Domitian's distributions paid for by executions and confiscation (67.4.4–5).

6. For "bigger is better," see M. Morgan, "Politics, Religion, and the Games
in Rome, 200–150 B.C.," *Philologus* 134 (1990): 30–31. In his discussion of the
difficulties in defining what is "wasteful," Veyne (*Bread and Circuses* 381) draws
attention to the difference between investment and what now seems to be irrational consumption (55–60) designed purely to express sovereignty (250–252,
365, 380–98). On the Principate's difference from rational bureaucracies, see
R. Saller, *Personal Patronage under the Early Empire* (Cambridge: Cambridge
University Press, 1982), 79. A rule of Caligula's was "Be frugal or be Caesar"
(Suet. *Calig.* 37). The very wide pay gap between lower and higher positions
reflects the elitist, hierarchical structure of ancient society that made vast resources available to a few; see D. MacKenzie, "Pay Differentials in the Early
Empire," *Classical World* 76 (1982): 267–73. Statistics in ancient fiction cannot
be treated as hard evidence since they are often exaggerated for literary effect,
and seemingly hard figures in nonfiction, too, may be no less a matter of effect,
though one that can still convey political truth; see Duncan-Jones, *Economy*
238–56. Heavy expense for *ludi* is recorded as early as the beginning of the
second century B.C. (Livy 40.44.12), and gladiatorial shows became more popular
as the liberal display of wealth was becoming more politically useful, though the
line separating reasonable liberality from irrational excess was at least initially
kept sharp by the Romans' own frugality; see H. Kloft, *Libertas principis* (Cologne: Böhlau, 1970), 35–37, 40–46, 67–69, 146–47.

7. Duncan-Jones, *Economy* 12, 146, 239 n4 (Pliny *Ep.* 10.39.1), 242; S. Bas-
tomsky, "Rich and Poor: The Great Divide in Ancient Rome and Victorian En-

gland," *Greece and Rome* 37 (1990): 38–39; Pliny *HN* 36.103 (a house priced at 14.8 million). Cf. I. Schatzman, *Senatorial Wealth and Roman Politics,* Collection Latomus 142 (Brussels: Latomus, 1975). In anecdotal variations, conspicuous consumption overshoots itself in opposite directions through demands too great to be met (the gourmet Apicius' suicide; Dio 57.19.5) or too great to be admitted (Caesar's concealment of what he paid for slaves; Suet. *Iul.* 47). On its public, competitive side, excess at Rome at times aimed at the intimidating effect of flamboyant destruction of wealth in potlatches; cf. Dio 58.22.2.

   8. Millar, *Emperor in the Roman World* 149. Tacitus manages to replace quantitative with qualitative political numbers much more subtly by inflating the relatively few suicides he mentions into an impression of pervasive violence through dramatic descriptions.

   9. E. Benveniste, *Indo-European Language and Society,* trans. E. Palmer (London: Faber and Faber, 1973), 161. On *éléments purements irrationneles* in ancient political economy, see T. Reekmans, "La Politique économique et financière des autorités dans les *Douze Cesars* de Suétone," in *Historiographia antiqua,* Commentationes Lovanienses in honorem W. Peremans, Symbolae Facultatis Litterarum et Philosophiae Lovaniensis, ser. A.6 (Louvain: Leuven University Press, 1977), 273, 305. The "irrational" economic values in political (as contrasted with market) capitalism and their connection at Rome to large-scale violence are discussed in J. Love, *Antiquity and Capitalism* (London: Routledge, 1991), 49–55, 194, 225–33. In these terms, acquisition, expenditure, and consumption of human life in arena games were part of the political economy, analogous to slaves in silver mines being "literally worked to death as quickly as possible to produce the maximum profit in the shortest time." The quotation is taken from E. Badian (*Publicans and Sinners* [Oxford: Blackwell, 1972], 33), who adds that "this, in fact, is one of the few examples known, of slavery at its theoretical extreme—a spectacle of human beings regarded as expendable objects." The last remark is an exact though not full description of bloodshed in the arena.

   10. Millar, *Emperor in the Roman World* 139–40. In modern society money is often felt to be inappropriate as a "gift," while being a somewhat more acceptable "present." Giving money seems to commercialize the gesture, and failure to spend time on selecting a special gift creates an impression of indifference; see D. Cheal, *The Gift Economy* (London: Routledge, 1988), 121–41. The heavily symbolic value of money at Rome perhaps made it appear to be a true gift rather than a mere payment when the emperor, for example, offered large donations to impoverished nobility or when Seneca identified his immense official wealth with the status it conferred.

   11. Duncan-Jones, *Economy* 245. Polybius (31.28), though, says that a good *munus* could cost 30 talents (about 700,000 sesterces). Conspicuous consumption was shamelessly quantified when scales were brought out to weigh unusually large fish or fowl served at fashionable dinners (Amm. Marc. 28.4.13). Elagabalus liked to hear the price of food served at his lavish dinners not merely mentioned but exaggerated, "to help the appetite" (*Hist. Aug.* 29.9).

   12. See A. J. Woodman, *Rhetoric in Classical Historiography* (London:

Croom Helm, 1988), 88, on modern economic and ancient rhetorical models as frames in which data take on meaning. The significance, as distinct from the accuracy, of statistics is one of the many aspects of typological truth in ancient historiography that aims at understanding, not at information. See D. Timpe, "Geschichtsschreibung und Prinzipat-Opposition," in *Opposition et résistances à l'empire d'Auguste à Trajan,* Entretiens sur l'Antiquité Classique 27 (Geneva: Fondation Hardt, 1987), 92–95. On ethnological *topoi* in the *Germania* erroneous in detail but (taken to be) a priori true of various cultures, see Bringmann, "Topoi" 59–78; and R. Urban, "Aufbau und Gedankengang der Germania des Tacitus," in *Beiträge zum Verständnis der Germania des Tacitus,* Teil 1, Abhandlungen der Akademie der Wissenschaften in Göttingen, ed. H. Jankuhn and D. Timpe (Göttingen: Vandenhoeck and Ruprecht, 1989), 92–94. A. J. Woodman discusses interchangeable modular descriptions of combat in "Self-imitation and the Substance of History," in *Creative Imitation and Latin Literature,* ed. D. West and T. Woodman (Cambridge: Cambridge University Press, 1979), 143–55.

    13. Duncan-Jones, *Economy* 137, 245n4.

    14. Ibid., 104, 245. On spending on games, see Millar, *Emperor in the Roman World* 193–94; and J. Drinkwater, "Gallic Personal Wealth," *Chiron* 9 (1979): 242.

    Large outlays entailed more subtle economic dilemmas. Because men in first-rate condition could best fulfill the games' public function, genuine care was provided for the health of some gladiators through medical attention, diet, and exercise. But heavy investment in a well-prepared *formosus gladiator* (and perhaps in his costly armor) was, after all, an extremely high-risk venture made on a peculiarly self-liquidating asset. The problem was cost-effectiveness. In the case of criminals sentenced to death or captives forced to fight without hope of survival, cost was minimal; the aim was simply disposal, and what otherwise would have been completely worthless could be made into a useful throwaway resource. On the other hand, entrepreneurs handling gladiators who commanded large fees and represented substantial investment would naturally want to protect themselves from the spectators' preference for blood by demanding a high and quick return to amortize their investment as rapidly as possible. Various measures taken to establish cost controls were responses to an inflationary spiral fed by these pressures from producer cost and consumer demand. The very high fee of 100,000 sesterces paid for veteran gladiators at games put on by Tiberius (Suet. *Tib.* 7.1) was perhaps compensation for the risk faced by skilled fighters (on a maximum of 12,000 set by law in the mid–second century, see Ville, *La Gladiature* 250; on the basis of tax receipts of 50 million sesterces, Ville estimates ten thousand to thirty thousand transactions per year involving gladiators, exclusive of many off the books [275]). In order to cover capital losses, the normal rental fee for a gladiator became a much larger sale price in the event he was killed or incapacitated (Gai. *Inst.* 3.146). For this reason, first-rank gladiators, who were not often matched against each other (Ville 322), would tend to survive and thus further increase in value, so that physical and economic survival of the fittest reinforced each other. As Ville observes, economics was swept aside by desire for prestige or for violence itself in cases of combat to the death *(sine missione),* and since freeing gladiators on public demand had the same effect as combat to the death, efforts to invalidate manumission under such circumstances were aimed at its economic effects (320–21, 327–28 n222).

The dynamics of the situation in these respects resemble the economics of modern sports, for example, astronomical salaries paid to predictably short-lived performers. As a general proposition, extra compensation for risk is rational; its specific level may be much less so. The risk/reward ratio in expenditure on gladiators perhaps fell somewhere between normal auto racing and a demolition derby played with expensive cars.

15. Val. Max. 3.2.24 (cf. Gell. *NA* 2.11), cited in Oakley, "Single Combat" 409; Weber, *Panem et circenses* 54–55.

16. Ville, *La Gladiature* 365–66. Concentration of public brutality, by quantity and quality, which is here temporarily wrapped in a strange appearance of sociability, is normally overt: for example, six thousand captives from Spartacus' army were crucified along a main road (App. *BCiv.* 1.14.120).

17. Ville, *La Gladiature* 366; on the ultimate appeal of arena combat coming from the fact of death itself rather than from skill in competition, see 320, 417, 423–24. In his general discussion of *l'ideologie et l'arène* (447–72), Ville remarks on the disturbing effects of the games, the fear they caused, and the "law of the jungle" (462) they represented. On the *Unschuldskomödie*, see below, chap. 5, n. 11.

18. H. A. Harris, *Sport in Greece and Rome* (Ithaca, N.Y.: Cornell University Press, 1972), 194–207. On racing, see Balsdon, *Life and Leisure* 314–24.

19. Friedlaender, *Sittengeschichte Roms* 81; J. M. C. Toynbee, *Animals in Roman Life and Art* (Ithaca, N.Y.: Cornell University Press, 1973), 17–23; on animal shows in general, see Balsdon, *Life and Leisure* 302–14. Ville (*La Gladiature* 144–46) points out that many thousands of animals shown by Titus seem to have been killed on a single day. For graphic portrayal of encounters with animals, see Robert, *Les Gladiateurs* 91 (no. 27), 150 (no. 114), 201–2 (no. 222), 213 (no. 252).

20. Friedlaender, *Sittengeschichte Roms* 78f.

21. The premise for such anecdotes is the merely normal cruelty in Nero's practice of sending messengers with official dispatches reading "Kill this man" or "This man is dead" (Dio 63.11.4). Compare Domitian's sinister tomb party (Dio 67.9). D. Sansone, in *Greek Athletics and the Genesis of Sport* (Berkeley: University of California Press, 1988), 46, notes that hunters prove prowess by sparing animals. Sovereign violence was displayed in an exceptionally outré manner when Commodus used specially designed arrows to decapitate ostriches so cleanly that their bodies continued to run for a time; see Toynbee, *Animals* 22. Martial's series of epigrams (1.6, 14, 22, 48, 51, 60, 104) treats the benign predator as a symbol of imperial clemency; see O. Weinreich, *Studien zu Martial,* Tübinger Beiträge zur Altertumswissenschaft 4 (Stuttgart: Kohlhammer, 1928), 90–112.

22. Friedlaender, *Sittengeschichte Roms* 90f; Coleman, "Fatal Charades" 67–73.

23. See Sansone, *Greek Athletics* 116–17, on gladiatorial violence as "intensification of the ritual sacrifice of energy." This is a partial explanation for what

Toynbee calls "one of the outstanding paradoxes of the Roman mind," namely, keen interest in animals coupled with equally keen pleasure in their "hideous sufferings and agonizing deaths" (*Animals* 21). Their suffering and death was pleasurable when tied to a show of human mastery, itself gratifying because of the threat animals presented in preindustrial societies (see Wiedemann, *Emperors and Gladiators* 62–65). If the animal that "previously was a source of fear turns into a game [*ludus*] when it dies" (*Latin Anthology* 187.10, cited in Wiedemann 65), then the game conversely is worth playing because of the fear it taps and the threat posed by every dangerous animal still at large. Wolves and other dangerous animals were bad signs when they penetrated the city. Pleasure at human death in the arena has the same explanation.

24. Compare Livy's repudiation (22.57.6) and Pliny the Elder's recognition (*HN* 28.12) of human sacrifice at Rome; see A. Giardina, ed., *The Romans,* trans. L. Cochrane (Chicago: University of Chicago Press, 1993), 5. On arena animals affectionately nicknamed Omicida, Innocentia, or Crudelis, see Matthews, *Roman Empire of Ammianus* 260. Official praise of a sponsor for having had ten bears killed *crudel (iter)* (Grant, *Gladiators* 113) is surprising and should perhaps be restored as *crudel (es)* (of the bears); see Coleman, "Fatal Charades" 50. The rationale of cruelty in Roman society is discussed in Wiedemann, *Emperors and Gladiators* 68–101.

Chapter 5. Sociology of Public Violence

1. C. Geertz, "Deep Play," in *Interpretive Social Science: A Second Look,* ed. P. Rabinow and W. Sullivan (Berkeley: University of California Press, 1987), 195–240.

2. Ibid., 204, 207, 234, 204, 211, 203. Reaffirmation of vitality and order through violence naturally has a sexual component. In speaking of the "deep identification of Balinese men with their cocks," Geertz notes that the word in Balinese has precisely the same dual sense it does in English (200). It is worth recalling that gladiatorial combat (like other games) was linked to ritual reaffirmation of communal vitality often entailing obscenity, that *gladius = penis,* and that gladiators were the objects of sexual admiration. Compare the striking passage from Prudentius (*c. Symm.* 2.1095–101) cited in Wiedemann, *Emperors and Gladiators* 152. After penetrating a gladiator's body, javelins acquired procreative power usefully applied to young women at marriage (Festus 55). When Nero, disguised as an animal, had been let out of a cage, he attacked the genitals of victims and was then "finished off" by his homosexual wife (Suet. *Ner.* 29; on a possible linking of Nero's behavior and his interest in gladiatorial combat in the version in Aur. Vict. *Caes.* 5.7, cf. DuFraigne's Budé edition with note *ad loc.*). On sexualized ritual killing, see Burkert, *Homo necans* 58–72. Claudius had the weapons of gladiators who had died at each other's hands made into little daggers for his own use (Suet. *Claud.* 34.2); Pliny the Elder's list of cures for epilepsy includes using game killed with a knife which had also been used to kill a man (*HN* 28.34). In both cases instruments of violence take on potency, with the daggers perhaps being sexual, too.

However some of these reports are assessed, violence at Rome at times seems pornographic not merely in the sense that the two tended to go together, as they often do. Beyond that, the peculiarly abstract, contrived quality that is so striking a feature of pornography suggests that it, like violence, is closely tied to a deeper principle of anomaly and excess as such. Substance is irrelevant, and idea becomes everything, hence the drive to think up novel forms and techniques of stimulation, such as depersonalized, external representations in pictures (Suet. *Tib.* 43–44) or magnifying mirrors (Sen. *QNat.* 1.16; Seneca remarks especially on unnatural objectification of sexual subjects). On secondary objectification of arena violence in mosaics, see Brown, "Death as Decoration" 208. H. Gugel, in *Studien zur Biographischen Technik Suetons,* Wiener Studien 7 (Vienna: Böhlau, 1977), 89, sees *eine gewisse Neigung zur Laszivität* in female gladiatorial matches and races "even between young women" (Suet. *Dom.* 4.1 and 4). On relatively exposed women gladiators, see Robert, *Les Gladiateurs* 188–89 ("The public wanted to see their heads and breasts"); on effeminate gladiators, see S. Cerutti and L. Richardson, "The *Retiarius Tunicatus* of Suetonius, Juvenal, and Petronius," *American Journal of Philology* 110 (1989): 589–94; on gladiators masquerading as women, see Merten, *Zwei Herrscherfeste* 71–75. In *Annals* 11.26 Tacitus remarks on the abstract, self-parodic "badness" for its own sake that sets in after all other substantive kinds of immorality have been exhausted: the scale of *infamia* and the unprecedented nature of *libidines* were what motivated Messalina's crowd.

3. Geertz, "Deep Play" 203–4, 208–9, 229–30, 232–33. On cockfighting as symbol of aggressive competition, see J. Winkler, *The Constraints of Desire* (New York: Routledge, 1990), 49. Cockfighting seems to have had little appeal at Rome; see M. Morgan, "Three Non-Roman Blood Sports," *Classical Quarterly* 69 (1975): 117–22.

4. Thuillier, *Les Jeux athlétiques* 69, 707n39, 710.

5. The effect this had on the tone of entertainment is illustrated by Polybius' account of a Greek chorus with flute players that left its Roman audience cold until the visitors took a few hints and turned the program into a mock brawl (30.22).

6. Thuillier, *Les Jeux athlétiques* 196, 243–46, 258–66, 591.

7. Ibid., 563n20. The word for boxing *(pygmē)* could be used for gladiatorial combat (Thuillier 267). The brutality of boxing stands out among the games in the *Aeneid* 5.362-484, with the winner driven at the end by a compulsion to kill (475–84).

8. Thuillier, *Les Jeux athlétiques* 586–93; on Pherseu as a simultaneously amusing and frightening death demon, see J.-P. Cèbe, *La Caricature et la parodie dans le monde romain antique des origines à Juvénal,* Bibliothèque des Ecoles Françaises d'Athènes et de Rome 206 (Paris: De Broccard, 1966), 29–30. Ville (*La Gladiature* 4–6) views the game in a more benign light.

9. R. Girard, *Violence and the Sacred,* trans. P. Gregory (Baltimore: Johns Hopkins University Press, 1977), esp. 87, 92, 117, 275–76. For a general discussion of recent theories of violence, see Hamerton-Kelly, *Violent Origins.*

10. Girard, *Violence and the Sacred* 8; cf. 18, 20, 79–82, 92–94. "Rites are in

a way vaccinations with the evil of violence against the evil of violence";
V. Nemoianu, "René Girard and the Dialectics of Imperfection," in *To Honor René Girard,* Stanford French and Italian Studies 34 (Stanford, Calif.: Anma Libri, 1986), 8. On the focusing of aggression on "legitimate targets" through military institutions to preserve internal social integrity, see Dixon, *Military Incompetence* 174. Evolution from raw violence to more stylized sport in the case of the Afghan game of bouz-kashi, which dates back to Genghis Khan, seems similar to what happened in gladiatorial games; see L. Routeau, "Le Bouz-kashi," in *Violence et vérité,* ed. P. Dumouched (Paris: Grasset, 1985), 499–503. "No longer sacrifice, not yet sport" (503)—this is a perfect characterization of liminoid states as well as of *munera.*

11. Girard, *Violence and the Sacred* 279–80, 85–88, 95, 36, 1, 312 (quotation), 39–67, 101–2. Some other parallels between Girard's violence and gladiatorial combat are worth listing. First, reciprocal violence and its discharge may be played out in games (93; cf. 86, 279). Second, intensity of violence is lessened by substitution of animal for human victims (278–80). On connections between war, sacrifice, and hunting, see Burkert, *Homo necans,* esp. 46–48. Though Burkert generally sees violence as an expression of innate aggression, response to external danger may be a factor (26, 50), and his definition of ritual fits well at several points with the Roman games (23). In his discussion in Hamerton-Kelly's *Violent Origins* (173), Burkert concedes that scapegoats, sacrificed by the group to avoid more serious external danger, cannot be explained by reference to hunting. The *Unschuldskomödie* (26) of the guilty "apology" owed by a hunter to the animal he kills is something like the last meal owed a condemned man (which gladiators, too, were given).

Third, like the scapegoat, the gladiator is a marginal figure beyond the pale of normal standards, and if he is not a condemned criminal, his innocence assures that violence against him is safe because it will not set off the ordinary chain of vengeance (Girard 12–14, 24–27). The violence of gladiatorial combat is likewise innocent because it is publicly sanctioned entertainment and ritualized self-defense (cf. Valentinian's killer-bear Innocentia; Matthews, *Roman Empire of Ammianus* 260). Gladiators were not scapegoats in a precise sense of the term, but it seems too much to deny that they were seen that way in *any* sense, as Wiedemann does (*Emperors and Gladiators* 34). On the general connection between gladiatorial combat and (the idea of) death, see Wiedemann 34–42, 91–93; on this combat's marginal, liminal location at the border between life and death, see 46–47. In seeing the loser lose, spectators experienced death with him, and in seeing the winner win, they escaped death with him.

Fourth, like unanimous violence, gladiatorial combat works preventively by driving out bad violence with good (Girard 19; 101–2). Fifth, the intensity of violence focused on the scapegoat is subject to sudden shifts of emotion, from savage hostility to awe and honor (78; cf. Tac. *Hist.* 1.69, on the unstable political hates and loves of the *vulgus mutabile*). If this did not usually fit the bloody mood of crowds at the arena (but compare the reaction to Pompey's exhibition of elephants; Dio 39.38.2–4; Pliny *HN* 8.20–21), it did parallel the ambivalent feelings of contempt and fascination aroused by gladiators. The fickleness of sporting and political crowds (often the same people) is thematically identified in Tacitus' treatment of Vitellius' fate; see C. Perkins, "Vitellius the *Spectaculum*: A Note on *Histories* 3.84.5," *Classical Bulletin* 66 (1990): 47–49.

Sixth, the aim of unanimous violence is to stabilize the status quo against the threat of disorder (Girard 280), and games (which could include gladiatorial shows) were vowed "si bellatum prospere esset resque publica in eodem quo ante bellum fuisset statu permansisset" (Livy 22.9.10). Seventh, violence ultimately discharged on the scapegoat can initially be represented by mock combat between members of society (Girard 119–23) as a type of "foreplay" sharpening the climax (34–36; on the relation of violence and sex, see above, n. 2). Gladiatorial combat fought with mock weapons had the same aim (on *paegniarii*, see Suet. *Calig.* 26.5). Eighth, violence of all against one carries the social sanction of collective action (Girard 100–101, 134) and occurs at a safe distance (268). Gladiatorial combat, too, is safely isolated in the arena, while the crowd embodies the social solidarity justifying violence and, in turn, reinforced by it. Gladiatorial violence, of course, is not itself collective, though it is shared collectively and the crowd might hold the combatant's life in its hands. Finally, collective violence is not chiefly a release of tension. On the contrary, the tension *is* the rite (103, 120, 132), and what is entertaining is the unusual violence. If aberrant, anomalous behavior is essential to the social meaning of ritual violence, then gladiatorial carnage, too, is not deplorably but necessarily brutal, and fear is inextricably woven into a sense of power (cf. Girard's remarks on *pharmakon* = "poison/medicine"; 95).

12. Human sacrifice has connections particularly with Gaul; see R. E. A. Palmer, *Roman Religion and Roman Empire* (Philadelphia: University of Pennsylvania Press, 1977), 153–88. Among the Gauls it could be a response to military danger or serious disease (Caes. *BGall.* 6.16.1), but in the account of a Roman general's fever subsiding as 130,000 Gauls are being killed in battle (Pliny *HN* 7.166), the overdose of violence is evidently not treated by Pliny the Elder as a factor in the cure.

13. Sall. *Cat.* 22; Dio 37.30.3; Plut. *Cic.* 10.4; Lincoln, *Discourse* 89–127, 142–59, 160–70. Though charges of this kind were stereotypes (J.-M. Pailler, *Bacchanalia*, Bibliothèque des Ecoles Françaises d'Athènes et de Rome 270 [Rome: Ecole Française de Rome, 1988], 801), Romans did frequently decapitate their enemies; see J.-L. Voisin, "Tite-Live, Capoue et les Bacchanales," *Mélanges de l'Ecole Française de Rome* 96 (1984): 616–18. In "Les Romains, chasseurs de têtes," in *Du châtiment dans la cité*, Collection de l'Ecole Française de Rome 79 (Rome: Ecole Française de Rome, 1984), 241–93, Voisin makes a case for head-hunting among the Romans and discusses the question of cruelty. Tacitus groups three instances closely together for effect in *Annals* 14.57, 59, 64. Severed heads have any number of uses: to establish identity for proof of death (Dio 60.32.4 [examination of teeth], 68.14.3; Tac. *Ann.* 14.64.2; Pseudo-Caes. *Spanish War* 39; App. *BCiv.* 2.15.105, 3.14.98, 4.2.7 [brought in for reward]; cf. Livy 24.14.7; Sall. *Iug.* 12.6); as objects of symbolic abuse (Plut. *Crass.* 33.1–4; App. *BCiv.* 3.3.26 [used as a ball]); to avoid abuse by preventing identification (Plut. *Ant.* 48.3); or to boost or undermine morale (Polyb. 11.18.6–7; Frontin. *Str.* 2.9.3–4, 2.9.5 [shot

into a city by ballista]; App. *BCiv.* 1.8.71 [heads of dead people cut off for display]).

14. M. Hengel, *Crucifixion in the Ancient World and the Folly of the Cross* (London: SCM, 1977); H.-W. Kuhn, "Die Kreuzesstrafe während der frühen Kaiserzeit," in *ANRW* II.25.1 (Berlin: De Gruyter, 1982), 648–793; Kiefer, "Der Römer" 82–86. On *cruciarii* mentioned together with gladiators and *venatio* in a show, see Cavallaro, *Spese* 14n27. Large-scale executions were carried out by crucifying victims spread horizontally along a main road (App. *BCiv.* 1.14.120). *Historia Augusta* Cassius 4.3 describes a no less horrific towering pole used on a large scale for executing criminals vertically by heat, smoke, and sheer terror from a fire lit at the bottom. Even if this is imaginary, it still is revealing as something that could naturally come to mind.

15. On the marginal victim chosen to be sacrificed at times of severe stress, see A. Henrichs, "Human Sacrifice in Greek Religion," in *Le Sacrifice dans l'antiquité,* Entretiens sur l'Antiquité Classique 27 (Geneva: Fondation Hardt, 1981), 233; and Coleman, "Fatal Charades" 70. On human sacrifice as a (liminoid) response to crisis and the link between human and animal sacrifice in connection with warfare, see Henrichs 213–18. In the *sphagia* offered just before battle, the act of killing was abstracted and performed with specially intense focus on imminent danger. The ritual was the task not of priests but of seers, probably owing to their association through divination with the supreme risk represented by war; the offering was made to unnamed gods; use of the victim's blood rather than flesh again directed attention to the fatal, as opposed to the life-giving, aspect of sacrifice; and fear of death came out even more clearly in occasional replacement of animals by human victims. The account of human sacrifice in Plutarch's *Themistocles* 13.2–3 (whose authenticity Henrichs questions; cf. Hughes, *Human Sacrifice* 111–15) touches on the use of anomalous ("irrational": *paralogon*) methods during crises. F. G. Bailey, in *The Tactical Uses of Passion* (Ithaca, N.Y.: Cornell University Press, 1983), 39, makes the interesting suggestion that displays of emotion in social life are similar to sacrifice in that they signal abandonment of reason and a shift to pure action for dealing with problems. For ritual atrocities and the genocidal *ver sacrum* in which all living things born during spring were sacrificed, see V. Pareto, *The Mind and Society,* vol. 2, ed. and trans. A. Livingston (New York: Harcourt Brace, 1935), 552–56. Polybius (10.15.4–5) remarks on orgiastic violence in which Roman soldiers slaughtered both people and animals in captured cities—exactly the human/animal overkill which furnished sport in the arena. The passage is cited in Harris, *War and Imperialism* 51; cf. Addendum 2.

Debasement of victims of political violence as less than human helps transform atrocity into sacrifice; cf. Lincoln, *Discourse* 98–100. Dehumanization is specifically recognized in the story of Caligula's keeping one of his victims in a cage (Sen. *De Ira* 3.17; Sen. *Ep.* 70.6; Dio 59.10.4; Procop. *Anecdota* 3.9–11). On public punishment as a symbol of public power especially through denial of the victim's humanity, see D. Potter, "Martyrdom as Spectacle," in *Theater and Society in the Classical World,* ed. R. Scodel (Ann Arbor: University of Michigan Press, 1993), 53–88. J.-M. David similarly explains mutilation of the corpses of

those executed *(sorte de lynchage posthume)* as a symbol of the emperor's absolute power; see David, "Du *Comitium* à la roche tarpeienne . . . ," in *Du châtiment dans la cité,* Collection de l'Ecole Française de Rome 79 (Rome: Ecole
Française de Rome, 1984), 173–75. The legitimacy which public mutilation establishes was readily turned against some emperors when they fell from power. The
terrifying possibility of personal abuse comes out very plainly in Seneca's remark
that men's worst fear is to become the victim of someone with greater power.
When he adds, after conjuring up dreadful tortures, that the public display of
superior power is what is so awful and urges blanket avoidance of offense to
people, it is clear that the political logic of cruelty, inside or outside the arena, lies
in notions of intensely competitive hierarchy *(Ep.* 14.3–7). I owe this reference
and point to Richard Saller.

Though status-ranking is purely notional, its social effect is entirely real.
Negatively, "everyone *is* inferior to the person he *thinks* feels contempt for him"
(Sen. *De Ira* 3.5.7; Sen. *Constant.* 10.3), and Seneca frequently remarks on the
many occasions at Rome for taking or giving offense *(De Ira* 2.24, 2.29, 3.10–11,
3.28.2, 3.30.2 [*moderate* benefits may be insulting], 3.37). Positively, "slave, ser-
pent or arrow kills a king; only a superior man can save an inferior," and "everyone can commit murder, no one can save except me [the emperor]" (Sen. *Clem.*
1.21.1, 1.5.4). This makes sense in a sharply defined hierarchy where assassination
can be devalued by treating it as an emblem of inferior status because violence
must be used. The emperor's supreme status then is expressed through power he
does not use (1.5.6: "Life is stolen from a superior, never given except to an
inferior").

Other, more domesticated sexual-political atrocities permit partial explanation along anthropological lines as well. Nero's homosexual rape of the young
Britannicus and of Aulus Plautius before having each of them murdered (Tac.
Ann. 13.17.2; Joann. Antioch, fg.90.M.v.87–93 [Dio 61.7.4]; Suet. *Ner.* 35.4) comes
close to the *Strafvergewaltigung* discussed by D. Fehling in *Ethnologische Überlegungen auf dem Gebiet der Altertumskunde,* Zetemata 61 (Munich: Beck,
1974), 18–27. The sneer over Plautius, a reputed lover of Agrippina—"*Now* let my
mother come and kiss my successor!"—is clearly a triumphant crow of sexual-
political power, possibly with an allusion to the rule that any successor eliminated is bound to be the wrong man (Dio 61.18.3), for, by the same token, anyone
who has been eliminated is sure not to be a successor. Gratuitous abuse for
homosexuality ultimately proved fatal to Caligula himself, assassinated by
Chaerea for making obscene gestures with his hand when Chaerea bent to kiss it
(Suet. *Calig.* 56.2; cf. Commodus' giving homosexual partners the names for
male and female sexual organs and then fondly kissing them, *Hist. Aug.* 10.8).
Seneca, in *De constantia sapientis* 18.2.3, pairs the story of homosexual insult to
Chaerea with one about Caligula's heterosexual machismo in taunting a man for
his wife's performance in bed. Sexual and political factors are closely combined in
the tale of Nero assessing the charms of Agrippina's corpse as he sipped a drink
(Suet. *Ner.* 34.4). For Nero, or for those who invented the story, familiar gloating
ridicule of a rival's corpse (Tac. *Ann.* 14.57.4, 59.3) is given added spice by talk of
incest. On sexual rivalry as a factor in Nero's elimination of Vestinus (Tac. *Ann.*

15.68–69), see W. Richter, "Tacitus als Stilist," in *Politik und literarische Kunst im Werke des Tacitus,* ed. G. Radke (Stuttgart: Klett, 1971), 125.

Though hostility does not figure in the near rape by Augustus and Caligula of women invited to dinner in the company of their husbands (Suet. *Aug.* 69.1; Suet. *Calig.* 36.2, cf. 24.1), sexual abuse of respectable people (married women again along with freeborn youths and Vestals in Suet. *Ner.* 28.1; Tac. *Ann.* 13.12.2, Dio 58.22.3) could have expressed political contempt through japing exercise of the power to take away other men's wives that could also be used more or less legitimately. Compare Corbier, "Divorce and Adoption" 57; and Edwards, *Politics of Immorality* 28, 47–48, 91–92. Dio explains the strange marriage of Messalina and Silius as mere perversity on her part, which he accentuates by coupling extremes of immorality in an odd hybrid promiscuous marriage: having acted like a prostitute in the palace and forced other distinguished women to do the same, she now wanted all her partners to be "husbands," too (60.31.1–2). Augustus was supposed to have found his own promiscuity most embarrassing when the issue of loose public morality came up (Dio 54.16.3–7), while the proposal to allow Caesar unrestricted rights of intercourse or marriage had an element of flattery of a fifty-year-old man's virility (Dio 44.7.3; cf. Suet. *Iul.* 50–52). Arbitrary restrictions on the sexual activity of others is no less a show of power, and so Caligula ordered a woman whom he had stolen from her husband and then quickly divorced to have no relations with other men (Suet. *Calig.* 25.2).

Additional light is perhaps thrown on such anecdotes by E. Goffman's discussion of the kind of risk taking that expresses itself through deliberately humiliating actions designed to create dangerous situations in which character and therefore status can be determined (*Interaction Ritual* 225, 248–58). The insulting behavior *(ludibrium)* of some emperors did, at any rate, stir up "action" in the competitive, high-risk world of politics at Rome.

The appearance of respectable people in public performances was regarded by some as another form of political humiliation (e.g., Tac. *Ann.* 14.14.4: Nero maliciously pressured people into social *delicta*). Palace prostitution with enforced participation by women from high society (Dio 59.28.9, 60.18, 60.31.1–3, 62.15.3–5) parallels forced performance in the theater or arena. In conjunction with such themes as seizure of a bride during her marriage ceremony (Dio 59.8.7) or forcing betrothal with an already married woman (59.12.1), this is a variation on the motif of the tyrant's lust (e.g., Polyb. 10.26.3–4), as is clear from Suetonius (*Dom.* 1.3). Nero's or Elagabalus' sexual insanity (the latter pondered surgery to create a vagina; Dio 80.16.7) seems deeply colored by the same tradition (e.g., Diegylis, king of Thrace, cut off the genitals of husbands and wives and exchanged them; Diod. Sic. 33.14). The odd story of Galba's reaction to the news of Nero's death (Suet. *Galba* 22) is a variation on the theme of sexual celebration, though without abuse of power, whereas Tiberius' rape and maiming of two youths (Suet. *Tib.* 44.2) is gross abuse, but not so clearly a show of power. It belongs with other cases in which abnormal psychological factors take over, such as Nero's sexual savaging of people bound to stakes (Suet. *Ner.* 29).

16. R. MacMullen, "Judicial Savagery in the Roman Empire," *Chiron* 16 (1986): 147–66. The entire following paragraph is based on this study, along with

G. Ville, "Les Jeux de gladiateurs dans l'empire chrétien," *Mélanges d'Archéologie et d'Histoire* 72 (1960): esp. 313–35; cf. P. Garnsey, "Why Penalties Become Harsher: The Roman Case, Late Republic to Fourth Century Empire," *Natural Law Forum* 13 (1968): 141–62. The growing expense of gladiatorial games was an initial inhibiting factor. See R. MacMullen, "What Difference Did Christianity Make?" *Historia* 35 (1986): 331; Ville 333–35. Ville suggests that the infrequency of the games then further helped reduce their importance (334). On pagan criticism of the games, see Ville 298n1; and Dio 71.29.

17. MacMullen, "Judicial Savagery" 164.

18. Ibid., 157; J.-P. Callu, "Le Jardin des supplices au Bas-Empire," and D. Grodzynski, "Tortures mortelles et categories sociales," both in *Du châtiment dans la cité,* Collection de l'Ecole Française de Rome 79 (Rome: Ecole Française de Rome, 1984), 313–59, 361–403. Suetonius has Tiberius so intent on ferreting out the truth of Drusus' death that an unfortunate friend who had arrived from Rhodes at the emperor's invitation was seized, tortured for any information he might have, and then executed to conceal the affair when Tiberius discovered his error (*Tib.* 62.1).

Chapter 6. Social Anomaly and Public Violence

1. *Oxymoronic* is the term used in R. Penella, "War, Peace, and the *Ius Fetiale* in Livy 1," *Classical Philology* 82 (1987): 233–37. At the end of Numa's reign Rome is "both *valida* and *temperata* in the arts of war and peace" (Livy 1.21.6), with *temperata* being both "well-organized" and "sober" or "disciplined." Rome is sober and capable of pursuing peace because she appreciates the dangers of strength and war, strong and militant because she appreciates their necessity. Though not including specifically apotropaic elements, fetial ritual still was a strongly cautionary procedure for assuring that war was only a last resort; see A. Watson, *International Law in Archaic Rome* (Baltimore: Johns Hopkins University Press, 1993), 8, 52–53.

2. Clavel-Lévêque suggests that the degree of lethality in gladiatorial combat was proportional to the level of external danger (*L'Empire en jeux* 76–77, 202). Danger demands action, and if games are ritual action, then the greater the threat they rehearse, the greater the risk—i.e., violence—they play out ritually. For estimates of reduced chances for survival in *munera* during the later Empire, see Ville, *La Gladiature* 319, 403–4.

3. Merten, *Zwei Herrscherfeste* 81, 84.

4. V. Turner, *Drama, Fields, and Metaphors* (Ithaca, N.Y.: Cornell University Press, 1974), 37–42, 78–79 (four stages), 129–36 (social arena); idem, *From Ritual to Theater* (New York: Performing Arts Journal Publications, 1982), 69, 92, 106.

5. Turner, *Forest of Symbols* 285. Circus shows of animals trained to be totally responsive to human instructions parallel exhibitions of animals or humans at Rome totally subject to the will of the authorities and work along the same lines; see Bouissac, *Circus and Culture,* esp. 6–8. Circuses, too, are marginal events, occasions for something odd ("it was like a circus"), yet also conventional

entertainment. The fluid status of circus animals creates classificatory anomaly (Bouissac 115–18) akin to the effect of carnivals (distorting mirrors, frightening rides) or freak shows. The circus is thus metacultural in rearranging rules while still falling under them: there is an "ambivalent response to the circus, namely, repression and fascination—enthusiasm produced by contact with freedom from culture, accompanied by the fear that this potential subversion may be generalized. That is to say, it is this very relevance of the circus to culture that accounts for the semi-rejection of the circus by the culture" (8). Bouissac isolates in circus acts a three-part dramatic sequence of situation/disruption/control in which ability to survive a test of instability caused by the disruption is put at stake. The successful acrobat appears superior to usual human norms, while the clown fills the role of inferior subjected to aggressive laughter (23–27, 37, 45–46, 97–101). In its own way the circus thus has the conservative aim (as gladiatorial combat does) of recognizing and repairing breaks in norms. Rigged combat, safety nets (40), or protective barriers are fail-safe devices for guaranteeing that disorder does not get out of hand. Exhibitionists like Nero or Commodus understood more truly that emperors were indeed godlike performers than critics did who saw in them only clowns. On the metaphoric messages conveyed by animal tricks, see 105–6; on the "cybernetic" (rigidly preset) messages in programmed circus body language (which gladiatorial maneuvers perhaps also "spoke" to a considerable degree), see 33.

6. Ville, *La Gladiature* 267–70. Compare Seneca's *De Providentia* 2.8 on admiration for a young man, especially if he is noble, who coolly takes the charge of a wild animal (though the passage may have normal hunting in view). A connection between military prowess and hunting would have been strongly felt in ancient society, since hunting was frequently an approved occupation of the elite when they were not waging war. In a sense hunting was war pursued by other means, so that while others at Rome could win fame only by injuring each other in court, Scipio's reputation for courage was enhanced by his vigorous hunting in Greece after a campaign had ended (Polyb. 31.29; cf. Plut. *Pomp.* 12.5). For a modern example with further speculation concerning psychological connections between hunting and warfare, see Dixon, *Military Incompetence* 268; on the military aspect of chariot racing, see Thuillier, *Les Jeux athlétiques* 516–17. Javelin games were the most immediately martial form of competition (Thuillier 306).

7. Cic. *Off.* 3.114: "Our soldiers either win or die." Hence the Romans refused to ransom captives after Cannae. Livy also draws attention to serious military purposes behind the games. Before the days when the circus was filled with extravagant displays of animals from everywhere on earth, military shows combined realistic maneuvers with the more artificial techniques of gladiators to produce the "tortoise" tactic that proved so useful in war (44.9.3–9). On the art of leaping between moving horses as a military skill, see Weiler, *Der Sport* 250; and Thuillier, *Les Jeux athlétiques* 97–109.

8. For these and the following passages, see Ville, "Les Jeux" 299–307. In deprecating gladiatorial combat, an edict of Constantine nevertheless still recognizes its value in times of war: "Bloody shows are not pleasing during civil peace and domestic tranquility" (cited in Ville 315).

9. When Valerius Maximus credits a consul, who used gladiatorial experts from a school to train legionaries, with "combining bravery with skill and vice versa" (2.3.2), the point seems not to be that the gladiators were not brave but that the troops needed skill. In any case, in real life the two were bound closely together. Advice shouted from the stands by spectators suggests knowledgeable as well as emotionally intense involvement; see Ville, "Les Jeux" 296n2.

10. Roman gladiatorial combat was so brutal as not to be sport in any ordinary sense, and for that reason it was not a completely satisfactory substitute for warfare. The Romans did not find any military value in (Greek) sports, while their own gladiatorial games were themselves really instruments of power; see Poliakoff, *Combat Sports* 108–9. R. Branham, in *Unruly Eloquence* (Cambridge, Mass: Harvard University Press, 1989), 95–103, notes that Lucian's keen sense of incongruity detected just this problem in Greek athletic competition. Anacharsis is sceptical about Solon's contention that sports foster martial virtue (Lucian *Anach.* 24–36). Solon's appeal to Spartan flagellation (which took its most bloody form in Roman times, attracted a good deal of public interest, and was presented in a theater built for the purpose) and to Athenian cockfighting (which everyone of military age had to watch; *Anach.* 37) brings the issue of violence into sharper focus. The barbarian Anacharsis' detached perspective on Greek culture helps highlight the incongruity further emphasized by his bemused laughter at how odd it all seems (cf. Horace's Democritus; *Epist.* 2.1.185–98). In pointing out that Spartan citizens engaging in sports are beaten as though they were criminals, Anacharsis is bothered by the same sort of systemic social anomaly that troubled critics of involvement in games on the part of respectable members of society (Lucian *Anach.* 39). A similar conflict in the meanings of combat with animals was noticed by dream interpreters: in some cities the nobility fought with animals, in most places condemned criminals did (Artem. 1.8).

11. G. Sissa and M. Detienne, *La Vie quotidienne des dieux grecs* (Paris: Hachette, 1989), 193; Vernant, "Theorie générale du sacrifice" 7. Guilt perhaps seemed less if captives were killed as sacrifices (Livy 7.15.10; App. *BCiv.* 1.14.117; Diod. Sic. 31.13; Florus 1.21.3). Hand-to-hand combat is thought to make the enemy a sacrificial victim in recompense for a treaty violation in Livy 4.19.3, and Dio reports but professes not to understand ritual execution of some captives (43.24.4, cf. 48.14.4; Suet. *Aug.* 15; Sen. *Clem.* 1.11.1). Mock display of gladiatorial skill with nonlethal weapons *(pugna lusoria)* or in comic versions—e.g., with deformed contestants—similarly provided a relatively benign version of the arena's serious business (Cèbe, *La Caricature* 123). In Lucan, on the other hand, the ritual element in gladiatorial combat intensifies the guilt of civil violence by theatricalizing it; see F. Ahl, *Lucan: An Introduction* (Ithaca, N.Y.: Cornell University Press, 1976), 82–115.

12. M. Wistrand, "Violence and Entertainment in Seneca the Younger," *Eranos* 88 (1990): 31–46; H. Harich, "De Nerone non Agitur: Zur siebenten Epistel Senecas an Lucilius," *Symbolae Osloenses* 65 (1990): 93–100; J.-F. Maisonobe, "Caton Gladiateur dans le *De Providentia* II.8," in *Philologie littératures et histoire anciennes,* Annales de la Faculté des Lettres et Sciences Humaines de Nice 35 (Nice, 1979), 235–57; Barton, *Sorrows* 23–24. A similar point is made by

Tacitus through accounts of violence spreading beyond the games. See A. Bäumer, *Die Bestie Mensch,* Studien zur Klassischen Philologie 4 (Frankfurt: Lang, 1982), 199–200; on "Destruktivität als erregendes Schauspiel," see 118–19. The decision mentioned by Seneca to release someone from a gladiatorial school (*Clem.* 2.6.3) is a purely personal act of clemency having nothing to do with pity, which he dismisses as irrational emotional distress at unpleasant situations. Though he is sensitive to the wider social effects of cruelty (e.g., *Clem.* 1.25.3–26.2) or of anger (*De Ira* 3.2), that is not what he has chiefly in mind here.

13. Coleman, "Fatal Charades" 61–65. R. Ehrman, in "Martial, *De Spectaculis* 8: Gladiator or Criminal?" *Mnemosyne* 40 (1987): 422–25, notes that the mythical forebears of both the Daedalus and the Prometheus killed in the arena had revolted against authority. The *De Spectaculis* follows the sequence of games put on by Titus to dedicate the Colosseum: (1–3) Caesar's splendid theater and its spectators, (4) public humiliation of *delatores,* (5–23, 27) games—(a) *venationes* in the morning, (b) execution of *damnati* at noon, (c) contrived animal acts, involving (i) men, (ii) women or (iii) wild beasts in mimes or mythical tableaux, (24–26) (a) water games, (28) (b) naval battle, (29–30) gladiatorial combat/*venatio,* (31) glory of Caesar. The original impact is entirely lost in transmuting what was preeminently action into a literary medium, but Martial is still able to reproduce the games' notional effect on the spectators. The result is a sociopolitical analysis centering on paradox (represented by the witty epigrammatic style), amazing permutations from one scene to another (represented by the epigrams' arrangement), and a recurrent factor of violence (spanning everything from the death of a boar to a criminal's blood-soaked, mutilated corpse no longer recognizably human after crucifixion and mauling by a bear). The political dimension of these three factors—the extraordinary, the abundant, the potent—appears overtly in the humiliation of *delatores* (4) and again in the poems which bracket the whole collection, describing at the start (1–3) the vast new building and the imperial unity in diversity of those in it and at the end (31) Caesar's power. Cf. L. Friedlaender, *M. Valerii Martialis Epigrammaton Libri,* vol. 1 (Leipzig: Hirzel, 1886), 137–38; Ville, *La Gladiature* 147–48.

The social dimension of the cleverness in these displays illustrates Mary Douglas' concept of "pollution," i.e., anomaly, a term she also uses (*Purity and Danger* 37–40). "Laughter, revulsion and shock" mark out different points on the "gradient of ambiguity" (degrees of anomaly), which includes such things as riddles and jokes, for "the structure of [pollution's] symbolism uses comparison and double meaning like the structure of a joke" (122). Cf. M. Douglas, "The Social Control of Cognition: Some Factors in Joke Perception," *Man* 3 (1968): 361–76, on the subversive effect of jokes and their creation of measured ritual, which, unlike truly obscene or monstrous ruptures, poses no ultimate threat. The contrast is essentially that between violent entertainment in its manageable aspect and as a real threat.

Impossible events in the arena belong formally to the genre of *miracula.* With their many forms of wordplay and their preoccupation with physical defects and other signs of social marginality, Martial's epigrams tap reactions at work also in communal rituals for identifying and rejecting what seems threatening; see

J. P. Sullivan, *Martial: The Unexpected Classic* (Cambridge: Cambridge University Press, 1991), 69. Weinreich (*Studien* 157–60) traces a thematic connection between emperors' anomalous power over animals in the arena (and elsewhere) and strange animal behavior in omens of imperial destiny. In Valerius Maximus (1.8.5 ext.), a mother whose baby was born as she was carried out for burial is said to have given birth after her own death (much as the deceased Arrachion won his match), while the baby was (almost) buried before being born. In proper meter, "altera iam fato functa parit; alter ante elatus quam natus est" makes a good riddle or epigram, to say nothing of oracle, and the event itself would do equally well as an omen. Compare the arena paradox of Mars amused at dwarfs' fierceness or of women gladiators doing the work of men (Stat. *Silv.* 1.6.51f). On the theme of "paradoxical" power so great that it can be exercised without violence (like political clemency), see Versnel, *Ter Unus* 225–26. The clean violence of Commodus' surgical arrowheads is a surreal refinement of this idea; above, chap. 4, n.21. For rhetorical wordplay inspired by one of his amazing feats of marksmanship in the arena, see Herodian 1.15.6.

14. Saller, *Personal Patronage* 38. Functional equilibrium theories of social order, however, do not necessarily deny conflict. A good part of divination's capacity to function effectively can be explained through the flexible, often conflicting interpretations it allows to come into play. What is excluded is revolutionary conflict.

15. Seneca's name in a graffito on the wall of barracks at Pompeii seems to echo his criticism. On objections to the games, see R. MacMullen, *Enemies of the Roman Order* (Cambridge, Mass: Harvard University Press, 1966), 349n30. Christian opponents often highlight the irrational contradiction in bloody games: e.g., Tatianus *Ad Gr.* 23; Prudent. *c. Symm.* 2.1091–93. For Seneca, too, they are a paradigm of endemic social contradiction at Rome, where "as in the gladiatorial schools they fight those they drink with" (*De Ira* 2.8.2–3; cf. Dio on civil war: "They recognized their opponents and wounded them, they called them by name and killed them," 41.59.2). On hopeless combat in the arena as a symbol of the futility of political conflict, see Sen. *De Ira* 3.42–43. The larger lesson Seneca draws from this leads him to elaborate a vision of society itself as a merciless zero-sum game ("no gain except at another's loss"; 2.8.2). Aristotle objects to Spartan training because, unlike true sports, it brutalizes (*Pol.* 1338B9), and Seneca notes that savage laws, too, actually increase the crime they are trying to suppress (*Clem.* 1.23). Livy claims that the games introduced by Antiochus in Syria at first seemed more terrifying than pleasing, though the public soon became accustomed to their brutality (41.20.11–13). Unpleasant aspects were occasionally noticed at Rome as well. Many were shocked at Drusus' passion for carnage (Tac. *Ann.* 1.76.3; on Claudius, see Suet. *Claud.* 34.1), and a specially sharp blade was named after him (Dio 57.13.1). Augustus intervened to stop the savagery of *munera* put on by Domitius (Suet. *Ner.* 4).

When the elephants in a show of Pompey went berserk from fear, after some initial terror (Plut. *Pomp.* 52.4 refers to an *ekplēktikōtaton* elephant fight), the crowd was carried away by pity and then by anger that he had brought them from Africa under false pretenses to be killed (Dio 39.38.2–4; Pliny *HN* 8.20–21; in *De*

Brevitate 13.6–7 Seneca criticizes the elephant show for its unnatural brutality). The facts again are not clear. Neither Dio nor Cicero, who was present (*Fam.* 7.1.3), says anything about danger to the public, and the remarkable human capacities that made the crowd feel kinship with the elephants' plight are heavily colored by folklorist notions of animal psychology. At the same time, the reports would be pointless unless such occasions were indeed felt to have negative as well as positive possibilities. Pliny the Elder's remark that Pompey's death later in Africa was "punishment" again illustrates the interweaving of ordinary and extraordinary: the show, an unexpected hitch, and Pompey's death are ordinary; the show's extravagance, the crowd's consciousness of abnormal brutality, and subsequent death are also "ominously" unusual—hence Pliny's remark.

Grant suggests that the absence of gladiators on coins reflects a sense of unease about what they represented (*Gladiators* 38). One possible explanation for the exceptionally lurid description of savage combat between men and animals in Lucretius (5.1308–49) is the ugly impression made on him by the *venationes* being presented on an increasingly large scale at Rome. If Echion's bloodthirsty anticipation of a gladiatorial show in the *Satyricon* is a depiction of cultural anomie, Petronius' criticism is aimed specifically at the games; see N. Slater, *Reading Petronius* (Baltimore: Johns Hopkins University Press, 1990), 46–47, 65–66. Wiedemann suggests that the supposed Etruscan origin of *munera* was a way of expressing the Romans' own moral ambivalence about the institution, as Etruscan culture was both alien and unwholesome (*Emperors and Gladiators* 32). He also notes that such criticism as there was from Christians and non-Christians alike did not start from humanitarian concern with victims but from bad moral or social effects on the public at large (128–64).

16. On gladiators as "birds of ill-omen," at once "assassins, future cadavers, kinds of suicide and hangmen," see Ville, *La Gladiature* 342n274; on representation of what may be an apotropaic gesture to ward off the effect of a gladiator's imminent death, see 419n139. Shrines in amphitheaters (Golvin and Landes, *Amphitheaters* 140) and the cult of Nemesis or Heracles are expressions of the danger faced much more directly by gladiators than by the public. Social classification, however, is fluid; the gladiator belongs to a marginal "they" yet is also an admirable individual with whom many could identify. Cf. Lincoln, *Discourse* 20. *Bestiarius* was used both for someone thrown to animals and someone who fought against them more or less professionally; see Thuillier, *Les Jeux athlétiques* 590 n95.

St. Paul naturally was sensitive to the outsider's role in the arena: "For I think that God displayed us apostles as supreme [criminals] condemned to death because we have become a spectacle to the world . . . weak . . . without rights . . . ill-clad, beaten up, vagabonds . . . the world's rubbish, the off-scouring of everything [or everyone]" (1 Cor. 4.9–13).

On restricted burial of gladiators to avoid pollution, see Grisé, *Le Suicide* 143. *Lanio* (mutilate), *lanius* (butcher), and *lanista* (gladiatorial entrepreneur) apparently all come from the same Etruscan root. Charioteers, too, though to a lesser extent, were both marginal and popular; on their reputation as users of illegal magic, see Amm. Marc. 28.4.25 with the note in Rolfe's Loeb edition. The ambivalent status of the gladiator's world is what made wild swings in the career of Asiaticus—he was sold for gladiatorial work in the arena and was later the recipient of a gold ring from the emperor (Suet. *Vit.* 12)—sensational and, for critics of the Principate, highly revealing of something very wrong. Popularity turned gladiators into objects of popular consumption suitable as commercial decoration—the GI Joes or Rambos of their day, as it were—on items like glass cups or lamps. See Clavel-Lévêque, "Rituels" 197; and Humphrey, *Roman Circuses* 193. Pliny the Elder (*HN* 35.52) mentions frequent displays of paintings on subjects having to do with the arena or theater. Though it could be thought of as the antithesis of warfare, the theater had some associations with violence and, more broadly, like the arena, was an ambivalent place, inasmuch as it, too, threatened social order; see Edwards, *Politics of Immorality* 98–136. Actors aroused both fear and fascination, and the punishment of an errant actor publicly beaten in three theaters (Suet. *Aug.* 45.4) symbolically assimilated theater to arena.

Those condemned to hard labor were literally marked as marginal by tattooing; see F. Millar, "Condemnation to Hard Labour in the Roman Empire, from the Julio-Claudians to Constantine," *Papers of the British School at Rome* 52 (1984): 128. Under the Republic, torture was not a formal judicial but rather an administrative measure used against marginal people to make a political point (Garnsey, "Penalties" 148–49), and later harshness against members of the upper classes had the same purpose (Suet. *Tib.* 51 mentions a knight condemned to the treadmill; Suet. *Calig.* 27 has many senators tattooed and sent to hard labor). In a sharply stratified society that favors severe penalties to protect status (Garnsey 159–61), the emperor is potentially the cruelest man of all.

17. Thuillier, *Les Jeux athlétiques* 611, 703; on the special provisions in Roman sports, see 639–75.

18. Ibid., 510f (charioteers), 267–68 (boxers); Rawson, "Chariot-Racing", 10, 16.

19. Thuillier, *Les Jeux athlétiques* 512–13; Ville, *La Gladiature* 246–70; B. Levick, "The *Senatus Consultum* from Larinum," *Journal of Roman Studies* 73 (1983): 108–15.

20. The foregoing borrows heavily from Barton, "Scandal" 2–3, 12–15, 23; cf. Barton, *Sorrows* 11–46. See Thuillier, *Les Jeux athlétiques* 536–39; on the marginality of modern boxers, see Oates, On *Boxing*. Ville (*La Gladiature* 335) notes that while few epitaphs record the profession of *lanistae*, many mention that of gladiators. Status shifted in relation to one or another social level: respectable people in comparison with gladiators, popular gladiators in comparison with gladiators without status or with *lanistae*.

21. A. Cameron, *Circus Factions* (Oxford: Clarendon, 1976), 184–92, 294–96. "Ubi plurima vulgi licentia in circum ac theatra effusi" (Tac. *Hist.* 1.72.3); Tac. *Ann.* 14.17.1, 11.13.1. See Z. Yavetz, *Plebs and Princeps* (Oxford: Clarendon, 1969), 11, 24f, on riots, many occasioned by games. After treating Roman military institutions, Valerius Maximus introduces his section on *spectacula* with this remark: "It is a very short move from military matters to urban camps, i.e., the theater. For they, too, have often caused pitched battles, and though created for

the worship of the gods and the pleasure of men, shows have outraged peace by staining both pleasure and worship with civil bloodshed for the sake of monstrosities on the stage [*scenicorum portentorum*]" (2.4.1). On rioting at sports events as an example of the fragile relation between social "frames," see E. Goffman, *Frame Analysis* (Cambridge, Mass.: Harvard University Press, 1974), 360. Robert (*Les Gladiateurs* 26–27) discusses associations of arena fans (*philoploi*: "weapon lovers").

22. On the tradition of abusive ritual slanging, see J.-P. Morel, "La Iuventus et les origines du theatre romain," *Revue des Etudes Latines* 47 (1969): 208–52; and A. Piganiol, *Recherches sur les jeux romains,* Publications de la Faculté des Lettres de l'Université de Strasbourg 13 (Strasbourg: Istra, 1923). The games' "office social est de rejouir les esprits des vivants et de provoquer, particulièrement au lendemain d'un deuil ou d'un danger, une réaction psychologique bienfaisante" (Piganiol 140). On the possible appearance of abusive slanging in gladiatorial combat, see Ville, *La Gladiature* 408. Laughter accompanies abuse, and beneath its different immediate aims (fertility, purification) there lies "une même préoccupation, qui est de promouvoir ou de defendre la vie" (Cèbe, *La Caricature* 20). On the piquant mixture of *seria et ioca,* see Dion. Hal. 7.72.10f. Clavel-Lévêque's Marxist reading sees in these conflicts class tensions simultaneously coming to expression and being managed by the ruling elite (*L'Empire en jeux* 123–28).

The pattern, in any event, is deeply embedded in the fabric of social institutions at many levels: private drinking parties, larger public meals, still larger and more overtly violent entertainment in the arena, and finally civil disorder. So far as the first of these stages is concerned, the formal principle of the symposium can be described as aggression and relaxation, competition and comradeship held together by group tension: The symposium is "deliberate provocation of forces which [a] festive gathering is capable of generating, and upon which there is an attempt to impose a rule which will prevent the appearance of dysphoric or aggressive attitudes, an ever-present danger in this type of social gathering. It is therefore a deliberate, controlled collective exploration of the universe of passions, not without anxieties about elements of contravention"; E. Pellizer, "Outlines of a Morphology of Sympotic Entertainment," in *Sympotica,* ed. O. Murray (Oxford: Clarendon, 1990), 179. The possibility of extreme violence at occasions of cameraderie epitomizes the paradox of antisocial social institutions; see W. J. Slater, "Sympotic Ethics in the *Odyssey,*" and J. D'Arms, "The Roman *Convivium* and the Idea of Equality," both in Murray 214–16, 314. Defining the symposium as *pharmakon phobou* and *meletē hēdonēs* (Pellizer 183) exactly captures the dual nature of gladiatorial combat—defensive yet entertaining—while the notion of "sympotic space" (Murray 7–9) corresponds in miniature to the arena seen as a special "killing space." The extension of Nero's disorderly private entertainments into society at large carried their tensions into the public sphere (Suet. *Ner.* 26). Given the personal nature of ancient politics, the notion that civil disorder is a large-scale party gotten out of hand (Tac. *Ann.* 13.25; Suet. *Ner.* 26) does not seem so strange, and in fact the crude expression of power through pointless gang violence in Nero's leisure-time street brawling is treated by the historians as anticipating what would be done at the highest political level; (see O. Murray, "The Affair of the Mysteries: Democracy and the Drinking Group," in Murray 158–60). Antony, too, went on nighttime brawls with Cleopatra at Alexandria in disguise (Plut. *Ant.* 29.1–2), and Antiochus' somewhat similar behavior, though harmless, seemed plainly mad (Polyb. 26.1; cf. Diod. Sic. 29.32). The staged character of insane behavior on the part of some emperors is discussed in relation to the concept of the festival in R. Herzog, "Fest, Terror und Tod in Petrons *Satyrica*," in *Das Fest,* ed. W. Haug and R. Warning (Munich: Fink, 1989), 140–43.

23. Clavel-Lévêque, *L'Empire en jeux* 2505–6.

24. E. Cizek, *Nero* (Paris: Fayard, 1982), 123f, 163–65, 360–61. In "Le Voyage de Neron en Grece," *Annuaire du College de France* (1985–86): 705–37, P. Veyne contends that in a *spirale d'inflation utopique* Nero pursued a radically new politics of the ruler's absolute personal superiority embodied in artistic "antivalues" inverting traditional norms. For a less dramatic view of Nero's liberal policy, especially his use of games for courting favor, see Griffin, *Nero* 42–48; and C. Manning, "Acting and Nero's Conception of the Principate," *Greece and Rome* 22 (1975): 164–75.

25. On Tacitus' view of games in general as a sign of weakness in the fiber of Roman society, see J. Deininger, "Brot und Spiele," *Gymnasium* 86 (1979): 286 (e.g., Tac. *Ann.* 1.54.2, 14.20f; Tac. *Hist.* 3.2.2). While wanting to degrade the nobility by forcing them into the games (Dio 61.17.3–19.4), Nero also sought to reduce the shame of games through the nobility's involvement (*Ann.* 14.14–20), policies by no means as incoherent as they sound, given the ambivalent attitude of Roman society. On the danger that role-change rituals may indeed destabilize society, see J. N. Bremmer and N. M. Horsfall, *Roman Myth and Mythography,* BICS suppl. 52 (London, 1987), 78–88. Political contradiction and irrationality permeate Tacitus' account of the Principate, ranging from Messalina's preposterous marriage to Silius (*Ann.* 11.27) to lesser, though no less revealing, incongruities such as removal of troops from Rome to improve military discipline by keeping them away from *ludi* and, at the same time, to learn whether civilian crowds could police themselves (13.24). In one way this is perfectly reasonable: what is a threat to the troops' discipline will naturally be a test of civilian *moderatio.* Still, given Tacitus' general picture of Roman society, the policy is bound to seem quite useless—all threat and no test. This quickly proves to be the case when troops have to be brought back thanks in good measure to fondness for violence at the highest levels of government by Nero himself (13.25).

In *The Collapse of Complex Societies* J. Tainter argues that very general categories such as "dysfunction" redescribe rather than explain, while narrower ones such as "contradiction" or "mismanagement" are too specific for true collapse, which in his view is best dealt with through the law of diminishing returns. When the cost of complexity begins to outstrip returns, the energy being expended is naturally reduced, and so long as costs continue to exceed returns the curve of an entire system goes into decline toward a new, lower level of complexity (91–197, esp. the graph of Roman civilization's curve at 125). Collapse is thus a self-adjusting mechanism. Still, in their own sphere—the sphere typical of Roman historical and political thought—narrower or broader explanations dealing with dysfunction or contradiction can be sound so far as they go and, in any case, are not precluded by explanation through diminishing returns but serve as specific causes of it. Moral decadence, dismissed by Tainter as "mystical" and "unscientific" (74–86), may in fact be a perfectly objective, though not exactly measurable, factor inasmuch as morale and attitude are crucial to the human behavior which ultimately explains all social categories, including "scientific" calculation of cost-effectiveness. Assuming that *munera* are examples of complexity in Tainter's sense, the conspicuous expenditure they entailed contributed to diminishing returns that were both qualitative and quantitative in nature. Tacitus' critique of political standards under the Principate and the contradiction seen by Seneca between social and antisocial consequences of violence in the arena combine nonmoral factors of public utility with considerations of moral decadence. Quantitative marginal utility also played a role, if the excessive expense of *munera* helped Christian moral sentiment reduce their scale in the later Empire, as philosophical objections had earlier helped Marcus Aurelius' effort to control costs.

26. On the incident as actually nothing more than a Mithraic initiation, see W. Allen, "Nero's Eccentricities before the Fire," *Numen* 9 (1962): 104–9. Cf. *Hist. Aug. Elagabalus* 6.5. In some later cases it becomes impossible to draw a line between religious motives on the one side and personal, political, or pathological ones on the other. When Commodus took violent religious rites to lethal extremes, he was perhaps still indulging a taste for cruelty (*Hist. Aug.* 9.5–6; 10.3 may be malicious parody). The even more bizarre stories about Elagabalus seem more likely to have been misinterpretations of religious devotion, though misinterpretation need not always have misrepresented the facts of what was done or its political meaning, whatever his real intentions may have been; see M. Frey, *Untersuchungen zur Religion und zur Religionspolitik des Kaisers Elagabal* (Stuttgart: Steiner, 1989), 14–44. Dio dismisses Elagabalus' wish to castrate as well as circumcise himself as plain effeminacy (80.11.1) and presumably thinks the same about reports that he sought a medical opinion on having a vagina made surgically (80.16.7).

27. Goffman, *Frame Analysis* 399. Actual and dramatic matricide overlap in Suetonius' *Nero* 39, and fake triumphs are manned by people made up to look like captives (Suet. *Calig.* 45, 47; Tac. *Agr.* 39.1). A gladiator armed with a wooden sword and fighting against Caligula fell on purpose but was stabbed by him with a real dagger (Suet. *Calig.* 32.2). The theatrical component in Roman public life is discussed in F. Dupont, *L'Acteur-Roi* (Paris: Belles Lettres, 1985), 19–40; and Barton, *Sorrows* 60–65.

In trying to understand how it was thought possible that metaphor and make-believe could threaten to become real, it is worth recalling that hypertrophic metaphor was, in fact, a central principle in another, deeply political kind of spectacle: Old Comedy. The "realized metaphor" around which Aristophanic scenes or entire plays were written created a grotesque *nouvelle realité* which had its genuinely unsettling side, featured a good bit of symbolic violence, and was an occasion for expressing serious social tensions; see P. Thiercy, *Aristophane: Fic-*

tion et dramaturgie (Paris: Belles Lettres, 1986), 103–9, 369. On the mutually subversive relationship between social reality and utopian possibilities in comedy ("En fait, la politique réelle avait commencé, à la fin du 5e.s., à *imiter la poésie*"), see J. Carriere, *Le Carnaval et la politique,* Annales Littéraires de l'Université de Besançon 212 (Paris: Belles Lettres, 1979), 106–7. The tension generated by conservative and subversive factors calling each other into question through parody or irony is discussed in S. Goldhill, "Comic Inversion and Inverted Commas: Aristophanes and Parody," in *The Poet's Voice* (Cambridge: Cambridge University Press, 1991), 167–222.

"Il poeta comico 'si diverte' a destrutturare il reale (critica del vissuto) e sui 'cocci' della realtà costruisce una situazione immaginaria che è il riflesso di un'intuizione organica e dominante. Le 'idee-immagini' non possono che trasformarsi in azioni sceniche. Il potere evocativo della parola sulla scena supera di gran lunga l' 'illusione di realtà' del testo letterario scritto. L'illusione di realtà sulla scena è costruita su un 'corto circuito' tra parola e fatti: il contenuto significativo della parola si traduce immediatamente in un mondo fittizio rappresentato sotto gli occhi dello spettatore senza mediazioni giustificative. Le metafore diventano situazioni reali, le opposizioni concettuali—giustizia/ingiustizia, abbondanza/miseria, etc.—si *incarnano*—in un senso ben più pregnante di quello dell'universo dell'utopia libresca—in personaggi, azioni, comportamenti; L. Bertelli, "L'Utopia sulla scena: Aristofane e la parodia della città," *Civiltà Classica e Cristiana* 4 (1983): 227. This is pertinent to the situation at Rome in that limited, metaphoric subversion of normal standards was an aspect of public performances more generally in ancient society. While losing nothing in theatrical vigor, then, the metaphoric reality of Nero's showmanship was augmented by what appeared to its critics—and perhaps to him, too—to be literal, seriously subversive political substance as well. An unusual combination of factors was needed to bring this about or at least to make some people fear that it was happening: the hothouse atmosphere of ruling circles largely free from restraint, autocratic power placed in the hands of a single person so as to couple aggression with licence, Nero's own tendency to carnivalesque modes of thinking. For a recent discussion of the relation between theater and reality, evidently puzzling to many Romans, see A. Betensky, "Neronian Style, Tacitean Content: The Use of Ambiguous Confrontations in the *Annals,*" *Latomus* 37 (1978): 432–35; and Manning, "Acting." Tacitus' account of the Pisonian conspiracy against Nero is read as sustained theater in A. J. Woodman, "Amateur Dramatics at the Court of Nero: *Annals* 15.48–74," in *Tacitus and the Tacitean Tradition,* ed. T. J. Luce and A. J. Woodman (Princeton, N.J.: Princeton University Press, 1993), 104–28. On power as essentially ostentatious or violent display of status, see R. MacMullen, *Corruption and the Decline of Rome* (New Haven, Conn.: Yale University Press, 1988), 58–96.

On potential subversion of order through liminoid suspension of rules, see Turner, *Process, Performance* 36–41; B. Babcock-Abrahams, "A Tolerated Margin of Mess: The Trickster and His Tales Reconsidered," *Indiana University Folklore Institute Journal* 11 (1974): 147–86; and S. Lasine, "Indeterminacy and the Bible: A Review of Literary and Anthropological Theories and Their Application to Biblical Texts," *Hebrew Studies* 27, no. 1 (1986): 62. See Bremmer, ed.,

Interpretations of Greek Mythology 138–46: festivals of disorder legitimate order by contrast, since in real life the utopia they represent would be an apocalyptic nightmare; "the utopian *cannot,* the dystopian *must not* exist in reality." On extreme situations permitted in myth but restricted in actual ritual, see Versnel, *Ter Unus* 143. If the idea of bisexuality expresses pure divinity, its reality is monstrous; see M. Delcourt, *Hermaphrodite* (Paris: PUF, 1958), 65. The impossible name Hermaphrodite constitutes a miniriddle, while the creature's abnormality is a true portent when it actually occurs. The rich tradition concerning sexual perversions of bad emperors perhaps takes some of its force from these ramifications in the notion of anomaly. On the special horror caused by hermaphroditic prodigies and their possible thematic connection with charges of sexual perversion during the Bacchanalia scandal, see Pailler, *Bacchanalia* 317n199.

28. Cavallaro, *Spese* 198–213.

29. R. Caillois, *Man, Play, and Games,* trans. M. Barash (Glencoe, N.Y.: Free Press, 1961), 130–38. Callois sees vertigo not as fear of danger but desire for it. Clavel-Lévêque writes, "La totalité de la culture se trouve alors en jeu" (*L'Empire en jeux* 2507). On a "taste of risk" in upper-class participation in arena games, see Grisé, *Le Suicide* 91. The risk, though, was ritualized, and Grisé suggests that either gentler forms of suicide than a sword thrust came into vogue or experts (slave, gladiator) were kept on call to do the job cleanly (101), as the Roman upper class "boudait le champ de bataille et s'embourgeoisait" (96).

30. C. Gnilka, "'Scholiastenweisheit' und moderne Exegese," *Wiener Studien* 81 (1968): 199–203. The last of these escalating stages, actual combat, was not part of the Floralia.

Chapter 7. Political Violence and Suicide

1. Robert, *Les Gladiateurs* 191 (no. 190), 305. The contradiction is felt more strongly in another epitaph: "After winning I died, contrary to fate" (224, no. 285). Even if death and victory do not coincide, there is still something awkward about epitaphs that record the dead man's earlier successes in a game of survival and even add the name of his killer (e.g., 165, no. 148).

2. E. Keitel, "Otho's Exhortation in Tacitus' *Histories,*" *Greece and Rome* 34 (1987): 73–82. Keitel suggests influence from the similar parody in Sallust's *Catiline*. Cf. S. Frangoulidis, "Tacitus (*Hist.* 1.40–43), Plutarch (*Galba* 26–27), and Suetonius (*Galba* 7.20) on the Death of Galba," *Favonius* 3 (1991): 1–10.

3. Kloft, *Libertas principis* 142. The real horrors of suicide must have been considerable, and Seneca seems irresistibly drawn to Cato's gruesome double harakiri, first by stabbing himself, then tearing open the wound after it had been treated (*Ep.* 24.8, 67.13, 70.19 ["the spirit which iron had not freed he pulled out with his hand"], 71.17, 95.72). At the same time, by transposing horror to a conceptual level, exempla have a positive protreptic effect, and a clean cool death like that of Tacitus' Otho helps disguise how hard dying may be. Marcellus, too, after calmly distributing gifts to his slaves, abstains from food, enters a steam tent, and dies "not without some pleasure." According to Seneca, he likened death to fainting (*Ep.* 77.5–9). Courage needs bolstering as well, and so Seneca

sets Cato's bloody resolve against the cowardice of Junius Brutus, who, after postponing execution by going to the bathroom, on being called out and ordered to bare his neck said, "I will, so long as I stay alive" (*Ep.* 82.12). This is a remark of "a man who should be condemned to live" in Seneca's opinion, apparently because he thought it had the effect (in modern terms) of someone ordered to a wall for execution saying, "I'll go, provided you don't shoot."

4. The rich, often euphemistic vocabulary for suicide is an indication of how complex its role and the role of violence more generally were in Roman society. See A. Draeger, *Über Syntax und Stil des Tacitus,* 3d ed. (Leipzig: Teubner, 1882), para. 252; Grisé, *Le Suicide* 21–28, 291–97; H. Furneaux, *Annales I–IV,* 2d ed. (Oxford: Clarendon, 1897), intro., 21; F. R. D. Goodyear, *The Annals of Tacitus, Books 1–6,* vol. 1 (Cambridge: Cambridge University Press, 1972), 1.3.3; and D. Daube, "The Linguistics of Suicide," *Philosophy and Public Policy* 1 (1972): 387–437 (French jokes about *etre suicide'* in connection with political murder concealed as suicide [Daube 389] are particularly pertinent to the compound of freedom and compulsion at Rome). For more general studies of suicide itself, see Grisé, esp. 307–16; A. van Hooff, *From Autothanasia to Suicide* (London: Routledge, 1990), which has a large collection of terms for suicide, a full list of instances, and some statistical analyses; J. Kany, "Le Suicide politique à Rome et en particulier chez Tacite," thèse Riems, 1970, a general survey with excellent remarks on political nuances in expressions for suicide, especially in Tacitus (175–85); A. Bayet, *Le Suicide et la morale* (Paris: Alcan, 1922), 271–316; R. Hirzel, "Der Selbstmord," *Archiv für Religionswissenschaft* 11 (1908): 75–104, 243–84, 417–76; M. Griffin, "Philosophy, Cato, and Roman Suicide," *Greece and Rome* 33 (1986): 64–77, 192–202; P. Veyne, "Suicide, fisc, esclavage, capital et droit romain," *Latomus* 40 (1981): 217–68; Bayet, "Le Suicide mutuel" 130–76; and A. Wacke, "Der Selbstmord im römischen Recht und in der Rechtsentwicklung," *Zeitschrift der Savigny-Stiftung für Rechtsgeschichte, Romanistische Abteilung* 97 (1980): 26–77.

5. For some legal provisions at Rome and general remarks on the sociology of suicide, see van Hooff, *Autothanasia* 80–85, 120–21, 166–73; on its "semi-institutional" nature, see 131.

Unbearable pressure of winner-take-all competition perhaps contributed to the social malaise inspiring Lucretius' reflections on the paradox of suicide through fear of death (3.79–82; cf. Sen. *Ep.* 24.22–23). Leo Strauss comments on the dialectical relationship between aggressive vanity and fear of death in *The Political Philosophy of Hobbes* (Chicago: University of Chicago Press, 1963), 13ff, 111f. On traditional forms of opposition through direct action and propaganda, see MacMullen, *Enemies* 1–99, esp. 4–5, 75–94 (on suicide and death as political weapons). Earlier Roman feeling that suicide was disgraceful posed a continuing problem (MacMullen 295n3, 310n23). MacMullen's genealogical tree of families prominent in opposition to the emperors (42–43) includes fourteen suicides.

In "Roman Elite Motivation: Three Questions" (*Changes* 13), MacMullen notes that suicide was one response to the pressure of peer expectations at Rome. The parallel economic "suicide" through excessive public benefaction, again due to pressure for status (20), was directly tied to actual suicide from *pudor aeris alieni,* with both belonging to the irrational motivations best penetrated through anecdotal evidence (23) because anecdotes are often defining cases.

General psychological and sociological factors at work in suicide were modified by the duress under which specifically political suicide took place, but the broad distinction between a wish to die and a wish to kill utilized by Giddens has some bearing on political suicide at Rome. The wish to die, motivated by failure to achieve ideals, is rooted in a sense of shame and fear of contempt; the wish to kill is caused by anger and desire for revenge against an enemy who can only be internalized. See A. Giddens, *Studies in Social and Political Theory* (New York: Basic Books, 1977), 297–321. These two alternatives represent the chief symbolic defensive and offensive choices possible at Rome. On Cato's aggressive suicide, see chap. 9.

Tacitus seems to bring out the same point in reporting the suicide of Ostorius (*Ann.* 16.15), a physically powerful military man of whom Nero was afraid. When the centurion sent to execute him arrived, he "turned the courage he showed against the enemy against himself." Münzer concludes that outright execution of fellow citizens was as a rule avoided at Rome so as to establish an unwritten precedent which could benefit winners in the event they became losers. After restraint had given way in the violence following the death of the Gracchi, during the Empire public execution again became taboo, though Tiberius made a deterrent point by permitting abuse of corpses. See F. Münzer, "Die Todesstrafe Politischer Verbrecher in der Späteren Römischen Republik," *Hermes* 47 (1912): 180–82.

6. Portia's self-wounding to prove that she could stand pain is a disguised "example" (as well as a threat) for Brutus, too (Plut. *Brut.* 13.3–6; cf. Antony's thanking a slave for the example he sets when he kills himself instead of Antony, Plut. *Ant.* 76.4). One of the many ambiguities in Nero's death is his repeated requests that someone else commit suicide first (Suet. *Ner.* 49.3). On death scenes, particularly those involving suicide, see G. Hutchinson, *Latin Literature from Seneca to Juvenal* (Oxford: Clarendon, 1993), 256–87.

Some of the wider ramifications of the culture of violence at Rome run along connections linking group military suicide, gladiatorial combat, and *devotio* traced in Bayet, "Le Suicide mutuel" 172–75. Gladiatorial combat could in effect be an enforced form of the first of these, while *devotio* was a voluntary solo version. See Grisé, *Le Suicide* 62, 63n18–19, 91, 103; and Barton, "Scandal" 19–23. In *devotio* a general himself becomes the sacrificial medium for absorbing danger, as do, on a different plane, those who commit suicide to defy the emperor (see Grisé 121, on passive suicide by fire as simultaneously an aggressive act of political arson). Individual suicide by way of protest is thus a private analogue to *devotio,* as *devotio* is a ritual analogue to private suicide. Religious officials who stay in Rome awaiting death at the hands of the Gauls are engaging in a passive form of suicide by *devotio,* though one has to strike a Gaul to trigger the massacre (Livy 5.41). While Germanicus' threat of suicide as he bargains with a mob was mostly bluff (Tac. *Ann.* 1.35) or pure funk, as it is in Tacitus' *Annals* 2.24.2, and Otho's actual suicide was genuine self-sacrifice (Tac. *Hist.* 2.47), the background of both lay in *devotio. Devotio,* in turn, is an inverted analogue—*self*-sacrifice—

of human sacrifice during crises: Decius does freely to himself what was done forcibly to a pair of Gauls and Greeks (Livy 22.57.6). Interest in the modulations of abnormal violence influenced accounts of Decius' death. In one version (Dio 7 Zonaras 7.26) it is directly caused not by the enemy but by one of his own men, and Livy links it to Manlius' execution (murder) of his own son in a type of vicarious *devotio*. Cf. Levene, *Religion in Livy* 220–23. Together all of this runs the gamut from *devotio* to suicide, vicarious suicide, vicarious *devotio*, sacrifice or execution.

Connections such as these helped make gladiators sacrificial figures. Even when suicide is an act of despair rather than defiance, it is still a form of violence directed against oneself and so, as a public statement, an abnormal act of mourning resorted to in the absence of normal means for expression; see Burkert, *Homo necans* 53. Public slaughter of animals at spectacles and ritual combat of humans in association with funerals are forms of aggression toned down by displacement onto substitute objects or subjects. See above, chap. 5, n. 11. The common factor running through all of these modulations is normal order breached by a threat—military, criminal, political—and then restored by counterviolence. H. S. Versnel, in "Self-Sacrifice, Compensation, Anonymous Gods," in *Le Sacrifice dans l'antiquité*, Entretiens sur l'Antiquité Classique 27 (Geneva: Fondation Hardt, 1981), 140, sees in *devotio* an elemental law of life for life enforced during crises. An unusual level of violence is represented also in the role played by horses, symbols of death in Indo-European cultures. "The element of furor, ecstasy and rapture realized by means of the uncheckable impetus of the frantic animal" was an element in *venationes*, too (Versnel 153).

For cases of group suicide during the fall of cities, see Addendum 2; J.-L. Voisin, "Tite-Live, Capoue et les Bacchanales," in *Mélanges de l'Ecole Française de Rome* 96 (1984): 619. Voisin contends that the case at Capua in 211 B.C. was not caused by defiant despair but by long-standing religio-political resistance against Rome; cf. Pailler, *Bacchanalia*, 279–85. In that case it was a principled act involving ritual, release, and revolution (or at least resistance) according to the typology of mass religious suicide applied to the events at Jonestown, Guyana, in 1978 by D. Chidester (*Salvation and Suicide* [Bloomington: Indiana University Press, 1988], 133). There, too, the instrument was a poisoned drink, death was seen as a crossing over to a better condition, and victims embraced to signify defiant solidarity ("bodies piled on bodies; families, friends, loved ones embracing, rows of bodies"; Chidester 161). At Capua poisoned wine was a Bacchic drink of immortality; participants joined right hands and shared a last embrace (Voisin 624–53). Other parallels attested from ancient instances include execution (murder) supplementing mass suicide and destruction even of animals in the community. A suicidal military oath taken by Samnites and enforced through murder in some cases is turned by Livy into a scene of mad carnage: "Some refusing to take the oath were cut down at the altars and now lying in the slaughter of animal victims were a sign to others not to refuse" (10.38–39). On suicide, at times by more than one person, as a traditional vehicle of Roman virtue, see J.-L. Voisin, "Education de la mort voluntaire a Rome," in *Sociabilité*, *pouvoirs et société,* Actes du Colloque de Rouen, 24–26 novembre 1983 (Rouen, 1987), 91–97.

Chapter 8. Political Game Rules

1. Asinius Gallus died because of similarly ambiguous starvation, Drusus because of plain execution by starvation (Tac. *Ann.* 6.23). A. Barrett, in *Caligula* (New Haven, Conn.: Yale University Press, 1989), 32, remarks on Agrippina that "there even seems to have been an attempt to force-feed her," but if this implies humanitarian desire to save Agrippina's life, it is hard to see why Tiberius would want to do that, except in the unhumanitarian sense of a current joke that during his reign life itself could be a punishment (Suet. *Tib.* 61.5). Agrippina died on Pandateria, where her mother, Julia (Augustus' daughter), had been exiled for a time, and reports of Julia's death, too, are uncertain: was it suicide or execution by starvation? (Tac. *Ann.* 1.53.1; Dio 57.18.1). To denigrate the value of a foreign representative's suicide by hanging, Caracalla had the body wounded to make it seem as though death was caused by execution (Dio 77.20.4); after Didius Iulianius' execution, conversely, it was given out that he had committed suicide (*Hist. Aug.* 8.7).

Since even those, like Agrippina, who were in a helpless position could still hope that damaging rumors would spread, the rationale of (useless) political resistance operated on the principle that violating a norm to show disdain for authority may be more damaging than any effect the violation itself has. "Enforcement of [professional] ethics . . . is a function largely of the visibility of the offense"; Abbott, quoted in Elster, *Cement of Society* 109. While the emperor and his rivals were not members of a group unified as a profession is, they did have a common vested interest in the political system. Some challenges forced the emperor to action he would have preferred to avoid, since by turning a blind eye on the behavior of those whose "profession" it was to be part of the elite at Rome, bothersome political issues could be circumvented. Augustus counseled Tiberius not to look for trouble provided critics did not go too far (Suet. *Aug.* 51); banned books attract attention, availability brings indifference (Tac. *Ann.* 14.50.2). Suicide thus could frustrate both official clemency and official attempts to conceal repression under a blanket of silence. The fine line between challenges that can be ignored and those that must be acknowledged is discussed in J. Scott, *Domination and the Arts of Resistance* (New Haven, Conn.: Yale University Press, 1991), 51: "Only when contradictions are publicly declared do they have to be publicly accounted for." Taking a deliberate push as an accidental bump (Scott 203) is a case of avoiding trouble by refusing to play, while giving a push, as some did by committing or refusing suicide, is issuing a public challenge. "By never speaking of someone whose existence one cannot plausibly claim to ignore, one can say as much as by talking about him constantly, as any husband whose wife is having an affair will know"; J. Elster, *Political Psychology* (Cambridge: Cambridge University Press, 1993), 93.

2. For a brief introduction, see T. Schelling, *Choice and Consequence* (Cambridge, Mass.: Harvard University Press, 1984), 213–42 ("Game theory is the

formal study of the rational, consistent expectations that participants can have about each other's choices"; 215); idem, *The Strategy of Conflict* (Cambridge, Mass.: Harvard University Press, 1960); and M. Shibuk, *Game Theory in the Social Sciences* (Cambridge, Mass.: MIT Press, 1982). J. Schellenberg, *Primitive Games* (Boulder, Colo.: Westview, 1990), is an especially useful, nonmathematical application of game theory to provide a "simple summary of the dynamics of a situation which may help it to be understood by outside observers" (144). Typical subjects are complicated, multifactor decisions of the kind that attracted the attention of Pliny (*Ep.* 8.14: pairings in voting on the alternatives of death, banishment, or acquittal) and Plutarch (*Pomp.* 58.4–5: those who want Caesar and not Pompey to disarm are a majority, but so are those who want both to disarm).

For some remarks on classical authors, especially Thucydides, see Schelling, *Choice and Consequence* 195–212. Xenophon, for example, knows all about the logic of bridge burning: insofar as taking a do-or-die position adds to the credibility of one's resolve, weakness actually enhances chances of victory (196). The literal military application is often mentioned by ancient authors (Amm. Marc. 23.5.4–6; Plut. *Crass.* 19.5; Dion. Hal. 9.31.3). Hannibal pitted captives against each other in a fight to the death before his troops to boost morale (Dio 14 Zonaras 8.23) by dramatizing the need for unyielding effort once bridges have been burned, as they had been for the Carthaginians in Italy (Livy 21.42; Polyb. 3.62–63). The principle applies more generally to any move for turning desperation into an asset: Virgil's "una salus victis nullam sperare salutem" (*Aen.* 2.354); burning corn (Caes. *BGall.* 1.5); committing atrocities to make reconciliation or pardon impossible (App. *Pun.* 18.118; Tac. *Hist.* 4.70.5); and throwing standards into the center of enemy formations where they can be retrieved only at great risk. Cf. Dio 8 Zonaras 8.1; Dio 21 Zonaras 9.29; Suet. *Iul.* 60. Political bridges, on the other hand, are better left standing by the party which thinks it may lose and is well advised to be less aggressive than its opponents (Tac. *Hist.* 1.90.2, 2.30.3, 3.9.4–5).

3. See Little, *Social Explanation* 55, 139, on dilemmas identified by game theory. See also Addendum 5.

4. On epigrammatic paradox in Cato's suicide, see chap. 9. The transition from the idiom of rhetoric to a fully theoretical grasp of social logic and its anomalies in their own right is especially marked in Mandeville, Gibbons, and Hobbes, whose epigrammatic style looks back to the past while also looking ahead conceptually to later developments in formal game theory. "The skill of making and maintaining Commonwealths consisteth in certain Rules, as doth Arithmetique and Geometry"; T. Hobbes, *Leviathan* (Cleveland: World, 1963), 203.

Highly elaborated literary epigrams characteristic of Silver Latin make extensive use of nominal sentences, whose relatively "primitive" form turns them into a peculiarly suitable vehicle for proverbial truth ("Red sky at night, sailors' delight," "per aspera ad astra," "nothing too much"); see E. Schwyzer, *Griechische Grammatik,* Handbuch der Altertumswissenschaft II.1.2 (Munich: Beck, 1950), 623. On ellipse as a sign of urgent truth and its use as an idiom in axioms, see

J. Hofmann, *Lateinische Syntax und Stilistik,* Handbuch der Altertumswissen-schaft II.2.2 (Munich: Beck, 1972), 424. The aphoristic style of medical writing, itself a transformation of proverbial wisdom, is treated as a link between generic ("scientific") truth and historical writing in J. Fineman, "The History of the Anecdote: Fiction and Fiction," in *The New Historicism,* ed. H. Veeser (New York: Routledge, 1989), 53–55. The timeless, analytic universalizing force of Tacitus' nominal sentences, especially *sententiae,* is discussed in P. Hernandez, "Contribution à l'etude stylistique de Tacite: La Phrase nominal (*Histoires,* I)," *L'Antiquité Classique* 57 (1988): 204–30.

In Livy the imponderables of history (e.g., that "those who finally won were closer to losing than those who did lose"; 21.1.2) retain a strongly religious dimension through the strange omens by which they are marked. For Tacitus, though religious mystery is largely secularized, the immanent historical anomaly which replaces it is still highlighted by dramatic portents and, at a subliminal level of style, by *variatio* periodically throwing language strangely off stride as well as by *sententiae* devoted particularly to bringing out unsettling truths. Though highly stylized and lending themselves to paradox-mongering, sharp antithetic epigrams were ideally tailored to spell out the simultaneously double-and-reverse mirror images projected by self-interest, anger, fear, or envy. If many epigrams serve the need of conventional moralism for clear-cut exemplary truths, in others rhetorical mannerism is a vehicle for genuinely shrewd moral insight into the opaque texture of events. Nor are moralism and moral diagnosis always mutually exclusive, as they can supplement rather than undermine each other by combining a grasp of, say, power under the Principate in a simple, heavily judg-mental paradigm of corruption on the one hand, with appreciation for the com-plexity and ambiguity of what paradigms cover on the other. See B. Williams, "Reading Tacitus' Tiberian Annals," *Ramus* 18 (1989): 140–66.

Quintilian illustrates a particularly tidy epigrammatic form called *anti-metabolē* from Cicero: "I don't live to eat, but eat to live" (*Inst.* 9.3.85). What we might call a looser, conceptual *antimetabolē* appears in another Ciceronian for-mula to the effect that religion and political power combine rightly when leading citizens safeguard religion by wise statesmanship and the state by wise religious policy (*Dom.* 1). Here contrasting elements fit together chiastically to express the efficiency of a self-sustaining system. An epigrammatic point more commonly comes from reversal of what seems right or expected ("It is bad to have an emperor who allows nobody to do anything, worse to have one who allows everyone to do anything"; Dio 68.1.3), and outright contradiction can be pro-duced by reversing one half of an antimetabolic *sententia,* e.g., "I eat to live and live to eat."

Rhetoric helped historians find ("invent") and articulate similar anomalous schemata elsewhere, for example, in civil war. "The troops were jumpy, their commander sluggish, and as though unable to think, he could use neither his tongue nor his ears, could accept neither the advice of others nor use his own, and being swayed this way and that by the enemies' shouts, countermanded what he had ordered, ordered what he had countermanded, and soon—as happens in a hopeless situation—everybody gave orders, no one obeyed" (Tac. *Hist.* 3.73.1);

"the ordinary troops were loyal to Vitellius, while officers inclined to Vespasian, hence the sequence of crime and punishment, mutiny and obedience, so that men who could not be controlled could be punished" (Tac. *Hist.* 4.27.3). Although the epigrammatic style in ancient historiography is omitted from consideration in Fineman's paper, Hayden White remarks on the analytic value of anomalous events and of the unusual ways of talking they call for: "[They are] . . . a means of identifying those aspects of historical sequences that conduce to the breaking, revision, or weakening of the dominant codes. . . . Whence their [New Historicists'] interest in what appears to be the episodic, anecdotal, contingent, exotic, abjected, or simply uncanny aspects of the historical record. . . . , These aspects of history can be deemed 'poetic'—in the sense of 'creative' (rather than that of 'fanciful' or 'imaginary') in that they appear to escape, transcend, contravene, undermine, or contest the rules, laws, and principles of the modes of social organization, structures of political superordination and subordination, and cultural codes. . . . they can be said to resemble poetic speech which, even though it may contravene the rules of both grammar and logic, not only *has* meaning, but also always implicitly challenges the canonical rules of linguistic expression prevailing at the time of its utterance"; H. White, "New Historicism: A Comment," in Veeser 301.

5. "*catch-22* . . . 1: a problematic situation for which the only solution is denied by a circumstance inherent in the problem or by a rule <the show-business [catch-22]—no work unless you have an agent, no agent unless you've worked—Mary Murphy>; *also:* the circumstance or rule that denies a solution. 2a: an illogical, unreasonable, or senseless situation. b: a measure or policy whose effect is the opposite of what was intended. c: a situation presenting two equally undesirable alternatives. 3: a hidden difficulty or means of entrapment"; *Webster's Ninth New Collegiate Dictionary.* Cf. J. Heller, *Catch-22* (New York: Modern Library, 1966), 46. Seneca is particularly attuned to catches: the tyrant "is driven by one set of contradictions into another; since he is hated because he is feared, he wants to be feared because he is hated" (*Clem.* 1.12.4).

Beyond the often trite rhetorical formulae, these epigrams represent a powerful tradition of critical analysis running back to Sophistic thought, one of whose many accomplishments was giving more rigorous, focused expression to awareness of the queer way in which things may be true. In quoting a riddle about a kind of violence that is both "fair and dishonest," the *Dissoi Logoi,* which epitomizes early Greek interest in antinomy, raises the unsettling problem of incoherent social norms. When boxers trick and assault opponents within the rules of the game, society is sanctioning what it also forbids (3[11], Diels; the situation, also noticed by Anacharsis [Lucian *Anarch.* 38–39], has special pertinence to the problem of violence in the arena noted by Seneca). In one particularly elegant paradox mentioned by Aristotle, a man both stupid and undisciplined can be counted on to do the right thing, because after stupidity has mistaken right for wrong, indiscipline is waiting to do what is right, since it does what it knows is wrong (*Eth. Nic.* 1146A27–31). Outlandish as this particular case is, getting at serious contradictions or dilemmas in the nature of things backward if need be has its uses, e.g., Ventidius' letting the Parthians think he was afraid they would invade along the route he in fact wanted them to take (Frontin. *Str.* 1.1.6). The strategy of taking a public position exactly opposite to one's true view presented a particularly nasty catch-22 to those who dealt with the emperors. It was a practice especially of the competent soldier Tiberius (Dio 57.1), while Caligula's contradictory attitudes are made to seem merely incoherent (Dio 59.4.2 and 5, 59.23.3; cf. Procop. *Anecdota* 13.13–14 [Justinian]; Pliny *Pan.* 66.5 [Trajan by way of contrast is candid]). Plutarch (*Quomodo adul.* 60C–61C) observes that since frankness precludes flattery, the clever flatterer flatters by means of frankness, telling the harsh Tiberius, for example, "Caesar, though no one dares say so, we all accuse you of being much too hard on—yourself."

6. The puzzle of voluntary enforced suicide has a counterpart in the political commonplace about voluntary servitude; see M. Vielberg, *Pflichten, Werte, Ideale,* Hermes Einzelschrift 52 (Stuttgart: Steiner, 1987), 117–21. Cf. P. Schmunck, "Studien zur Darstellung des Endes von Galba, Otho und Vitellius in den Historien des Tacitus," *Symbolae Osloenses* 39 (1964): 38–82, esp. 57–73: "Das Leben schien schwerer zu bewältigen als das Sterben" (59). That is exactly the sentiment entered in his diary by Admiral Ugaki, who himself committed suicide at the end of World War II, as he reflected on the death of a comrade: "The saying goes, to die is easy, but to live is hard"; Ugaki, *Fading Victory,* trans. M. Chichya (Pittsburgh: University of Pittsburgh Press, 1991), 280.

On a resolute style of suicide as substitute (symbolic) aggression, see Schmunck 65; and A. Giddens, *Central Problems in Social Theory* (Berkeley: University of California Press, 1979), 149: "The dialectic of control operates even in highly repressive forms of collectivity or organization. . . . *An agent who does not participate in the dialectic of control, in a minimal fashion, ceases to be an agent.* . . . all power relations, or relations of autonomy and dependence, are reciprocal. . . . A person kept thoroughly confined and supervised, as an individual in a strait jacket, perhaps has lost all capability of action, and is not a participant in a reciprocal power-relation [hence the symbolic political point in forcible prevention as well as imposition of suicide at Rome]. But in all other cases . . . power relations are two-way. This accounts for the intimate tie between agency and suicide. Self-destruction is a (virtually) always-open option, the ultimate refusal that finally and absolutely cancels the oppressive power of others; hence suicidal acts themselves can be understood as concerned with the exercise of power." Cf. Strauss, *Political Philosophy* 13f, 111f; and Grisé's apt quotation of Schopenhauer: "Far from negating the will to live, suicide is a passionate affirmation of it" (*Le Suicide* 92).

The rationale of "do by dying" (not "do or die") depends on symbolic values akin to those in Arrachion's triumph. "What the challenge to a duel [i.e., decisive conflict] says, symbolically, is that to accept this insult is to lose standing, without which life is not worth living (the ideal code, seldom rigorously followed, of the warrior aristocrat). Who wins the duel is symbolically irrelevant; it is the challenge that restores honor. If the challenger loses, he paradoxically wins his point by demonstrating that he is willing to wager his physical life in order to preserve his honor, his name. The very logic of the duel makes its status as an ideal apparent; any code that preaches assertion of standing and honor at the expense of life itself is likely to have many lukewarm adherents in a pinch" (Scott, *Domination* 37). By replacing the possibility of death with its certainty, political suicide takes this logic one step further. On the topos of suicide as a paradoxical way to escape death, see van Hooff, *Autothanasia* 279n15. The internal anger at work in suicide is most noticeable in mass self-destruction after defeat in war (Addendum 2), characterized by Appian in one instance as carried out "in insane anger" (*Gallic History* 11). Holocausts (App. *BCiv.* 4.4.25) or suicide on funeral pyres thus are symbolic gestures of aggressive arson.

Chapter 9. The Tactics of Political Suicide

1. Versnel, *Ter Unus* 225–26. In stories about Domitian, never more genial to people than just before ordering their execution (Suet. *Dom.* 11; Dio 67.1.3, 77.22.2), concealment is used only to reveal power all the more decisively. The tactic was a specialty of Tiberius (e.g., Dio 57.1.1; Tac. *Ann.* 3.22.2, for confusingly mixed signs of anger and clemency). Everything is reversed yet again, though with less drastic consequences, when apparent exercise of power conceals the actual safety of its target (e.g., Tac. *Ann.* 15.69.3; Suet. *Calig.* 54.2; Dio 57.11.2; *Hist. Aug.* Antoninus Geta 7.4; in *Hist. Aug.* Gallieni Duo 12.5, the false threat is in a good cause).

2. Marsh, *Reign of Tiberius* 286.

3. Dio says no more about an official dismissed by Caligula than that he committed suicide in distress (59.20.3). For natural death thought worth mentioning, see Tac. *Ann.* 14.12.4. Uncertainty about natural or accidental death, suicide, or murder (Pliny *Ep.* 3.9.5; Vell. Pat. 2.102.1; Plut. *Rom.* 27.3–4; Plut. *Aem.* 37.2; App. *BCiv.* 1.3.20; Tac. *Ann.* 3.19.3) took on special political significance under the Principate. The theme recurs in Ammianus Marcellinus (28.6.24, 29.2.13). Suicide was suspected in the death of Orgetorix (Caes. *BGall.* 1.4), as it or murder was in some other remarkably "opportune" deaths (Livy 6.1.7, 23.30.12). The romantic death of Sophoniba was hard to classify as either execution or suicide (Livy 30.15.1–8). Van Hooff (*Autothanasia* 11–14) notes that statistics based on ancient evidence are largely worthless because of selectivity, in addition to incompleteness and inaccuracy. In reflecting reporters' special interests, reports constitute a reasonably reliable guide only to the ideology of suicide. Since the frequency of suicide generally decreases in wartime, its apparent rise during the late Republic and earlier Empire may merely show that the historical tradition records a very restricted point of view.

4. Actual suicide under direct supervision, termed *mors cum arbitro* by Kany ("Le Suicide politique" 18–20), is the next thing to execution. A. Mehl, in *Claudius,* Studia et Testimonia Antiqua 16 (Munich: Fink, 1974), 87, holds that Claudius naturally did not ask, since all that mattered was that Messalina was dead. Having given her an opportunity to stand trial, he believed that she had committed suicide to escape inevitable condemnation. Claudius was tricked into condemning Asiaticus on much the same grounds (Dio 60.29.6). In Tacitus' *Annals* 11.2.2 Claudius asks Poppaea's husband why she has not joined them at dinner and is told that she has died. This is apparently news to the emperor, though

Poppaea had been forced to commit suicide by his own wife, Messalina, whose similar fate later is again only partially known to him. Suetonius (*Claud.* 39) combines the two incidents.

5. Other potentially ugly aspects of suicide by proxy come out in the death of Hadrian. Though not acting under duress from anyone else but from a wish to escape painful disease, he nonetheless became aware of the political paradox that he could still kill others, while being unable to kill himself (Dio 69.22.3; the dilemma is purely medical in the case of Mithridates, who had developed such immunity to poison that "though eager to kill himself, he could not," Dio 37.13). Hadrian's intention becomes known after he orders a slave to kill him, and he is urged not to carry out his plan. In anger at the unwarranted interference, he demands death for those who have revealed his intention and then requests poison from his doctor, who promptly kills himself to escape the order. After a brief recovery, Hadrian finally does die (*Hist. Aug.* 24.8–25.6).

The generic term *percussor* (hit man) covered both "killer" or "assassin" and friend or servant (e.g., a gladiator) who could be asked to deliver the fatal blow efficiently (Suet. *Ner.* 47.3). It is not clear which of the two Seneca's wife has in mind when she calls for the *manum percussoris* (Tac. *Ann.* 15.63.2). The jingle *successores/percussores* in *Nero* 43.1 (replacements ready to step into positions whose occupants have been terminated by the emperor's hit men) was perhaps a current grim joke. Compare the play on *hospitem/hostem* in reference to shifting political fortunes and loyalties (Cic. *Div.* 2.79; Livy 6.26.3; Tarquin, too, comes *hostis pro hospite*, Livy 1.58.8), which result in the paradoxical deaths of people at the hands of their best friends during proscriptions (Dio 47.5.2–3; in 48.29.3 the point is that the same person is friend or foe depending on political alliances of the moment). Seneca plays on the oddity of such a last service at the hands of a faithful servant by wondering "who could have *servaverit* his master more splendidly" than the slave who killed Vettius (*Ben.* 3.23.5). The slave "served" his master by "saving" him by not "saving" his life. C. Gracchus, too, was killed by a slave who then killed himself (Vell. Pat. 2.6.6; App. *BCiv.* 1.3.26; cf. Cassius: Dio 47.46.5; Labeo: App. *BCiv.* 4.17.135; Brutus: Vell. Pat. 2.70.2–5; Dio 47.49.1–2; App. *BCiv.* 4.17.131; Varus "forces" a freedman to kill him, Vell. Pat. 2.71.2).

In some of these cases, others besides the loyal executioner are inspired to die as well. Exemplary suicide comes into the picture when the bystander asked by Antony to kill him kills himself instead and Antony then follows suit (Dio 51.10.7). Mutual suicide either in a military setting or among relatives usually shows more planning. Thus Juba and Petreius agree to single combat so they will appear to have died in battle, and after dispatching Petreius, Juba has a slave kill him (Pseudo-Caesar *African War* 94; their deaths are placed at a banquet in App. *BCiv.* 2.14.100). Adjusting reports to make a political point rendered the facts as uncertain in many of these cases as the true cause of death often was under the emperors. The younger Marius either killed himself or was killed by a friend or slave (App. *BCiv.* 1.10.94; Vell. Pat. 2.27.4–5; Diod. Sic. 38–39.15); Fimbria is said to have killed himself (Diod. Sic. 38/39.8.4) or to have been killed by a slave, who then killed himself (App. *Mith.* 9.60); when a friend refuses to help Brutus commit suicide, another does so or Brutus himself acts (Plut. *Brut.* 52); it was not certain that Cassius' servant had actually been ordered to kill him (Plut. *Brut.* 43.5–6; App. *BCiv.* 4.15.113); C. Gracchus is killed by a servant who duly killed himself, or perhaps both were killed (Plut. *C. Gracch.* 17.3). Varying accounts of Hannibal's suicide were also current (Plut. *Flam.* 20.5).

6. Suicide is a frequent topic of anecdotes because it creates marginal situations whose moral and political logic need probing. Another interesting taxonomy of death comes up in Livy (26.15). After killing his wife and children "so they would not suffer indignity," a Capuan leader demands that he be executed, as many of his fellow citizens already have been. When the Romans refuse and he kills himself, suicide becomes the equivalent of execution, as the murder of his loved ones was equivalent to their own suicide (cf. Ligarius and his wife, App. *BCiv.* 4.4.23). Valerius Maximus has a case of execution demanded and granted after the death of a political associate (4.7.4). In Lucan, Vulteius regrets that the children and parents of his men are not present to be included in the impending mass suicide (4.503). Exposure of newborn children on news of Germanicus' death (Suet. *Calig.* 5) seems to have been protective murder, surrogate suicide, and symbolic protest all in one.

7. P. Garnsey, *Social Status and Legal Privilege in the Roman Empire* (Oxford: Clarendon, 1970), 47–48. The Vestal Virgins' special status made it politically convenient to do some careful juggling in dealing with them. Suetonius mentions three different ways of handling the problem raised by their unchastity. Vespasian and Titus used strategic ignorance and simply ignored the scandal; Domitian first granted *liberum mortis arbitrium* and later had the chief Vestal executed by live burial and the men involved executed or exiled (Suet. *Dom.* 8.3–4). As a rough substitute for suicide, live burial falls between plain execution and complete inaction, and so Domitian's several measures make up a repertory of violence—indirect (suicide), direct (execution), and symbolic (exile). In Dionysius of Halicarnassus (9.40.3–4) when a Vestal is buried alive, while one of the men implicated commits suicide and another is executed, the burial of the Vestal and the suicide of one man are each in its own fashion equivalent to the direct execution of the other man. Two wives found guilty of drinking too much also suffer alternative but equal fates: one is beaten to death, the other starved to death by her relatives (Pliny *HN* 14.89).

8. On the declamatory manner in Tacitus' account of Drusus' death, see R. H. Martin and A. J. Woodman, eds., *Tacitus, Annals Book IV* (Cambridge: Cambridge University Press, 1989), 124. In Leo Bruce's *Case without a Corpse* the victim is tricked into staging a practical joke by claiming to be guilty of murder, then pretending to commit suicide with what is only a sleeping potion. When poison is substituted by the killer, suicide and murder become not only real but identical, there is only one corpse where two are expected, and suicide conceals murder. Though the building blocks in the two situations fit together differently, both involve intricate interplay between appearance and reality: in the one, no murder, only suicide, but suicide which is murder; in the other, no attempt on Tiberius, but one on Drusus, whose suicide was in fact murder, though not by Tiberius but by Sejanus. The narrative possibilities of apparent suicide are exploited by Xenophon of Ephesus in *Anthia and Habrocomes* 3.6.4–5; cf. Suet.

Ner. 2.3. In another ingenious plan for murder, after meat is cut with a blade poisoned on one side, the contaminated portion is given to the victim as the killer eats the safe half (*Hist. Aug.* Marcus Antoninus 15.5). Tacitus mentions a second intricate plot devised by Sejanus in *Annals* 4.54. When Agrippina is offered fruit at dinner by Tiberius, if she refuses, the implicit accusation of attempted murder gives him grounds for taking offense (as happened, Suet. *Tib.* 53); if the fruit is poisoned and accepted, she is gotten rid of (as happened later by other means). That she might spoil everything by just accepting the harmless fruit need not be considered, as that would be far too natural a response.

Murder concealed as suicide from a sense of guilt comes up in Suetonius' *Vitellius* 6, and Nero thought of using the trick to cover his mother's murder (Suet. *Ner.* 34.3; Tac. *Ann.* 14.7.6, 10.3). Tacitus' account of the whole affair (*Ann.* 14.3–8) evinces a good deal of interest in the planning and detection of criminal schemes (14.3), in analysis of evidence (14.6), and in the flaws of Nero's cover-up (14.11). In accordance with Tacitus' own purposes, strong parodic elements run throughout, highlighting the bumbling execution of the plot and its helpless chief criminal ("the attempted murder had gone just far enough to remove any doubt about who was guilty"; 14.7.1). Perseus' poison plot against Demetrius is equally melodramatic (Livy 40.5, 40.24). The story of Siccius' death hinges on elaborate detective work, including careful analysis of evidence at the scene of the crime (Dion. Hal. 11.27; Livy 3.43; Dio 5 Zonaras 7.18). Dionysius also devotes several pages to ingenious arguments from probability in a complex case of fraud (11.33–34).

9. E.g., the case of Piso (Tac. *Ann.* 3.16.1). The following paragraph in the text borrows substantially from Marsh, *Reign of Tiberius* 289–95. Though not involving suicide, alternative reports in Suetonius' *Divus Augustus* 27.4 appear to reflect efforts at public disinformation. A man allegedly tortured on the spot, with his eyes torn out by the emperor in person, and then executed was in Augustus' own version jailed for attempted assassination, exiled, and lost in a shipwreck or killed by robbers. Thinking that delay would be dangerous, yet fearing the *invidia* caused by open execution of Blaesus, Vitellius settled on poison, only to have the crime betrayed to (justifiably) paranoid power watchers at Rome by the evident pleasure he had shown earlier in visiting his victim (Tac. *Hist.* 3.39.1). Domitian's frequent inquiries about the dying Agricola again made people doubt that anyone would be so eager to learn sad news (Tac. *Agr.* 43.2). The ominous hints dropped by Tacitus himself, e.g., that Agricola was poisoned (*Agr.* 43), show how death could be a tool for managing public relations in historiography as well. Public opinion was at best unfocused, whatever opinion counted was to be found chiefly among the elite, and attempts on the emperor's part at direct influence required explanation rather than justification because his power was beyond serious question. See Veyne, *Bread and Circuses* 298–302.

10. Mehl, *Claudius* 30–32.

11. On this legal point and complications in its application, see E. Koestermann, *Annalen 4–6* (Heidelberg: Winter, 1965), *ad* 6.29.1; Bayet, *Le Suicide et la morale* 276–77; Grisé, *Le Suicide* 251–57; and Wacke, "Der Selbstmord" 52–53.

Restrictions were introduced shortly after Tiberius' time. Naming the emperor in a will was thought useful, too, with (Tac. *Ann.* 16.17.5) or without suicide (Tac. *Agr.* 43.4; Tac. *Ann.* 14.31.1).

12. Insofar as refusal to respond to insults is not a sign of strength but a defensive strategy, it is only a less drastic way of dropping out of the game than suicide is. Submission or suicide are, in fact, alternatives in *De Ira* (see Addendum 6). The value of not taking offense even if you have power (e.g., Sen. *Clem.* 1.3–4) is bolstered by Seneca with numerous examples of indifference to insults (*De Ira* 3.11.4, 23). The wise man's total disregard of abuse (Sen. *Constant.* 5–12) solves the problem more radically, but only by bringing normal politics to an end. When Caesar's troops demand discharge with the real intention of showing his dependence on them, he pretends to take the demand seriously and then calls their bluff—i.e., he refuses to be provoked—by granting it (Dio 49.13–14.4, cf. 42.53–55.1; App. *BCiv.* 2.13.93). Variations on the trick have a place on the battlefield. Tullus frustrated a false ally's plan to paralyze the Roman army through sudden withdrawal from battle by pretending that *he* had given the order for them to do so. The strategy, classified in Frontinus under "On Concealing Reverses" (Frontin. *Str.* 2.7.1–2; Dion. Hal. 3.23.6–25), is partially reversed in the next case (*Str.* 2.7.3): when some of his troops are wiped out, Sulla prevents panic by claiming that he had put them into a dangerous position because they planned to defect.

13. In *De Ira* 3.1.5 and 3.6.5, frustrated ambition leads to suicidal anger against oneself, which Seneca treats as a vice. The notion, common in modern psychiatry, that suicide is actually aggression against someone else is given more definite legal form in the treatment of suicide by slaves or soldiers. See Wacke, "Der Selbstmord" 70–76 (esp. 73), 65–66; Grisé, *Le Suicide* 270–81; and Veyne, "Suicide" 235–42, 267. Sociologically, Cato's anger is a symptom of Durkheim's *anomie,* due to disrupted social order and causing unrestrained ambition or suicidal anger; see E. Durkheim, *Suicide,* trans. J. Spaulding and G. Simpson (New York: Free Press, 1951), 252–53, 284–85.

The right of slaves, as human beings, to dispose of themselves is formally recognized ("licet enim etiam servis naturaliter in suum corpus saevire"; *Dig.* 15.1.9.7). But the concession comes in the narrow context of the effect that attempts at suicide have on the *peculium.* Moreover, as Wacke observes, *licet* is not the same as *decet* (70n185), and since considerations of status which made legal acknowledgment of suicide indispensable for free men are irrelevant here, the situation is both socially and legally awkward. If a slave who attempts suicide "has such audacity toward himself, he will have it toward others, too" (*Dig.* 21.1.23.3). Not only must he be labeled defective goods for any prospective buyer (21.1.1.1), but "audacity" *(audere)* means that he is a dangerous person. The general principle that suicide may be presumptive evidence of bad conscience does apply to others as well (48.21.3.6), but a slave's attempt on himself is linked closely to murder (Wacke 63–64, 72–73). A negative version of the principle, involving fault by omission, holds slaves who are in a position to prevent their master from killing himself liable for failure to do so (*Dig.* 29.5.1.22). Proper freedom of action on the part of slaves in denying a master his freedom to kill himself is the obverse of the improper initiative they show in feeling free to kill themselves. The slave ordered by Hadrian to kill him was thus in a very difficult position ("preventing a master from killing himself is as bad as doing it yourself"; Sen. *Ep.* 77.7). Crucifixion of slaves for refusing to give their master poison became a subject of declamatory rhetoric, a sure sign that the situation was felt to be anomalous (Sen. *Controv.* 3.9). An abstract, a priori notion of implicit guilt for aggression is even more apparent in the law calling for execution of all slaves in a household where any slave kills his master (cf. Tac. *Ann.* 14.42). A similar generic conception of evidence taken from slaves by torture in Greece is discussed in P. DuBois, *Torture and Truth* (New York: Routledge, 1991), 47–68. Though its unreliability was clearly recognized, such evidence was treated as uniquely trustworthy because of the instrumental social role which made slaves, so to say, accessory not to guilt in particular cases but to truth in the legal system as such. The *servus poenae* was a free man who after losing all rights through condemnation to capital punishment became a slave owned by no one *(sine domino),* could never be freed, and thus lived as a nonperson whose body existed solely for abuse.

Military decimation works on the same principle, and when adjudged equivalent to desertion, suicide or attempted suicide of soldiers was punishable by death or annulment of a will. Though reasons for treating the military as a special class are evident and motives for suicide in particular cases were in practice taken into account, there is something slightly odd about executing someone who has failed to kill himself. An exceptionally grotesque case from nineteenth-century England is mentioned in A. Droge and J. Tabor, *A Noble Death* (San Francisco: Harper, 1992), 6. After being saved and patched up, a man who had cut his throat was sent to the gallows, but since hanging broke his wound open again and restored his breathing, the aldermen decided to have the wound closed in order to carry out the sentence.

The provisions in Roman law follow from treating slaves and soldiers as representatives of the formal social roles they fill relative to those in authority. Each group is defined abstractly as a class that, as a matter of social logic, is dangerous and must therefore be dealt with by an equally abstract axiom of outbidding threats through calculated overkill. Similar generic ways of thinking helped rationalize bloodshed in the arena. Less rigidly but on the same principle, political suicide was regulated by the system of power relationships between the emperor and his rivals among the elite. Their guilt, too, could be an abstract matter of suspect status or, rather, of guilt defined by intention, and when intention characterizes a class, all of its members are guilty. The same rationale had cosmic warrant when Tiberius executed people on the basis of horoscopes showing that they were in point of astrological fact (guilty of being) dangerous (Dio 57.19.2–4). Dio mentions "a strange charge" that led to condemnation of someone who had squandered his property perhaps to avoid being rich (62.27.2; cf. 59.14.4). Nero reasoned that since he was now poor, he must want to be rich (as all slaves were presumed to want their masters dead) and therefore was guilty of aiming at power. Several people, too, Tacitus claims, were stripped of rank on the grounds not that they hated the emperor but that they were thought to do so

(*Ann.* 15.71.2). For presumed intention, see Dio 52.38.3. "The man who makes love to his wife as though she were another woman is an adulterer" (Sen. *Constant.* 7.4).

Political assassins constituted another actually potential class. Vitellius liquidated all those involved in the murder of Galba, not to honor him but "for present self-defense and future vengeance" (Tac. *Hist.* 1.44.2). Claudius did the same with the killers of Caligula, "not as an avenger but as though he had caught his own assassin plotting against him" (Dio 60.3.4). Later, as a warning to his own freedmen, Domitian executed Nero's for having failed to protect him (Dio 67.14.4). Like the corresponding execution of immediate relatives of someone who has been assassinated or of those whose own attempt at assassination has failed (Suet. *Ner.* 36.2), this goes beyond mere personal vengeance to become a political imperative. Julius Caesar's and Augustus' "I like treachery but can't praise traitors" (Plut. *Sayings of Romans* Augustus 2), or Antigonus' admission that he loved those who were betraying but hated them once they had done so is another consequence of thinking along generic lines, while also expressing the essential ambivalence of treason: the beneficiary either (both) values the advantage offered him or (and) fears the precedent. That is why slaves were both rewarded and executed for (treacherously) turning in treasonous masters. Compare Epaphroditus, executed by Domitian for having helped Nero commit suicide (Suet. *Dom.* 14.4; cf. Dio 67.14.4).

A general tendency to think generically about classes rather than about individuals is behind the strongly hierarchical and rigid notion of social slots at work in stereotypical roles, especially of slaves, on the stage. People are, as it were, pieces whose value is predetermined by the rules of the game they play (cf. *to lēstrikon kai stasiōdes;* Joseph. *BJ* 2.235). In A. Zinoviev's satire on Soviet social logic, when a gesture of protest by self-immolation fails due to watered gasoline, the would-be suicide is taken by the police to the station and nearly beaten to death; see Zinoviev, *Yawning Heights,* trans. G. Clough (New York: Random House, 1979), 567. If protest is conceptually inadmissible, as self-possession and other kinds of initiative on the part of slaves or soldiers were in Rome, then even attempted suicide can be a capital crime. By the same token, applying for permission to emigrate may be a crime punishable by exile; see P. Watzlawick, *The Invented Reality* (New York: Norton, 1984), 192. The slave who revealed treason on the part of Brutus' sons was granted freedom by him as a savior of Rome and was then crucified for informing on his masters, whose categorical prerogatives made patriotism as illegal as treason; scholion to Juv. 8.266f, cited in Hengel, *Crucifixion in the Ancient World* 56n10. Another slave was rewarded with freedom for turning in his master during the proscriptions, then killed for betraying him (Livy *Per.* 77), and Cicero mentions a man who, after helping defend a town he is visiting against attack, is arrested for violating a law prohibiting noncitizens from walking on the walls (*De Or.* 2.100).

14. On the possibility that Cremutius Cordus' death by starvation was designed to leave room for a last-minute reprieve, see B. Baldwin, *The Roman Emperor* (Montreal: Harvest Home, 1980), 105. On suicide as a threat or bargaining chip, see Grisé, *Le Suicide* 89–90; Germanicus' dramatic gesture (Tac. *Ann.*

1.35) should be added to Grisé's list, and the case in Seneca's *De Brevitate Vitae* 20.3 should perhaps be omitted, unless Turannius was threatening to starve himself to actual death. Exile, which preserves the options both of subsequent execution and recall for the emperor, gives its victim no tactical leverage.

15. Ville, *La Gladiature* 236. Symmachus mentions a large group of Saxons who committed suicide to escape the arena (*Epistulae* 2.46). On the motif of spectacular suicides, see Vell. Pat. 2.120.6, with T. Woodman's note in *Velleius Paterculus: The Tiberian Narrative 2.94–131* (Cambridge: Cambridge University Press, 1977), ad loc. Catulus' suicide by suffocation from charcoal fumes concentrated in a newly plastered room attracted attention (App. *BCiv.* 1.8.74). Plutarch (*Mar.* 44.5) says nothing about wet plaster, only charcoal fumes, while Jovian's mysterious death is said to have been due to one or the other, either to fumes from new plaster or to a head swollen from breathing in too many charcoal fumes (Amm. Marc. 25.10.13). The suicide of a governor's assassin by dashing his head on a rock merits mention in Tacitus' *Annals* 4.45.2.

16. And considerable malice as well: see Grisé, *Le Suicide* 89, 135–36, on suicide in protest carried out near people who are the target of protest in order to infect them directly with pollution. Like some of the notes commonly left behind in modern suicides, the body delivered an accusatory message. Cicero thought of killing himself at Octavian's hearth, according to Plutarch (*Cic.* 47.6), and the *flamen dialis* who kills himself under political duress in a temple (Val. Max. 9.12.5) augments his murderers' guilt with sacrilege by transforming the suicide they are forcing on him into human sacrifice (cf. Sen. *Clem.* 1.9.4). Slaves who killed themselves at public altars to avoid fighting animals in the amphitheater evidently also wanted to add a suggestion of unholy sacrifice to protest (Diod. Sic. 36.10.1–3).

The husband denied refuge in his wife's house during proscriptions probably killed himself on its doorstep with the same idea in mind (Livy *Per.* 89); similarly, Bibulus bares his neck to Caesar's men and invites a blow to fix guilt on him (App. *BCiv.* 2.2.11). Feelings of admiration rather than guilt seem to have been inspired by the suicide of a Roman which so impressed those sent to arrest him that they did not dare to approach his body (Diod. Sic. 37.27.2), but Coriolanus' mother openly threatened to leave a curse by killing herself (Dion. Hal. 8.53.2). Norbanus did kill himself in the center of an agora on Rhodes while deliberations were going on concerning Sulla's demand for his surrender (App. *BCiv.* 1.10.91). Accusatory suicide in effect inverts forced suicide designed to avoid guilt that would be incurred by direct execution. When an unchaste Vestal, no longer virgin but not a normal woman either, was starved to death in an underground chamber, the small symbolic portions of food left with her absolved society from guilt either for killing her or for permitting her to live (Plut. *Num.* 10.3–7; execution by a draught of hemlock in Greece perhaps had the same aim). If one's own guilt for murder could be avoided this way, it could be pinned on someone else through accusatory suicide.

17. Dio, too, says that he killed himself in order to be believed (64.11). Plutarch has a trooper kill himself to convince Otho not to give up (*Otho* 15.3). This is yet another of the forms taken by *devotio*, whose suicidal aspect is sym-

bolized in the swords pointed at their own throats by troops swearing an oath of loyalty to death (Amm. Marc. 21.5.10). The pledged suicide of soldiers is a vow to die in battle; the threatened suicide of generals is a political lever. The tribune who committed suicide though he had been acquitted of complicity in a conspiracy against Nero may have been acting in protest or from guilt at its failure; another tribune "spoiled the pardon he had accepted," perhaps by a showy suicide (Tac. *Ann.* 15.71.2).

18. Lintott, *Violence* 16–21; Grisé, *Le Suicide* 74–76. Wives and husbands and other relations share exile as well; see Tac. *Ann.* 15.71.3; Tac. *Hist.* 1.3.1; Dio 55.10.14. Mistreatment of surviving relatives (e.g., Dio 58.22.3, 59.10.4, 29.7; Joseph. *AJ* 19.190–200; Suet. *Calig.* 59) was a threat that could be forestalled by joint suicide. On couples dying together, not always by suicide: Portia/Brutus (on one account she had killed herself before his death; Plut. *Brut.* 53.4–5); Calpurnia/Antistius, Servilia/Lepidus (Vell. Pat. 2.26.3, 2.88.3); Tac. *Ann.* 6.29.1 and 4; Tac., *Hist.* 2.59.1; Dio 58.4.6, 59.10.6; Plut. *De garr.* 508B [Tac. *Ann.* 1.5 has a different version]; Philo *Leg.* 61. Apicata's suicide after Sejanus' death was perhaps not a gesture of loyalty, as they had been divorced for some years (van Hooff, *Autothanasia* 151). Cornelius Sabinus may have committed suicide defiantly after the execution of his fellow conspirator Chaerea and was in any case motivated by personal loyalty (Dio 60.3.5; cf. Joseph. *AJ* 19.273). Velleius Paterculus comments on the frequent loyalty of wives to husbands during the proscriptions (2.67.2). Several multiple suicides of relatives appear among the melodramatic events of the times (App. *BCiv.* 4.3.15–6.51; Livy 40.4; cf. Dio 47.10.7, 62.17.4; Tac. *Ann.* 16.33.2; Diod. Sic. 34/35.4.1). Polybius' instances of multiple suicide include father/son/*erōmenos* (5.28.7–8; cf. Dio 72.14.3) and entire family (5.54.3–5); compare the quasi–double suicide of father and son in Suetonius' *Divus Augustus* 13.2 and Dio 51.2.6. Accounts of a dog jumping into a river to be with the body of its executed master (Dio 58.1.3) and a guilty soldier killing himself and his horse (75.1.2) are sentimental folk versions of the motif.

The parallel between Lucretia and a daughter killed by her father to protect her from rape (Dion. Hal. 11.37.5–6, 41.2) suggests that murder can stand for suicide. Many of these family tragedies are scaled-down versions of mass suicide (see Addendum 2). On joint suicide deliberately performed as an exemplum, see R. G. Mayer, "Roman Historical Exempla in Seneca," in *Seneque et la prose latine*, Entretiens sur l'Antiquité Classique 36 (Geneva: Fondation Hardt, 1991), 142. Thematic variation then generates an inverted pattern of relatives sundered by *dis*loyalty. The motif of *perfidia punica* makes an appearance in this connection when Hasdrubal tries to stop his wife from bargaining for her own and their children's lives with the Romans. As Carthage falls and he is the one who submits to Scipio, she commits suicide with them in outrage at his betrayal (Dio 21 Zonaras 9.30; App. *Pun.* 19.131; Polyb. 38.20.7–10 [text incomplete]). In an incident especially useful to Tacitus, when a father is dragged into court "dirty, unkempt and manacled" directly from exile by his son (*Ann.* 4.28), though his misery is not voluntary, the scene takes some of its force from the tradition of symbolic self-abasement to protest injustice. That aspect of the situation is sharpened by Tacitus' phraseology *(reus pater accusator filius)* and then further underscored by his remark that since they had the same name, the case was, outrageously, Vibius Serenus versus Vibius Serenus.

19. Still another form of bargaining-suicide is more clearly "devotional." To stop retreat or inspire assault, a general may throw his standard toward the enemy and plunge ahead shouting, "Help me, Romans!" or "Here is where I die!" (App. *BCiv.* 2.15.104, 1.7.58, 2.21.152; App. *Hisp.* 5.27; Livy 6.8.3, 25.14.7, 26.5.15; Dion. Hal. 8.65.5, 9.31.3; Frontin. *Str.* 2.8.1–5; Plut. *Sull.* 21.2; Plut. *Aem.* 20.1–2).

20. Tacitus himself occasionally devalues suicide with depreciatory remarks. The flattery of Nero found in Piso's will after his suicide was due to "love of his wife" (*Ann.* 15.59.5), but any sympathy which that may create is reduced when Tacitus adds that she was a worthless, though attractive woman stolen from a friend's marriage and that her shamelessness along with her former husband's passivity simply made Piso's infamy all the greater. Tigellinus' suicide in the baths among "concubines and kisses" was perhaps intended by him to be a gesture of contemptuous indifference but is treated by Tacitus as itself contemptible (*Hist.* 1.72.3). Petronius' may be contemptible too, though less clearly so (Schmunck, "Studien" 71–72). Libo's last feast (*Ann.* 2.31) does him no credit either. These are cases not of politically useless opposition but of suicide not counting because it is morally worthless.

21. On the significance of *amicitiam renuntiare* and the various grades of displeasure it registered, see R. Rogers, "The Emperor's Displeasure," *Transactions and Proceedings of the American Philological Association* 90 (1959): 224–37. Vistulius similarly kills himself because of a breach in friendship with Tiberius (Tac. *Ann.* 6.9.2), and Lollius drinks poison after Gaius Caesar renounces *amicitia* (Pliny *HN* 9.118). When his renunciation of friendship with Gallus had a domino effect ending in suicide (Suet. *Aug.* 66.2), Augustus—sincerely or not— "shed tears that he was unable to be angry with a friend without fatal results." It could be politically most convenient that renunciation "was not tantamount to injunction of suicide, even if some offenders out of their own character made that response" (Rogers 237).

22. K. Bradley, *Slaves and Masters in the Roman Empire,* Collection Latomus 185 (Brussels: Latomus, 1984), 21–45, 113–43.

23. Ibid., 79–80, 45.

Chapter 10. Political Anomaly and Suicide

1. See Addendum 6; on juridical and philosophical aspects, see M. Griffin, *Seneca: A Philosopher in Politics* (Oxford: Clarendon, 1976), 129–71. Tacitus is perhaps using the language of accounting, if not of gaming, when he says that in merely exiling someone for a second hostile act the emperor "entered it as clemency" (*trahebat ad clementiam; Ann.* 12.52.2). Clemency was, in fact, an important factor also in the symbolic political game conducted through competition in the arena. It regulated the emperor's dealings with the people, its medium was again violence which could be employed in various ways as a vehicle of power, and power was again exercised through disposal of life and death. But as befitted a relationship less focused and direct than that with the Senate, clemency was

exercised on a third party. The idiom of the arena located power very precisely when it spoke of officials as doing the killing (Juv. 3.37, *occidunt populariter*), though decisions could be influenced by the crowd or the emperor (e.g., Dio 77.19.4). Public displeasure at prominent figures for "cruelty" was often due to the symbolic meaning of their reluctance to spare defeated combatants on popular demand. The crowd makes demands or requests—the ambivalence between the two being exactly the political point—which the emperor then permits or refuses. Claudius brought on a gladiator the spectators were especially keen to see in action (Suet. *Claud.* 21.5); Domitian characteristically only "allowed" them a choice of four imperial fighters (Suet. *Dom.* 4.1); Titus, also characteristically, provided both favorites when two champions were called for (Mart. *Spect.* 20.1–2) and offered to give a *munus* wholly at the public's pleasure, not his own (Suet. *Tit.* 8.2); Messalina's influence was sufficient to save a lover of hers, though Claudius and the crowd wanted him killed after he had lost a match (Dio 60.28.2). Paradoxes that naturally arise in subtle politico-sporting moves of this kind are illustrated in Martial's *De Spectaculis* 29. After a pair of gladiators had fought to a standoff, the crowd wanted a draw and *missio,* but the rules called for a clean decision, which Titus then made by declaring both victorious, though neither had won and both in a sense had lost. This second game of clemency within the primary game seems to be the background for a somewhat obscure story about Claudius (Suet. *Claud.* 21.6). When some naval combatants saluted him with "Hail, emperor! Those who are about to die salute you!" and he added "Or not," they refused to fight on the grounds of having been spared. After dithering for a time about killing them all, he finally induced them to fight through a combination of threats and promises. In Dio's version nothing is said about Claudius' response, the salute itself is apparently an unsuccessful invitation for reprieve, and when the combatants have to take part in a naval battle, they do no more than go through the motions until being forced to kill each other (60.33.4).

2. Cf. Cic. *Att.* 8.9A.2, 9.16.2, 10.4.8; Cic. *Phil.* 2.116. In Pliny the Younger's *Panegyricus* 3.4, too, clemency is close to cruelty. *De clementia* 1.17.2 compares clemency, which Seneca is recommending, to a placebo through which political disease can be alleviated. Though Caesar spared those who laid down arms, he never put aside a hidden sword, whereas others who were initially not so generous stopped the killing after a while (Sen. *Ben.* 5.16.5). According to Dio (43.12.3–13.2), since Caesar deviously got rid of people he had not openly executed or pardoned, his clemency was a shrewd tactic maximizing opportunities for defense and attack (38.11.3–6). M. Lossau, in "Suetons Clementia Caesaris," *Hermes* 103 (1975): 498, notes the pairing of clemency and arrogance in *Iul.* 73–79.

3. This last rule parallels the payoff or payback advantage of revenge over gratitude (Tac. *Hist.* 4.3.2; cf. Sen. *Clem.* 1.7.3: failure to get revenge is a sign of weakness; Dio 8 fg.36.14: we are more pained by injuries than pleased by favors). Most of what is in the analyses in Dio had been worked out in Seneca's *De clementia,* where Livia also advises the harassed Augustus (1.9.4–6), and Seneca talks about a ruler's vulnerability to innate human violence (1.1.1 and 3, 8.2) and

about the uselessness of strict justice, because it would decimate the population (1.6.1, 10.1) and by stirring resentment actually augment the ruler's danger (1.8.6–7, 11.4, 23). Clemency is the safer course because it wins favor (1.1.5, 3.4), if nothing else through the subjects' self-interest (1.4.1).

4. Burning incriminating letters unread and uncopied was a political ritual (Dio 59.4.3, 60.4.5, 67.11.2, 71.28.4). Augustus also claimed to have burned letters in Antony's possession but kept them for later use (Dio 52.42.8), and the order that evidence concerning his earlier career be destroyed protected him as much as it did others (App. BCiv. 5.13.132). Cf. Plut. Sayings of Romans Pompey 7; Plut. Pomp. 20.4; Sen. De Ira 2.23.4. The motive for being slow to believe the worst about others is not charity but concern about one's own safety (Sen. De Ira 2.24.1), and that is true also for feigning ignorance of insults (2.33.1). For the Golden Rule in Roman politics, see M. Vielberg, "Ein Übersehener Historiographischer Topos aus der Vulgärethik: Tac. Hist. 1.16.4," Hermes 119 (1991): 121–23.

"Defensive avoidance is manifested by lack of vigilant search, selective inattention, selective forgetting, distortion of the meaning of warning messages, and construction of wishful rationalizations that minimize negative consequences"; I. Janis and L. Mann, Decision Making (New York: Free Press, 1977), 50. "Cultivated inability to hear or comprehend can be a genuine strategic advantage" (Schelling, Strategy 17), inasmuch as ignorance removes responsibility or ability to make decisions and preserves freedom of action—for example, settling an argument over the telephone about where to eat by simply saying what restaurant you are going to and hanging up (Schelling 146). Antigonus refused to take action on a conversation in Seneca's De Ira 3.22.1, while Galba's culpable ignorance left him talking on a dead line when he "prayed to the gods of an empire no longer his" (Tac. Hist. 1.29.1; perhaps an allusion to evocatio, e.g., Livy 5.21). Preserving freedom of action in one way is actually an aggressive, take-it-or-leave-it tactic for pressuring others. Avoiding decisions by retreating is a more cautious approach used by Caesar when he stayed away from the Curia and Rome to avoid having to do something about an awkward situation (Dio 50.2.4). It is not surprising that the move comes up repeatedly in connection with the devious Tiberius, who pretended to be at home ill in order to avoid making any definite moves (Dio 57.3.2) or attended games infrequently to avoid public pressure (Suet. Tib. 47). His mysterious retreat to Capri perhaps can be partly explained as tactical isolation, too. Dio does in fact connect it with a desire to escape from Livia's meddling in public and domestic affairs (57.12.6); compare P. Schrömbges, Tiberius und die Res Publica Romana (Bonn: Habelt, 1986), 140, on the serious political difficulties within the imperial family. Tiberius did not so much stay in Capri as stay away from Rome, turning back on one occasion from fear of "the people's power" (Suet. Tib. 72.2), presumably the pressure they could exert. Sejanus' control of access to Tiberius suggests a new style of management through deliberately restricted communication, without, however, anything like real loss of contact; see G. Houston, "Tiberius on Capri," Greece and Rome 32 (1985): 179–96. Tacitus' report that Tiberius would urge others to assume the responsibility of administering provinces "but forget that he himself prevented

Arruntius from going to Spain for ten years" (*Ann.* 6.27.3) scores a point about his deviousness, though the forgetfulness may simply have been administrative finesse.

Closely related to this—not breaking the connection but mumbling into the phone—is the purposely opaque language both on Tiberius' part and on that of senators (Tac. *Ann.* 1.11.2–3) to assure ignorance of policy and thereby escape the need for decisions which might be regretted on both sides. "To speak at all is to give some other [person] power over us, and some assert their own power by refusing to speak at all [e.g., Tiberius' or Paetus' *taciturnitas;* Tac. *Ann.* 1.74, 14.12.1], to speak intelligibly [e.g., senators; Tac. *Hist.* 1.85.3] or (so far as this is possible) within any frame of reference they cannot unilaterally prescribe"; J. Pocock, *Politics, Language, and Time* (Chicago: University of Chicago Press, 1971), 24. Claudius' obtuseness, Nero's frivolity, and Caligula's brainstorms perhaps all included a measure of the same tactic. Nero's initial indifference to reports of rebellion is explicable as strategic ignorance, though Suetonius' account suggests mere blind self-confidence (*Ner.* 40). Tacitus depicts Vitellius' refusal to accept bad news as stupid pretense (*Hist.* 3.36.1, 54–56: *stulta dissimulatio;* on his "ostrich policy" of shielding himself and the public from bad news to sustain morale, see Z. Yavetz, "Vitellius and the 'Fickleness of the Mob,'" *Historia* 18 [1969]: 567). The "astonishing silence" surrounding him (*Hist.* 3.54.1) reappears in the defensive pretended ignorance through which those present when Britannicus was murdered (*Ann.* 13.16) tried to escape involvement; Agrippina, who had also been there, later again realized that the best defense against danger may be ignorance (*Ann.* 14.6.1). As these examples show, deliberate ignorance, pathological denial, and dishonest appeasement (e.g., Dio 59.16.9–11) are not easily kept apart; cf. Dixon, *Military Incompetence* 65, 141–42.

5. This tension between an emperor's intentions in dealing with individuals and the requirements imposed on him by political reality can also be understood in light of the distinction between relational and systemic levels made with reference to patronage in T. Johnson and C. Dandeker, "Patronage: Relation and System," in *Patronage in Ancient Society,* ed. A. Wallace-Hadrill (London: Routledge, 1989), 219–41. As systemic exploitation for Marx coexists with voluntary individual relationships between labor and capital (232), so a good-faith agreement made by the emperor not to execute members of the elite was rendered vacuous by the larger political system that gave him real power and was presupposed by the agreement.

The whole of *De clementia* is an excellent example of the uneasy relationship between system and individual. In 1.2 Seneca is advancing carefully over slippery terrain. The value of clemency to guilty people is obvious, but complications immediately set in. Since clemency is possible only after something wrong has been done, it seems to be the only virtue that is useless to those who are innocent. An analogy with medicine helps put a better face on things: as the sick "use" medicine, but healthy people too "honor" it, so while the guilty "appeal" to clemency, the innocent "cherish" it. This still leaves it largely negative in nature: the parallel to sickness is guilt, and it is not clear why the innocent should be concerned about that. But they in fact are, because sometimes "fortune" (bad political luck) takes its place, and then even they are guilty. Moreover, clemency can help not only innocence but virtue *(virtus)*, since "due to political conditions it happens that even praiseworthy actions can be punished [*possint laudata puniri*]." In contrast to bad luck, virtue is activism which, Seneca concedes, can bring guilt, even if the cause is admirable. Clemency and the political reality it deals with are like an optical illusion, changing shape depending on how we see or think of it. Seneca's aim is to influence Nero's perspective by showing that clemency is a good thing for rulers, but he can no more avoid implying the facts of power than he can oblige Nero's better self through flattery without constantly reminding him of his absolute authority. The problem is already implicit in Seneca's ominous remark at the end of 1.1: "There is no one so confident in his innocence that he is not also pleased to see clemency open and ready for human errors." Here "errors" diplomatically cover everything from guilt to innocence, real or otherwise. It is impossible even to talk about clemency without disclosing the internal tensions that compromise its application in particular cases, especially when they involve emperors like Nero ("We can hope and trust, Caesar, that this [a regime of clemency] will largely come true. Your kindness of heart will spread"; 2.2.1). After promising to spare Cinna in a dramatic face-to-face interview, Seneca's Augustus challenges him "to let *amicitia* between us start today; let us compete to see if I have given you life or you owe it to me [*an tu debeas*] in better faith." (1.9.11). Cinna presumably does not understand that, personal gestures aside, "the man who owes his life [*debet*] has lost it" (1.21.2).

6. Adolf Hitler, *Mein Kampf,* trans. R. Manheim (Boston: Houghton Mifflin, 1943), 288. Seneca remarks that Augustus became merciful only after the necessary killing had been done (*Clem.* 1.11.1–2). On the subject of leniency to Carthage, too, some recommended unconditional surrender first, "then we will see" (App. *Pun.* 9.64). The dilemma of either destroying or pardoning an enemy comes up in Livy 8.13.14–17, and the risks in the latter policy are somewhat laboriously rationalized away on the grounds that high spirit makes a defeated enemy worth sparing (8.21.9). It also makes him dangerous (cf. the alternative rules for arena combat: "My advice is to kill the man you defeat"; "I saved many lives when I needn't have, hoping that someone would return the favor" [Robert, *Les Gladiateurs* 113, 305–6]). A highly artificial debate on clemency is conducted through paradigmatic single-line exchanges between Nero and Seneca in *Octavia* 436–532. Friendship through intimidation is a formula for imperialism in Tacitus' *Histories* 4.57.2, and Cicero takes a similarly hard line (*Off.* 1.88): clemency is justified only if severity for the public good is a live option. Cf. Cic. *ad Brut.* 1.2a.2: Brutus' desire for clemency is a bad thing, because unless healthy toughness eliminates an empty show of mercy, civil war will never end; *ad Brut.* 1.15.10: clemency is praiseworthy but out of place in the current war when freedom is at stake and severity is needed to deter others. Cicero holds that even measures taken against children are justified, as the other side would do the same. In *Histories* 3.66 the risks of clemency are canvassed from the opposite perspective, that of its intended recipients. Backers of Vitellius think of "the danger and humiliation they face, the sheer faith they must put in the victor's whim [*libidine*]" if they come to terms. Neither Vespasian's pride *(superbia)* nor the pity

felt by Vitellius' defeated men will allow Vitellius himself to return to private life, and the harsh language of *libido* or *superbia* leads up to the paradox that under the circumstances victors "have freedom only to kill." Just such considerations had already been seen at work from the victor's own point of view (2.63): an attempt at clemency was thwarted by the charge that it was motivated by a desire for good reputation purchased at the price of danger to the emperor posed by those who were being treated too gently.

7. The Budé text in the next sentence catches the same paradox (*an mortem rei perderent;* "whether they were losing the death of a defendant"), and the wide range of proposed readings in the paragraph reflects the inherent anomaly of what Seneca is trying to say. The passage is discussed in W. Suerbaum, "Der Historiker und die Freiheit des Wortes," in *Politik und literarische Kunst im Werke des Tacitus,* ed. G. Radke (Stuttgart: Klett, 1971), 64n8. Cf. Lucan 2.156–57: "They stole their own death from the bloody victor"; in a somewhat similar turn of thought, accommodating those who want to die is a "loss" to their killer (4.277). The incident of a man "accused of having stabbed himself" (Suet. *Claud.* 16.3) may not have involved political resistance so much as political status; see Grisé, *Le Suicide* 252n28.

8. See U. Vogel-Weidemann, "The Opposition under the Early Caesars," *Acta Classica* 22 (1979): 95.

9. My use of this concept along with some related terminology depends largely on the version in F. Modigliani, "Liquidity and Uncertainty—Discussion," *American Economic Review* 39 (1949): 203–8, where the notion is given a very specific and technical economic application.

10. See Addendum 7. Cf. Thuc. 2.62.3: "It is worse to lose what you have than to fail in trying to get what you do not." The "endowment effect," "status quo bias," or "loss aversion" is discussed in R. Thaler, *The Winner's Curse* (New York: Free Press, 1992), 63–78; cf. D. Kahneman and A. Tversky, "The Psychology of Preferences," *Scientific American* 246, no. 1 (1982): 160–73.

11. These points and terminology come from Little, *Social Explanation;* and Schellenberg, *Primitive Games* 24, 49, 67, 73, 131, 143. Side payments added as compensation to facilitate fine adjustments increase the range of possible agreement and create an "exchange bonus" by enhancing the bargaining process itself (Schellenberg 122–24, 243–44). This formal analysis of what is seen by participants as "not free lunch but extra dessert" is particularly pertinent to Roman society, where donatives of carefully estimated size were given to carefully selected groups by the emperor, who just as carefully, in turn, might be named co-heir in wills.

The monetary aspect of voluntary suicide, too, in effect constituted a side payment adding an overall exchange bonus to the system. The value of property that could be confiscated in the event of formal execution was conceded in the form of a valid will by one party (the emperor) to induce suicide by the other. What is more, the trade-off permitting victims to preserve property at the cost of their lives was sweetened for the authorities when part of an estate had to be left to the emperor or his henchmen to ensure preservation of the rest (Tac. *Ann.* 14.31.1, 16.11.1, 17.5; Tac. *Agr.* 43.4). The anecdote in Suetonius' *Vitellius* 14.3, which does not involve suicide, reduces the general pattern to farce: when a knight being led off to execution assured the emperor that he had made him his heir, Vitellius examined the will and, finding that a freedman was named co-heir, had him executed, too. Compensation for death through preservation of property was thus an odd reverse life insurance policy under which suicide assured payment. Moreover, the looser considerations of equity that can be accommodated through side payments introduce another of the factors beyond purely selfish utility which in fact motivate people but tend to be excluded by game theory. At Rome such considerations included genuine concern for family status so that when the emperor occasionally made gratuitous payments to impoverished members of prominent families, he was attempting to keep some players in the game and sustain the system as a whole. Refusing to extend aid, then, and confiscating wealth indiscriminately were moves in the opposite direction. The value of suicide was subject to moral depreciation as well.

12. Schelling, *Strategy* 22. A statue of Commodus with bow tensed ready to shoot was set up opposite (facing?) the Curia to intimidate senators (Hdn. 1.14.9). Antoninus' habitual affectation of anger occasioned a jest which he greatly appreciated for its truth to the falsity of appearances. He looked, someone said, "like a man who is angry" (Dio 77.11.1 [2]), either because he just really was and therefore normally looked that way, or because he was not but wanted to look that way. The often threatening facial expressions mentioned by historians are a symptom of the highly personal, face-to-face nature of much ancient political life (Tac. *Agr.* 45: Domitian and the Senate). Spontaneous or artificial, they inevitably became a political language, e.g., Tiberius' angry mien (Tac. *Ann.* 1.12.3) or the faces of others read by him (1.7). Physiognomic descriptions by the historians take added force from the same background. Quite aside from serious theories on the relationship of appearance to character, it is natural to be curious about what famous people look like, all the more so if they are notorious, and to make inferences about their attitudes from their appearance. Reading body language is connected with social competition at Rome in M. Gleason, "The Semiotics of Gender: Physiognomy and Self-Fashioning in the Second Century C.E.," in *Before Sexuality*, ed. D. Halperin, J. Winkler, and N. Zeitlin (Princeton, N.J.: Princeton University Press, 1990), 389–415.

13. Livia sets out the advantages of variously measured penalties in Dio 55.18.2–4, 20.5–7. Further refinements included an inverse exile consisting of restriction *to* Rome thought up by Claudius (Suet. *Claud.* 23.2) and the smoother Tiberian version, in which assignments of provincial offices were "forgotten" so the appointee did not go. See Addendum 8.

Some remarks of F. G. Bailey in *Stratagems and Spoils* are highly pertinent to these exact adjustments in the conflict between emperor and Senate. Before commenting on how political situations "seem to tremble on the brink of disorder and disintegration, yet . . . there is an over-all order and regularity" (109), he notes that lack of clarity permits a choice of strategies. "One regular move is simple and straightforward: you maintain your honour and you remove another man's honour with the least ambiguity by murdering him. . . . But murders are the extreme form of competitive interaction: they constitute encounters which form the punctuation marks in a series of competitive interactions. There are certain moves beforehand, which either lead up to murder or which may bring victory without the final drastic action. These moves consist in taking followers and allies away from your opponent, by undermining his political credit or outbidding him" (91). "Somewhat less violently, the leader may bring new personnel into the arena or create roles for existing personnel, making them depend directly on himself [at Rome this would include creation of senators, powerful freedmen, and other appointees beholden to the emperor]. . . . an opponent may be harassed or attacked directly and ruined financially through litigation [a regular procedure in Rome carried out by *delatores*]. . . . A more subtle tactic is to 'entrust' the intermediate leader with some task at which he will probably fail" (79). Germanicus (Tac. *Ann.* 2.5.1) and Piso perhaps both fell victim to this trick at the hands of Tiberius.

14. MacMullen, *Enemies* 243. On the paradoxical relation of emperor and Senate, see Veyne, *Bread and Circuses* 406–14; and Kany, "Le Suicide politique" 169–70. Though he called senators *domini* (Suet. *Tib.* 29), Tiberius was offended when the term was addressed to him (27), and unpleasant implications went equally with its sincere or ironic uses. Augustus forbade his children to use the word "either in jest or seriously" (Suet. *Aug.* 53.1), because even at play it had a jarring sound, encouraged wrong attitudes, and occasioned quarreling all too reminiscent of their elders' serious behavior. The emperor's generosity to impoverished noble families (Edwards, *Politics of Immorality* 183–86) served his own interests in the same way that *clementia* did, by keeping useful players in the game.

Traditional interlocking rights and obligations operative in upper-class Roman society brought complicated psychological, moral, and social factors into play; for a highly nuanced analysis of the very similar two-sided Greek concept of "shame" combining competitive self-regard and cooperative other-regard, see D. Cairns, *Aidos* (Oxford: Clarendon, 1993), 95–103 (96n144, on the importance of perceived intention; cf. Sen. *De Ira* 2.28.5, 2.30.1, 2.32.2); 140–41; 272–87 (constraint imposed by fear of others' opinion is analogous to the effect of *invidia* on the emperor, while the social logic of supplication is akin to that of *clementia*, notably in the balance between calculated self-interest and genuine altruism and the dangers restraint may entail); 433–34 (personal relationships reflected in facial expression and intensifying a symbolic sense of political "face"). See D. Shotter, "Tacitus' View of Emperors and the Principate," in *ANRW* II.33.5 (Berlin: De Gruyter, 1991), 3269–71; and M. Morford, "How Tacitus Defined Liberty," in *ANRW* II.33.5, 3420–50.

15. This affects Tacitus' concept of biography in the *Agricola*, which salvages political engagement by showing how an honorable man can take particular circumstances into account without being obliged to court Stoic martyrdom or become a mere collaborator; see A. Dihle, *Die Entstehung der Historischen Biographie*, Sitzungsberichte der Heidelberger Akademie der Wissenschaften, Philosophische-historische Klasse 1986.3 (Heidelberg, 1987), 31–32; and G. Petersmann, "Der 'Agricola' des Tacitus: Versuch einer Deutung," in *ANRW* II.33.3 (Berlin: De Gruyter, 1991), 1785–806. When political decisions are entirely inter-

nalized in the form of moral resolve, principled intransigence can score points only if the game is abandoned and thus, in Tacitus' view, merely assures futility by making the game irrelevant.

On suicide in Flavian epic portrayed as a symptom of political disorder and itself largely futile, e.g., in orgies of mutual suicide, see D. McGuire Jr., "Textual Strategies and Political Suicide in Flavian Epic," *Ramus* 18, nos. 1–2 (1989): 21–45, esp. 37–39. The suicide of Maeon before the eyes of Eteocles in Statius is not only phrased so as to conflate suicide with assassination in a politically suggestive way (31); its performance also recalls public suicides at Rome. If illusory resistance is one horn of the dilemma, dishonest compliance is the other. In a system where everyone has reasons to be dishonest, it seems dishonest not to be dishonest, hence the (honest) indignation of Thrasea's dishonest detractors at his honesty (Tac. *Ann.* 16.22.4). If everyone is implicated, everyone is guilty, but then everyone is innocent (Tac. *Ann.* 6.44.5; Tac. *Hist.* 3.61.3; cf. Sen. *De Ira* 2.10.4). Tacitus' remarks about guilty silence under Domitian point to a "psychologically baffling culture of hypocrisy [which] is sustained by a feeling of guilt from complicity: since everybody is both victim and perpetrator of these practices, nobody can denounce them" (Elster, *Cement of Society* 109). That is the idea behind the claim that Nero wanted to reduce his own shame by pressing others to join him in public performances (Tac. *Ann.* 14.14.3). Seneca may have such cases in mind when he speaks of those led to do wrong by others (*Clem.* 1.6.3, 2.7.2).

16. Analysis along maximax/minimax lines evaluates outcomes that are known, as they generally were at Rome owing to disparity of power between Senate and emperor. When it comes to actually choosing a course of action whose outcome is unknown, assessment is replaced by gamble, which in Modigliani's model is rationalized by inverting the outcome curves so they no longer diverge toward extremes of loss or gain but converge at a point marking the least damaging result when favorable and unfavorable outcomes are taken into account. Somewhat more risk may have to be incurred here than under the best of the worst cases, but by way of compensation there is a chance of faring better if the best case occurs. This intersection of the inverted and now aptly named "regret curves" represents, formally, the position of someone like Corbulo, whose rueful last words may well express regret for a fatal miscalculation. Given the power relationship in which he, like many players in Rome, found himself, the principal possibilities included (a) the best outcome (he takes power, if that is what he had in mind), (b) the best of bad outcomes (Nero respects and continues to exploit his subordinate status), and (c) the worst outcome (he is liquidated). By gambling or presuming on *b* and meeting Nero unprotected, he discounted *a*, which he may not have been interested in anyway, and invited *c*. Had he dealt with Nero from a distance or come with protection, his evident caution would have risked losing something from the accommodation in *b* by aggravating Nero's suspicion. But that need not have had serious consequences, since suspicion was the rule in any case, and it would have left option *a* open or at least excluded *c*. Careful hedging of bets was the tactic used successfully by the Flavians against Vitellius and by others in the jockeying for power that went on between the provinces and Rome. Tiberius, too, calculated risks and rewards along this line if

he really did initially hesitate to assume power out of fear (Addendum 5). The power sharing proposed at the time would then be the best of a bad situation, and in weighing various outcomes he decided that while by hesitating he risked losing what he could get by simply accepting compromise, that tactic also left opportunities for some much larger gains.

17. Petronius' "imitation of vice" was perhaps designed to create the impression that he had no political ambition, as Otho's imitation of fear would have created an impression of justified self-defense. On the former, see A. J. Woodman, ed., *Velleius Paterculus: The Caesarian and Augustan Narrative 2.41–95* (Cambridge: Cambridge University Press, 1983), 144. "Imitation vice," though, would be a more penetrating idea if Tacitus means that in Neronian circles one got ahead by being or pretending to be *bad*. Cf. Tac. *Ann.* 11.26. One measure of Vitellius' deficient initiative is that the prospect of power could fire his ambition only halfway into "wanting rather than hoping" (*ut concupisceret magis quam ut speraret; Tac. Hist.* 1.52.4).

18. Schelling, *Strategy* 54, 207–54. "He, thinking I was about to kill him in self-defense, was about to kill me in self-defense, so I had to kill him in self-defense" (232). Futile as this is, it is still a calculated response; uncalculated outbursts of violence due to nervous fear with a multiplier effect on both sides (218–19) were a likely factor in some cases of unnecessary suicide (perhaps followed by equally useless nervous expressions of clemency by the emperor) or in some instances of unnecessary execution (e.g., the friend invited by Tiberius to Rome, then caught up in his frenzied suspicions, arrested, tortured for evidence, and finally executed to cover up the error; Suet. *Tib.* 62.1). Suicidal political power as a more general proposition is treated in E. Dutoit, "Le Thème de 'la force qui se détruit elle-même,'" *Revue des Etudes Latines* 14 (1936): 365–73.

On suicide understood as a moment of supreme rage in which personal liberty can be forever preserved, see W. Rutz, "Amor Mortis bei Lucan," *Hermes* 88 (1960): 462–75. In view of its potential contradictions, Seneca admits suicide only as a reasoned last resort. While the powers that be can see death as a favor granted ("Let the moderate tyrant kill; under my regime death is requested"; *Thyestes* 247; cf. life under Tiberius as punishment, Suet. *Tib.* 61.5), to those without power it seems to be a civil right ("a man who prevents suicide is worse than a murderer"; Sen. *Phoenissae* 98–101). Lucan's extreme ideological position leads him to treat Caesar's clemency as a calculated attack on integrity through denial of death (Rutz 470–71), so that the more frenetic suicide is, the more it dramatizes the political dilemmas of Roman society. Thus the irrationality in Vulteius' avowedly "mad" outburst (Lucan 4.474–580) comes initially from the incoherent sound of what he is saying: "No life is short if a man has time enough to kill himself" (478); "No one is forced to die willingly" (484); "People don't realize that they have swords for escaping slavery" (579). The effect of these startling *sententiae* is then reinforced by the mutual suicide which he and his men actually carry out, in what amounts under the circumstances to a second civil war within one of the factions engaged in the primary civil war: "He thanked them all, but as he died returned the special favor of the man who killed him by killing *him"* (546); "The proof of comradeship was to *kill* at one blow" (565). Amid all of this extraordinary behavior, Vulteius then wishes for an offer of clemency solely in order to be able to reject it and thereby demonstrate that the Caesarians are not dying in despair at defeat (509–12), though in fact they are defeated and committing suicide because they have given up hope. "Wish [to do] what you must do" (487) is perilously close to the high-minded fatuity of Pliny the Younger's "Order us to be free and we will be" (*Pan.* 66.4). Vulteius' attitude, however, is politically rational, too, because he has calculated its effect on the morale of both sides and on the Caesarians' posthumous fame. Still, conceptually as well as practically, the recurrence and extravagance of such scenes show that suicide was a natural (and "poetic" in White's sense of the word; "New Historicism") epitome of profound political contradictions at Rome, doubly so in that those who want to destroy liberty seem no less in the grip of its most extreme forms.

19. This is essentially the rationalization given to treason when Vespasian is told that he has to "take refuge in power," i.e., "defend" himself (*confugiendum est ad imperium;* Tac. *Hist.* 2.76.3), because "those who think about power have already committed treason" (*qui deliberant, desciverunt,* 2.77.3; cf. Plut. *Galba* 4.4). The concept of the preemptive strike is discussed in Sallust (*Cat.* 52.3–4) and Aulus Gellius (Gell. *NA* 6.3.26–33, 41–42: *occupare*). By the same token, because giving up power is dangerous for those who hold it, exercising it can be treated as a matter of plain self-defense and survival (Thuc. 2.63.1–2; Dio 52.17.1–2, 18.3). Fear on the one side, hatred or anger on the other, again camouflage each other when Poppaea's taunts and threats at once "terrified and incensed" Nero (Tac. *Ann.* 14.61.2, 62.1).

Corresponding to this combination of defensive and aggressive reactions is the complex motivation at work in the axiom "It is natural for people to hate the person they have harmed" (Tac. *Agr.* 42.3; cf. "the more unjust reasons for hatred are, the more bitter they are," Tac. *Ann.* 1.33.1). What Tacitus has in mind is not guilty conscience but self-defensive fear of danger from others due to their self-defensive reaction to one's own intentions toward them in the course of aggressive competition. Hating or fearing a victim is thus the obverse equivalent of hating a benefactor ("so long as gifts can be repaid, they are pleasing; with anything beyond that gratitude is replaced by hatred"; *Ann.* 4.18.3), insofar as our obligation to others which makes us fear benefactors seems no less a threat than is the anger of others toward ourselves which makes us fear our victims.

Tacitus, who has a specially sharp eye for involuted patterns, remarks on a case of preemptive vengeance that comes very close to aggression rationalized as self-defense. Atrocities during a rebellion were committed specifically as anticipatory vengeance for punishment that the rebels knew would come (*Ann.* 14.33.2). This envisages a perpetual-motion treadmill on which the normal cause-effect relationship loops back on itself to form a vicious circle. Instead of an action-reaction sequence, subsequent reactive vengeance is foreseen as provocative action transforming the initial action into a queer preemptive, reactive countervengeance. Compare "Get your retaliation in first," a slogan of the Lions Rugby Union team touring South Africa (I owe this parallel to Denis Feeney). On the paranoid logic of those caught up in violence, see Girard, *Violence and the Sacred* 54.

20. Kany, "Le Suicide politique" 211.

21. For remarks on Tacitus' sense of anomaly in history, see D. Timpe, "Die Absicht der Germania des Tacitus," in *Beiträge zum Verständnis der Germania des Tacitus,* Teil 1, Abhandlungen der Akademie der Wissenschaften in Göttingen (Göttingen: Vandenhoeck and Ruprecht, 1989), 124–27: "In diesem Rahmen [of the Principate and Roman historiography] könnte auch dem Fremden, dem Unerwarteten und Entlegenen etwas abgewonnen werden, wenn eine Bezugsachse gefunden wurde."

The story of Caesellius Bassus' death links political absurdity and illusion with outright mental delusion and (in one version) with suicide. "The future made a fool of Nero" when a madman, who had taken a dream about Dido's hidden treasure as quite certain, induced the emperor to send ships to pick it up. Prudent people were sceptical, but everyone else believed, including those who used the story in declamations extolling Neronian prosperity, certain of his own credulity. And Nero indeed did begin to spend the windfall so that, in a typical antithesis setting illusion against reality, "expectation of wealth was a cause of public deficit." After futilely scouring the countryside in company with a crowd of soldiers and local farmers assigned to help, Bassus regained his senses. Then, entertaining the final delusion that he had never had delusions, he wondered why his dreams were never wrong before and committed suicide "to escape fear and shame" or, according to another report, lost his own property through confiscation (Tac. *Ann.* 16.1–3). These are normally serious motives for suicide, and under the circumstances mental disturbance makes them no less compelling than real guilt would, since it is the emperor who has been deceived. In a sense the suicide is the only sane part of the whole affair, and that is just as crazy as the events it caps.

22. Compulsion and freedom converge even more dramatically in the "voluntary," semisuicidal death of some martyrs; see Droge and Tabor, *Noble Death* 2–3. Like some of those being helped to carry out enforced suicide, Perpetua even steadied the hand of the gladiator detailed to execute her.

Epilogue

1. For discussion of the relationship between alternative models of social reality, see P. Boyer, ed., *Cognitive Aspects of Religious Symbolism* (Cambridge: Cambridge University Press, 1993), 9–13; and I. Morris, *Death-Ritual and Social Structure in Classical Antiquity* (Cambridge: Cambridge University Press, 1992), 3–21.

2. R. LaPiere, quoted in E. Noelle-Neumann, *The Spiral of Silence,* 2d ed. (Chicago: University of Chicago Press, 1993), 94, in a discussion of the wider concept of public opinion. Those who found themselves in the arena were generally not mainstream members of society, but some had once been, and the role of the "public eye" (230), mercilessly focused in the arena, is to scrutinize deviants and declare them scapegoats (111), whether they come from within or without. An example of self-justifying mass violence, less official but still at work in modern societies, cited by Noelle-Neumann in this connection, is a "demonstra-

tion concerning the death of a victim of police brutality [in which] it is impossible to defend the policeman," who is a disposable symbol guilty of what group opinion, justified or not, condemns.

3. Illustration and discussion appear in Brown, "Death as Decoration" 204–5. For more elaborate sculptural monuments, see Robert, *Les Gladiateurs* 55–64. With the involvement, both direct and indirect, implied by *ferrum misit,* compare *ferrum adhibere* (strike) and *ferrum (optimum) dare* (sponsor a show). See Petron. *Sat.* 45; and Sassi, *Il linguaggio gladiatorio* 72, 103. Bulls, too, were both "furnished" and more directly "let loose" by the sponsor (Robert 315), who is again thought of as the direct agent when he is credited with "laying low an army of fighters in the arena" (142) as well as providing them.

Addendum 1: Legal Antinomy

1. J. G. C. Anderson, *Tacitus: Germania* (Oxford: Clarendon, 1938), 26.1.

2. On Seneca's similar worries, see Introduction, n. 8. If everyone is guilty to some degree (Sen. *Clem.* 1.6), then clemency seems no less necessary than laudable. It is laudable for inspiring Golden Age harmony under a beloved ruler (1.3–5, 1.13, 2.1–2). But the idea that "if society thinks it is good [i.e., respects law], it will be" (1.23.2) becomes much less uplifting when feelings of innocence fostered by infrequent punishment are due to recognition that since evil simply cannot be dealt with, it is necessary to look the other way and talk about "clemency" (see Addendum 6). The air of vast but fragile social pretense in this is strengthened by Seneca's historical parallel: a proposal to have slaves and freedmen wear different clothing was turned down because it would betray how few masters there were (1.24.1). Seneca is uncomfortable with overexact philosophical distinctions hindering realistic action, but he concedes that permissiveness is as cruel as excessive severity (1.2.2) and tries to keep clemency separate from *tristitia* or *misericordia,* which he dismisses as automatic "misting of the eyes" in pity for the worst criminals, lacking judgment, and therefore actually unjust (2.5–6).

3. Levick, *"Senatus Consultum"* 97–115; on the paradox in Roman law of escaping *infamia* by incurring it—e.g., highborn women avoiding penalties for adultery by registering as prostitutes, and thus dropping out of the game—see 110–14. See D. Daube, "Fraud No. 3," in *The Legal Mind,* ed. N. MacCormick and P. Birks (Oxford: Clarendon, 1986), 2–9. In her discussion of the Larinum decree and of Dio 56.25, J. Gardner, in *Being a Roman Citizen* (London: Routledge, 1993), concludes that *infamia* came from the money earned by gladiators and other disreputable people (135–54), though even those who did not take money still seemed "unproductive" (152).

4. R. Katzoff, "Tacitus, *Annales* 1.74: The Case of Granius Marcellus," *American Journal of Philology* 92 (1971): 683.

Addendum 2: Orgiastic Violence

1. Compare P. Veyne, *"Humanitas:* Romans and Non-Romans," in *The Romans,* ed. A. Giardina, trans. L. Cochrane (Chicago: University of Chicago Press, 1993), 362.

2. Rhetorical and poetic conventions for scenes of carnage are discussed in R. Funmari, "Tacito e il linguaggio 'espressionistico': Un saggio di commento a *Hist.* 2.70," *Athenaeum* 67 (1989): 584–94.

3. Compare A. Ziolkowski, "*Urbs Direpta,*" in *War and Society in the Roman World* (London: Routledge, 1993), esp. 86–90. The problem that rape would not be possible after wholesale slaughter was easily solved by reversing their order.

4. On Livy's view of mass suicide as a reprehensible dropping out of history by entire cities, see Voisin, "Tite-Live" 621–23.

5. A. Gowing, *The Triumviral Narratives of Appian and Cassius Dio* (Ann Arbor: University of Michigan Press, 1992), 247–69.

6. N. Denyer, "The Case against Divination: An Examination of Cicero's *De Divinatione,*" *Proceedings of the Cambridge Philological Society,* n.s. 31 (1985): 9.

7. Cited in Lincoln, *Discourse* 101. On a similar attitude in Spanish culture, see Mitchell, *Violence and Piety* 31. Was earnest religious recklessness of this kind a factor in the parody of divination when sacred chickens would not produce auspices favorable for a battle that Publius Claudius wanted to fight and he threw them overboard, with the suggestion that they might try drinking if they would not eat? (Suet. *Tib.* 2.2). Suetonius sees in the incident nothing but a shocking "practical joke during a crisis," worth coupling with an instance of pure *ludibrium:* when Claudius' sister later had trouble making her way through heavy traffic in Rome, she wished aloud that her brother would come back to life and thin out the population by losing another fleet (*Tib.* 2.3).

8. Elster, *Cement of Society* 192–202.

9. Tambiah, *Culture, Thought* 60–86. Throughout the book, Tambiah discusses the application of performative communication to analysis of ritual and the role played by magical, homeopathic influences.

Addendum 3: The Ambivalent Triumph

1. J. Scheid, "The Priest," in *The Romans,* ed. A. Giardina, trans. L. Cochrane (Chicago: University of Chicago Press, 1993), 82–84.

2. Cf. D. Ochs, *Consolatory Rhetoric* (Columbia: University of South Carolina Press, 1993), 95–101. If death is implicit in celebrations of triumph, celebration of life and power may no less be part of funeral rites. Though new constitutional issues had developed, the principle is at work later in "The king is dead; long live the king!"

"The ritual [involving the king's effigy and corpse] became expressive of great dyadic tension: the triumph of death versus the triumph over death . . . grief versus joy"; R. Huntington and P. Metcalf, *Celebrations of Death* (Cambridge: Cambridge University Press, 1979), 166 (on the contrast between "hall of honor" and "hall of grief" in France, see 169). Parallels between the symbolism of French and Roman public funerals are examined in R. Giesey, *The Royal Funeral Ceremony* (Geneva: Droz, 1960). Tension between life and death was especially salient in the marginalizing phase of public funerals when what the dead leader represented was gotten rid of. On the similarity between rituals of burial and of marriage, see S. Lonsdale, *Dance and Ritual Play in Greek Religion* (Baltimore: Johns Hopkins University Press, 1993), 239.

3. M. Hornum, *Nemesis, the Roman State, and the Games* (Leiden: Brill, 1993), 9, 27–28, 74–90; on Nemesis stepping on prostrate human figures or animals, see 34–35, 65, 86–87; on Nemesis holding arena weapons, see 67. Arena weapons and a ruler or set of scales held by Nemesis (63–68) can represent both human political power and the inscrutable divine power that fate exercises over life; the epithet "unconquerable" (69) similarly applies to both.

4. Ibid. 73, 76, 241–42. The two-sided confident *show* of past victory and present power joined with anxious *hope* for future success is compared by Faraone to "the annual parades in the former Soviet Union in which destructive nuclear weapons (usually hidden away under lock and key for the rest of the year) are paraded through the streets of the capital giving the populace a confidence in their security as well as a deepest fear of the unpredictability of such awesome power in their midst" (*Talismans* 138–39). The roots of this pattern, which run deep in ancient culture, can be traced through residual apotropaic rituals in the triumph back to other forms of apotropaic gestures. On the conjoined negative/positive facets in the very notion of protective magic—getting rid of evil, admitting good—see Faraone 24, 77. To get rid of evil, the magic has to be deadly, and that leads to the second negative/positive possibility: that the protective agent acts against its wielder (see 15n48, 26, 58). Hermes, for example, becomes the averter of thieves but himself remains a thief, and Apollo is both healer and bringer of disease (63). There is a curious political parallel to the alarming possibility of Apollo's turning his bow against the wrong target (120–21) in the sight greeting senators as they left the Curia: a statue of Commodus holding a bow ready to shoot (see above, chap. 10, n12).

Faraone's distinction (borrowed from Tambiah) between descriptive and prescriptive approaches to deity separates the good things we can be sure of from the bad things we can only hope to escape (120–21). Mars is an ambivalent deity closely linked to the violence represented by heads set up as apotropaic "trophies" in whose confident display there is also anxious awareness of dangers inseparable from the apotropaic process itself (38, 47, 119). "Fighting fire with fire" by means of apotropaic animals (36–53) that protect *from themselves* involves the same homeopathic principle operative more subtly in playing games in the arena with violence. What is more, the peculiar "comic" effect associated with "out of place" apotropaic figures (121) reappears in *venationes* and other playful, yet disturbing forms of violent entertainment in the arena.

5. Cavallaro, *Spese* 10–11.

6. Cf. Merten, *Zwei Herrscherfeste* 33–36, 94–99.

7. Hardie, *Virgil's Aeneid* 135–36, 154. On the failure of idealized imperialism amid the violence of real life, see R. O. A. M. Lyne, "Vergil and the Politics of War," *Classical Quarterly* 33 (1983): 188–203, reprinted in *Oxford Readings in Vergil's Aeneid*, ed. S. J. Harrison (Oxford: Clarendon, 1990), 316–38. "*Vis temperata* is a chimaera," writes Lyne (337–38); likewise, the social usefulness of violence in the arena later seemed chimeric to some observers of Roman society.

For prose, see Sen. *QNat.* 3.5–6 pref.; Sen. *Ep.* 87.23 ("What is crime on a small scale, on a large scale merits a triumph"), 90.26, 94.61–67, 95.30–31.

8. M. Sperber, quoted in K. Hondrich, *Lehrmeister Krieg* (Reinbek, Ger.: Rowohlt Taschenbuch, 1992), 40–41.

9. Mitchell, *Blood Sport* 36–37, 44–46. *Manliness* may be a better term than *bravery* since the prize is sometimes the bull's testicles (21).

10. Ibid. 166, 148, 29, 111, 2, 171, 167–73, 24–25. Augustine's portrayal of the disgust felt by aficionados of bloody sport is cited by Mitchell (167); cf. Pl. *Resp.* 439E–440A.

11. Mitchell, *Blood Sport* 111, 148–49, 90, 81, 103–11, 78.

12. Ibid. 79–80, 67, 77–81, 33, 91–103. Cf. Addendum 2.

13. Specific points of contact with *munera* are examined by Mitchell (ibid. 159–68). In Sagunto the old Roman amphitheater is still used for bullfights (19). On the erotic dimension of orgiastic public violence, see 79, 154–75 (with voyeurism [167] especially pertinent to arena games, ancient and modern); on the connection between what is sexually forbidden and performers' marginal social status, see 66–74. Boasting of injuries and deliberately courting death at fiestas (30, 46) are additional evidence for a suicidal facet, and in Spain, since the public itself may be directly involved in risk taking, both represent the spread of "accidental" violence from ring into society (5–6, 23, 145–46; on "participatory theater," see 29; compare the moral and emotional implicating of spectators in the death of gladiators).

Involvement took less direct form at Rome, though troops were needed there to maintain order, as they were in Spain (Mitchell 146). A passage like Suetonius' *Caligula* 35 suggests that action in the stands could be as interesting as that in the arena. On partisan clubs outside the arena, see Mitchell 4; on conspicuous consumption, its redistributive function, and the prestige it brought for wealthy patrons who supported games to project some of their own values, see xii (twenty-five thousand bulls killed in a year), 74–77, 85–91, 144; on comic-grotesque forms of violence, perhaps providing emotional relief (xiii) as they did at Rome, see ix (dwarfs), 21 (bulls yoked together), and 157–58 (women fighters). Plazas temporarily darkened during night games (21) increased danger in a way that *munera* given at night probably did not, unless lighting for the latter created an effect like that of the ghostly moonlit battle described by Tacitus (*Hist.* 3.23.3).

In Roman combat of man against man and Spanish combat of man against animal, a clean kill was and is expected. But while gladiators and matadors know when to stop the mayhem, animals do not, and so killing of men by animals or of animals by animals can involve particularly horrendous carnage through which the danger faced by men is authenticated. Encounters between bulls and other animals not only provide a full dose of real danger (disemboweled horses stumbling on their own entrails; cf. Mitchell 185n26 on veterinary first aid in the ring: guts stuffed back with a fist, bellies sewed up with twine, and anything still hanging out snipped off with scissors). Butchery aside, gore in Spain carries larger messages of political pride, as it did in Rome: for example, the Spanish bull routs a Bengal tiger to shouts of "¡Viva Espana!" and patriotic songs from the crowd (147).

Addendum 4: Political Monstrosity

1. L. Fiedler, *Freaks* (New York: Simon and Schuster, 1978).
2. Ibid. 43. On the erotic attraction of dwarfs, see 51–58, 137–53.
3. Ibid. 47–68, on dwarfs consulted as well as kept in later centuries. A. Vassileiou, in "Crispinus et les conseillers du prince (Juvenal, *Satires*, IV)," *Latomus* 43 (1984): 27–68, identifies Domitian's confidant as a diminutive adult and reads *pravo* for *parvo (capite)*. See W. Slater, "Pueri, Turba Minuta," *Bulletin of the Institute of Classical Studies of the University of London* 21 (1974): 133–40.
4. "Barnum for President," *Punch*, Sept. 1, 1855, 89; *Fraser's*, Feb. 1855, 220. On the emperor's accepting unworthy associates or taking part in their activities to humiliate the elite by showing his power, see Edwards, *Politics of Immorality* 131–36, 193. The notion of divinatory monstrosity instills specific force into political abuse: "Vitellius himself was the chief *ostentum*" (Tac. *Hist.* 3.56.1); Catiline, too, was *monstrum illud atque prodigium* (Cic. *Cat.* 2.1.1). A full collection of instances in Cicero can be found in F. Guillaumont, *Philosophe et augure: Recherches sur la théorie cicéronienne de la divination*, Collection Latomus 184 (Brussels: Latomus, 1984), 187–89. Claudius used *prodigium* as a sneer in one of his speeches (E. M. Smallwood, *Documents Illustrating the Principate of Gaius Claudius and Nero* [Cambridge: Cambridge University Press, 1967], 369, col. II.15), and several insults in Seneca's *Apocolocyntosis* (3, 5, 11) exploit Claudius' own "ominous" appearance.

On dwarfs or pygmies employed as grotesque gladiators and their frequent appearance in popular art, see Cèbe, *La Caricature* 346, 350–51. As a manifestation of fear and insecurity, public curiosity about anatomical oddities was a disguised form of much more openly hostile "physiognomic" ridicule directed at an enemy's ugliness or of the desire to make him ugly through mutilation (e.g., the lynching of Vitellius accompanied by *ludibrium* at his physical defects; Suet. *Vit.* 17). Physiognomic description for its part can double as verbal caricature. See Cèbe 129–41; E.-M. Schenck, *Das Bilderrätsel* (Hildesheim: Olms, 1975), 80–90; and M. Rambaud, "Recherches sur le portrait dans l'historiographie romaine," *Les Etudes Classiques* 38 (1970): 423–24.

Tiberius' baldness was the target of elaborate ridicule at a festival prominently attended by bald men and five thousand servants with shaved heads bearing torches to make the sea of skulls shine. Inscrutable as ever, Tiberius did nothing (Dio 58.19.1–2). Domitian was more sensitive about his baldness (Suet. *Dom.* 18), as were Caligula and Caesar. It was a capital crime to look down on Caligula from above (Suet. *Calig.* 50), and he had the heads of men with full hair forcibly shaved (35.2). Caesar's baldness was also the subject of jibes (Suet. *Iul.* 45.2). Hostility, especially of a joking kind, is volatile, and feelings about personal appearance can take strange turns. A conspirator against Claudius was banished instead of executed, in view of the small size and great ugliness that made him seem ridiculous rather than dangerous (Dio 60.27.5).

5. G. Williams, *Change and Decline* (Berkeley: University of California Press, 1978), 153–92, 219–30; Barton, *Sorrows* 85–189. On irrationality as a threat to a culture's validity, see Lasine, "Indeterminacy and the Bible" 67; Babcock-Abra-

hams, "Tolerated Margin of Mess" 157, 161, 186 (the trickster as an essentially ambiguous figure). Nero and Caligula did in some respects exercise a tricksterlike personal freedom or irresponsibility whose supreme moments were readily used by a hostile historical tradition to expose systemic anomalies in the Principate.

Addendum 5: Political Game Moves

1. Schelling, *Strategy* 17–18.
2. Elster, *Cement of Society* 135.
3. On the misrepresentation of Tiberius' policy in the sources, see Schrömbges, *Tiberius* 77–85.
4. E. Koestermann, *Annalen,* vol. 2 (Heidelberg, 1965), 4.21.2.

Addendum 6: Clemency

1. For similar ambiguities of surrender *in dicionem (potestatem)* or *in fidem,* see Watson, *International Law in Archaic Rome,* 48–53. Though free to act as it pleases, Rome is restricted by the implicit appeal in the latter, the paradox being that there is much the man who can do anything cannot do (Dio 52.38.1).
2. Lyne, "Vergil and the Politics of War" 327, 336n33.
3. Z. Maoz, *Paradoxes of War* (Boston: Unwin Hyman, 1990), 107–18.
4. Griffin, *Seneca* 315–66.
5. Augustus' *Res Gestae* 3.2 includes the statement, "When foreign peoples could safely be pardoned, I have preferred to spare rather than destroy them." For a discussion of clemency and power starting from these lines ("It would be difficult to imagine anything more terrible with their fierce and merciful smile"), see Veyne, "*Humanitas*" 354–63. On the sinister side of clemency, see M. Charlesworth, "The Virtues of a Roman Emperor," *Proceedings of the British Academy* (1937): 112–13. The essential link tying clemency to power rather than to mercy or justice comes out in yet another way in Seneca's remark that even innocent people may need clemency (*Clem.* 1.1.9–1.2.1). As A. Borgo notes, Seneca's own situation can be seen in this somewhat nervous line of thought; see Borgo, "*Clementia:* Studio di un campo semantico," *Vichiana* 14 (1985): 63. What was in the Republic an informal system of favors to help keep the system going becomes in *De clementia* a full-blown theory of absolutism, finally, Seneca argues, no less dependent on restraint. See B. Mortureaux, "Les Idéaux stoïciens et les premières responsabilités politiques: Le 'De Clementia,'" in *ANRW* II.36.3 (Berlin: De Gruyter, 1989), 1680. On the interrelation among envy, (in)gratitude, and clemency, see Barton, *Sorrows* 118–19, 133n133.

The logic of clemency is explored with the help of game theory in S. Brams, *The Theory of Moves* (Cambridge: Cambridge University Press, 1994), 67–84, and in Maoz, *Paradoxes of War* 254–57. The meeting between Germanicus and Piso is a case of the "provocative deterrence" (Maoz 85) which may damage the *stronger* party. Piso sets his face to conceal fear; Germanicus, who is normally too mild *(clementior),* sets his to avoid open threats. But when Germanicus cannot dissemble, Piso reacts with "hostile defensiveness," and the two part in hatred (Tac. *Ann.* 2.57.2–3). The counterpart to this trap is provocative weakness inadvertently inviting attack. On the paradoxical notion of restraint by which a victim or rival "permits" the other party to be generous, see Brams 73, 138.

Addendum 7: Loss Aversion

1. In Dion. Hal. 8.74.4, concern with what is not ours rather than with what is, is transformed into *Schadenfreude* when poor people are more pleased at others' loss than at their own gain. Tacitus notices this reaction (cf. *Hist.* 1.38.3: "The chief incitement of bad people was that good ones were dismayed") and corresponding pain at another's success (*Hist.* 2.20.1; cf. 1.8.1).

2. J. Short Jr. and L. Clarke, eds., *Organizations, Uncertainties, and Risks* (Boulder, Colo.: Westview, 1992), 29. On opposing motivation from fear of failure or from hope of success, see Dixon, *Military Incompetence* 222. Conservative attitudes made the ancient intellectual tradition somewhat less sanguine about the "healthy" character of the latter and more prone to what Dixon labels "pathological" fear of failure (239).

3. For a rough ancient equivalent of "smart or lucky," that is, "brave or lucky" *(fortior an felicior)*, see W. Bloomer, *Valerius Maximus and the Rhetoric of the New Nobility* (Chapel Hill: University of North Carolina Press, 1992), 171–72. *Virtus* is a personal quality, especially military skill, while *felicitas* or *fortuna* is the superhuman dimension of success. See R. Combes, *Imperator* (Paris: PUF, 1966), 213–14. Even though the Romans tended to make success a function of *virtus* (A. Keanevey, "Sulla and the Gods," in *Studies in Latin Literature and Roman History III*, Collection Latomus 180 [Brussels: Latomus, 1983], 46–49), the former was still a divine gift, and in reflecting on the relative importance of each in the lives of great men, Romans recognized that while risk seeking is justified when *fortuna* accompanies *virtus*, a reliable connection is exceptional. It is true that *virtus* deserves (causes) success in some cases (Sall. *Iug.* 95.4), *fortis* can be closely coupled with *felix* (Combes 216–19), and when Sulla rated luck over bravery in his own career (Val. Max. 6.9.6) he was not discounting the latter. But risk (luck) and control (virtue) can also be contrasted. Then the divine element added to human capacity brings with it the possibility of failure, as *fortuna* becomes "chance" as well as "success" and virtue calls for a prudent measure of risk aversion. The Romans knew enough about war to give what Clausewitz called friction its full due: "There is no human affair which stands so constantly and so generally in close connection with chance as War. But together with chance, the accidental, and along with it good luck, occupy a great place in War"; C. von Clausewitz, *On War,* trans. J. Graham (Harmondsworth, Eng.: Penguin, 1968), I.20.

Addendum 8: Degrees of Penalty

1. The notion of moral and political "dead space" furnished Tacitus with a favorite formula for bringing out futility or incongruity more generally, especially that of civil war: in civil disorder the populace must "appeal for peace though there is no war" (*Hist.* 1.63.2); "they did not seek peace though they had given up war" (*Hist.* 3.31.2); "war had stopped more than peace had begun" (*Hist.* 4.1.1);

Germans "love idleness and hate quiet" (*Germ.* 15.1); Galba was a man "more without vices than with virtues" (*Hist.* 1.49.2); Tiberius "feared liberty and hated adulation" (*Ann.* 2.87); Tiberius did not "look for outstanding virtue though he hated vice" (*Ann.* 1.80.2); the Armenians were "more without a master than free" (*Ann.* 2.4.2); "though already deprived of life by awareness of her doom, she [Octavia] had not yet found rest in death" (*Ann.* 14.64.1). For somewhat similar patterns as a political phenomenon in reference to the Soviet system, see Elster, *Political Psychology* 70–100. Soviet Russia again provides parallels for V. Rudich's study of dissimulation; see Rudich, *Political Dissidence under Nero* (London: Routledge, 1993).

2. Garnsey, "Penalties" 143–44. As a rule, execution was avoided among the upper class in accordance with an inverse, iron rule: Do not do to others what you do not want them to do to you. On graded penalties, see Millar, "Condemnation to Hard Labour" 124–47.

Selected Bibliography

Abt, V. J. Smith, and E. Christiansen. *The Business of Risk.* Lawrence: University Press of Kansas, 1985.

Ahl, F. *Lucan: An Introduction.* Ithaca, N.Y.: Cornell University Press, 1972.

Allen, W. "Nero's Eccentricities before the Fire." *Numen* 9 (1962): 104–9.

Auguet, R. *Cruelty and Civilization.* London: Allen and Unwin, 1972.

Aymard, J. *Essai sur les chasses romaines.* Bibliothéque des Ecoles Françaises d'Athènes et de Rome 171. Paris, 1951.

Babcock, B., ed. *The Reversible World.* Ithaca, N.Y.: Cornell University Press, 1967.

Babcock-Abrahams, B. "A Tolerated Margin of Mess: The Trickster and His Tales Reconsidered." *Indiana University Folklore Institute Journal* 11 (1974): 147–86.

Bailey, F. G. *Stratagems and Spoils.* New York: Schocken Books, 1969.

Balsdon, J. P. V. D. *Life and Leisure in Ancient Rome.* New York: McGraw-Hill, 1969.

Barrett, A. *Caligula.* New Haven, Conn.: Yale University Press, 1989.

Barthelemy, S., and D. Gourevitch. *Les Loisirs des Romains.* Paris: Société d'Edition d'Enseignement Superieur, 1975.

Barthes, R. "The World of Wrestling." In *Mythologies,* translated by A. Lavers, 15–25. New York: Hill and Wang, 1972.

Barton, C. "The Scandal of the Arena." *Representations* 27 (1989): 1–36.

Barton, C. *The Sorrows of the Ancient Romans.* Princeton, N.J.: Princeton University Press, 1993.

Bäumer, A. *Die Bestie Mensch.* Studien zur Klassischen Philologie 4. Frankfurt: Lang, 1982.

Bayet, A. *Le Suicide et la morale.* Paris: Alcan, 1922.

Bayet, J. "Le Suicide mutuel dans la mentalité des Romains." In *Croyances et rites dans la Rome antique,* 130–76. Paris: Payot, 1971.

Beard, M. "Priesthood in the Roman Republic." In *Pagan Priests,* edited by M. Beard and J. North, 19–48. London: Duckworth, 1990.

Betensky, A. "Neronian Style, Tacitean Content: The Use of Ambiguous Confrontations in the *Annals.*" *Latomus* 37 (1978): 419–35.

Bettini, M. *Anthropology and Roman Culture.* Translated by J. Van Sickle. Baltimore: Johns Hopkins University Press, 1991.

Bloomer, W. *Valerius Maximus and the Rhetoric of the New Nobility.* Chapel Hill: University of North Carolina Press, 1992.

Bollinger, T. *Theatralis licentia.* Winterthur, Switz.: Schellenberg, 1969.

Boone, E., ed. *Ritual Human Sacrifice in MesoAmerica.* Washington, D.C.: Dumbarton Oaks, 1984.

Bouissac, P. *Circus and Culture.* Bloomington: Indiana University Press, 1976.

Bradley, K. *Slaves and Masters in the Roman Empire.* Collection Latomus 185. Brussels: Latomus, 1984.

Bremmer, J. N., ed. *Interpretations of Greek Mythology.* Totowa, N.J.: Barnes and Noble, 1986.

Bringmann, K. "Topoi in der taciteischen Germania." In *Beiträge zum Verständnis der Germania des Tacitus,* Teil 1., Abhandlungen der Akademie der Wissenschaften in Göttingen, edited by H. Jankuhn and D. Timpe, 59–78. Göttingen: Vandenhoeck und Ruprecht, 1989.

Broda, J., D. Carrasco, and E. Moctezuma. *The Great Temple of Tenochtitlan.* Berkeley: University of California Press, 1987.

Brophy, R., III. "Deaths in the Pan-Hellenic Games: Arrachion and Creugas." *American Journal of Philology* 99 (1978): 363–90.

Brophy, R., III, and M. Brophy. "Deaths in the Pan-Hellenic Games II." *American Journal of Philology* 106 (1985): 194–97.

Brown, S. "Death as Decoration: Scenes from the Arena on Roman Domestic Mosaics." In *Pornography and Representation in Greece and Rome,* edited by A. Richlin, 180–211. New York: Oxford University Press, 1992.

Brundage, B. *The Jade Steps.* Salt Lake City: University of Utah Press, 1985.

Burkert, W. *Homo necans.* Translated by P. Bing. Berkeley: University of California Press, 1983.

Caillois, R. *Man, Play, and Games.* Translated by M. Barash. Glencoe, N.Y.: Free Press, 1961.

Callu, J.-P. "Le Jardin des supplices au Bas-Empire." In *Du châtiment dans la cité,* Collection de l'Ecole Française de Rome 79, 313–59. Rome: Ecole Française de Rome, 1984.

Cameron, A. *Circus Factions.* Oxford: Clarendon, 1976.

Cavallaro, M. *Spese e spettacoli.* Antiquitas 34. Bonn: Habelt, 1984.

Cèbe, J.-P. *La Caricature et la parodie dans le monde romain antique des origines à Juvénal.* Bibliothèque des Ecoles Françaises d 'Athènes et de Rome 206. Paris: De Broccard, 1966.

Cizek, E. *Nero.* Paris: Fayard, 1982.

Clavel-Lévêque, M. *L'Empire en jeux.* Paris: CNRS, 1984.

Clavel-Lévêque, M. "L'Espace des jeux dans le monde romain." In *ANRW* II.16.3, 2405–563. Berlin: De Gruyter, 1986.

Clavel-Lévêque, M. "Rituels de mort et consommation de gladiateurs." In *Hommages à Lucien Lerat I,* Annales Littéraires de l'Université de Besançon 29, edited by H. Walter, 189–208. Paris: Belles Lettres, 1984.

Coleman, K. "Fatal Charades: Roman Executions Staged as Mythological Enactments." *Journal of Roman Studies* 80 (1990): 44–73.

Conrad, G., and A. Demarest. *Religion and Empire*. Cambridge: Cambridge University Press, 1984.

Corbier, M. "Divorce and Adoption as Roman Familial Strategies." In *Marriage, Divorce, and Children in Ancient Rome*, edited by B. Rawson, 47–78. Oxford: Clarendon, 1991.

Crook, J. "Patria potestas." *Classical Quarterly* 17 (1967): 113–22.

Croon, J. "Die Ideologie des Mars Kultes unter dem Principat und ihre Vorgeschichte." In *ANRW* II.17.1, 246–75. Berlin: De Gruyter, 1981.

Daube, D. "Greek and Roman Reflections on Impossible Laws." *Natural Law Forum* 12 (1967): 1–84.

Daube, D. "The Linguistics of Suicide." *Philosophy and Public Policy* 1 (1972): 387–437.

Daube, D. *Roman Law: Linguistic, Social, and Philosophical Aspects*. Edinburgh: Edinburgh University Press, 1969.

Deininger, J. "Brot und Spiele." *Gymnasium* 86 (1979): 278–303.

Dixon, N. *On the Psychology of Military Incompetence*. London: Cape, 1976.

Douglas, M. *Purity and Danger*. New York: Praeger, 1966.

Droge, A., and J. Tabor. *A Noble Death*. San Francisco: Harper, 1992.

Dumezil, G. *Archaic Roman Religion*. Vol. 1. Translated by P. Krapp. Chicago: University of Chicago Press, 1970.

Duncan-Jones, R. *The Economy of the Roman Empire*. Cambridge: Cambridge University Press, 1974.

Dupont, F. *L'Acteur-Roi*. Paris: Belles Lettres, 1985.

Dutoit, E. "Le Thème de 'la force qui se dètruit elle-même,'" *Revue des Etudes Latines* 14 (1936): 365–73.

Duverger, C. *L'Esprit du jeu chez les Aztèques*. Paris: Mouton, 1978.

Eckstein, A. "Human Sacrifice and Fear of Military Disaster in Republican Rome." *American Journal of Ancient History* 7 (1982): 69–95.

Edwards, C. *The Politics of Immorality in Ancient Rome*. Cambridge: Cambridge University Press, 1993.

Ehrman, R. "Martial, *De Spectaculis* 8: Gladiator or Criminal?" *Mnemosyne* 40 (1987): 422–25.

Elster, J. *The Cement of Society*. Cambridge: Cambridge University Press, 1989.

Elster, J. *Logic and Society*. New York: Wiley, 1978.

Elster, J. *Political Psychology*. Cambridge: Cambridge University Press, 1993.

Elster, J. *Solomonic Judgments*. Cambridge: Cambridge University Press, 1989.

Faraone, C. *Talismans and Trojan Horses*. New York: Oxford University Press, 1992.

Fears, J. "The Theology of Victory at Rome." In *ANRW* II.17.2, 736–826. Berlin: De Gruyter, 1981.

Fehling, D. *Ethnologische Überlegungen auf dem Gebiet der Altertumskunde*. Zetemata 61. Munich: Beck, 1974.

Festinger, L. *A Theory of Cognitive Dissonance*. Evanston, Ill.: Row Peterson, 1957.

Fiedler, L. *Freaks*. New York: Simon and Schuster, 1978.

Fineman, J. "The History of the Anecdote: Fiction and Fiction." In *The New Historicism,* edited by H. Veeser, 49–76. New York: Routledge, 1989.

Finley, M. *The Ancient Economy.* 2d ed. London: Hogarth, 1985.

Foucault, M. *Discipline and Punish.* Translated by A. Sheridan. New York: Pantheon, 1977.

Fox, R. Lane. *Pagans and Christians.* New York: Knopf, 1987.

Frey, M. *Untersuchungen zur Religion und zur Religionspolitik des Kaisers Elagabal.* Stuttgart: Steiner, 1989.

Friedlaender, L. *Sittengeschichte Roms.* 10th ed. Vol. 2. Leipzig: Hirzel, 1922.

Funmari, R. "Tacito e il linguaggio 'espressionistico': Un saggio di commento a *Hist.* 2.70." *Athenaeum* 67 (1989): 584–94.

Garnsey, P. *Social Status and Legal Privilege in the Roman Empire.* Oxford: Clarendon, 1970.

Garnsey, P. "Why Penalties Become Harsher: The Roman Case, Late Republic to Fourth Century Empire." *Natural Law Forum* 13 (1968): 141–62.

Geertz, C. "Deep Play." In *Interpretive Social Science: A Second Look,* edited by P. Rabinow and W. Sullivan, 195–240. Berkeley: University of California Press, 1987.

Gennep, A. van. *The Rites of Passage.* Translated by M. Vizedom and G. Caffee. Chicago: University of Chicago Press, 1960.

Giddens, A. *Central Problems in Social Theory.* Berkeley: University of California Press, 1979.

Giddens, A. *Studies in Social and Political Theory.* New York: Basic Books, 1977.

Girard, R. *Violence and the Sacred.* Translated by P. Gregory. Baltimore: Johns Hopkins University Press, 1977.

Goffman, E. *Frame Analysis.* Cambridge, Mass.: Harvard University Press, 1974.

Goffman, E. *Interaction Ritual.* Chicago: Aldine, 1967.

Golvin, J.-C., and C. Landes. *Amphithéatres et gladiateurs.* Paris: CNRS, 1990.

Gordon, R. "The Veil of Power: Emperors, Sacrifices, and Benefactors." In *Pagan Priests,* edited by M. Beard and J. North, 201–31. London: Duckworth, 1990.

Gowing, A. *The Triumviral Narratives of Appian and Cassius Dio.* Ann Arbor: University of Michigan Press, 1992.

Grant, M. *Gladiators.* London: Weidenfeld and Nicholson, 1967.

Griffin, M. *Nero.* London: Batsford, 1984.

Griffin, M. "Philosophy, Cato, and Roman Suicide," *Greece and Rome* 33 (1986): 64–77, 192–202.

Griffin, M. *Seneca: A Philosopher in Politics.* Oxford: Clarendon, 1976.

Grisé, Y. *Le Suicide dans la Rome antique.* Montreal: Bellarmine, 1982.

Grodzynski, D. "Tortures mortelles et categories sociales." In *Du châtiment dans la cité,* Collection de l'Ecole Française de Rome 79, 361–403. Rome: Ecole Française de Rome, 1984.

Hamerton-Kelly, R. G., ed. *Violent Origins.* Stanford, Calif.: Stanford University Press, 1987.

Hardie, P. *Virgil's Aeneid: Cosmos and Imperium.* Oxford: Clarendon, 1986.

Harich, H. "De Nerone non Agitur: Zur siebenten Epistel Senecas an Lucilius." *Symbolae Osloenses* 65 (1990): 93–100.

Harris, H. A. *Sport in Greece and Rome.* Ithaca, N.Y.: Cornell University Press, 1972.

Harris, W. *War and Imperialism in Republican Rome, 327–70 B.C.* Oxford: Clarendon, 1979.

Hengel, M. *Crucifixion in the Ancient World and the Folly of the Cross.* London: SCM, 1977.

Henrichs, A. "Human Sacrifice in Greek Religion." In *Le Sacrifice dans l'antiquité,* Entretiens sur l'Antiquité Classique 27, 195–242. Geneva: Fondation Hardt, 1981.

Herzog, R. "Fest, Terror und Tod in Petrons *Satyrica.*" In *Das Fest,* edited by W. Harg and R. Warning, 120–50. Munich: Fink, 1989.

Hirzel, R. "Der Selbstmord." *Archiv für Religionswissenschaft* 11 (1908): 75–104, 243–84, 417–76.

Hopkins, K. *Death and Renewal.* Cambridge: Cambridge University Press, 1983.

Hughes, D. *Human Sacrifice in Ancient Greece.* London: Routledge, 1991.

Humphrey, J. *Roman Circuses.* Berkeley: University of California Press, 1986.

Jarrett, S. *Rereading the Sophists.* Carbondale, Ill.: Southern Illinois University Press, 1991.

Jocelyn, H. D. "The Roman Nobility and the Religion of the Republican State." *Journal of Religious History* 4 (1966): 89–104.

Johnson, T., and C. Dandeker. "Patronage: Relation and System." In *Patronage in Ancient Society,* edited by A. Wallace-Hadrill, 219–41. London: Routledge, 1989.

Kany, J. "Le Suicide politique à Rome et en particulier chez Tacite." Thèse, Reims, 1979.

Keitel, E. "Otho's Exhortation in Tacitus' *Histories.*" *Greece and Rome* 34 (1987): 73–82.

Kiefer, O. "Der Römer und die Grausamkeit." In *Kulturgeschichte Roms,* 66–105. Berlin: Aretz, 1933.

Kloft, H. *Libertas principis.* Cologne: Böhlau, 1970.

Kolendo, J. "La Répartition des places aux spectacles et la stratification sociale dans l'Empire Romain." *Ktema* 6 (1981): 301–15.

Lasine, S. "Indeterminacy and the Bible: A Review of Literary and Anthropological Theories and Their Application to Biblical Texts." *Hebrew Studies* 27, no. 1 (1986): 48–80.

Latte, K. *Römische Religionsgeschichte.* 2d ed. Handbuch der Altertumswissenschaft 5.1. Munich: Beck, 1967.

Lemosse, M. "Les Eléments techniques de l'ancien triomphe romain et le problème de son origin." In *ANRW* I.2, 442–53. Berlin: De Gruyter, 1972.

Levene, D. *Religion in Livy.* Leiden: Brill, 1993.

Levick, B. "The *Senatus Consultum* from Larinum." *Journal of Roman Studies* 73 (1983): 97–115.

Lincoln, B. *Discourse and the Construction of Society.* Oxford: Oxford University Press, 1989.

Lintott, A. *Violence in Republican Rome.* Oxford: Clarendon, 1968.

Little, D. *Varieties of Social Explanation.* Boulder, Colo.: Westview, 1991.

Love, J. *Antiquity and Capitalism.* London: Routledge, 1991.

Lyne, R. O. A. M. "Vergil and the Politics of War." *Classical Quarterly* 33 (1983): 188–203. Reprinted in *Oxford Readings in Vergil's Aeneid,* edited by S. J. Harrison, 316–38. Oxford: Clarendon, 1990.

MacMullen, R. *Changes in the Roman Empire.* Princeton, N.J.: Princeton University Press, 1990.

MacMullen, R. *Corruption and the Decline of Rome.* New Haven, Conn.: Yale University Press, 1988.

MacMullen, R. *Enemies of the Roman Order.* Cambridge, Mass.: Harvard University Press, 1966.

MacMullen, R. "Judicial Savagery in the Roman Empire." *Chiron* 16 (1986): 147–66.

Maisonobe, J.-F. "Caton Gladiateur dans le *De Providentia* II.8." In *Philologie littératures et histoire anciennes,* Annales de la Faculté des Lettres et Sciences Humaines de Nice 35, 235–57. Nice, 1979.

Manning, C. "Acting and Nero's Conception of the Principate." *Greece and Rome* 22 (1975): 164–75.

Maoz, Z. *Paradoxes of War.* Boston: Unwin Hyman, 1990.

March, J. "Bounded Rationality, Ambiguity, and the Engineering of Choices." In *Rational Choice,* edited by J. Elster, 142–70. Oxford: Blackwell, 1986.

Marsh, F. *The Reign of Tiberius.* New York: Barnes and Noble, 1931.

Matthews, J. *The Roman Empire of Ammianus.* London: Duckworth, 1989.

Maurin, J. "Les Barbares aux arènes." *Ktema* 9 (1984): 102–11.

McGuire, D., Jr. "Textual Strategies and Political Suicide in Flavian Epic." *Ramus* 18, nos. 1–2 (1989): 21–45.

Mehl, A. *Claudius.* Studia et Testimonia Antiqua 16. Munich: Fink, 1974.

Merten, E. *Zwei Herrscherfeste in der Historia Augusta.* Antiquitas 4.5. Bonn: Habelt, 1968.

Millar, F. "Condemnation to Hard Labour in the Roman Empire, from the Julio-Claudians to Constantine." *Papers of the British School at Rome* 52 (1984): 124–47.

Millar, F. *The Emperor in the Roman World.* Ithaca, N.Y.: Cornell University Press, 1977.

Mitchell, T. *Blood Sport.* Philadelphia: University of Pennsylvania Press, 1991.

Mitchell, T. *Violence and Piety in Spanish Folklore.* Philadelphia: University of Pennsylvania Press, 1988.

Modigliani, F. "Liquidity and Uncertainty—Discussion." *American Economic Review* 39 (1949): 201–8.

Moore, S., and B. Myerhoff, eds. *Secular Ritual.* Assen, Neth.: Van Gorcum, 1977.

Münzer, F. "Die Todesstrafe Politischer Verbrecher in der Späteren Römischen Republik." *Hermes* 47 (1912): 161–82.

Murray, O., ed. *Sympotica.* Oxford: Clarendon, 1990.

Nardoni, D. *I gladiatori romani.* Rome: Edizioni Italiane di Letteratura e Scienze, 1989.

Nemoianu, V. "René Girard and the Dialectics of Imperfection." In *To Honor*

René Girard, Stanford French and Italian Studies 34, 1–16. Stanford, Calif.: Anma Libri, 1986.

Newbold, R. "Cassius Dio and the Games." *L'Antiquité Classique* 44 (1975): 589–604.

North, J. "Diviners and Divination at Rome." In *Pagan Priests,* edited by M. Beard and J. North, 51–71. London: Duckworth, 1990.

Oakley, S. "Single Combat in the Roman Republic." *Classical Quarterly* 79 (1985): 392–410.

Oates, J. C. *On Boxing.* Garden City, N.Y.: Doubleday, 1987.

Pailler, J.-M. *Bacchanalia.* Bibliothèque des Ecoles Françaises d'Athènes et de Rome 270. Rome: Ecole Française de Rome, 1988.

Pearson, J. *Arena.* London: Thames and Hudson, 1973.

Penner, H. "Rationality, Ritual, and Science." In *Religion, Science, and Magic,* edited by J. Neusner, E. Frerichs, and P. Flesher, 11–24. New York: Oxford University Press, 1989.

Piganiol, A. *Recherches sur les jeux romains.* Publications de la Faculté des Lettres de l'Université de Strasbourg 13. Strasbourg: Istra, 1923.

Pocock, J. *Politics, Language, and Time.* Chicago: University of Chicago Press, 1971.

Poliakoff, M. *Combat Sports in the Ancient World.* New Haven, Conn.: Yale University Press, 1987.

Price, S. R. F. *Rituals and Power.* Cambridge: Cambridge University Press, 1984.

Rawson, E. "Chariot-Racing in the Roman Republic." *Papers of the British School at Rome* 49 (1981): 1–16.

Rawson, E. "*Discrimina ordinum:* The Lex Julia Theatralis." *Papers of the British School at Rome* 55 (1987): 83–114.

Rawson, E. "Religion and Politics in the Late Second Century B.C. at Rome." *Phoenix* 28 (1974): 193–212.

Reekmans, T. "La Politique économique et financière des autorités dans les *Douze Cesars* de Suétone." In *Historiographia antiqua,* Commentationes Lovanienses in honorem W. Peremans, Symbolae Facultatis Litterarum et Philosophiae Lovaniensis, ser. A.6, 265–314. Louvain: Leuven University Press, 1977.

Robert, L. *Les Gladiateurs dans l'Orient grec.* Amsterdam: Hakkert, 1971.

Rogers, R. "The Emperor's Displeasure." *Transactions and Proceedings of the American Philological Association* 90 (1959): 224–37.

Rosenstein, N. "*Imperatores Victi:* The Case of C. Hostilius Mancinus." *Classical Antiquity* 5 (1986): 230–52.

Rosivach, V. "Mars, the Lustral God." *Latomus* 42 (1983): 509–21.

Rudich, V. *Political Dissidence under Nero.* London: Routledge, 1993.

Rutz, W. "Amor Mortis bei Lucan." *Hermes* 88 (1960): 462–75.

Saller, R. "*Patria potestas* and the Stereotype of the Roman Family." *Change and Continuity* 1 (1986): 7–22.

Saller, R. *Personal Patronage under the Early Empire.* Cambridge: Cambridge University Press, 1982.

Sansone, D. *Greek Athletics and the Genesis of Sport.* Berkeley: University of California Press, 1988.

Sassi, M. *Il linguaggio gladiatorio.* Bologna: Patron, 1992.

Saylor, C. "Funeral Games: The Significance of Games in the *Cena Trimalchionis.*" *Latomus* 46 (1987): 593–602.

Schatzman, I. *Senatorial Wealth and Roman Politics.* Collection Latomus 142. Brussels: Latomus, 1975.

Schele, L., and M. Miller. *The Blood of Kings.* New York: Braziller, 1986.

Schellenberg, J. *Primitive Games.* Boulder, Colo.: Westview, 1990.

Schelling, T. *Choice and Consequence.* Cambridge, Mass.: Harvard University Press, 1984.

Schelling, T. *The Strategy of Conflict.* Cambridge, Mass.: Harvard University Press, 1960.

Schmunck, P. "Studien zur Darstellung des Endes von Galba, Otho und Vitellius in den Historien des Tacitus." *Symbolae Osloenses* 39 (1964): 38–82.

Schrömbges, P. *Tiberius und die Res Publica Romana.* Bonn: Habelt, 1986.

Schutz, A. *Collected Papers.* Vol. 2. Edited by A. Brodersen. The Hague: M. Nijhoff, 1971.

Scott, J. *Domination and the Arts of Resistance.* New Haven, Conn.: Yale University Press, 1991.

Scullard, H. *Festivals and Ceremonies of the Roman Republic.* Ithaca, N.Y.: Cornell University Press, 1981.

Shibuk, M. *Game Theory in the Social Sciences.* Cambridge, Mass.: MIT Press, 1982.

Skorupski, J. *Symbol and Theory.* Cambridge: Cambridge University Press, 1976.

Smith, J. Z. *Imagining Religion.* Chicago: University of Chicago Press, 1982.

Stier, H. "Augustusfriede und römische Klassik." In *ANRW* II.2, 3–54. Berlin: De Gruyter, 1975.

Strauss, L. *The Political Philosophy of Hobbes.* Chicago: University of Chicago Press, 1963.

Syme, R. "Scorpus the Charioteer." *American Journal of Ancient History* 2 (1977): 86–94.

Tainter, J. *The Collapse of Complex Societies.* Cambridge: Cambridge University Press, 1988.

Tambiah, S. *Culture, Thought, and Social Action.* Cambridge, Mass.: Harvard University Press, 1985.

Thaler, R. *The Winner's Curse.* New York: Free Press, 1992.

Thomas, Y. "Vitae necisque potestas." In *Du châtiment dans la cité,* Collection de l'Ecole Française de Rome 79, 525–45. Rome: Ecole Française de Rome, 1984.

Thuillier, J.-P. *Les Jeux athlétiques dans la civilisation étrusque,* Bibliothèque des Ecoles Françaises d'Athènes et de Rome 256. Rome: Ecole Française de Rome, 1985.

Timpe, D. "Geschichtsschreibung und Prinzipat-Opposition." In *Opposition et résistances à l'empire d'Auguste à Trajan.* Entretiens sur l'Antiquité Classique 33, 65–102. Geneva: Fondation Hardt, 1987.

Toynbee, J. M. C. *Animals in Roman Life and Art.* Ithaca, N.Y.: Cornell University Press, 1973.

Turner, V. *Drama, Fields, and Metaphors*. Ithaca, N.Y.: Cornell University Press, 1974.

Turner, V. *Forest of Symbols*. Ithaca, N.Y.: Cornell University Press, 1967.

Turner, V. *From Ritual to Theater*. New York: Performing Arts Journal Publications, 1982.

Turner, V. *Process, Performance, and Pilgrimage*. New Delhi: Concept, 1979.

Turner, V. *The Ritual Process*. Chicago: Aldine, 1969.

van Hooff, A. *From Autothanasia to Suicide*. London: Routledge, 1990.

Vernant, J.-P. "Théorie générale du sacrifice et mise à mort dans la *thysia* grecque." In *Le Sacrifice dans l'antiquité*, Entretiens sur l'Antiquité Classique 27, 1–39. Geneva: Fondation Hardt, 1981.

Versnel, H. S. *Inconsistencies in Greek and Roman Religion*. Vol. 2. Leiden: Brill, 1993.

Versnel, H. S. "Self-sacrifice, Compensation, Anonymous Gods." In *Le Sacrifice dans l'antiquité*, Entretiens sur l'Antiquité Classique 27, 135–94. Geneva: Fondation Hardt, 1981.

Versnel, H. S. *Ter Unus*. Leiden: Brill, 1990.

Versnel, H. S. *Triumphus*. Leiden: Brill, 1970.

Veyne, P. *Bread and Circuses*. Translated by B. Pearce. London: Penguin, 1990.

Veyne, P. "*Humanitas*: Romans and Non-Romans." In *The Romans*, edited by A. Giardina, translated by L. Cochrane, 342–69. Chicago: University of Chicago Press, 1993.

Veyne, P. "Suicide, fisc, esclavage, capital et droit romain." *Latomus* 40 (1981): 217–68.

Veyne, P. "Le Voyage de Neron en Grece." *Annuaire du College de France* (1985–86): 705–37.

Ville, G. *La Gladiature en Occident des origines à la mort de Domitien*. Bibliothèque des Ecoles Françaises d'Athènes et de Rome 245. Rome: Ecole Française de Rome, 1981.

Ville, G. "Les Jeux de gladiateurs dans l'empire chrétien." *Mélanges d'Archéologie et d'Histoire* 72 (1960): 273–335.

Vogel-Weidemann, U. "The Opposition under the Early Caesars." *Acta Classica* 22 (1979): 91–107.

Voisin, J.-L. "Education de la mort voluntaire a Rome." In *Sociabilité, pouvoirs et société*, Actes du Colloque de Rouen, 24–26 novembre 1983, 91–97. Rouen, 1987.

Voisin, J.-L. "Les Romains, chasseurs de têtes." In *Du châtiment dans la cité*, Collection de l'Ecole Française de Rome 79, 241–93. Rome: Ecole Française de Rome, 1984.

Voisin, J.-L. "Tite-Live, Capoue et les Bacchanales." In *Mélanges de l'Ecole Française de Rome* 96 (1984): 601–53.

Wacke, A. "Der Selbstmord im römischen Recht und in der Rechtsentwicklung." *Zeitschrift der Savigny-Stiftung für Rechtsgeschichte, Romantische Abteilung* 97 (1980): 26–77.

Watson, A. *International Law in Archaic Rome*. Baltimore: Johns Hopkins University Press, 1993.

Watson, A. *The Law of Persons in the Later Roman Republic.* Oxford: Clarendon, 1967.

Weber, C. *Panem et circenses.* Dusseldorf: Econ, 1983.

Weiler, I. *Der Sport bei den Völkern der Alten Welt.* Darmstadt: Wissenschaftliche Buchgesellschaft, 1981.

Weinreich, O. *Studien zu Martial.* Tübinger Beiträge zur Altertumswissenschaft 4. Stuttgart: Kohlhammer, 1928.

White, H. "New Historicism: A Comment." In *The New Historicism,* edited by H. Veeser, 293–302. New York: Routledge, 1989.

Wiedemann, T. *Emperors and Gladiators.* London: Routledge, 1992.

Williams, B. "Reading Tacitus' Tiberian Annals." *Ramus* 18 (1989): 140–66.

Williams, G. *Change and Decline.* Berkeley: University of California Press, 1978.

Wistrand, M. "Violence and Entertainment in Seneca the Younger." *Eranos* 88 (1990): 31–46.

Woodman, A. J. "Amateur Dramatics at the Court of Nero: *Annals* 15.48–74." In *Tacitus and the Tacitean Tradition,* edited by T. J. Luce and A. J. Woodman, 104–28. Princeton, N.J.: Princeton University Press, 1993.

Woodman, A. J. "Nero's Alien Capital: Tacitus as Paradoxographer." In *Author and Audience in Latin Literature,* edited by T. Woodman and J. Powell, 173–88. Cambridge: Cambridge University Press, 1992.

Woodman, A. J. *Rhetoric in Classical Historiography.* London: Croom Helm, 1988.

Woodman, A. J. "Self-imitation and the Substance of History." In *Creative Imitation and Latin Literature,* edited by D. West and T. Woodman, 143–55. Cambridge: Cambridge University Press, 1979.

Yavetz, Z. *Plebs and Princeps.* Oxford: Clarendon, 1969.

Index

Index of Passages Cited in Text

WISCONSIN STUDIES IN CLASSICS

General Editors
Richard Daniel De Puma and Barbara Hughes Fowler

E. A. THOMPSON
Romans and Barbarians: The Decline of the Western Empire

JENNIFER TOLBERT ROBERTS
Accountability in Athenian Government

H. I. MARROU
A History of Education in Antiquity
Histoire de l'Education dans l'Antiquité, translated by George Lamb
(originally published in English by Sheed and Ward, 1956)

ERIKA SIMON
Festivals of Attica: An Archaeological Commentary

G. MICHAEL WOLOCH
Roman Cities: Les villes romaines by Pierre Grimal,
translated and edited by G. Michael Woloch,
together with A Descriptive Catalogue of Roman Cities
by G. Michael Woloch

WARREN G. MOON, editor
Ancient Greek Art and Iconography

KATHERINE DOHAN MORROW
Greek Footwear and the Dating of Sculpture

JOHN KEVIN NEWMAN
The Classical Epic Tradition

JEANNY VORYS CANBY, EDITH PORADA,
BRUNILDE SISMONDO RIDGWAY, and TAMARA STECH, editors
Ancient Anatolia: Aspects of Change and Cultural Development